MW01225961

Reengineering
Nursing and Health Care
The Handbook for Organizational Transformation

Suzanne Smith Blancett, EdD, RN, FAAN
Editor-in-Chief
The Journal of Nursing Administration
Philadelphia, Pennsylvania

Dominick L. Flarey, PhD, MBA, RNC, CNAA, CHE
President
Dominick L. Flarey and Associates, Inc.
Health Care Management Consultants
Niles, Ohio

AN ASPEN PUBLICATION®
Aspen Publishers, Inc.
Gaithersburg, Maryland
1995

Library of Congress Cataloging-in-Publication Data

Reengineering nursing and health care: the handbook for
organizational transformation / edited by Suzanne Smith Blancett,
Dominick L. Flarey.
        p.   cm.
Includes bibliographical references and index.
ISBN 0-8342-0660-9
1. Nursing services—Administration. 2. Organizational change.
3. Health services administration. I. Blancett, Suzanne Smith.
II. Flarey, Dominick L.
[DNLM: 1. Nursing Services—organization & administration—United
States. 2. Delivery of Health Care—organization & administration—
United States. 3. Organizational Innovation. 4. Quality Control.
WY d16 R327 1995]
362.1'73'068—dc20
DNLM/DLC
for Library of Congress
94-44207
CIP

Copyright © 1995 by Aspen Publishers, Inc.
All rights reserved.

Aspen Publishers, Inc., grants permission for photocopying for limited personal or
internal use. This consent does not extend to other kinds of copying, such as copying for
general distribution, for advertising or promotional purposes, for creating new collective
works, or for resale. For information, address Aspen Publishers, Inc., Permissions
Department, 200 Orchard Ridge Drive, Suite 200, Gaithersburg, Maryland 20878.

Editorial Resources: Ruth Bloom
Cover Design: Jay Robbins

Library of Congress Catalog Card Number: 94-44207
ISBN: 0-8342-0660-9

Printed in the United States of America

1 2 3 4 5

Table of Contents

Contributors

Rella Adams, PhD, RN, CNAA
Senior Vice President, Nursing
Valley Baptist Medical Center
Harlingen, Texas

Linda Bartkowski-Dodds, MS, RN
Nurse Manager
Ambulatory Treatment Unit and
    Endoscopy Unit
Stanford Health Services
Stanford, California

Heather Beebe, MBA
Associate
APM Management Consultants
Chicago, Illinois

Marjorie Beyers, PhD, RN, FAAN
Executive Director
American Organization of Nurse
    Executives
Chicago, Ilinois

**Suzanne Smith Blancett, EdD, RN,
    FAAN**
Editor-in-Chief
The Journal of Nursing Administration
Philadelphia, Pennsylvania

Carol Boston JD, MS, RN
Senior Consultant
Work Transformation Services
Hay Management Consultants
Chicago, Illinois

Roberta Carefoote, MSN, RN
Director of Quality Management
Health Spring
Reston, Virginia
Former Senior Manager
The Moore Group
Washington, D.C.

Barbara A. Donaho, MA, RN, FAAN
Former President and Chief Executive
    Officer
St. Anthony's Hospital
St. Petersburg, Florida

**Dominick L. Flarey, PhD, MBA,
    RNC, CNAA, CHE**
President
Dominick L. Flarey and Associates, Inc.
Health Care Management Consultants
Niles, Ohio

Julie Fleury, PhD, RN
Assistant Professor
Department of Adult and
    Geriatric Health
University of North Carolina at
    Chapel Hill
Chapel Hill, North Carolina

**Nancy Mansheim Formella, MSN,
RN**
Assistant Administrator
St. Luke's Hospital—A Mayo Affiliate
Jacksonville, Florida

Rose M. Gerber, PhD, RN
Associate Professor
University of Arizona College of
    Nursing
Tucson, Arizona

Lisa E. Gray, MSHA, RN
Director of Nursing, Information
    Management
Valley Baptist Medical Center
Harlingen, Texas

Susan D. Guild, MS, RNC, NNP, PNP
Clinical Nurse Specialist
Ob/Gyn Nursing
Strong Memorial Hospital
University of Rochester Medical
    Center
Rochester, New York

**Leanne M. Hunstock, MBA, MEd,
RN, CS, CNAA**
Assistant Vice President
Patient Care Services
National Medical Enterprises, Inc.
Santa Monica, California

Judy M. Lanigan, MA, RN
Assistant Director of Nursing
Psychiatric Service Line Administrator
Division of Patient Care Services
Stanford Health Services
Stanford, California

**Rebecca Wrede Ledwin, MS, RNC,
PNP**
Clinical Nurse Specialist
Ob/Gyn Nursing
Strong Memorial Hospital
University of Rochester Medical
    Center
Rochester, New York

**Patti Ludwig-Beymer, PhD, RN,
CTN**
Director, Special Programs
Research Institute
Lutheran General HealthSystem
Park Ridge, Illinois

**Jo Anne S. Maehling, MSN, RN,
CNAA**
Senior Administrative Consultant
Youngstown Osteopathic Hospital
Youngstown, Ohio
Instructor
The Pennsylvania State University
University Park, Pennsylvania

Jo Manion, MA, RN, CNAA
Consultant
Manion & Associates
Altamonte Springs, Florida
Member, Development Team
Lakeland Regional Medical Center
Lakeland, Florida

Jody Mechanic, MS, RN
Research Associate
Division of Patient Care Services
Stanford Health Services
Stanford, California

Doris A. Milton, PhD, RN
Director of Nursing Research
Samaritan Health System
Phoenix, Arizona

Tim Porter-O'Grady, EdD, PhD, RN, FAAN
Senior Partner
Tim Porter-O'Grady Associates, Inc.
Senior Consultant
Affiliated Dynamics, Inc.
Assistant Professor
Emory University
Atlanta, Georgia

Dawn P. Rinehart, MN, MBA, FACHE
Chief Quality Officer
Sarasota Memorial Hospital
Sarasota, Florida

Deborah M. Sanford, MBA, RN
Project Manager
Ob/Gyn Nursing
Strong Memorial Hospital
University of Rochester Medical Center
Rochester, New York

Julie W. Schaffner, MSN, RN
Vice President
Patient Care Services
Lutheran General Hospital
Park Ridge, Illinois

Kerry A. Shannon, MS
Director
Coopers & Lybrand, L.L.P.
Chicago, Illinois

Diane Shindoll, BSIE
Management Engineer
Sarasota Memorial Hospital
Sarasota, Florida

Eric Six, MD, FACS, ABQAURP
Medical Director
Staff Neurosurgeon
Valley Baptist Medical Center
Harlingen, Texas

Carolyn Hope Smeltzer, EdD, MSN, RN, FAAN
Principal
APM Management Consultants
Chicago, Illinois

Bruce D. Smith, MBA
Vice President
Information Systems
Lutheran General HealthSystem
Park Ridge, Illinois

Leann Strasen, DPA, RN, FACHE
Senior Vice President
National Medical Enterprises
Santa Monica, California

Mary Crabtree Tonges, MBA, MSN, RN
Consultant
The Center for Case Management, Inc.
South Natick, Massachusetts

Stephen L. Ummel, MA
President and Chief Executive Officer
Lutheran General HealthSystem
Park Ridge, Illinois

Carol A. Veihmeyer, MBA, RN, CNAA
Managing Associate
Health Care Operations Improvement
    Practice
Coopers & Lybrand, L.L.P.
Atlanta, Georgia

Joyce A. Verran, PhD, RN, FAAN
Professor and Division Director
Adult Health Nursing
University of Arizona College of
    Nursing
Tucson, Arizona

Thomas H. Watkins
Managing Principal
Société Watkins Limited
Roswell, Georgia

Phyllis M. Watson, PhD, MEd, RN
Senior Vice President/Patient-Focused
    Development
Chief Nurse Executive
Lakeland Regional Medical Center
Lakeland, Florida

Terri Winter, MS, RN
Night Clinical Resource Nurse
Ob/Gyn Nursing
Strong Memorial Hospital
University of Rochester Medical
    Center
Rochester, New York

Gail A. Wolf, DNS, RN, FAAN
Vice President
Patient Care
Shadyside Hospital
Pittsburgh, Pennsylvania

Karen Zander, MS, RN, CS
Principal and Co-owner
The Center for Case Management,
    Inc.
South Natick, Massachusetts

Foreword

Tomorrow's health care delivery system will look totally different from today's. Even the most innovative organizations of today are only in a transitory state and will be subjected to the pressures imposed by governmental directives, technological innovations, and emerging social structures.

One must acknowledge that today's delivery system has the same basic organizational structure that has existed for over 50 years. The hospital has been the primary core, with multiple new businesses being developed to support the financial base. The major shift to wellness, prevention, and a cost-effective health care plan requires a focus on cost-effectiveness across the total continuum of care, with health care professionals making every effort to use the most appropriate human and technological resource in the most appropriate setting. Consequently, reengineering is essential! It must start with an understandable vision of what future is to be created. Change for change's sake or tinkering with the current structure will not result in a new organization that is prepared to be a key player in the delivery of health care to a community.

The challenge to be faced by all health care professions is how to orchestrate the changes. How can the transition be managed? What can be accomplished incrementally? Is it necessary to take revolutionary steps? The process will also challenge individual and organizational value systems. Successful outcomes will be contingent on the level of commitment to achieving solid human relationships. Organizations are composed of people; thus, their achievements are dependent on human relationships. The product of health care organizations is delivered to human beings, and the success of that service depends on human relationships. Reengineering will be successful only if people accept and willingly implement the change; that occurs when there is value placed on each health care worker's individual contribution to the ultimate outcomes.

The magnitude of the work of reengineering requires that staff be given support when their usual work patterns and thought processes are disrupted and that they be challenged to create and support a new vision and a new organization. These requirements place everyone in a position of risk, but without risk, reengineering will not happen and we will not create a new order.

The authors of this book have addressed the critical elements of reengineering from their perspective, and the result is a comprehensive presentation. Their shared knowledge provides the reader with sound information about a complex subject and sets the stage for action. This book is about innovation, radical change, and courage—courage to break from old assumptions about how care is delivered and to recreate the health care system for the future. To the authors I say, "Thank You"; to the readers I say, "Go for it!"

Barbara A. Donaho, MA, RN, FAAN
Former President and Chief Executive Officer
St. Anthony's Hospital
St. Petersburg, Florida

Preface

In 1993, reengineering gurus Michael Hammer and James Champy defined reengineering as the radical redesign of an organization's processes, organization, and culture. They set forth the major goal of reengineering as a quantum leap in performance—radical improvements that follow from entirely new work processes and structures.

Since the release of Hammer and Champy's book—*Reengineering the Corporation: A Manifesto for Business Revolution*—reengineering has become the hottest new management strategy in the business world. Everyone is scrambling to learn all they can about this innovative approach to managing for the future. Health care organizations are no exception. In fact, the imperative to reengineer in nursing and other health care professions is essential as we enter the new era of health care reform. The looming reality yet ambiguity of reform challenges health care leaders as never before to totally reengineer their business, beginning with process reengineering through organizational reengineering and transformation.

While new and exaggerated definitions of reengineering are emerging in the literature, we have developed this book around Hammer and Champy's basic concepts. We believe their theory and methodologies are the most valid because they are based on sound, logical business principles that can safely guide businesses in their quest to reengineer.

Health care organizations are reengineering for survival. A few have begun reengineering projects and are demonstrating remarkable outcomes in quality, efficiency of service, and cost containment. Many more are gathering information about this innovative strategy, which promises to be popular and effective for decades to come. We think reengineering will be the key strategy hospitals employ to meet the new challenges of a reformed health care system. Reengineering is not just a fad, but rather a revolutionary new management strategy that will stand the test of time and become the management innovation of the 1990s.

Reengineering projects are undertaken by interdisciplinary teams composed of members from all areas of the organization, including physicians. Since the primary product of health care organizations is patient care, nurses will be leaders in reengineering as well as being the professionals most affected by this new, revolutionary management strategy.

Even now, a few nurse executives and nurse managers are taking the lead in health care organizations to pioneer reengineering efforts, which will continue into the 21st century as success stories are made public. Through reengineering, nursing departments will be integrating with other departments to create a seamless organization of health care services. Consequently, nurse executives and nurse managers, as well as health care executives and managers, must learn and develop skills in reengineering.

Health care executives, managers, and educators will find this book helpful in their work because it operationalizes the concepts of reengineering into the health care and nursing arenas. It provides comprehensive theories, methodologies, and cutting-edge strategies for successful reengineering in health care and nursing; it also provides nurse executives, nurse managers, and other health care providers with a comprehensive reference for approaching, implementing, and evaluating their own reengineering projects. The book is divided into two parts. Part I presents theories and methodologies of reengineering applied to nursing and health care, while Part II presents a variety of health care reengineering case studies, from patient care delivery, to facilities design, to information systems. The chapter authors represent a wide range of health care professions, and many chapters were written by interdisciplinary teams of authors.

As we complete this writing project, we thank our contributing authors who took the time to share their experiences and to help advance our understanding of the many uses of reengineering in health care. We also appreciate the support we received from our families, especially Ethel, Joe, and Virginia. Finally, we dedicate this book in loving memory to Dominick Phillip Flarey, whose life was taken suddenly during this project, reminding us that life is precious and short, so we must live our dreams today.

Suzanne Smith Blancett, EdD, RN, FAAN
Dominick L. Flarey, PhD, MBA, RNC, CNAA, CHE

▪ Part I ▪

Reengineering
Nursing and Health Care:
Theories, Methods, and Issues

■ 1 ■

Changing Paradigms: The Impetus To Reengineer Health Care

Suzanne Smith Blancett, EdD, RN, FAAN
Dominick L. Flarey, PhD, MBA, RN, C, CNAA, CHE

> The old paradigm is failing. Costs per problem solved are skyrocketing. This trend is just beginning. It will take two decades to be fulfilled but during the last decade of this century, it will begin its ascent. Too many people in this country cannot afford health care as it is now configured.[1(p.173)]

How did we get in the predicament of needing to take dramatic, revolutionary, radical measures to save our organizations? In retrospect, health care providers see the harbingers of change—warning signs that, taken individually, seemed manageable. It is now clear how seemingly discrete issues and problems related to health care were parts of the same picture—a malfunctioning system that is being treated with first aid instead of surgery.

Because many internal and external factors were not adequately managed, the organization and delivery of health care became the business of everyone—the government, the public, business, and insurance companies. Health care providers are assailed by competition, a global marketplace, radical technical innovation, and major attitudinal shifts about work, employees, and leadership.[2(p.93)]

COST

A critical factor that brought the health care system to the forefront of public and private scrutiny was its increasing share, approaching 15 percent, of the gross national product.[3] General economic recession and inflation certainly had a part in spiraling health care costs. As all costs related to care delivery increased (e.g., costs of products, services, salaries, construction, unreimbursed care, and capital equipment), they were passed on to consumers, most often to the government and insurance companies.

An offshoot of the government's effort to curb expenses through reimbursement mechanisms was competition among providers. The health care industry's initial response was to procure new equipment, new facilities, and new services, in an attempt to remain competitive and attract new business. In the face of decreasing profit margins and reduced inpatient bed occupancy, these efforts further contributed to the cost of doing business.

STRUCTURE

The bureaucratic organizational structures of health care institutions also contributed to waste and economic inefficiency. Built on 19th century principles, hierarchical organizational structures were "not designed to operate in today's highly competitive global markets, let alone take them successfully into the 21st century."[4(p.46)] Bureaucratic structures, with their focus on "specialization, uniform policies, standardized jobs, a career of promotions, impersonal relationships, and coordination from above . . .,"[5(p.18)] work well with a passive labor force and a stable environment. These types of organizations are not good at perceiving and reacting to threats to their well-being. They stifle productivity and operational efficiency. The hospital has also added a unique twist to the bureaucratic structure. "The 'business' of hospitals (caring for patients) was separated from the financial management of the enterprise," which further encouraged development of the hospital as a highly labor-intensive, highly segmented business.[3(p.23)]

STAKEHOLDERS

Along with the imperative to decrease costs came changing expectations of the American public and other stakeholders in adequate and effective health care. Better educated and informed, consumers wanted a more active part in the management of their care. More consumers joined the ranks of the working poor or the uninsured. The increasing number of working poor—noninsured and underinsured—was also stimulating change. Currently, 37 million Americans are uninsured; that is one in seven people, mostly from low-income families.[6] Unable to afford care, they use the emergency department for both primary and nonurgent care. In addition to increasing hospital costs for unreimbursed care, this practice has brought an ethical issue before the public, as incidents of mistreatment of these uninsured patients occurred. The image of the health care institution was changing from concerned, community caretaker to inept, fragmented, inefficient, and perhaps unethical provider. Those with health insurance coverage often had their company-sponsored health care benefits decreased; consumers were directly paying larger percentages of their health care bill. Knowledge coupled with increasing personal cost led many consumers to begin questioning what they were getting for their health care dollar. They started demanding better service and better outcomes, in large part by lobbying their elected officials.

The work force was also changing. Better educated workers felt entitled to find personal fulfillment and meaning from their jobs. A hierarchical reporting system and the bureaucratic fragmentation of work processes into tasks were not personally fulfilling or satisfying. We had ". . . successful people producing results, but with no time in which to arrange themselves and change others."[7(p.29)] Administrators found the work environment and its structure challenged from within as well as from without.

Another stakeholder no longer satisfied with a passive role in health care is the third-party payer—the government, business, and insurance companies. Through regulation and economic pressure, payers are assuming a significant and more overt influence on the delivery of health care services. Their influence comes from regulating and negotiating how much and what types of care will be reimbursed. "Employers, insurance companies, and government are all now experimenting with ways to slow the rising costs, in effect trying to place ceilings on what Americans spend for health care."[6(p.13)]

MANAGED COMPETITION

These and other factors led to a ground swell for health care reform. In 1992, President Bill Clinton, along with numerous congressional candidates, were elected on their pledge to enact health care reform. There was no doubt that the health care system problems had to be faced. Exactly how became the turning point. The government and payers, convinced that fee-for-service and prospective payment systems were not the answer, moved toward capitated payment systems. A major element of the Clinton administration's plan for national reform rests on the concept of managed competition. Jack Hole, a physician and economist, states:

> . . . under managed competition, most doctors and hospitals would join prepaid plans such as health maintenance organizations that would compete for the business of large consumer groups. By rewarding doctors for prudent care and publicizing comparative medical results, this approach should help move medical care back to where most things that are done to patients actually improve their health. By drastically reducing waste, we can avoid or at least delay rationing.[6(pp.289–290)]

Capitated payments and managed care mandate that health care institutions rethink their basic operation if they are to survive. Predictions are that capitation may decrease inpatient utilization by 50 percent.[8(p.30)]

An integral part of capitated care for a designated population (an increasingly large part of institutional revenue) is the mandate to identify and manage outcomes. Managed care buyers are selecting their provider institutions on the basis of quality and effectiveness. Government is increasing public disclosure of morbidity and mortality rates as well as data from facility inspections and from physician malpractice and licensure actions; "Major employers and employer health coalitions are developing regional data bases, implementing comparative quality assessment systems, hiring consultants to pick superior providers, and contracting in exclusive provider arrangements with select hospitals for specialized services. . . ."; and voluntary accreditation agencies (e.g., the Joint Commission on Accreditation of Healthcare Organizations) are expanding the types of facilities they review and implementing outcome indicators for clinical services.[9(p.119)]

ALLIANCES

There have been many institutional responses to competition and economic constraints. A major industry initiative is formation of strategic partnerships, alliances, and networks. Health care institutions are establishing services and acquiring or partnering with others to provide a broad range of comprehensive services for specific patient populations under managed care. Physician/hospital groups are forming to more adequately integrate patient care services as well as to share the financial risks and rewards of a capitated system. Large health care corporations continue to buy and sell health care agencies with targeted services, seeking the right mix of services necessary to excel in a rapidly changing environment. The explosion in numbers of multiprovider networks is seen in the growth of health maintenance organizations (HMOs) from a handful in 1970 to 590 in 1990 and the growth in multihospital systems from 268 in 1985 to 307 in 1990.[3(p.23)]

REDESIGN

The redesign of health care delivery models was a major institutional initiative to control costs, improve patient satisfaction, and use resources efficiently. Encouraged by a multimillion dollar project grant from the Robert Wood Johnson Foundation and the Pew Charitable Trust, hospitals started restructuring their systems in an effort to remain viable and responsive to many competing customers (e.g., government, physicians, staff, and payers). A major model of care delivery to emerge was patient-focused care. Its main components were decentralization of key services to the unit level; delivery of care by teams (ranging from a nurse partnered with a nursing assistant to interdisciplinary groups); and managed care measured by predefined expected outcomes during the course of an illness.

QUALITY

Total quality management (TQM) and quality improvement programs also emerged from pressure, first, from external forces. The demand of third-party payers and consumers to know what they were getting for their health care dollar, limited resources, and the subsequent internal pressure to eliminate inefficient work processes that did not add value, led to quality initiatives. Since teams are an integral part of a formal TQM program and most of the restructured systems used teams to deliver care, the critical role of front-line staff in making operations more efficient and effective became apparent. Staff development expanded beyond the acquisition of clinical skills to include team building, empowerment, delegation, budgeting, and governance.

THE FUTURE

While these initiatives have certainly addressed some basic economic and delivery problems, the question is: Is it enough, and is it adequate for the future?

> Every day in hospitals across the country, CEOs [chief executive officers] and other senior managers sit at their desks and try to improve costs and service performance. They pull the "levers" that they have been taught to pull to change the organization. But these levers do not seem to be connected to anything. Significant change continues to elude us. We reach out to new techniques like total quality management or continuous quality improvement, throw resources at them, and hope for the best.[10(p.21)]

In terms of the present, is it enough? The answer is no. Donna Shalala, Secretary of Health and Human Services, stated:

> There has been a great deal of discussion about the recent report by the Department of Labor showing that health care inflation in 1993 slowed to 5.4 percent. Let's remember, however, that medical prices still rose twice as fast as all other consumer prices . . . that this slowdown is a temporary reaction to the debate over health reform in Washington.[11(p.2F)]

Thus, varying degrees of pressure for reform from government are likely to continue.

What about the future? Are current initiatives and strategies for addressing issues related to limited and shrinking resources, quality imperatives, and a competitive environment sufficient to meet the needs of an uncertain future? Are we creating flexible approaches adaptable to whatever comes along, or are we simply replacing an antiquated and static approach with one that is equally soon to be outdated?

The fact that health care leaders are ambivalent about reform and the degree of change they have to make in their institutions is seen in a recent report. The Health Care Forum Leadership Center queried health care opinion leaders on three future health care scenarios. The first scenario—"continued growth/high technology"—has health care consuming 17 percent of the gross national product (GNP) by 2001, with high technology proliferating, but at a high cost. Health care reform does not occur, and patchwork managed care grows, as do medical indigence and unequal access. The second scenario—"hard times/government leadership"—has a frugal universal access system with significant rationing of services based on cost-benefit and outcomes research. Heroic lifesaving measures decline and researchers adopt a more frugal approach to innovation. Health care's percentage of GNP declines to 11 percent by 2001.[12]

The third scenario is "new civilization," in which

> . . . dramatic changes in science, technology, society and government hasten health care change. Care broadens its focus from the person to the community and the environment. National health reform favors managed care through a government/business partnership with discretion at the community level. This partnership would provide basic coverage for all with an emphasis on the continuum of care, health promotion and social HMOs. High tech and alternative therapies are common. Health care consumes 12 percent of the GNP in 2001.[12(pp.7–8)]

Interestingly, it was this third scenario that 87 percent of the leaders preferred; however, they thought it was the least likely to occur. Instead, they felt the reality would be "hard times/government leadership." This preference and expectation is an interesting paradox to consider. Our health care leaders can envision an ideal future but expect the worst. One has to suspect that this dual type of thinking probably exists in their management of their organizations too. Many administrators show an

> . . . unwillingness to think rigorously and patiently about themselves or their ideas. . . . When leading an organization into the future, executives come to a fork in the road. As they come face to face with their organizations' needs to reinvent themselves, many executives hope for the best and opt for the prudent path of change.[13(p.104)]

Change is traumatic. Why put an organization and its people through radical change if simple adjustments will accomplish results? This attitude of not reacting quickly and doing nothing too dramatic seems to be borne out by a recent American Hospital Association (AHA) study.[14]

The AHA reports that hospital actions taken in anticipation of what national health care reform might require have led to "controlling costs by managing better within fixed budgets, forming new partnerships with other providers and coming up with innovative solutions to community health problems."[14(p.1)] These efforts caused a decline in total hospital expenses for 1993 of 8.1%, down from 10.2% the prior year.[14(p.1)] However, the AHA report points out that the decrease in costs resulted from a decline in almost all measures of hospital use and a continuing shift from inpatient to outpatient services. Thus, although health care executives have taken many initiatives to solve system problems related to economic delivery of care, initiatives that merely produce incremental improvements in the existing system might not be enough for the future.

How can one adapt to a future in which the only certainty is unpredictability, complexity, and turbulence, coupled with scarce resources? If health care is to not only survive, but also prosper, all aspects of our organization have to change—structures, human resource procedures, information technology, and management and worker skills and attitudes. We must find ways to empower staff who are doing the work, so that they can design and adjust their work, its processes, and their organizational connections. We must change the education received by managers so that it emphasizes the human side of the enterprise. We must learn how to cross organizational boundaries—interdisciplinary, interdepartmental, and intradepartmental.

What kind of organizational model can do all this? Perhaps the organization of the future will be the intelligent organization, a market-based confederation of entrepreneurial teams, structured to support and coordinate self-managing groups and teams.[5] The new architecture of the intelligent organization

> . . . lets people connect laterally, between specialties, geographies, or products, whether within or outside the boundaries of a particular organization . . . the intelligent organization creates clear visions of possible futures and acts quickly and effectively in a locally adaptive, yet coordinated way.[5(p.20)]

The intelligent organization has three essential ingredients: freedom of choice, responsibility for the whole, and limited corporate government. The first element—freedom of choice—is based on widespread sharing of information so workers can make intelligent decisions. It implies that workers have freedom of speech, freedom of association, and the rights to make contracts with each other and to keep promises. It reinforces Drucker's contention that "knowledge is the only meaningful resource today [and that without] knowledge employees cannot, in effect, be supervised."[15(p.14)]

> We are entering a period that demands that we operate in such a way as to empower the incalculable assets of human intelligence and cre-

ativity. The major distinction, for example, between old and new methods lies not in the methods themselves, but in the ability to integrate human beings into meaningful work. The new world requires humans to function as essential information and idea resources, creating solutions we have never seen before. In this kind of situation, human labor is no longer a disposable commodity, but a unique creative resource, in which an individual's development is as valuable as the organization's growth.[16(p.265)]

Responsibility for the whole is about leaders helping staff and teams achieve their highest potential so that they are integrated into and committed to the whole. It involves equality and diversity, voluntary learning networks, and democratic self-rule.

The final element, limited corporate government, acknowledges the fact that no central management team can design an organizational structure fluid enough to get the work done in the most efficient and effective manner.

It has to be done on the fly by the choices of all the people at work, people establishing the connections they need to get the work done . . . the primary role of the [corporate] center is to create the conditions that empower those doing the work to build systems to run their operations effectively.[5(p.21)]

Contemplating how we get from today's health care organization to the intelligent organization of the future is critical. Change of this magnitude is not an easy process; it is a mixed blessing representing growth, opportunity, and innovation but also threat, disorientation, and upheaval.[2(p.93)] Resistance will abound. "Conflict has its human and organizational costs, but it is also essential fuel for self-questioning and revitalization."[17(p.59)] The savvy administrator will have to head off and defuse resistance due to top management skepticism; physician, staff, and/or union resistance; turf battles; redesigned management and staff roles; and the costs of physical renovations and information management systems.[18]

The rate of change in health care is unprecedented. Driven by technological and economic forces, health care is being retooled and reshaped for the 21st century. The change and challenges we are about to face in the new world of health care will be intensely different from those we have confronted in the past several decades. The following changes will drive the need to reengineer the delivery of health care:

1. **Care delivery**
   - Third-party payers will force a massive shift of care delivery away from the acute care setting and into the home, subacute care facilities, and outpatient centers.

- The hospital as we know it will become extinct; the largest delivery system will be home health care.
- In the next five years, the acute care inpatient census will be at least 50 percent of what it is today.
- Clinic services will be the second largest delivery system of care. Many types of clinics will emerge, offering communities a wide array of care services. Clinics will be strategically placed in malls, schools, and churches.
- Prior to the year 2000, the average length of hospital stay for acute care will be three days.
- Hospitals will become triage centers with the primary objective of making rapid diagnoses and stabilizing patients. Most future inpatient units will be what we now know as critical status units; our typical medical-surgical units will be virtually empty.
- Obstetric care will also shift from the acute care setting. Birthing centers will become vogue. Home births will flourish once again and be attended by nurse-midwives, a back-to-the-future phenomenon.
- All but the most complex surgery procedures will be done in free-standing, outpatient surgery centers where such procedures can be done more cost-effectively.

2. Reimbursements

- We will live in a world of managed care. Local and regional networks of managed care providers will compete vigorously to be agents for patient care services. Health maintenance organizations (HMOs) and preferred provider organizations (PPOs) within a managed care framework will be commonplace.
- Fixed payment structures will prevail. Financial resources for care will be paid out in fixed rates regardless of the amount of care required. Capitation will thus be the major driving force for changes in medical and nursing practice patterns.

3. Physician practice patterns

- Physicians will be active participants in some type of integrated delivery system. The most popular will be physician-hospital organizations (PHOs) where physicians and hospitals work together in strong partnerships to negotiate the delivery of care with managed care networks and mutually develop strategic plans for the delivery of high-quality, cost-effective care. Fixed-rate payment systems will force these partnerships and drive more and more changes in the way care is delivered, including the judicious use of resources.

- As our system continues to transform itself, fully integrated care delivery systems will emerge. We will witness high levels of integration whereby physicians become employees of organizations and are contracted to provide a continuum of services. Private physician practices will be a rarity.

4. Physician extenders

- In this new era, we will witness the emergence of many nonphysician providers, such as nurse-practitioners and nurse-midwives. Our government will fund and encourage the use of such providers in an ongoing effort to hold down health care costs. Reimbursement incentives will exist for organizations and group practices with nonphysician providers.

5. Prevention

- The current focus on disease will shift to a focus on disease prevention, health promotion, and wellness.
- Many and varied health prevention programs will be developed. Nurses will play key roles in patient and public education and many will practice in primary prevention practices. There will be great financial incentives for organizations and physician group practices to practice preventive medicine as healthy populations use less capitated dollars for care.

6. Practice patterns

- Medical guidelines and protocols or pathways will be standard. These will be developed to assist the care team in delivering expedient, more efficient health care services. These pathways will become major financial initiatives in a capitated payment system, because length of stay and use of resources will be reduced.
- A major focus on quality and outcomes will prevail.
- Network payers will stringently monitor quality and outcomes. Organizations and practitioners who cannot meet these established standards will likely be excluded from managed care networks, PHOs, and other integrated delivery systems.
- The driving force for all care delivery will be based on nationally accepted patient outcomes and quality indicators.

7. Continuum of care

- Networks will mandate that providers offer a full continuum of services to patient populations. An overwhelming emphasis on a full continuum of care services will be the driving force for the formation of group practices, integrated delivery systems, and organizational and system affiliations and mergers.

RECREATING HEALTH CARE

There are three keys to the future of any organization: anticipation, innovation, and excellence.[1] These three keys coincide well with the need to recreate health care organizations. Anticipation focuses on gathering information to allow the organization to be in the right place at the right time for innovation and excellence.[1] These keys to the future are found in the philosophy of reengineering. Through reengineering, organizations will recreate themselves to be successful in the emerging age of reform.

The following chapters in this book present a process for the work of reengineering—a process that will help organizations to ". . . continuously adapt their bureaucracies, strategies, systems, products, and cultures [and become] masters of organizational reengineering."[2(p.93)] Through reengineering, organizations will find "ways to make infrastructure completely flexible [and thereby], in theory, never become inefficient."[17(p.59)]

REFERENCES

1. Barker J. *Paradigms: The Business of Discovering the Future.* New York: Harper Business; 1992.
2. Lowenthal J. Reengineering the organization: A step-by-step approach to corporate revitalization. Part I. *Qual Prog.* 1994;27(1):93–95.
3. Helppie RD. A time for reengineering. *Comput Healthcare.* 1992;10(1):22–24.
4. McManis GL. Reinventing the system. *Hosp Health Networks.* 1993;67(19):42–48.
5. Brown T. The intelligent organization. *Industry Week.* 1994;243(6):17–21.
6. Eckholm E, ed. *Solving America's Health Care Crisis.* New York: Time Books; 1993.
7. Bredin J. Parker's offense on defense. *Industry Week.* 1994;243(8):29–30.
8. Cerne F. Shaping up for capitation. *Hosp Health Networks.* 1994;68(7):28–37.
9. Holden EF, Coile RC. Viewpoints: The futurist's perspective. In: England E, Glass RM, Patterson CH, eds. *Quality Rehabilitation: Results-Oriented Patient Care.* Chicago: American Hospital Publishing, Inc; 1989:103–121.
10. Lathrop J. *Restructuring Health Care: The Patient-Focused Paradigm.* San Francisco: Jossey-Bass, Inc., Publishers; 1993.
11. Shalala DE. There sure is a health crisis. *Sarasota Herald Tribune.* January 30, 1994: p. 2F.
12. Curtin L. Sign of things to come. *Nurs Manage.* 1992;23(7):7–8.
13. Goss T, Pascale R, Athos S. The reinvention roller coaster: Risking the present for a powerful future. *Harvard Business Rev.* 1993;71:97–108.
14. American Organization of Nurse Executives. Growth in hospital expenses slows as cost-cutting efforts reap dividends. *AONE News.* 1994;3(1):1,5.
15. Brown T. Peter Drucker: Managing in a post-capitalist marketplace. *Industry Week.* 1994;243(1):13–18.

16. Land G, Jarman B. Moving beyond breakpoint. In: Ray M, Rinzler A, eds. *The New Paradigm in Business: Emerging Strategies for Leadership and Organizational Change.* New York: Jeremy P. Tarcher/Perigee Books; 1993.

17. Morris D, Brandon J. Reengineering the hospital: Making change work for you. *Comput Healthcare.* 1991;9(11):59–64.

18. Murphy R, Papazian-Boyle L. Seven barriers to work reengineering for patient centered care. *Hosp Manage Rev.* 1993;12(11):1.

■ 2 ■

Reengineering:
The Road Best Traveled

Dominick L. Flarey, PhD, MBA, RN, C, CNAA, CHE
Suzanne Smith Blancett, EdD, RN, FAAN

The dogmas of the quiet past will not work in the turbulent future. As our cause is new, so must we think and act anew.

—Abraham Lincoln

"Despite a decade or more of restructuring and downsizing, many U.S. companies are still unprepared to operate in the 1990s."[1(p.104)] Businesses have failed to keep pace with the rapid changes occurring in technology, customer needs, and quality service. Consequently, companies attempt to compete in today's turbulent environment while operating with archaic systems and processes. The result has been the demise of many large and small corporations. The business of health care is no exception.

Can business as we know it today survive? Is there a prescription for success? The answer is yes. The secret to revitalizing American business is reengineering. Reengineering is new. As the hottest trend in management today,[2,3] it is an intense method that focuses on the radical redesign of systems and processes to achieve quantum leaps in performance and defined outcomes. This chapter provides an in-depth discussion of the fundamentals of reengineering, as well as a methodology for operationalizing the concept. Case studies from industry are also presented.

THE REENGINEERING REVOLUTION

As with any emerging management trend, reengineering is being defined in endless ways. Despite its dilution, reengineering in the purest sense has been defined and operationalized. There is really only one concrete, far-reaching definition of reengineering. This definition was developed by the gurus of reengineering, Michael Hammer and James Champy. Thus, the substance of this book has been built on their working philosophy, definition, and concepts of reengineering.

Hammer and Champy define reengineering as "the fundamental rethinking and radical redesign of business processes to achieve dramatic improvements in critical, contemporary measures of performance, such as cost, quality, service, and speed."[4(p.32)] Reengineering is not about fixing processes; rather, it is about starting over from scratch.[4]

It is an innovative, far-reaching concept that touches every element of an organization. It is about reinvention—the recreation of processes, work, and systems. It directly impacts the very core of businesses and organizations. As such, reengineering drives major change, leading to radical transformation of the organization. When processes are reinvented, a rippling effect occurs. A few of the major organizational elements that are revitalized as a direct result of reengineering are:

1. governance and management structures
2. organizational culture and climate
3. quality initiatives
4. standards of work performance
5. compensation and benefit packages
6. labor relations
7. measurements of customer satisfaction
8. vendor relationships
9. employee recognition and reward
10. overall service delivery.

The impacts on these elements are examined in detail throughout this book.

To fully understand and appreciate the concept of reengineering, it is necessary to examine its core features. "At the heart of reengineering is the notion of **discontinuous thinking**—of recognizing and breaking away from the outdated rules and fundamental assumptions that underlie operations."[1(p.107)] True reengineering means breaking with the past. It means that the old and often comfortable ways of doing things must be abandoned. It requires a radical shift in the way we think about work, our processes, our systems, and our entire business. This type of nonlinear thinking leads to change that is basic and irreversible. "The reason is that something happens in the mind; there is a new mind set, a new mental model, a new set of measures . . . the more nonlinear the change, the more irreversible it is. Top management recognizes that it is burning its bridges, and that there is no way back. "But they have to understand that their bridges are probably burning anyway."[5(p.52)]

Reengineering then is a genesis in itself. It means asking this question, "If I were recreating this company today, given what I know and given current technology, what would it look like? Reengineering a company means tossing aside old systems and starting over. It involves going back to the beginning and inventing a better way of doing work."[4(p.31)] Reengineering then, is synonymous with reinvention. Reinvention is not about changing what exists; it is about creating what is not.[6] Reengineering is a process that gives us permission to be innovative, creative, and sometimes even a bit eccentric. It encourages us to tap our innermost skills and allows us, finally, to discard sacred cows and the traditional bureaucracies of the American corporation.

Another core feature of reengineering is its **cross-functional approach** to work.[2] Processes rarely operate independently, and systems certainly do not. The way in which businesses operate and work is accomplished is an interactive process. Processes and systems are in constant play with one another, and each significantly affects the ways in which the others operate. Reengineering, a global concept, impacts multiple business processes and, thus, multiple functional divisions. It focuses on reinventing these processes and systems in an integrated fashion, not in isolation.

Reengineering is also about **major, radical change**. It seeks quantum leaps in performance and outcomes. As a general rule, reengineering targets a 20 percent to 50 percent change in processes, with an equally planned transformation in costs, quality, timeliness, and satisfaction.[7] Thus, it is distinctly different from traditional total quality management and continuous quality improvement. In those methodologies, processes and systems are examined, and the focus is on "fixing" or making incremental improvements in them. Such initiatives are not as radical or bold as reengineering. This premise is substantiated by research data showing that traditional quality improvement programs generally result in changes of 2 percent to 5 percent.[7]

Another feature of reengineering is its **futuristic imperative**. True reengineering starts from the future and works backward.[2] It requires executives and managers to undergo an intense future-oriented analysis. It means having a vision of what could be, as well as specific goals and objectives for realizing the vision. It means rethinking what the business is[3] and what it must become for future success and viability. This concept of rethinking is vital to the success of any reengineering project. In order to "rethink" the business, reengineering focuses on defining desired outcomes and working backward to realize them.[8]

One essential feature for reengineering is that it must be a phenomenon that works from the top down to be successful.[2] Executive management must be fully committed to the concept and display a passion for transformation through reengineering. Reengineering requires the dedication of substantial amounts of fiscal and human resources, as well as time. It is not a quick-fix solution to old problems; it is about innovation and creation. Executives must understand the scope of reengineering and their need to reengineer the business. This philosophy and commitment must be sustained and communicated to everyone in the organization. Management support is critical to the overall reengineering process; it is a core feature. A reengineering initiative without ongoing, visible support from top management has no chance of success.

Exhibit 2–1 summarizes the core features and philosophies of reengineering. To reengineer successfully, it is essential that everyone involved in the project have a solid, fundamental understanding of these core elements. These elements also provide guidelines for ongoing assessment of whether or not reengineering is occurring. We recommend a frequent review of the elements throughout the reengineering process, along with an analysis of the total project. Adherence to the core features will help ensure that reengineering, not some other initiative, is being accomplished.

WHAT REENGINEERING IS NOT

Now that we have examined what reengineering is, it is necessary to reiterate what it is not. Such an examination will further clarify the core features and elements of reengineering. Careful attention must be given to what reengineering is not, because much misconception exists in the business world today. Many boast of reengineering efforts and projects, but in reality, few fulfill the definition of reengineering set forth in this chapter. Projects that are not reengineering do not reap the enormous gains and radical changes inherent in the methodology. Too

---

Exhibit 2–1 Core Features and Philosophy of Reengineering

1. **Radical change**—The focus is on radical change in processes and systems.
2. **Discontinuous thinking**—It involves a radical departure from dysfunctional ways of doing and thinking; it means breaking old assumptions and rules.
3. **Innovation**—The emphasis on creativity and recreation, going where no one has gone before.
4. **Dramatic improvements**—The major imperative is realization of quantum leaps in defined outcomes, yielding dramatic not just incremental improvements in processes and systems.
5. **Start-from-scratch initiative**—The focus is on what can be, rather than what is.
6. **Genesis effect**—It is a birth, a new beginning, a time of creation.
7. **Cross-functional**—This is a synergistic process, crossing multiple functions and boundaries.
8. **Futuristic**—The emphasis is on future operations, not on the present or past, which demands visionary thinking and leadership.
9. **Driven from the top down**—This effort requires the absolute commitment and continuous support of top-level management to be successful.
10. **Organization focused**—All elements of the organization are readily involved and positively affected.

often, executives and managers say they have reengineered and, when gains are small or nonexistent, develop a belief that reengineering does not work. This judgment is erroneous and often dissuades others from committing to the reengineering revolution. Reengineering is not about:

- accomplishing incremental or small-scale change
- reducing full-time equivalents (FTEs) to control costs
- switching vendors or changing products
- offering contests, slogans, or gimmicks
- providing quality improvement initiatives
- remodeling the physical plant
- restructuring the organization
- improving processes
- developing new services
- automating existing processes
- improving systems
- decreasing services
- marketing
- initiating mergers or joint ventures

Although many of these items may well be techniques or outcomes of reengineering, in and of themselves, they are not essential features. As mentioned previously, reengineering does impact the entire organization.

> Reengineering triggers changes of many kinds, not just of the business process itself. Job designs, organizational structures, management systems—anything associated with the process—must be refashioned in an integrated way. In other words, reengineering is a tremendous effort that mandates change in many areas of the organization.[1(p.112)]

The key to successful reengineering is to stay focused on the core features and elements of the process. The greatest mistake is to focus on the peripheral organizational elements. Confusion and frustration will generally result, and the overall objective of making radical changes and quantum leaps in performance will never be realized.

THE NEED TO REENGINEER

Why should organizations reengineer at all? Why invest heavily in the resources and time necessary to reengineer processes, systems, and organizations? Hammer and Champy[4] provide some insight into these questions by highlighting three major forces that have significant impact on the new business world.

The first major force is customers. Customers today are decidedly different from those of yesterday. Today's business customers have very unique needs and demand considerable individuality. They will go to great lengths to seek out companies who are very responsive to their needs and expectations. Making small improvements in service initiatives is not enough. Customers demand more. They are the central driving force today for businesses to reengineer their operations. Our environment today is consumer driven and will remain so well into the next century.

The second major force driving the imperative to reengineer is competition. Competition is widespread and constantly evolving. Today, many competitors focus on narrowly defined products and services with expert quality. Growing competition mandates that businesses reinvent themselves if they are to remain in the race.

The third force is change. While change is perceived as a constant, it is occurring in the new business world at accelerated rates. Over the past decade, people have become so accustomed to change that it is now viewed as a normal process. Becoming comfortable with change can be very damaging. Change today is occurring faster than people can comprehend it or keep pace with it. One striking example close to home is the rapid change occurring in health care. Driven by a national agenda for reform, this change is unparalleled by any other in current experience. Such change is causing health care organizations across the country to scramble for reengineering initiatives that will help ensure future viability.

When is the best time to reengineer? The answer is simple. The most appropriate time is when the organization is doing well and the required resources are readily available.[9] If reengineering is a last resort, chances are good that it will fail, because reengineering is an all-or-nothing proposition.[1] It requires intense commitment and resources, as well as time. Reengineering cannot be accomplished in a day. Organizations on the brink of failure do not have the time or the capability to mobilize the required resources.

Consequently, reengineering must be planned for well in advance. It needs to be written into the organization's strategic plan[7] and planned for as a major initiative toward organizational transformation. It must become a routine management strategy. To survive into the next century, organizations must constantly reengineer their businesses. One method of incorporating reengineering into the constant, overall operations of the organization is to frequently address the following questions:

- What are our customer's needs, requirements, and expectations?
- What trends and changes are clearly affecting our business?
- What is the current environment of competition like?
- Which elements of our current processes and systems are not adding value?

- What is the future vision for this organization?
- What are the organizational goals and objectives for realizing the vision?
- How can current performance or products be reinvented or recreated?
- What radical changes can be made to ensure our future success?
- How flexible and fluid is the organization?
- How do we envision our future? Where do we want to be 5 years from now?
- What major paradigm shifts in the world are predicted to occur over the next decade, and how will they affect our business?

Frequently addressing these questions will most certainly lead organizations to many reengineering initiatives. These questions or imperatives focus heavily on a total recreation of the organization. It is necessary, when reengineering, that we look at the effects of strategic processes on the organization as a whole.[9] "Many current business processes are based on decisions made by functional departments in an effort to optimize their own performance, with little attention to the impact on overall organizational effectiveness."[10(p.17)] Such thinking evolved from 200 years of industrial management.[4] Reengineering means breaking from this mind-set and moving away from the division of labor toward an integrated approach to organizational functioning.

The imperative for change throughout the organization is the key to future business success. Such change can be achieved through reengineering. Thus, the fundamental reason to reengineer is to blend the interactive components of the organization into a synergistic whole.[11] Once an integrated organizational system is created, it is structured around customers and the accomplishment of key strategic objectives, rather than around functions and departments.[12] The greatest need to reengineer is to create an integrated organization that can respond quickly to customers and the constantly changing business environment. Thus, reengineering is a major change initiative. Through reengineering, a new infrastructure is created to accommodate continual change.[13]

THE NEED TO REENGINEER HEALTH CARE

There is no business today as complex as health care. The health care environment is changing at unprecedented speed. Unfortunately, health care organizations lag far behind other businesses in terms of their innovations, redesign, and ability to recreate themselves. The outcome has been the demise of many health care organizations over the past decade. If health care organizations cannot mobilize themselves for dramatic and radical change in the coming era, they will fail.

The need to reengineer in health care is paramount. To deal effectively with the coming global transformation of our health care system, all health care organizations will have to reengineer. Some major indicators for a rapid reengineering initiative are declining profits, customer dissatisfaction, and difficulty competing successfully for managed care contracts.[9] Health care organizations experiencing such difficulties have little time to begin a reengineering initiative.

In health care, the same industrial definition and concepts of reengineering apply as in other businesses. The definition of reengineering has been somewhat expanded for use in health care: "the radical redesign of the critical systems and processes used to produce, deliver, and support patient care in order to achieve dramatic improvements in organizational performance within a short period of time."[9(pp.28–30)] While the definition is really not different, it does place an emphasis on the delivery of care.

When reengineering in health care, it is important to focus on the major imperatives for successfully confronting the changing environment. "The mandates for health care providers are clear: develop organized, integrated systems of care; reduce waste and inefficiencies; focus on primary care and prevention; and improve quality and outcomes. In essence, we need to reinvent the delivery system."[12(p.42)] In reinventing the system, the major imperative for a reformed system is to build community health networks.[9] Reengineering is an excellent tool for this overwhelming challenge; other major imperatives for reengineering in health care are detailed in Chapter 1.

A METHODOLOGY FOR REENGINEERING

Several methodologies have been developed for reengineering.[4,7,14,15] All of them are organized, concrete, and proven to work. Their similarities are striking and their differences are few. The distinguishing feature among them is their degree of complexity. On the basis of the overwhelming imperatives to reengineer health care delivery, we have developed a methodology that is focused and can be easily applied to health care reengineering projects. The major distinguishing factor in our methodology is its concrete simplicity. This feature will allow health care organizations to reengineer with the speed necessary to survive the current health care revolution. When applied appropriately, it will provide for effective and successful reengineering of processes and organizational systems in health care. Our methodology consists of seven major steps:

1. internal and external assessment
2. visioning
3. planning
4. starting from scratch
5. testing

6. evaluating
7. revisiting

Internal and External Assessment

Before reengineering can happen, it is paramount that a comprehensive analysis of the organization's internal and external environment be undertaken. This analysis lays a solid foundation for the overall reengineering effort. Internal assessment means taking a long, hard, critical look at the organization. It means facing the realities of the evolution of the organization and its current status. It is often a painful process, but a necessary one if radical change is to occur. For successful reengineering, the assessment must be honest.

The assessment process must be a group effort of the organization's management team. Everyone must participate. It is imperative that executive management lead the assessment initiative to demonstrate the commitment that is essential to the reengineering effort. The most effective means to this goal is a management retreat, which further establishes the commitment by top-level executives and brings the management team together for a common cause and purpose. It also provides a social setting where participants can more freely interact and share their perceptions of the current internal environment.

The first task of internal assessment is to thoroughly assess the culture of the organization.[7] Some of the initial questions that must be answered in cultural assessment are:

- What is our current culture like?
- Is our culture a barrier to change?
- What are the values of the organization?
- How did our culture evolve?
- How did our organization get to where it is today?
- What are the organization's sacred cows?
- How do employees perceive the culture?
- What is the prevailing attitude of the employees toward the organization?
- How does our culture affect the way we lead?
- How does our culture affect the work life of the employees?
- How has our culture negatively affected the organization?
- Are people satisfied with the current culture?

Once the cultural assessment is complete, the team can begin a more in-depth diagnosis of the organization.

The best approach is through a diagnosis that generates a complete picture of how the organization really works. What assumptions are we making about our strategic position and customer needs that may no longer be valid? What functional units are most influential, and will they be as important in the future as they were in the past? What are the key systems that drive the business? What are the core competencies or skills of the enterprise? What are the shared values and idiosyncracies that comprise the organization's being? If explored in-depth, these types of questions generate responses that, taken together, paint a picture of how things really work.[6(p.106)]

The next step in the internal assessment of the organization is a focus on customers. Questions need to be answered:

- Who are our customers, and what are their needs?
- What do customers expect from us?[2]
- What is the status of customer satisfaction?
- How has the organization traditionally related to our customers?
- What are their perceptions of the organization?

Then the assessment must honestly identify what is dysfunctional in the organization. Questions that need answering include:

- What are the major dysfunctions in the organization?
- How has the dysfunction affected the organization's processes?
- In what way is the dysfunction slowing down the organization in achievement of its goals and objectives?

To complete the internal assessment, the following questions must also be answered by the management team:

- What is the current quality of our service?
- What is the overall leadership style?
- What are the strengths and weaknesses of our systems and processes?
- To what degree is the organization integrated?
- What is the degree of the division of labor?
- What is the financial status of the organization?
- What is our relationship with our medical staff?
- How do employees relate to one another?
- How is performance recognized and rewarded?
- How is performance measured?
- How is information communicated in the organization?

- What is the degree of employee satisfaction with the organization?
- What is the speed of our service delivery?
- What are our costs?
- What inefficiencies exist in the organization?
- What prevents the organization from moving forward?

Once all of the components of the internal assessment have been completed, a clear and compelling picture of the organization will emerge.

A comprehensive assessment of the external environment must also be completed. This evaluation is essential so that the management team can fully understand the nature of the health care business and the need to act quickly to confront the realities of our changing health care system. An external assessment must include answering the following compelling questions:

- What are the major changes occurring in our health care system?
- What is driving these changes?
- What is the role of government in health care reform?
- What is the federal reform agenda?
- What type of reform is occurring in our state government?
- Who are our competitors?
- What threats do our competitors pose to the organization?
- What do consumers want today in a health care system?
- What are our community's needs for health care services?
- Are these services meeting the community needs?
- In what ways are our competitors superior to us?
- What are our relationships with our vendors?
- How do our costs compare with those of other health care organizations?
- What is the image of the organization in the community?
- How does our medical staff perceive the organization?
- What is our relationship with payers?
- What external community services does our system offer?
- What is our length of stay or service like?
- How does our length of stay compare with other health care organizations?
- What are the outcomes of our recruitment efforts?
- What is the extent of our public relations efforts?
- Who supports our organization?
- What major external factors threaten the viability of the organization?

Completing the external environment assessment clarifies the need for the organization to undergo a total transformation through reengineering. It provides perspective on the opportunities, strengths, and weaknesses of the organization and the threats to its success, and it stimulates thought on how the organization must position itself for viability and future success.

Visioning

The internal and external assessments prepare the management team for the next major step in the reengineering process—visioning. The most important, difficult, and challenging aspect of this step is to be truly visionary, which requires the management team to tap their creative powers. Most health care organizations do not have a clear vision of what they want their new organization to look like after reengineering.

While visioning seems complex, it really is a simple concept. It involves imagination and creativity. Because this step is so essential to the reengineering process, a visioning retreat should be established for the purpose of bringing the management team together, with the overall objective of creating the new organization.

The first step in the visioning process is to accept the realities of the internal and external assessments. The team needs to thoroughly discuss its dissatisfaction with what currently exists and to make a commitment to change the organization. The assessment phase clearly paves the way for visioning. It reminds the team of past mistakes and drives its thinking beyond the status quo.

The visioning session begins with the question: If there were absolutely no obstacles or restraints, what would our organization look like? From here, the brainstorming begins. It is essential that the chief executive lead the visioning session to further support the concept that top management is fully committed to the reengineering initiative. It also places the chief executive in a new light, in the role of transformational leader.

Following the visioning session, the brainstorming material must be concisely developed into a vision statement for the new organization. It should read smoothly and should clearly identify the structure and characteristics of the new organization. Exhibit 2–2 presents a vision statement that was developed by a health care organization's management team under the leadership of one of the authors. This vision statement was developed in an overall process for organizational transformation through reengineering. The vision then is a clear picture of the future organization.

There are certain organizational imperatives for creation of the vision. The vision must be created by the entire management team, not just a choice few. This strategy will foster a real ownership by the team for the vision. The vision must be realistic, tangible, and not so far-fetched that it cannot come to fruition. Most

Exhibit 2–2 Vision Statement for an Acute Care Osteopathic Hospital

The Medical Center will be a model organization known for providing holistic health care founded within the principles, teachings, and philosophy of osteopathic medicine. Our patients will receive the highest quality health care provided by a staff of physicians, administrators, professional nurses, and clinicians and by support staff committed to excellence in service delivery and continuous improvement. To establish a model organization, the members of the Medical Center Board, its physicians, administration, and staff associates will work together, unified under these guiding principles:

- *Respect for the individual*—Each staff associate, manager, and physician is regarded as the most valued resource of the Medical Center; individuals in the organization and each customer will be treated with respect and dignity.
- *Teamwork*—The organization will work synergistically as a place without walls or barriers, to progress and change. All members of the organization will respect and value one another's ideas. Management and staff associates will work in partnership to drive the organization forward, unified, to face the challenges of today and the future.
- *Learning*—The organization will value learning and education to the highest degree, continue to support the programs established in osteopathic medicine, and establish and maintain programs that further the education and skill development of managers and staff associates.
- *Trust*—The foundation for every relationship between members of the organization is trust; in order to foster trust among staff, communication will be open and forthcoming.
- *Partnership and collaboration*—The organization will focus attention on working with the leadership of the surrounding communities to provide quality health care services for all those it serves and will seek out ventures with other health care providers that will extend opportunities for the organization to grow and expand the delivery of the specialized services of osteopathic medicine.
- *Continuous improvement*—The organization will support and foster change as a means to continue to improve the work environment and all aspects of its operations in the delivery of health care services.
- *Fiscal responsibility*—The organization will operate in a manner that maintains quality in service delivery while providing these services at a reasonable cost. All members of the organization will control the costs of operations and avoid misuse and waste. As a result of maintaining a sound fiscal base, the organization will secure the viability to continue to provide health care services to this community well into the future.

important, the vision must be constantly and clearly communicated to everyone in the organization and to key players outside the organization, such as the community, vendors, and payers. The vision statement should be posted in easily accessible places throughout the organization.

The vision is the foundation for the transformation of the organization. It will never be realized, however, unless the employees believe in its promise. This can only happen when management is a role model and advocate for the vision. Communicating the vision is not enough; the management team must make it a visible, viable part of daily operations.

When the vision is created, important questions should be discussed.

> Have you thought about your business thoroughly enough that, despite its complexities, you can explain how it hangs together and moves ahead in dynamic interaction with its environment? And there's another question, even more veiled in thinking about vision: are you smart enough and wise enough to make sense out of this business and its marketplace?[16(p.62)]

Without a strong, clear vision, the organization will remain stagnant, and transformation will not occur. Without vision, there is no future for the organization. The major advantages to visioning are:

- It clearly describes what the organization will become.
- It provides a road map for reengineering.
- It provides a compass for the organization in its transformation.
- It provides consensus in the organization.
- It defines what systems and processes need to be reengineered.

Planning

The next phase of the total reengineering initiative is planning. In this phase, the management team comes together and develops concrete, strategic plans for making the vision a reality. This phase, which focuses on what needs to be done to realize the vision, is difficult and challenging.

Planning must focus on four major imperatives for transformation and realization of the vision statement:

1. Increase the quality of all services delivered.
2. Dramatically improve the work environment for employees.
3. Increase customer satisfaction.
4. Develop efficient and effective processes that contribute to care delivery in a cost-effective way.

The planning session must be intense and must tap the skills and abilities of the management team, and the session must be led by top management. A new way of thinking must prevail. "When a company reinvents itself, it must alter the underlying assumptions and premises on which its decisions and actions are based."[6(p.98)] This is the time to face and relinquish the fear of change, to welcome change as a wonderful opportunity to become better. This is also a time for further identification of sacred cows. They must go; everything must seem possible.

The planning session begins by brainstorming what processes and systems need reengineering to transform the organization and realize the vision. As the session continues, the management team identifies what must be accomplished. These imperatives are then translated into major reengineering projects. From here, multifunctional teams are formed to tackle each reengineering project. A team leader is elected, and team members volunteer to participate.

Then, the teams need to meet in small planning groups and begin writing the project plan. The goals and objectives of the project must be established. This team session includes planning for recruitment of staff members to join the teams. The team should identify any constraints that will exist and develop a plan to overcome them. An initial budget should be developed on the basis of resources required for the project. A timetable for the project should also be developed at this time. A project can take from a few months to four years, with the typical project taking 9 to 12 months.[9]

A facilitator should be chosen for each team. In addition, executive management must commit to sponsoring a team-building seminar for the project team members. The rewards of such an effort will surely outweigh the costs. See Chapter 7 for discussion of team formation and dynamics in reengineering.

Project teams are resource intensive. They must meet frequently, and executive management must commit to providing them with the human and fiscal resources necessary for reengineering. All teams should meet together once a month to share their progress.

Starting from Scratch

The very core of reengineering is found in the phase of starting from scratch. The previous phases lay the foundation for this critical point in the process. In this phase, actual reengineering of processes occurs. This phase is the most time intensive of all the steps in the reengineering initiative, the most challenging, and the most enjoyable. Hammer and Champy[4] advocate one tool for process reengineering: a blank sheet of paper.

Once processes have been identified for change, the reengineering team must recreate the process, not simply attempt to improve it. If improvement is what you want, then improvement is what you will get. However, if dramatic change with outcomes of speed, quality, efficiency, and effectiveness is the desired outcome, then the process must be reengineered.

Reengineered processes need to look very different from traditional ones[4] because reengineering is about radical change and dramatic improvements, innovation,[3] and recreation. To reengineer, the teams go to the drawing board, start with a blank sheet, and totally recreate the process.

To assist in process reengineering, the following guidelines should be adhered to:

- Delete everything that does not add value; this is the essence of re-engineering.[3]
- Let no organizational facet be immune to change or elimination.
- Be innovative—break all assumptions.[3]
- Focus on the breadth of the process.[14]
- Innovate mental work, and do not replicate physical work.[17]
- Focus on total customer satisfaction.[11]
- Coordinate the management of change into the new process.[18]
- Focus on the objectives of process reengineering.[19]
- Recreate processes so that workers make the decisions.[4]
- Remodel the work flow to streamline the business operations.[15]
- Incorporate automation, which is a key enabler in process reengineering.
- Design work into process teams.[4]
- Focus on keeping the process simple.
- Cut out all redundancy in the new process.
- Implement quality initiatives in the new process.[20]
- Set up the process for ongoing, continual improvements.[20]
- Define desired outcomes of the new process.
- Draw a flowchart for the new process.
- Redesign the work of the new process.
- Constantly add value to the process.
- Destroy the division of labor in the process.
- Redesign many jobs into one.[4]
- Challenge the process as it is being created, and constantly rethink it.

Learning to reengineer processes comes by doing. There is no secret formula or magical trick to it. The guidelines above will be helpful in the recreation of processes. Another major imperative to focus on while reengineering processes is the development of goals. Exhibit 2–3 presents the 12 major goals of the reengineering of health care systems. These goals should be used as an additional support to process reengineering and the overall organizational transformation initiative. These defined goals provide further structure for the reengineering of processes and of the organization.

Exhibit 2–3 Goals for Reengineering

---

1. **Synergy**—a focus on integration of systems and processes so that the whole will be greater than the sum of its parts, with all systems and processes working together in harmony
2. **Organizational transformation**—realization of a radically changed and transformed organization through reengineering, with the organizational imperatives for transformation driving the reengineering effort
3. **Change**—prevalence of change throughout the project, with change expected, planned, and managed
4. **Success**—organizational success now and in the future
5. **Reconfiguration**—the ability of the organization to successfully downsize without compromising quality, to become "lean and mean"
6. **Partnerships**—development and thriving of partnerships, with customers, vendors, and payers
7. **Efficiency**—emphasis on timely delivery of services
8. **Effectiveness**—care delivery resulting in excellent clinical outcomes, with a primary objective of quality patient care
9. **Role redesign**—redesign of the role of management to that of transformational leader
10. **Competitiveness**—emphasis on being highly competitive in the marketplace, especially in managed care
11. **Systems thinking**—functioning of the organization as an open, interactive system rather than in specialized isolated divisions
12. **Knowledge**—a focus on cultivation of knowledge, producing an organization where constant learning is promoted and valued

---

Testing

Once teams have completed the creation of new processes, the testing phase can begin. In this phase, a performance model of the newly reengineered process is developed.[7] The model is presented to the staff most involved. Education, training, and motivation for the new process are led by the project team. All staff education should include problem cause-and-effect analysis, rudimentary statistical process control, and group problem-solving techniques.[21] Further plans are developed for the implementation of the new process; these include automation and physical redesign of facilities, as appropriate.

Time frames for testing the process innovation must also be established. They should be realistic and not rushed. Staff must be afforded ample opportunity to buy into the new process and make it work. One of the major reasons for failure of reengineering projects is that the organization was not ready to make a commitment to the time and energy required to test the new process.[7]

Reengineering is an organized response to change,[18] so some resistance is to be expected. Resistance can be minimized by ongoing communication, staff involvement in team ad hoc committees, and education about change and how to deal with it. The testing process requires much time. Employees must become desensitized to the magnitude of change, not necessarily to the new process. The management and reengineering team can assist in this change process by demonstrating their commitment to the new process and/or system and by demonstrating that it is highly valued by the organization. The prevailing attitude must be that constant stimulation through new goals and process configurations fuels the fires of creativity and productivity.

Evaluation

The implementation evaluation is the next phase of the project. In this phase, the reengineering team and the employees systematically evaluate the new processes over a defined time frame. To assist in the evaluation process, it is necessary to define outcomes for the project. Exhibit 2–4 presents broad-based outcomes that can be established for any reengineering project in health care. These outcomes should then be concisely analyzed against the realized outcomes of the project. Specific outcomes for each newly developed process must also be established.

Evaluation must be carefully planned and ongoing. Critical indicators must be developed and measured frequently. The evaluation phase is enjoyable, as the organization begins to realize the fruits of its labor. The reengineering project must also be evaluated against the vision statement. Is the vision becoming a reality? If reengineering was done correctly and with commitment and support of the management team, it will be easy to see the vision unfold.

Revisiting

The last phase of the initiative is to periodically revisit the reengineering process. As change continues in the health care environment, the methodology for reengineering must constantly be revisited. As change occurs, environments are affected, and the need for more internal change becomes manifest. Our health care system will never be static; it will constantly evolve. As it evolves, the organization must be positioned for more change. The reengineering process is the strategy that can be used to drive needed change in the future.

CASE STUDIES

To fully appreciate the scope and depth of reengineering, it is helpful to examine case studies. Reengineering is new, so few case studies have been published.

Exhibit 2–4 Outcomes for Reengineering

1. **Transformation**—evidence of radical change in processes, systems, and within the organization, with changes positive, transformational, and measurable
2. **Simplicity**—simplified processes and systems with complexities of former processes nonexistent
3. **Cost reductions**—demonstrable reductions in overall and specific costs, as a result of process innovation
4. **Cultural transformation**—recreation of the culture of the organization with change no longer feared or a barrier to innovation
5. **Quality**—enhancement of the quality of all services delivered by the organization, with measurable improvements in quality
6. **Expediency**—improved time of response to the customer as a predominant element of the organization, with services delivered in a realistic and timely fashion
7. **Satisfaction**—increase in overall satisfaction of all identified customers of the organization, with improvement in satisfaction over time
8. **Increased market share**—establishment of a competitive organization, with increased market share in the community and improved ability to acquire managed care network contracts
9. **Focus on customer**—complete dedication of the organization to providing service to customers
10. **Viability**—establishment of the organization as strong, financially sound, and well on its way to future success

Most of these cases have been from industry rather than from health care, because reengineering has its birth in general industry. The following is a very brief synopsis of noteworthy cases from industries that have successfully reengineered.

An excellent case study of effective reengineering in the IBM Credit Corporation was presented by Hammer and Champy.[4] Prior to reengineering of the processes for this organization, the process for client application for credit to final approval was composed of five major steps, with many different employees involved. It generally took from six days to two weeks to approve an application. The duration of this process was unacceptable to customers and gave them ample time to obtain financing elsewhere. When the corporation examined the process, it found that the actual application approval process took only 90 minutes.

Management soon realized that the problem was not the required tasks or the people doing the work; instead, it was the process that was inefficient and causing them to lose market share. The management team set out to reinvent the process. In its recreation, or reengineering, the corporation replaced specialists with generalists. Instead of the application being sent to five or six specialists for piecemeal task completion, one generalist now processes the entire application.

The outcomes were very impressive. Evaluation of the reengineered process showed that application process time was reduced to four hours, the number of positions was reduced, and the number of processed applications increased over one hundredfold. This is an excellent example of process innovation with far-reaching outcomes. The core elements of this reengineering process were: speed, simplicity, cost reductions, and customer satisfaction.

Hammer and Champy[4] provide us with another example of successful reengineering—Ford Motor Company. Ford's accounts payable department employed 500 people prior to reengineering. To reduce costs and downsize the operation, Ford initiated a reengineering project. The procurement process, which included accounts payable, purchasing, and receiving, was eventually targeted for reengineering. The old process was extremely complex, was redundant with unnecessary checks and balances, and involved a slow, time-consuming system overloaded with forms and papers and many people processing receivables in a piecemeal fashion.

Ford reengineered the procurement process, and the change and outcomes were radical. The new process is simple. The authorization for payment of receivables is accomplished at the receiving dock through automation when products are received. Ford broke all of its traditional rules and assumptions. The outcome of the recreated process is speed and dramatic cost savings. Ford now has only 125 people in its vendor payment process.

Another excellent example from industry is that of GTE.[2] When it reengineered, GTE looked at its telephone operations business. These particular operations accounted for the majority of the company's annual revenues. An organizational analysis indicated that GTE needed to enhance its customer service. Reengineering took place on the basis of the new assumption that customers want one-stop shopping—"one number to fix an erratic dial tone, question a bill, sign up for call waiting, or all three, at any time of the day."[2(pp.41–42)]

In its reengineering initiative, the company created a customer care center and piloted it. The project encompassed a massive physical redesign and automation of processes to link up the various services. New software was developed to allow operators free access to data bases so they can handle all of the customer requests. In the reengineering process, GTE eliminated enormous amounts of work, and the pilot studies showed a 30 percent increase in productivity.

The reengineering in health care is just beginning. In Part II of this book, many dynamic case studies from pioneering health care organizations and businesses that have successfully reengineered are presented. As reengineering becomes more common and studies of reengineering are published and reviewed, it will become apparent that reengineering is not just a new fad, but rather, a solid methodology for driving radical, needed change in health care delivery.

CONCLUSION

Time is not standing still for our health care system. The system is in rapid transition and transformation. Health care organizations cannot accept or deal effectively with the radical changes about to overcome them without a solid methodology for changing and transforming themselves. Does such a methodology exist? The answer is yes—and it is found in reengineering. "Reengineering is new and it has to be done," asserts Peter F. Drucker, the most eminent of management experts."[2(p.41)] Nothing could be more true or applicable for our health care delivery system today.

Reengineering is a journey—a long and often painful one. It is about that which organizations fear the most—change. It is often expensive, time-consuming, energy draining, and complex. It is also innovative, invigorating, transformational, empowering, and enlightening. For today's health care organizations, it is the road best traveled.

REFERENCES

1. Hammer M. Reengineering work: Don't automate, obliterate. *Harvard Business Rev.* 1990;68(4):104–112.
2. Stewart TA. Reengineering: The hot new management tool. *Fortune.* 1993;128(4):41–48.
3. Coan T. Start-from-scratch thinking: The prerequisite for reengineering. Presented at the annual conference of the American Organization of Nurse Executives; April 11, 1994.
4. Hammer M, Champy J. *Reengineering the Corporation: A Manifesto for Business Revolution.* New York: Harper Business; 1993.
5. Sheridan JH. The huntmaster's solution. *Industry Week.* 1994;243(5):49, 50, 52.
6. Goss T, Pascale R, Athos A. The reinvention roller coaster: Risking the present for a powerful future. *Harvard Business Rev.* 1993;71(November/December):97–108.
7. Wachel W. Reengineering: Beyond incremental change. *Healthcare Executive.* 1994;9(July/August):18–21.
8. Easton R. Reengineering health information management: The first steps. *J AHIMA.* 1992;63(6):50–57.
9. Bergman R. Reengineering health care. *Hosp Health Networks.* 1994;68(3):28–36.
10. Tonges M, Lawrenz E. Reengineering: The work redesign-technology link. *J Nurs Adm.* 1993;23(10):15–22.
11. Lowenthal J. Reengineering the organization: A step-by-step approach to corporate revitalization. Part I. *Qual Prog.* 1994;27(1):93–95.
12. McManis GL. Reinventing the system. *Hosp Health Networks.* 1993;62(19):42–46.
13. Morris D, Brandon J. Reengineering the hospital: Making change work for you. *Comput Healthcare.* 1991;12(11):59–64.

14. Hall G, Rosenthal J, Wade J. How to make reengineering really work. *Harvard Business Rev.* 1993;71(6):119–131.
15. Morris D. You may be a target for business reengineering. *Comput Healthcare.* 1991;12(3):31–32.
16. Beckham JD. The vision thing. *Healthcare Forum.* 1994;37:60–68.
17. Duck JD. Managing change: The art of balancing. *Harvard Business Rev.* 1993;71(6): 109–118.
18. Morris D, Brandon J. Reengineering: More than meets the eye. *Comput Healthcare.* 1992;13(11):52–54.
19. Helppie RD. A time for reengineering. *Comput Healthcare.* 1992;13(1):22–24.
20. Greising D. Quality: How to make it pay. *Businessweek.* 1994;3384:54–59.
21. Bernd DL, Reed MM. Reengineering women's health services. *Healthcare Forum.* 1994;1:63–67.

■ 3 ■

Reengineering in a Reformed Health Care System

Tim Porter-O'Grady, EdD, PhD, FAAN

The rate of change in health care is unparalleled in any other time in the history of the American health care system. Driven by technological and economic forces, the whole of health care is being retooled for the 21st century.[1] Under the gun to better utilize resources and to expand services to all Americans, the leadership has focused on change at all levels of the system.[2]

The health care revolution has already begun, regardless of what is occurring with federal and state legislation. Private reconfiguring of service relationships has created a number of structures that support the integration of a wide variety of players.[3] Physician-hospital organizations are emerging, exemplifying the interdependence of their relationship in any future model.[4] The economics of the relationship is changing the character of their interaction, and the financial association between them is redefining the way service is provided and paid for.

Delivery of service, too, is in the midst of retooling.[5] Subscriber-based approaches to health service are changing the focus from treatment of illness to prevention and reduction of the service and cost impact of illness on the system. The goal in the framework of capitated (price of service's prenegotiated and capped rate) fixed-rate service is to maximize the margin between reimbursed services and how much and what kind of service is provided.[6] The drive to use high technology and resource-intensive services because they are available is no longer a viable strategy. Using more resources than necessary can have a tremendously negative impact on the cost of care in a fixed-payment model, stretching resources beyond the ability to justify this practice.[7] The demand on the practitioner is to judiciously determine how best to use resources and then do so at the appropriate level of intensity at the time service is provided.

Professional practice of medical care and health care is now a much more studied undertaking. Gone are the days when professionals made independent clinical and critical judgments about patients, their health status, and what to do

37

about it solely on the basis of good clinical analysis. Now, a much clearer delineation regarding the merits of certain clinical decisions must be undertaken. Justification must be compared to clinical benchmarks, which serve to normalize the interaction and create a framework for developing a behavioral standard that is both acceptable and replicable.[8] Ostensibly, such practices will normalize clinical decisions and actions and create a standard of service and care that is both cost acceptable and clinically beneficial.[9]

None of this occurs without great noise. Physicians, use to a great degree of clinical independence, are now required to submit their work to review, at a number of levels, by both payers and providers. Unconvinced that such reviews address the service needs of the patient, physicians object to the control over clinical judgment that such processes require, including the resources and time they take from the physician's own work. Clinical accountability for both efficacy and efficiency, it seems, is the objectionable part of this scenario and one that is difficult to accommodate.[10]

In a health care system where other health professionals are accustomed to intruding into the physician's clinical practice, it is a challenge for physicians to adapt to and trust the value of more partnership orientations.[11] Ultimately, it will become their essential reality. Also, looking at health care as health practice rather than medical practice will call for a significant change in the orientation of physicians to their own role.

Health care leaders, too, are confronted by a reality they are not fully prepared for. While they grudgingly acknowledge the need for change, substantive change in roles and behavior is slow in coming.[12] Often, it is apparent in many redesign efforts that the executive leaders see a need for the organization and its players to change but that they view that need apart from any real change in their own roles. The style and content of the work of such leaders often undergo precious little change, which inadvertently reinforces the perceptions in the staff that the reorganizational change is not substantive and does little to alter the fundamental relationships in the organization.

The shift in paradigm, however, is not forgiving of those who do not wish to undertake the essential changes necessary to meet the conditions of transformation.[13] It must be remembered that reengineering is a response to a global shift in life and reality. If the printing press moved whole societies out of the middle ages, the computer is inexorably moving this world into a new age. The movement is unrelenting and is not optional. The direction of change is already set. It is, however, unclear what the territory of the transformation looks like just beyond the field of view. For a people accustomed to defining goals and points of arrival, it is challenging not to know enough to define what arrival might look like in the emerging reality.[14]

Health care providers are reengineering for the journey,[15] but the effort does not appear to be directed toward a permanent outcome. They are uncertain whether what they are doing can sustain their efforts. Health care professionals must be willing to adapt and alter their activities as the evidence suggests new directions or turns in the road. They can no longer construct permanent structures or establish fixed relationships, because circumstances may change both.[16] What does not work must be quickly abandoned for a different strategy. Data will be the new cornerstone of work and activity and will continuously tell us the relationship between our actions and the results of our efforts. Rewards will be tied to that relationship and to our drive in achieving it.[17]

Success in confronting the vagaries of the journey will depend heavily on how the passage is constructed, and it will require an understanding of what is or is not essential. Health care providers cannot get tied up with inconsequential issues and thus must focus clearly on what they are attempting to do. They must not delude themselves into believing they are on the right path when they are not, which is a real challenge because they have a history of doing just that. Health care professionals must also sort out the fashionable and short term from the consequential.[18]

Reengineering cannot be about strategy and other applied activities. It assumes that every action is subject to assessment and review. Workers cannot be distracted or coerced by false promises of security, benefit, or permanence in a time when none can be assured. The reengineering transformation is about competence for roles, commitment to the work, movement toward defined outcomes, and a flexibility in work content that will challenge the stability and control that leaders once believed assured our understanding and our value[19] as health care providers.

Leaders most notably have much to do in the transformation. Most of what was once asked of leaders (managers) is now meaningless and superficial. The leader is no longer the organizational gatekeeper, the supervisor, the overseer. This notion assumed a parental relationship between the bossed and bosses. Adulthood will be expected of all the players—both leaders and staff. Adult-to-adult interchanges will be the character of communication. More decentralization of services and work will call for more staff independence and interdependence without a great deal of supervision.[20] Those who are unclear about the demands of their accountability simply will not be there. The "lean" organization cannot afford the "fat" of roles not clearly related to their outcomes.

LOOKING OVER THE HORIZON

To which signs of change should reengineering activities be directed? Without clarity of vision, outcome is uncertain. No one can be sure of the long-term outcome. As health care providers ride the winds of change, they must, like seers of old, depend on reading the signs to learn and tell us about the direction they are taking.[21] Some of these directions are already clear.

- The world is quickly becoming a global community driven by economic and technological forces creating connections not previously conceived.

- There is no ascendant society that does not become so at the expense of a descendant group. The earth is a global system; a broken part in one place affects all parts of the system.

- The health of society and the health care system are not separable. If society's ills are not addressed, they always end up in the health care system.

- Broad-based partnerships are the response of the age to the changing global circumstance. Competition is no longer between entities on the global stage but instead operates within; the entity competes with its own standards and pushes them to ensure the highest possible excellence in either product or service.

- Organizations and systems are configuring around their core and rebuilding their structures from the center (core) out. They are removing from their structures anything that impedes their relationship with the core and the achievement of defined outcomes.

- The workplace is increasingly constructed to create stakeholder relationships with all staff. There is a mounting recognition that the system is dependent on the skills and talents of those closest to the point of productivity or service. If ownership is not experienced there, it does not matter where else in the organization it exists.

- The recipient of service is a partner in the enterprise. In that person are the answers to the questions of process and value and the potential to alter and grow toward a more valid and valuable organism. In health care the recipients of service are the owners. It is the obligation of the staff to always keep them in control of their own circumstances.

Everywhere one looks in America today, corporations, systems, and government are attempting to recreate themselves.[16] Their urge to retool is overwhelming in its breadth and depth. The desire to succeed on a larger stage has driven all the players at every level of society to discern what their work means and how important it is in the course of doing business. Reengineering is a vehicle that provides the methodology for fundamental retooling at every level.

The real question is, retooling for what? If efficiencies and cost reduction, profit and service effectiveness are the only goals of reengineering, it will be a short-term experience, falling to the same ruin of many a former failing fad. There must be a much more substantial reason for undertaking such fundamental change.

At the bottom of the reengineering effort is the understanding that an organization is being created *for a fundamentally different world.* The organization of the future does not look the same, because it will not behave the same. The driving forces of change evidenced by the tremendous impact of technology are creating an entirely new scenario for how people organize and how work gets done. In old models, where the driving force was the configuration of work tasks and the people who do them, shifting the players and structures was a standard process. The relationship in the workplace is no longer solely between a person and a machine; it is instead an interactive process that moves the players into the technology itself and creates a virtual community—a concept that is mostly foreign to the present players. This scenario is especially true in health care services.

Technology makes it possible to create a world data base to which every person has access.[22] Today through commercial programs and tomorrow through more specific technological pathways, health care providers will have access to information related to health care from every place in which it is generated. Scanning the whole range of variables and options related to health care activities will provide information to persons that educate and inform but, even more, will draw them to conclusions they might not have seen for themselves in the past.

Clinicians will have available, in complex data bases, information about patient needs, illness, diagnostics, therapeutics, and a range of differential functions that provide a primary framework for decision making.[23] Today's clinical processes, in many instances, will be antecedent to the machinery of decision making of tomorrow. Current structures fail to take into consideration that this information architecture leads to decentralizing of patient services and calls for an emphasis in the continuum of care that is not institutional or even acute in its orientation.

Indeed, much of health care will not be institutionally based. Reconfiguring and reengineering the hospital to be more effective and efficient, as is the case in a majority of current approaches, without consideration of the institution's ultimate diminishment, is a waste of good effort. The goal of reengineering should not be the more efficient hospital. Instead, its outcomes should relate to a changed relationship of acute care activities along a much broader service continuum of which the hospital will be a smaller part.

This understanding changes the reality within which reengineering activities proceed. Instead of moving structure, jobs, and functions around an institutional chessboard, the issue becomes changing careers and responsibilities within an entirely different circumstance. The challenge to all players no longer becomes, "What will my job be in all this change?" Instead, the question becomes, "What does my career path look like and how am I prepared to meet it?" This approach is real reengineering at both the personal and organizational levels.

Technology will affect not only the context of care, but also the content of the clinical role. Much more interdependence and broader service relationships will emerge as care is provided in a number of different circumstances. Clinical knowledge regarding one's work will be vital. Just as vital will be the need to relate, communicate, interact, and contribute to a team-based approach to service delivery. In this new workplace, the health care provider will have a stronger relationship with persons in other disciplines in greater numbers than with those in the provider's discipline.[24]

Two questions emerge. (1) How do the disciplines work together? (2) How is this configuration managed effectively? In redesign, moving workers closer to the point of care is almost a credo. What happens thereafter, however, is as important as getting the players together. Much of the redesign effort today often reflects the creation of some amorphous cross-trained and cross-referenced worker who has no identity other than that in the work and role assigned. For the professional health care worker, issues related to personal and professional identity and contribution complicate this delineation.

The professional health care worker does not always identify with the organization those accountabilities he or she sees in the role. Regulatory processes have historically supported the belief in individual accountability and have often done so at the expense of protecting the patient. While this approach may affect our sensibilities when we think of cross-training, the seeds of accountability and obligation are embedded in the professional role, thus driving a relationship with the patient, not the organization. The individual professional looks to his or her profession for the guidelines that facilitate the use of personal judgment and the application of the profession's standards of service. Good leaders understand this and incorporate this expectation into the accountability of staff roles and into the perspective of leaders regarding accountability. Doing this early in the relationship between management and staff creates the kind of partnership necessary to fully invest the worker into ownership of the work process.[25]

While not unique to health care, the professional equation is a significant factor in the success of reengineering and team-based efforts. There are those who suggest that the professional component is obstreperous and an impediment to the ability to engineer services around the patient's needs. Often, the argument is narrowly directed to health care professionals who are not physicians, causing the argument to lose its strength. There is simply no reason not to harness the professional's sense of social obligation and direct him or her to the planning and purposes of good patient care that advances the work of the professions and enhances their relationships in the interests of good patient care. Any future success in reengineering work will depend on incorporation of this concept. This task is less intensive and less expensive than trying to eliminate professionals or diminish their impact on redesign efforts.[26]

THE MANAGER'S ROLE

Managing this emerging focused relationship among the various work groups creates a whole new set of challenges for the manager. In team-based approaches, the manager role is less directive and more facililtative. Expectation of leadership in this scenario calls for a broader commitment to development and growth of the staff in arenas like problem solving, effective communication, self-directed strategies, and quality-driven, problem-solving processes. There is considerably less focus for the manager on the content of work and increasing attention to the context of work and all that is necessary to support staff in their efforts.[27]

Future managers will be well acquainted with data base systems and the impact and management of great aggregates of information.[23] The manager will be required to collect and generate much service and resource information for the clinical teams in order to provide them with the information they need to validate their work process and to evaluate their effort in terms of outcomes. The reengineered health care workplace will be very computer dependent and information intensive. Clinical and resource information must be readily available in a form that can be quickly accessed and immediately applied. Linkage of clinical data across the continuum of care will be essential to ensure an appropriate data flow across the service configurations in the health care system.

The manager's role in team effectiveness becomes a major focus of the position. Teams must be internally driven and self-directed if they are to maintain the relationships and integrity necessary to their work and affiliations.[28] In the course of human relationships, however, there are breakdowns in communication, interaction, and effectiveness, all of which affect outcomes. The manager is constantly examining these characteristics and assessing the appropriate responses to them. In the manager's effort to facilitate team effectiveness, the team's requisite to address both its issues and the mechanisms it uses are a part of the developmental and leadership role of the manager. It is clear, therefore, that reengineering for the future calls for a significant shift in the role of the leader and the emergence of different expectations for that role. It can no longer be narrowly focused and functional in its application. A broader view of the system and its interactions is an essential characteristic if the manager of today becomes the leader of tomorrow.

A TRANSFORMED STRUCTURE FOR CHANGE

Reengineering work and the workplace means altering the structure of work as much as changing its content. It is not possible to retool the work and the environment without a consequential impact on the structure of decision making and of authority. One of the significant components of a successful work system is the clarity of accountability of its members and the effectiveness of their decisions. A reengineered structure will demand that the system supports ensure primary accountability at the point of service[15]—point-of-care design. This design is a major shift in the critical organizational structure of the health care facility.

Traditional models of organization simply cannot be sustained in a continuum-based approach to delivery of health care services.[29] Furthermore, an organizational structure that does not create a seamless linkage of all its arenas of decision making can't possibly integrate the continuum of services. The attempt to reengineer the work of health care without restructuring the organizational design will result in behaviors and practices that cannot be sustained. Older concepts of structure must give way to newer examplars of organization. Because of the collateral nature of relationships in interdisciplinary systems, it will be necessary to change the hierarchical notions of decision making and design. The structure of administration and of health care systems must be reformatted to support the decision making that occurs at the point of care. Increasingly, because of the need for health care decisions to be made close to the point of care, design must support the move to flatten administrative structure. There will necessarily be a reduction in the number of manager roles in a decentralized health care system. Diminishing the role of the intermediate manager and reducing the number of executive managers will be a common occurrence in this restructuring.

The emerging centrality of the role of the front-line manager will be emphasized in the emerging health care system. Roles once reserved for executive leadership now become standard for the first-line manager. Operating the service within the continuum demands an ability to integrate with other services and players and facilitate a broadly based service network that is self-directed and relatively interdependent. The management of complex information and the generation of important financial, service, and quality data will be essential skills for this individual. The old concept of the superclinician-manager simply will not work in a role that will demand a more sophisticated understanding of systems, financing, and leadership processes.

In point-of-care designs, one emphasis of restructuring roles is reduction of the total number of executive roles to the minimum necessary to link the organization together. Fewer positions that are defined as directional will be necessary when the role of the leader becomes more service oriented and facilitative in its content. As in business, the majority of health care or work decisions will be made in the clinical settings by those closest to the service. This obligation will include an understanding of the financial, service, and quality impact on those decisions on both patient and organization by the service providers themselves. Furnishing support and information to the providers will become a central component of the leader's role. Helping the provider to recognize the parameters of decision making and also to explore alternatives to resource-intensive practices will be an essential characteristic of the role.

Point-of-care design will require the organization to focus its energy and resources on linking systems in a manner that economically and effectively supports the point-of-care activities. Linkage between the hospital board of directors and the service provider will be essential to the efficiency of the organization. Old notions of compartmentalized or unilateral decision making at the governance and administrative levels can't work in a highly integrated organization. Such organizations increasingly depend for their success on the decisions of those at the service end of the decision continuum farthest from the traditional place where governance decisions were made. Besides compartmentalizing decision making, such traditional approaches isolate players and have reduced the investment of workers in decisions that affect what they do.

Seamless structures join decision making at every place in the system, forcing the players to deal with all the issues that affect the quality and viability of decisions made on behalf of the organization. Integrated structure ensures that boards include service providers (in addition to the token or independent physician role) and that service decision makers include those with governance accountability. Building this seamless approach ensures integration but challenges the traditional sensibilities of the old status-based organizational models.[30]

Some basic principles of the integrated organizational system are emerging to provide a framework of values for health care reengineering efforts:

1. Building the continuum of care actually *drives the reengineering effort.* Building the organization around the point of care is the basic requisite of successful reengineering efforts.

2. All the players must be integrated into the processes and structures that affect what they do. No role is exempt from the reengineering effort. Whatever role does not support the effort constrains it.

3. The focus of health care service is not simply on quality and cost, but also on value, which takes into consideration the contribution of both cost and quality to desirable outcomes. It is the balance between the two, however, that ensures the appropriate delineation of value.

4. Physicians do not operate outside the reengineering effort. Accountability requires that physicians be integrated into the decision-making processes of reengineering and are not excused from its obligations and outcomes.

5. Reorganizing efforts reflect the value of partnership in building the system. Hierarchy does not serve as a basis for rebuilding the organization. Defining role and mutual accountability are at the center of partnering processes and provide the foundation for establishing relationships within the context of partnership.

6. Equity between roles and persons is an essential value in redefining relationships in health care. Unilateral or status-based decision making belies the fact that the success of health care organizations will now depend increasingly on the decisions of their clinical providers at the point of service and along the continuum of care.

7. Accountability is the driving energy behind all reengineered roles. All outcome measurement depends on a clear delineation of accountability. Individual and team-based accountabilities serve as the base line for measuring the contribution to the goals and purposes of the organization. Accountability lies at the center of measuring value and effectiveness between provider and patient and between health care service and payer.

8. The principle of ownership is of growing importance in reengineering efforts. All players, regardless of their roles, are stakeholders in the process. Each worker has a role that affects outcome and influences the effectiveness of the health care process. Because of the economies of restraint, no organization can afford to have people on board who do not substantially contribute to the purposes and outcomes of providing efficient health care.

It is clear that the application of new principles reflects a reformatted workplace and calls for leadership to recognize an altered approach to both structuring and managing the health care workplace in the near future. This is not business as usual, and an understanding of roles and behaviors that enhance worker investment and point-of-care decision making is required. Building a skill base for such activities is an essential characteristic of the role of the leader in a reengineered organization.

1. The manager must now incorporate different leadership skills into the role in order to increase effectiveness without taking away ownership from staff for the decisions for which they are accountable.

2. Facilitation of functions rather than direction of activities becomes more important in accountability-based systems. Coaching, developing, and evaluating processes become more fundamental to the success of the enterprise and the role of the players, without removing their obligation for obtaining effective outcomes.

3. The process of integration of both persons and systems moves to the center of the role of the manager. The fit of the pieces of the organization and its care processes is critical to the success of its work. Organization of work processes and integration of efforts along the continuum of care are essential to effective subscriber-based patient care. That linkage between components of the care-giving network is a central thrust of the emerging work of the manager.

4. Coordinating the system and players in the delivery of health care is becoming a seriously challenging role. The manager must be able to use the information system and the health care delivery approach as a basis for determining efficacy, efficiency, and effectiveness. If the variables that af-

fect health care service are not well managed, the ability to adjust and make essential change is severely compromised. The leader must be able to respond in a manner that is fast, fluid, and flexible, as the demands of the consumer and the results of the collected data indicate.

5. The ability to respond to the increasing number of variables affecting the delivery of health care services at a level of immediacy not experienced before is now a key component of the manager's role. Unlike the past expectation, which allowed ample time for analysis, immediate response demands the ability to make quick decisions about the data and to risk what the response will be. Increasing comfort with high levels of risk and a greater number of variables will be essential to the role of the manager.

6. Managing within the continuum of care requires a different role for the manager. Interdisciplinary teams and point-of-care decision making will not require the tightly defined supervisory role of the manager so familiar in institutional models of health care. Much more interdependence will require more support services and less intervention in the daily processes of care giving.

7. The skill level of the manager becomes critical to the effectiveness of the role for the future. Most managers in health care are not prepared for their role; most learn their role on the job. What is necessary today is preparation for the changing demands of the role. It requires skills substantially different from those that were expected and rewarded in the past. A stronger orientation to systems, data management, outcomes, worker support, and accountability approaches requires further development of the first-line manager.

The role of the first-line manager continues to expand in patient-centered and continuum-focused approaches. Local decision making will be the critical point of the majority of decisions that affect what the health care system does. The ability of that leader to manage those processes and link them to other components of the health care continuum is critical. Roles and functions once expected only in the executive position now become constituents of the role of the service manager. Increasingly, the transition of authority and accountability to the front lines of decision making reflects the structuring of the organization around the places where health care services are delivered. The competence of leadership there is accelerating the importance of both the role of the position and the skills of the person who occupies it.

The new paradigm challenges our very concepts of health care and the relationships necessary to facilitate it. It does no good to imagine the continuation of industrial model ideas of organization and assembly line service or product systems. Those times are past. Health care providers must all mourn the loss and find embedded deep within the loss the seeds of a new era in work relationships and configurations. The challenge for all is simply to be available to the opportunities embedded in the change. This openness and response to the transformation process serve as the foundation for our readiness to take on new roles and accountabilities as all work to create a true health-based delivery system.

REFERENCES

1. Altman S. Health care in the nineties: No more of the same. *Hospitals.* 1990;64(4):64.
2. Anderson H. Hospitals seek new ways to integrate health care. *Hospitals.* 1992;66(7):26–36.
3. Shortell S. Creating organized delivery systems: The barriers and facilitators. *Hosp Health Services Adm.* 1993;33(4):447–466.
4. Goldsmith J. Driving the nitroglycerin truck: The relationship between the hospital and physician. *Healthcare Forum J.* 1993;36(2):36–40.
5. Cummings S, O'Malley J. Designing outcome models for patient-focused care. *Semin Nurse Managers.* 1993;1(1):16–21.
6. Buerhaus P. Economics of managed competition and consequences to nurses. *Nurs Economic$.* 1994;12(1):10–17.
7. Eckhart J. Costing out nursing service: Examining the research. *Nurs Economic$.* 1993;11(2):91–98.
8. Watson G. *Strategic Benchmarking.* New York: John Wiley & Sons, Inc; 1993.
9. Contrad D. Coordinating patient care services in regional health systems: The challenge of clinical integration. *Hosp Health Services Adm.* 1993;38(4):491–508.
10. Johnson R. The entrepreneurial physician. *Health Care Manage Rev.* 1992;17(1):73–79.
11. MacStravic S. Warfare or partnership: Which way for health care. *Health Care Manage Rev.* 1990;15(1):37–45.
12. Beckham D. The longest wave—Fad surfing. *Healthcare Forum J.* 1993;36(6):78–82.
13. Moeller D, Johnson K. Shifting the paradigm for health care leadership. *Front Health Service Manage.* 1992;8(3):28–30.
14. Wheatley M. *Leadership and the New Science.* San Francisco: Berrett-Koehler Publishers; 1992.
15. Hammer M, Champy J. *Reengineering the Corporation: A Manifesto for Business Revolution.* New York: Harper Business; 1993.
16. Peters T. *Liberation Management.* New York, NY: Harper & Row; 1992.
17. Flynn AM, Kilgallen ME. Case management: A multidisciplinary approach to the evaluation of cost and quality standards. *J Nurs Care Qual.* 1993;8(1):58–66.
18. Porter-O'Grady T. Patient-focused care service models and nursing: Perils and possibilities. *J Nurs Adm.* 1993;23(3):7–15.
19. Argyris C. *Knowledge for Action.* San Francisco: Jossey-Bass, Inc, Publishers; 1993.
20. Byrne J. The horizontal corporation. *Business Week.* 1993;3351(December 20):76–81.
21. Nauert R. Planning an alternative delivery system. *Top Health Care Financ.* 1992;18(3):64–71.

22. Barnet R, Cavanagh J. *Global Dreams: Imperial Corporations and the New World Order.* New York: Simon & Schuster, Inc; 1994.

23. Tapscott D, Caston A. *Paradigm Shift: The New Promise of Information Technology.* San Francisco: Jossey-Bass, Inc, Publishers; 1993.

24. Luthans F, Hodgetts R, Lee S. New paradigm organizations. *Organizational Dynamics.* 1994;22(3);5–19.

25. Nielson D. *Partnering with Employees.* San Francisco: Jossey-Bass, Inc, Publishers; 1993.

26. Porter-O'Grady T. Work redesign: Fact, fiction, and foible. *Semin Nurse Managers.* 1993;1(1):8–15.

27. Neubauer J. Redesign: Managing role changes and building a new team. *Semin Nurse Managers.* 1993;1(1):26–32.

28. Katzenbach J, Smith D. *The Wisdom of Teams.* Boston: McKinsey & Co; 1993.

29. Kofman F, Senge P. Communities of commitment: The heart of the learning organization. *Organizational Dynamics.* 1993;22(2):5–23.

30. Porter-O'Grady T. Building partnerships in health care: Creating whole systems change. *Nurs Hlth Care.* 1994;15(1):34–38.

■ 4 ■

The TQM–Reengineering Link

Roberta Carefoote, MSN, RN

Picture this scenario:

Your leader returns from a management conference and excitedly talks about reengineering the organization to make it more competitive under health care reform. Shortly after the discussion begins, one executive speaks out and suggests that this "reengineering" approach sounds a lot like your existing total quality management (TQM) process. All eyes turn to you, the quality coordinator, when the financial executive convincingly states that reengineering is just the newest label in the quality movement. "Isn't that so?" she asks, looking to you for confirmation of her statement. You stand, with marker in hand, ready to talk about and illustrate the relationship between quality and reengineering.

You mentally organize your presentation, keeping in mind that you are speaking to executives familiar with TQM and individuals who have little tolerance for lengthy presentations or long-winded speakers. You elect to start with a definition of the two terms and then move to a discussion of their similarities and differences; you can end with how TQM and reengineering work together and an overview of the situations where reengineering can be beneficial. The mental outline seems to "fit" the audience and the time frame for the meeting. You begin!

DEFINITIONS

The acronym TQM was initially coined in 1985 by the Naval Air Systems Command to describe its Japanese-style management approach to quality improvement. Today, just about everyone has a definition for TQM. Simply stated, however, TQM is a management approach to long-term success through customer satisfaction.[1] Inherent in the definition and approach are four tenets that have resonated to many as the right prescription for health care.[2] These tenets are as follows:

1. There is value to proactive and continuous change and improvement, rather than acceptance of the status quo.
2. There is value in involving those closest to the work in the change process.
3. There is value in applying analytical tools to problem solving to ensure better decision making.
4. There is value in listening to the customer as the first step to process improvement.

These four tenets form the underpinnings of TQM and have led many administrators and regulators to adopt the tools and techniques of TQM in health care organizations.

For some, reengineering is a more recent term that was first used a few years ago to describe a blending of several methodologies.[3] Others, however, point to 1990 when Michael Hammer, an information technology consultant, wrote about obliterating outdated work processes and radically redesigning them to achieve dramatic improvements in organizational performance.[4] He called this approach reengineering and underscored three elements—work processes, radical change, and dramatic improvement. Hammer went beyond a definition of the term to put forth seven principles that could "jump start" a reengineering effort in an organization. Collectively, these principles form the underpinnings of a reengineering process, much as the four tenets form the basis for TQM.

The seven principles of reengineering are:

1. to organize work around outcomes rather than tasks, in order to enable one person to perform all the steps in a process
2. to have those who use the output of the process perform the process, in an effort to capitalize on the benefits of specialization
3. to subsume information-processing work into the real work that produces the information, that is, to have the person, unit, or organization that produces information process that information
4. to treat geographically dispersed resources as though they were centralized, by using data bases and telecommunication networks
5. to link parallel activities as they occur, instead of integrating their results once they are completed
6. to put the decision point where the work is performed and build control into the process
7. to capture information only once, at the source.

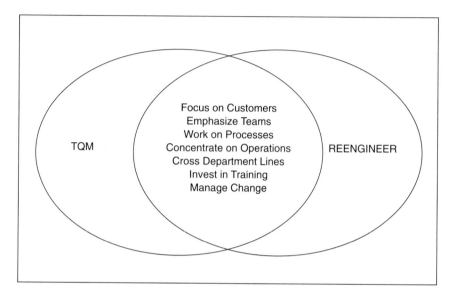

Figure 4–1 Quality and Reengineering: Where Is the Common Ground?

SIMILARITIES

It is easy to see why individuals link TQM and reengineering in conversation. Even though both approaches have unique attributes, there is also much in common (Figure 4–1). They both start with customer needs and work backward to achieve their objectives. While the customers may differ depending on the objective being pursued, it is clear that a high priority is placed on determining customer expectations before any action is taken to change operations. Both approaches emphasize the need to pull people together who are involved in the processes under review. As a result, teamwork and skills are essential to successful implementation. Both methods focus on the processes that support an organization's mission and, for the most part, focus only on those processes that cross departmental or functional lines. Operational processes that fall within the sole domain of one department may be examined by using TQM tools and techniques, but it is the cross-functional processes that are common to both TQM and reengineering. Both approaches require that a significant amount of time and resources be devoted to training and educating individuals on principles, tools, and techniques. Because both approaches are relatively new in the United States, training in the use of TQM and reengineering is not common in educational settings and is often left to the employer and work setting. Finally, both approaches deal with behavioral and operational change, thereby demanding a conscious plan of action for managing the change effort.

Thus, five elements common to TQM and reengineering are (1) a focus on the customer, (2) emphasis on teamwork, (3) orientation to process, (4) educational requirement, and (5) change management. The extent of overlap between the two approaches can serve to confuse the uneducated as well as the educated. However, when one begins to delve further into the subject, it is clear that each approach has a uniqueness that sets it apart despite the commonality.

DIFFERENCES

Reengineering is not the same as TQM or any other manifestation of the quality movement, according to Hammer and Champy.[5] In at least five areas, the differences between TQM and reengineering are significant (Figure 4–2).

Emphasis

Where TQM purports to improve a process—clinical or operational—reengineering purports to reinvent the process. Where TQM focuses on removing the waste and non–value-added work from existing practices, reengineering focuses on devising a new process. In brief, TQM works to make a better organization and reengineering works to make a different organization. The critical difference is that reengineering is about "beginning with a clean sheet of paper"[6(p.28)] and not about improving, enhancing, or modifying a business.[4]

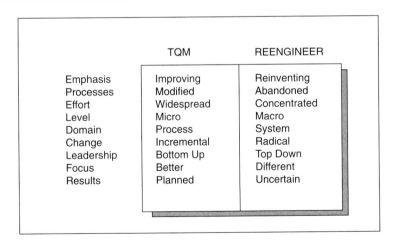

	TQM	REENGINEER
Emphasis	Improving	Reinventing
Processes	Modified	Abandoned
Effort	Widespread	Concentrated
Level	Micro	Macro
Domain	Process	System
Change	Incremental	Radical
Leadership	Bottom Up	Top Down
Focus	Better	Different
Results	Planned	Uncertain

Figure 4–2 Quality and Reengineering: What Is the Difference?

Assumptions

Even though both TQM and reengineering emphasize processes, a key difference lies in the assumptions about those processes. TQM assumes that a process can benefit from improvement but that it is fundamentally sound. There is little if any challenging about whether the process should be continued. Rather, the focus is on streamlining and making the process more efficient and effective. In reengineering, there is a "rejecting of the conventional wisdom and received assumptions of the past."[6(p.28)]

Reengineering does not make any assumptions about the existing process. Instead, you start with a blank page and ask yourself, "If you were to design the ideal process today, what would it look like?" In effect, you are not constrained by what exists; you are free to let your imagination and knowledge of the current environment drive the development of an ideal process. A reengineering process takes nothing for granted; ". . . it ignores what is and concentrates on what should be."[4(p.33)]

Leadership

TQM strives to change the management style and the culture of an organization and for this reason requires everyone's participation. While leadership commitment and support are critical to TQM, it cannot be accomplished solely by management; it requires the widespread effort of everyone working together toward a common goal. Extensive employee participation and buy-in are also important to ensure that an accurate analysis of work processes occurs and that proposed changes are adhered to.[7] This comprehensive grass roots or front-line involvement is often referred to as a "bottom-up" approach. It emphasizes the involvement of staff at all levels of the organization, with an emphasis on individuals who actually carry out the "work" of the organization.

Reengineering does not seek to change an organization's culture; its focus is to dramatically improve performance in one or more areas. For this reason, reengineering efforts can be concentrated in areas that require significant, not incremental, change. This means that reengineering must be led by people with the authority to oversee a process from end to end or top to bottom,[8] individuals capable of seeing the "big picture" and the organization as a whole.[5] This "top down" concentrated approach requires individuals at the level of the chief executive officer, chief operating officer, or department director to assume an active role. It requires that the best people—individuals that managers hate to spare—be pulled together to participate in the effort.[8] Successful reengineering projects have consumed between 20 percent and 60 percent of the time of top executives.[9] These individuals are the driving force behind the reengineering effort.

Focus

In TQM, there is a need to avoid the "world hunger" syndrome, in which quality improvement teams attempt to tackle large complex processes or projects. To be effective, TQM should be used to address "manageable" projects, which are often translated at the operational level as micro rather than macro processes. A macro process is one that is likely to involve several interrelated or connected processes to form a system.[10] Consequently, a micro process is one that does not involve a system of care or operations.

Reengineering is not bound by "world hunger" concerns—quite the contrary. Its focus is to make drastic or quantum leaps in improvement,[5] which can only be accomplished if macro processes or systems are examined. In health care, reengineering does not focus on an admitting process or emergency department procedures, says John Kralovec, vice-president of the First Consulting Group (Long Beach, CA). "We're talking about much larger organizational strategic processes such as arranging care, delivering care and managing care."[6(p.30)]

Change

TQM emphasizes continuous quality improvement, with many incremental changes collectively having an impact on an organization's positioning with its customers.[6] Reengineering emphasizes radical change that should not be undertaken by the uninitiated or uncommitted. According to Hammer,[4] reengineering cannot be planned meticulously and accomplished in small and cautious steps. It's an all-or-nothing proposition with a sometimes uncertain result.

Five features that clearly distinguish reengineering from TQM and other quality management initiatives are (1) reinventing processes, (2) rejecting conventional wisdom, (3) directing from the top, (4) focusing on macro processes, and (5) radically changing operations. These differences need to be understood if one is to appropriately determine the most effective approach in any given situation.

EXAMPLES

To move from the abstract to the concrete, it is helpful to visualize a situation in which TQM is employed and another in which reengineering is utilized. To do so, picture a 150-bed nursing facility in a midwestern state where the administrator has been practicing according to quality management principles for over one year and the staff are comfortable addressing customer issues by using a team format. Early in the year, it becomes evident that staff are unhappy with the process used to serve resident meals. The meals are often served late, which results in delayed and shortened staff breaks and disgruntled employees.

A quality improvement team is assembled with the charge of streamlining the serving process while maintaining resident satisfaction with the dining experience. Staff from the dietary, housekeeping, laundry, recreation, nursing, and social work departments are pulled together to assess the problem and recommend a plan of action. In this situation, TQM is employed to address a manageable topic in a narrowly defined area. The serving process under review is believed to be sound but in need of improvement, and the knowledge and commitment of front-line staff are required to improve operations. The recommended plan of action is expected to change day-to-day operations, but management does not anticipate radical changes. Given this situation, a TQM approach is appropriate.

During the same period at this 150-bed facility, it also becomes evident that residents are not receiving sufficient fluids throughout the day to ensure adequate hydration. Staff notice an increase in urinary tract infections as well as several complaints about the smell of concentrated urine. When staff are asked about the resident hydration system, it becomes clear that such a system does not exist. Residents are offered fluids at mealtimes, at midmorning and afternoon breaks, and sometimes during recreational and personal activities, but there does not appear to be any consistency in the manner, type, or amount of daily fluid offered to the residents. Management staff from the appropriate departments are called together to design a resident hydration system that is simple and easy to understand and follow—one that, when consistently applied, will result in a decrease of urinary tract infections and complaints about urine smells.

In this situation, reengineering is employed to address an issue at the macro level, an issue that touches many staff and consists of a number of subprocesses in several departments. In effect, management is asked to create a system where one does not exist. Any thoughts about current practices are abandoned in favor of a clean sheet of paper and the objective of creating the "ideal" system for hydrating residents. The new system will require management's knowledge about facility operations, and, although the outcome is uncertain, it is likely that there will be significant changes in personnel roles and functions in a number of departments. Given this situation, a reengineering approach is appropriate.

You stop to catch your breath and see how your colleagues are responding to this information. Just about everyone is awake and alert, and you are besieged by questions about the material presented thus far. How does an organization support both TQM and reengineering approaches? How do you know in advance if TQM or reengineering is the most appropriate approach? How long does a reengineering effort take? Who in health care has successfully undertaken a reengineering project, and what were the costs and results? Recognizing the time constraints of this morning's meeting, you agree to continue and talk about the relationship between TQM and reengineering as well as some of the situations that might call for reengineering. Presentations about case studies in health care and the specifics about using reengineering in your organization are advanced to next week's agenda.

THE RELATIONSHIP

An organization can support both TQM and reengineering approaches, and, in some respects, it is helpful if an organization has adopted TQM before it tackles a reengineering project.[8] A TQM environment is one that is already customer oriented, committed to teamwork, and focused on processes—an environment in which the leadership recognizes that continuous education and change are essential if an organization is to succeed in the current fast-paced dynamic marketplace. These TQM attributes will help to minimize the amount of time it takes to get a reengineering project up and running.

Remembering that both TQM and reengineering focus on cross-functional business processes, it is useful to envision a process continuum (Figure 4–3) with improvement (TQM) at one end and redesign (reengineering) at the other end. Process restructuring—something more than improvement but less than redesign—captures the overlap between TQM and reengineering. In using this continuum, it is clear that TQM and reengineering are two ends of the same business process spectrum. Questions about their simultaneous use in an organization are thereby unnecessary; both approaches are essential to ensuring that business processes are in line with customer expectations and needs. Sometimes an organization is in need of a small incremental change, and at other times an organization is in need of radical drastic change.

WHEN TO REENGINEER

Hammer suggests that an organization should reengineer only when it must or when it is driven to; otherwise, it should be improved.[4] When an organization is in need of a 10 percent change in performance in one of its processes, it does not need to be reengineered. TQM efforts are likely sufficient to bring about such a change. Take this brief test before you undertake a process change:

- Do you believe that your business processes are fundamentally sound?
- Are you looking for small incremental changes in performance?
- Are you looking to make your organization better?
- Are you looking for manageable projects with somewhat predictable outcomes?

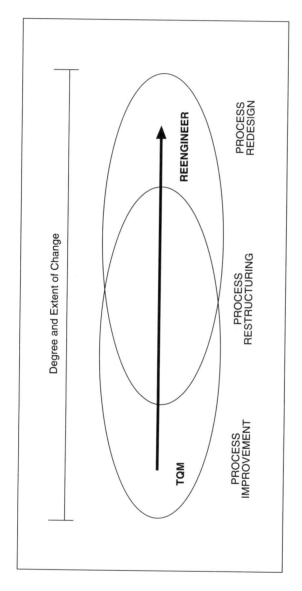

Figure 4–3 Quality and Reengineering: The Process Continuum

- Are you looking to actively involve your staff in decision making and empower them to make changes?
- Are you willing to devote 10 percent to 20 percent of your time to the effort?

If you answered yes to these questions, try TQM tools and techniques.[11–13] Reengineering is used only when a need exists for heavy blasting, when demands dictate blowing up the old and starting anew.[5] Reengineering is used when periodic quantum leaps are required, rather than continual improvement.

On the basis of the collective experiences of Hammer and Champy, three kinds of situations might lead to reengineering.[5] The first situation is when an organization finds itself in deep trouble, for example, a nursing facility that, amid stiff competition, has only a 30 percent occupancy rate. The facility may find that it has no choice but to reengineer if it is to remain solvent. The second situation is when an organization is not yet in trouble but can foresee trouble in the near future. In this case, you might imagine a single home care agency that is operating smoothly in the current competitive environment. Recognizing that managed care is just around the corner, it may elect to reengineer its business practices to fully prepare for this eventuality and keep its market share. The third situation is when an organization is operating at peak efficiency and is envied by others. The organization may be a leader in its field and wants to ensure that it keeps this competitive advantage. It may reengineer in order to set a different standard of care, thereby making it more difficult for other organizations to compete successfully. Regardless of the situation, reengineering is not for the weak or the timid. It requires significant commitment by the leadership and recognition that drastic and radical change will result.

CONCLUSION

TQM and reengineering are relatively new approaches in America[8] and they are even newer applications in health care.[6] This newness and the lack of significant literature on the subject[6] has left many administrators confused about the similarities and differences between the two approaches. Information contained in this chapter clarifies these differences by defining the terms, describing the similarities and overlap, and contrasting five key elements. The link between the two approaches is clarified by the premise that TQM and reengineering are two ends of a continuum and that both are needed in an organization. The trick is to determine when to improve a process and when to start over. While there is no clear-cut answer to this question, a general guideline is suggested—if in doubt, improve; if that fails, reengineer.

Your leader calls the meeting to an end and thanks you for your presentation on reengineering. On leaving the meeting room, you find that not only is the leader excitedly talking about reengineering the organization, she is joined by almost one-half of the executive team. The discussion centers around picking an area to reengineer, and it is easy to see that mental plans are under way to reinvent several key business processes. While you are secretly thrilled by their interest, you realize that your brief educational session this morning has only served to raise their awareness about reengineering. There will be a need for more in-depth discussion about reengineering at your place of employment. You return to your office to plan for next week's meeting and part two of your reengineering presentation—the realities of a reengineering project!

REFERENCES

1. Bemowski K. The quality glossary. *Qual Prog.* 1992;25(2):20–29.
2. Health Care Advisory Board. *Total Quality Management.* Volume II. Washington, DC: The Advisory Board Co; 1992.
3. Lowenthal J. Reengineering the organization: A step-by-step approach to corporate revitalization. Part 2. *Qual Prog.* 1994;27(2):61–63.
4. Hammer M. Reengineering work: Don't automate, obliterate. *Harvard Business Rev.* 1990;68(4):104–112.
5. Hammer M, Champy J. *Reengineering the Corporation: A Manifesto for Business Revolution.* New York: Harper Business; 1993.
6. Bergman R. Reengineering health care. *Hosp Health Networks.* 1994;68(3):28–36.
7. Health Care Advisory Board. *Total Quality Management.* Volume I. Washington, DC: The Advisory Board Co; 1992.
8. Stewart TA. Reengineering: The hot new managing tool. *Fortune.* 1993;128(4):41–48.
9. Hall G, Rosenthal J, Wade J. How to make reengineering really work. *Harvard Business Rev.* 1993;71(6):119–131.
10. *New World Dictionary of the American Language. Second College Edition.* Cleveland, OH: World Publishing Co, Inc; 1974.
11. Growth, Opportunity, Alliance of Lawrence/Quality, Productivity, Competitiveness. *The Memory Jogger—A Pocket Guide of Tools for Continuous Quality Improvement.* Methuen, MA:GOAL/QPC; 1988.
12. Joint Commission on Accreditation of Healthcare Organizations (JCAHO). *An Introduction to Quality Improvement in Health Care.* Oakbrook Terrace, IL:JCAHO; 1991.
13. Leebov W, Ersoz CJ. *The Health Care Manager's Guide to Continuous Quality Improvement.* Chicago, IL: American Hospital Publishing, Inc; 1991.

∎ 5 ∎

Process Reengineering: Strategies for Analysis and Redesign

Jo Anne S. Maehling, MSN, RN, CNAA

Process reengineering: it is logical, creative, and complex all at the same time. This phenomenon is a paradox to some degree, since reengineering aims to simplify work processes, not complicate them. Where the challenge and complexity lie is in organizing the reengineering effort, understanding business processes, unleashing the creativity of the reengineering team, and managing the organizational changes required to execute the reengineering plan. The focus of this chapter is to describe methods used to understand business processes and how these methods can be applied in health care. It also describes how to identify which processes to target for change and examines what reengineering teams must understand about their current processes in order to generate new ones through reengineering.

UNDERSTANDING BUSINESS PROCESSES IN HEALTH CARE

Over the years, health care has become so highly specialized that many of the jobs people perform are oriented to a single task or function. There are multiple small departments and elaborate hierarchies. Methods have not changed for decades, and waste, delays, bottlenecks, and problems continue to contribute to the high costs of health care. To some degree, the current processes were never engineered to begin with; they just evolved. When considering the large number of processes and the complexity of the processes used to deliver patient care in the variety of care settings, it can be overwhelming to try to decide what needs to be reengineered or to determine where to start.

Clearly, experience is limited, as are examples of reengineering in health care. Many organizations are still developing their continuous quality improvement programs; they have not begun to think about reengineering their organizations.

However, given the issues facing the health care industry today, many organizations are incorporating reengineering into their business design strategy.

Some specific examples of reengineering in health care are described in this book; one popular example is the concept of patient-centered care. Patient-centered care is the redesign of patient care in the acute care setting so that hospital resources and personnel are organized around the patients' health care needs. Organizations that have adopted this design examined the core components of patient care and redesigned work, which resulted in the elimination or radical change of many of the current processes. Layers of management were eliminated, and highly specialized single-function jobs were reconfigured to create cross-functional roles.[1] Several aspects of this redesign concept are radical and different. Imagine a hospital without nurses' stations or one where patients are admitted directly to the unit where care is provided, whether it is short term (i.e., same day surgery) or long term (one to several days), thus eliminating the admissions office department. In this design, duties once performed by phlebotomists, electrocardiogram technicians, intravenous therapy teams, respiratory therapy technicians, or unit secretaries are completed by staff who are cross-trained and multifunctional.

Nursing departments are somewhat dismantled and nursing professional staff are part of a care team that is under the direction of a patient care center leader. The care center leader is responsible for a variety of care professionals (e.g., nurses, therapists, and social workers), not just one category of personnel. The care center leader is usually someone with a clinical background, often in nursing, or sometimes in a field such as physical therapy. In large, focused-care units, there is a leader and an assistant leader; at least one of the leaders is a nurse. If the focused-care center is small, requiring only a leader, then the leader is a nurse.

Some consider this concept an outcome of reengineering patient care in the acute hospital setting, but some argue that patient-centered care is only an initial attempt to do limited reengineering.[1] Despite the controversy and the limited data on the cost benefits of patient-centered care, these changes are certainly a beginning approach to rethinking how patient care can be delivered.

For most organizations that attempt reengineering, a starting point is to define core business processes, along with evaluation of the organization's business goals and corporate strategy. This assessment may include identifying product lines and evaluating customer needs, the marketplace, and competition. A primary focus can also be examination of processes that have a high impact on the overall success of the business. Specifically, in health care, it may require definition of patient populations and development of a comprehensive understanding of the processes used to provide the service called patient care. Simply put, any organization must ask the question: What are the critical processes that must be executed to provide the service, produce the product, and operate the support infrastructure of the business?[2]

In their book, *Reengineering the Corporation: A Manifesto for Business Revolution,* Hammer and Champy[3] suggest developing a process map to describe the natural business activities of a company. Process maps display a clear and comprehensive picture of the work that an organization performs. Developing a process map does not require a long period of time, but it can be a challenge because it does not allow people to think of work by department or function, which are usually easy to identify. It requires people as members of a team to think of the work as global or high-level processes that are less clearly defined, cross the grain of the organization, and are more abstract.[3]

Banca di America e di Italia, a retail banking company that radically reengineered its processes, used the process map concept to categorize its critical processes into "families." Examples of families included payments, deposits, withdrawals, and money orders. They analyzed how they currently performed these processes and uncovered several opportunities to radically change the way banking was done. For example, when they examined the check-deposit transaction process, they found that there were 64 activities, 9 forms, and 14 accounts. After reengineering, activities were reduced to 25, using 2 forms, and 2 accounts.[4]

To define core processes in health care, it is helpful to first look at the fundamental components of patient care in the context of a care delivery model. This approach can be useful in attempting to develop a process map to categorize processes or create families of services that are provided for patients. Components of this model may apply to many levels of care—preventive, restorative, or supportive. The model can also be applied to care given in an acute care hospital as well as other care settings. While not all health care providers will fit exactly into this model, its usefulness is in creating a framework for understanding key aspects of patient care.

An example of the care delivery process is shown in Figure 5–1. The elements required to provide patient care are not described by departments or functions but are more global in nature. In the past, we have tended to view and execute the six elements in the model as individual functions rather than as a dynamic set of core processes. Herein lies the challenge to look at the care delivery components in a more conceptual manner.

For any provider, element 1 consists of the processes required for patients to gain entry and, subsequently, to exit the system. The next high-level process, element 2, is to create a record of the event or encounter. This record encompasses both past and present data and serves to represent the entire patient record data base. It is one of the unique elements of the care delivery model that interconnects with all of the other five elements.

Elements 3 and 4 encompass the activities necessary to identify problems and diagnose illness. From these elements flow the treatment plan and implementation (element 5). Element 6 relates to the ongoing monitoring and evaluation of the patient and the care provided. This last element includes planning to meet

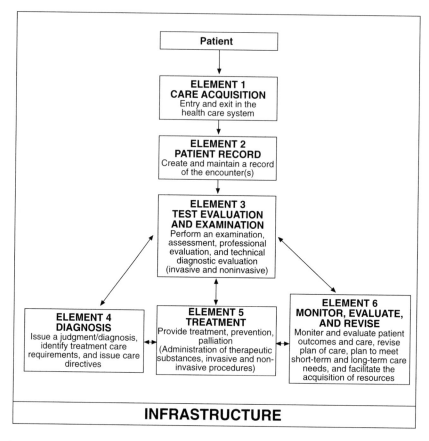

Figure 5–1 The Care Delivery Model

short-term and long-term care needs and facilitating the acquisition of resources to meet these needs. Surrounding these elements are the processes that create the infrastructure and support the execution of the care. Examples of support processes would include housing and feeding patients and producing bills for services.

Process maps often result in identifying a small number of basic processes. Within these limited basic processes are the numerous subprocesses that are performed to conduct one's business. Embedded in the care delivery model are subprocesses, tasks, or functions that are performed to accomplish the primary element. Exhibit 5–1 shows the care delivery model elements and their subprocesses. It illustrates the nature of the many types of work and processes performed in providing patient care.

For example, to complete a diagnostic evaluation, a test may be performed. Subprocesses and tasks would include scheduling the test, transporting the patient, obtaining physician interpretations, producing the report, and communicating the results. Numerous subprocesses, tasks, and functions can be included within the elements.

Integrated within the care delivery model is nursing practice. Nursing practice centers around the delivery of direct care to patients, daily monitoring and management of care, and planning and evaluating patient care. Nursing is therefore embedded within many of the elements of the care process. In this context, nursing can no longer be thought of as a department or entity unto itself. Rather, nursing works in collaboration with many disciplines for the delivery of high-quality care.

IDENTIFYING REENGINEERING OPPORTUNITIES

Once global processes and their associated subprocesses are identified, reengineering teams can explore which processes to change. Profitability and survival in the marketplace can certainly be a driving force toward determining focus.

In the company AT&T, the reengineering team chose to examine a core business line, the Global Business Communication Systems, which sells the telephone system known as the PBX. They selected this process because the business unit was in danger of being dissolved if its performance continued to stagnate and overall performance did not improve.[4] Hallmark Corporation, while still doing well, foresaw the future demands of the marketplace and realized that it needed to dramatically reduce the length of time it took to produce new products and get them to retailers.[3] The approach in both of these examples was, first, to look at the core processes used to produce the services or product, and, second, to identify measures of performance (e.g., outcomes, profitability, and ability to compete in the marketplace) as the determining factor for deciding where to start.

According to Hammer and Champy,[3] three factors can be used to determine priority for deciding which processes to target for reengineering: ". . . dysfunction, impact, and feasibility."[5] While this is not a specific formula for all reengineering projects, it can be used as a guide for teams trying to make choices. Let us see how these criteria can be applied to examples of processes typically performed in health care.

Dysfunction

Often, the most obvious dysfunctional processes are known by the members of an organization. If you are rekeying, recopying, and performing multiple tasks

Exhibit 5–1 Subprocesses of the Care Delivery Model

	Element 1	Element 2	Element 3	Element 4	Element 5	Element 6	Infrastructure / Support Processes
Infrastructure / **Support Processes**	Entry and exit into the health care system	Create historical and current patient information database and record of encounter	Perform an exam/assessment/professional and technical diagnostic evaluation	Issue a judgment or diagnosis; Identify treatment care requirements; Issue care directives	Provide treatment/prevention/palliation	Perform ongoing monitoring evaluation, revision of plan of care; Plan to meet short- and long-term care needs, and facilitate acquisition of resources to meet needs	**Infrastructure** / **Support Processes**
Clean and Maintain the Environment	Admission process	Initiate and maintain current encounter data input	Schedule tests; Perform tests	Issue physician orders	Schedule and perform surgical procedures	Perform daily monitoring and evaluation of patient and care	**Facility Maintenance** / **Staff Education, Orientation, and Training**
Prepare and Deliver Food to Patients	Emergency Room triage and registration	Store and maintain past medical records	Notify and perform consultations	Order transcription	Administer therapeutic agents (medications, IVs, radiation)	Plan discharges	**Communications Processes among Staff (Report, Meetings, Memos)**

Exhibit 5–1 continued

Human Resource Management, Hiring, Employee Relations	Outpatient registration	Retrieve past medical records	Perform tests	Assist other professions ordering care and treatment for patients	Perform rehabilitative therapies (physical, occupational, and speech)	Perform utilization and peer review	Communications processes among staff (report, meetings, memos)
Performance Evaluations, Salary Administration	Short stay and same day surgery registration	Code encounters for payment	Report test findings	Communicate diagnosis	Health teaching, health promotion	Assist long-term care placement	
	Discharge from services	Transcribe dictated encounter events	Obtain tissue and blood samples for exam	Obtain patient treatment preference and consent	Provide respiratory therapy		
	Bill and Collect Payment for Services	**Management of Fiscal Affairs, Budget, and Planning**		**Transport Patients**	**Order, Deliver, and Receive Supplies**		**Scheduling Staff**

that require approvals and the processes appear fragmented, then the process is probably dysfunctional.

Consider the transfer of patients from the intermediate care (stepdown) area to a general care unit. Every day in hospitals throughout the country, staff spend a majority of their day moving patients from one location to the other. In this process, there are delays, bottlenecks, lost articles, and miscommunication resulting in errors. The question to be asked is: Does this process add any value to patient care, or does it just create problems? Perhaps, health care providers need to look further at the elements that comprise this process.

Impact

When searching for processes that have a substantial impact on the organization, what comes to mind are those that affect the length of stay, customer satisfaction, and the cost of care. For example, problems with scheduling, performing diagnostic tests, and obtaining results can certainly increase an inpatient stay. If these processes still take days to complete, resulting in an increased length of stay, and if there is still a considerable amount of waste, fragmentation, rework, and redundancy, then perhaps it is time to rethink how things are done.

Feasibility

Changing major aspects of an organization is no easy task. These processes affect many people and are more difficult to change. Feasibility entails determining the likelihood of success in the reengineering effort. If the proposed changes require major costs or will be met with extreme resistance, then perhaps the change should start in other areas. The dilemma any organization faces is wanting to do that which will achieve the most dramatic results. However, such changes can be the most disruptive to the status quo.

UNDERSTANDING PROCESS REQUIREMENTS

Once the core processes are identified and processes are targeted for change, reengineering teams must not rush to the design table. The next step is to clearly understand the current processes and then move forward to their reinvention. Teams will need to ask important questions about the core elements and their subprocesses:

- What is required to receive or admit a patient into a program or facility?
- How many tasks and people does it take to perform this function?

- What are the costs?
- What is the quality of care, and how much time does it take to achieve the output?
- Do the steps in the process add value to the output, or does the entire process and its output add any value for the customer?
- Is this process necessary?
- How is information technology being utilized?

To search for answers to these questions and to organize reengineering team activities so that process requirements can be understood, the initial step is documentation of the current process. This documentation does not need to be extensively detailed. What is important is to get an overall picture of what happens, including what is done, who does it, and other relevant aspects (e.g., forms and equipment) of the process. The next step is to quickly identify the costs, performance measures, problems, bottlenecks, and issues that surround this process. This step can help identify the financial benefit of the proposed changes.

Then two key questions are asked: (1) What are the assumptions? (2) What steps are required? At this point, the reengineering team must search for the reasons why things are done a particular way. When the team probes further, they begin to uncover the critical outputs of the process studied and its true purpose, which will set the stage for the creative design of the new process. Often the true requirement for a process is as simple as paying the bill, performing the treatment, obtaining the blood sample, communicating the order, or changing the level of intensity of care the patient now requires. However, the extensive processes involved in accomplishing these key outputs are elaborate.

An example of this approach is applied to examination of the process for the transfer of a patient from an intermediate care unit to a general patient care unit. In Table 5–1, an abbreviated version of documentation of this process illustrates how to identify the process tasks, who performs them, where they are performed, the time elements involved, and the problems and issues associated with the tasks and the process. In many organizations, this process could take 16 or more steps, involving sometimes seven or eight people. The time to complete the transfer can range from 1.5 hours to 4 hours or longer. The problems and issues associated with this process are numerous. Costs can be estimated by considering the number of people, salaries, time element, and associated costs of lost article replacement, errors, and waste.

In Table 5–2, the reengineering team looks further into the process to search for the assumptions that are embedded in the current processes, clarify the requirements, and determine if tasks add or do not add value to the output of the process. This analysis revealed that our assumptions led us to believe that things

Table 5–1 Documenting the Current Process

Transfer from Intermediate (Stepdown) Care to General Care

Process Tasks	Who	Where	Timing	Problems
1. Patient is evaluated to determine level of care required	MD, RN	Patient bedside	15 minutes to several hours	MD rounds late or is in surgery, MD doesn't follow unit discharge criteria, need lab results to issue transfer orders
2. Physician writes order for patient transfer in chart and places in nurses station	MD	Patient chart in nurses station	5 minutes to 30 minutes	Can't find chart, MD gets interrupted with pages or phone calls
3. Unit secretary transcribes order	Unit secretary	Nurses station	30 minutes to 1.5 hours	Chart placed in wrong area, unable to read MD handwriting, transcription errors
4. Unit secretary calls admissions to notify of transfer and to obtain bed on general unit	Unit secretary, admissions clerk	Nurses station, admissions office	5 minutes to 30 minutes	Can't get admissions on the phone, bed unavailable
5. Unit secretary transcribes order for transfer and additional orders	Unit secretary, RN	Nurses station	30 minutes to 1 hour	Confusion regarding start of new orders and transfer orders
6. Admissions calls general unit for bed assignment	Admissions clerk, unit secretaries, charge nurse, RN	Admissions office, nurses station	30 minutes to 2 hours or longer	Phone lines busy, people not available
7. Charge nurse/supervisor of general unit assigns bed	Charge nurse, RN	Nurses station	5 minutes to 30 minutes	Unable to find charge nurse, bed not available, disagreement with assignment
8. Bed is assigned	Admissions clerk, secretaries, RN	Nurses station, admissions office	5 minutes	Other departments are not notified of change resulting in errors and waste (i.e., dietary—meals delivered to wrong place; pharmacy—medication delivered to wrong place)

continues

9. Nurse from stepdown calls general unit nurse to give report	RN in both areas	Nurses stations on both areas	5 minutes to 30 minutes or longer	Nurse not available
10. Nurse prepares patient for transfer, collects belongings, and transfers patient	RN, aide in stepdown	Patient room	15 minutes to 1 hour	Patient and family concerns about new environment, articles lost or forgotten, meals missed during transfer process, medications delayed, escort not available

Table 5–2 Identifying Assumptions and Requirements

Process Tasks	Assumptions	Requirements	Adds Value/Does Not Add Value
1. Patient is evaluated to determine level of care required; physician writes order and places in nurses station	• Physician cannot write an order to transfer the patient	• A decision or judgment needs to be made by the physician that a less intense level of care is required	Yes
2. Unit secretary calls admissions and calls occur between units to make bed assignments	• Bed assignments must be made through admissions • Units must control the assignments of beds	• Patient needs to be assigned a new bed	No
3. Report is given from transferring unit nurse to receiving unit nurse	• Verbal report must be given between nurses	• Nurses caring for patients need information	Yes
4. Patient belongings are gathered and patient is moved	• Patients must move to another room to have the level of care changed	• Patients need to be safely moved to other areas with all their belongings	Yes, patients need to be moved safely but . . . do they need to move?

must be done this particular way. The assumptions are that beds can only be assigned by a central department, that nurses must give verbal reports to each other, and that the patient must be moved to an entirely different area if the level of care is to change. When the requirements are examined, it becomes apparent that the primary desired outcome is to change the level of intensity of care for a patient. It was erroneously assumed that this elaborate series of tasks was required to accomplish the desired outcome.

Uncovering the necessary requirements of key processes moves the reengineering team into the creative process of identifying a new approach. In this next phase, teams must achieve breakthrough thinking to be different and creative in their design approaches. They must also focus heavily on considering technology as a key enabler to design of the new process. Again, using the transferring process as an example, teams may decide not to move the patient to change the level of care. They may explore other alternatives that would explore the role technology can play and seek alternatives that are more simplistic and cost-effective.

CONCLUSION

In summary, the methods described are strategies recommended for process reengineering. Reengineering teams must perform process analysis with an approach somewhat different from that used in continuous quality improvement, which seeks to improve current processes. It is not just improving the existing state but innovation and invention that achieve breakthrough results. Like continuous quality improvement, reengineering must include administrative support of risk taking to give teams the willingness and safety to unleash their creative ideas.

Process reengineering is no easy task. It does not, however, have to be laborious and extensive, and it does not take years to achieve dramatic improvements. It must be methodical and directed to focus on the most important elements that drive the business. This chapter illustrates methods of accomplishing process reengineering. These methods require a primary focus on identifying core business process, targeting dysfunctional subprocesses, and, most important, understanding processes and their requirements.

REFERENCES

1. Bergman R. Reengineering health care. *Hosp Health Networks.* 1994;68(4):28–36.
2. Guha S, Kettinger W, Teng J. Business process reengineering: Building a comprehensive methodology. *Information Systems Manage.* 1993;10(2):13–22.

3. Hammer M, Champy J. *Reengineering the Corporation: A Manifesto for Business Revolution.* New York: Harper Business; 1993.
4. Hall G, Rosenthal J, Wade J. How to make reengineering really work. *Harvard Business Rev.* 1993;71(6):119–131.
5. Randall R. The reengineer. *Planning Rev.* 1993;21(3):18–21.

■ 6 ■

Management and Organizational Restructuring: Reforming the Corporate System

Dominick L. Flarey, PhD, MBA, RN, C, CNAA, CHE
Suzanne Smith Blancett, EdD, RN, FAAN

Inherent in the concept of reengineering is radical change. When a change occurs through process reengineering, change ensues throughout the organization. To successfully reengineer, organizations must redesign their management roles and restructure traditional hierarchal, bureaucratic and line-reporting relationships. A new organizational structure that will support ongoing reengineering needs to be created.

When creating a new organizational structure, it is important to keep in mind that, as processes and systems are reengineered, major components of restructuring and role redesign will evolve. Thus, restructuring and role redesign will change as the organization is recreated. This chapter details the planned and evolving changes occurring in organizational structures and management roles as an imperative and as outcomes for reengineering processes and systems. Leadership imperatives and matrix structures are also discussed.

RECREATING MANAGEMENT ROLES

To support an environment for organization-wide reengineering, management roles need to be recreated. Although changes in various responsibilities will evolve as an outcome of reengineering, the imperative for strong leadership remains constant. The most important leadership skill for driving reengineering is communication. Since reengineering is a change initiative, communication must be ongoing and sensitive to the information needs of various stakeholders in the reengineering process. Open communication will increase confidence and trust in the staff, which can lead to increased risk-taking behavior and creativity. This

---

Note: *The authors thank Jack Kenneson, BSME, mechanical engineer, for typesetting the figures in this chapter.*

communication allays employee fears and ensures that everyone in the organization understands how change will occur.

Two additional characteristics must also be designed into the leadership role if reengineering is to be successful. Leaders must become visionaries and motivators for the change initiative.[1] These characteristics require leaders to maintain accountability for the overall rethinking of the organization and to constantly provide the staff with the motivation necessary to bring the vision to reality.

In terms of role structure, reengineering initiatives require a different approach than other, more recent projects for initiating change, such as total quality management, continuous quality improvement, and quality circles. In those approaches, change is generally initiated from the bottom of the organization, with staff driving the project while receiving support from top management. In reengineering, the initiative must be led by one person or a group at the top level of management; if it is led from the bottom up, it will be blocked by organizational barriers.[2] This phenomenon is due in large part to the radical change inherent in the reengineering project.

"'Who fills the leader's role?' The role requires someone who has enough authority over all stakeholders in the process(es) that will undergo reengineering to ensure that reengineering can happen."[1(p.104)] This requirement is essential because the reengineering process crosses many organizational boundaries. As a consequence, issues of turf protection need to be successfully confronted and resolved. Thus, the leader must possess the inherent authority to make reengineering happen. The top leadership is accountable for the judicious allocation of resources and must make them available if reengineering is to succeed. When organizations recreate themselves through major reengineering initiatives, many new roles emerge. Hammer and Champy[1] define five major new roles that are created through and developed by reengineering initiatives:

1. **Leader**—A leader must emerge who can oversee the entire project[2] and ensure that it happens. This reengineering leader, in most instances, should be the chief executive officer or the chief operating officer, so that top management will continue to be engaged and committed to the project. This top-level leadership will also solidify the perception by the entire organization that top executive management is truly living out their responsibility to lead the organization through its recreation.

2. **Process owner**—Process owners are generally the managers who are responsible for specific processes. The major imperative for their role is to facilitate process reengineering and to ensure the integration of departments that is necessary to recreate the organization. They must think differently and support the facilitation of an organization-wide change initiative. It is their responsibility to remove the traditional barriers and

boundaries that have slowed the organization down in its past attempts to respond swiftly to the changing external environment.

3. **Reengineering team**—The reengineering team is the group that actually reengineers processes and systems. Its membership generally consists of multidisciplinary representatives throughout the organization. As reengineering team members, they take on a true leadership role. One of their primary responsibilities is to sell the change concept to everyone in the organization and to be role models for change. These members lead by doing and, as a direct consequence, motivate others to cooperate with the actual reengineering process.

4. **Steering committee**—The steering committee is generally made up of senior and middle managers who assume accountability for developing policy and standards related to reengineering efforts. They also serve as the primary body responsible for the ongoing evolution of the project. Their other major responsibility is to evaluate the need for additional resources for reengineering and to ensure that such resources are available to the reengineering team.

5. **Reengineering czar**—Every organization that reengineers needs a full-time leader who is an expert in process reengineering and serves as a teacher and mentor to the reengineering team. This new leader must also be well versed in the use of specific tools for process reengineering, as well as in the tools and statistical analyses used to evaluate reengineering projects. In this role, the reengineering czar serves as an internal consultant to the organization for its reengineering initiatives.

As previously discussed, one of the major roles of management in any reengineering effort is to help others work through change.[3] Creating an environment for change is the single most important task for driving success in reengineering. Based on this change imperative for change movement, it is essential that the organization's leaders undergo major shifts in the transformation of their roles.

Flarey identified 15 paradigm shifts in the role transformation of the nurse manager.[4(p.42)] Such transformations are applicable for all leaders involved in reengineering projects. These shifts demand that leaders change roles from

1. manager to leader
2. director to coach
3. boss to mentor
4. quality assurance to continuous quality improvement
5. department perspective to organizational perspective
6. clinical audits to research

7. coordinator to project manager
8. participatory management to self-governance
9. turf protection to collaboration
10. control to partnership
11. planning to strategic vision
12. vertical management to horizontal management
13. budgeting to fiscal accountability
14. status quo to innovation
15. department focus to product-line focus.

The authors believe that shifts to these new roles will support the overall reengineering initiatives by the organization and also assist in recreating the organizational culture and climate for ongoing reengineering and change processes. We believe reengineering cannot happen unless this transformation occurs. Such a transformation must be led by top executive management through intense management education and development, as well as role modeling.

THE NEW NURSE MANAGER

The one role that has undergone change and will continue to transform itself in the future is that of the nurse manager.[5] In the context of reengineering, this transformation becomes more critical. The business of health care organizations is the delivery of patient care. This primary product is delivered at the bedside. Consequently, many of the reengineering initiatives in health care are focused on the delivery system of care. Care is delivered by nurses. Thus, the nurse manager role is pivotal to the successful recreation of care delivery and of the organization.

Nurse managers must be included in all phases of the reengineering initiatives and should be assigned a leadership role on the reengineering team. For reengineering to successfully drive change in the delivery of patient care at the bedside, the nurse manager role must be redesigned.

Flarey[5] has identified ten visionary outcomes for the transformation of the nurse manager role. Exhibit 6–1 presents these defined outcomes. These outcomes drive the redesign of the nurse manager role, which must be led by the nurse executive and supported by the chief executive officer and the chief operating officer. Based on these visionary outcomes, coupled with the support and direction of executive management, nurse managers can actually redesign their roles to facilitate the change necessary in the practice environment to support ongoing reengineering of the delivery system. Redesign of the nurse manager role is not an option; it is a must if health care organizations are to successfully recreate themselves to deal with the new environment.

Exhibit 6–1 Ten Role Outcomes for Nurse Managers

1. ***Postentrepreneurial style***. the ability to relinquish bureaucratic styles of leadership; more employee-person centered, with core characteristics of innovation, efficiency, and reward of outcomes; authority derived from expertise and experimentation.[1]

2. ***Empowerment***: ability to empower self and staff for quality patient outcomes; ability to influence organizational policy development as related to patient care.

3. ***Vision***: ability to foresee the growth and development of nursing and management practice and strategically to plan to assist processes.

4. ***Enhancement of image***: ability to identify self as a professional nurse and manager, perceiving self as a leader and enhancing the profession of nursing within the profession, community, and organization.

5. ***Flexibility***: ability to adapt to turbulence in the institution and the practice environment; ability to assess outcomes and design new and better processes in patient care and management to achieve quality and superior service.

6. ***Clinical expertise***: ability to identify with those who are managed; staying close to the client and the practice environment to manage the delivery of health care effectively.

7. ***Analytic thinking***: ability to problem solve effectively using logic and decision support systems and models; ability to conduct research in nursing and management.

8. ***Leadership role identity***: ability to see self as a leader, mentor, and nurse/patient advocate; ability to assist in meeting institutional goals and objectives through effective performance; ability to "get things done."

9. ***Autonomy***: ability to practice nursing and management in a highly decentralized environment without alienation of executive leadership.

10. ***"Change Master"***:[2] ability to identify, cope with, introduce, and assimilate change successfully in the practice environment.

(1) Moss-Kanter R. *When Giants Learn To Dance: Mastering the Challenge of Strategy, Management, and Careers in the 1990s.* New York: Simon & Schuster, Inc; 1989.

(2) Moss-Kanter R. *The Change Masters: Innovation and Entrepreneurship in the American Corporation.* New York: Simon and Schuster, Inc; 1983.

Source: Reprinted from Flarey D, Redesigning Management Roles: The Executive Challenge, *Journal of Nursing Administration,* Vol. 21, No. 2, pp. 40–45, with permission of J.B. Lippincott Company, © 1991.

THE MATRIX STRUCTURE

The hospital, ostensibly a part of the free-market economy, yet resembling it only to the extent of capital needs and profitability, must operate differently from general businesses, requiring new ideas, management approaches and information systems that allow managers to find their way effectively in a hybrid, quasi-free enterprise environment.[6(p.23)]

This phenomenon is certainly true for health care organizations that are undertaking radical changes through reengineering. The successful recreation of the organization through reengineering requires a hybrid structure. This concept is supported by the gurus of reengineering, Hammer and Champy.[1] A hybrid organization structure is one that combines the characteristics of both a product structure and a functional structure. In this structure, functions important to each product or market are decentralized, whereas other functions are centralized.[7]

Because health care organizations are so complex, it is advisable to go beyond a traditional hybrid structure to a matrix structure to support reengineering. For reengineering, health care organizations need an organizational chart that assigns priority to functional activities and product lines simultaneously. "The unique characteristic of the matrix organization is that both product and functional structures are implemented simultaneously in each department."[7(p.242)]

Figure 6–1 details our version of a matrix structure for reengineering in health care organizations. In this structure, the organization retains a semblance of some traditional vertical line reporting around major functions such as: (1) patient care services, (2) ancillary and plant services, (3) finance, (4) medical affairs, (5) human resources, and (6) managed care.

Horizontally, a team-based structure that crosses the traditional, functional boundaries is developed. This team-based structure focuses on ongoing, major imperatives for recreating the organization through reengineering. For health care organizations to recreate themselves and to develop and support an environment for reengineering, we propose that the hospital component of the matrix structure should be developed around the following self-directed teams:

1. **Reengineering team**—This team is the top-level team and is the pivotal point of the horizontal structure. There is an open relationship between the reengineering team and all of the other established teams. Thus, the process between teams is interactive, and the teams support each other in goal attainment. The reengineering team is led by a reengineering executive who reports to the chief executive officer or the chief operating officer.

2. **Patient care team**—This team exists to oversee the integration and recreation of the organization's patient care delivery system. It constantly seeks to reengineer the delivery system on the basis of imperatives of quality, speed and efficiency, customer satisfaction, and cost control. The team is instrumental in assessing the delivery system and identifying opportunities for reengineering.

3. **Operations improvement team**—This team is challenged with assessing the internal environment and seeking ways to reengineer processes to improve specific and overall operations in the organization. It is multi-

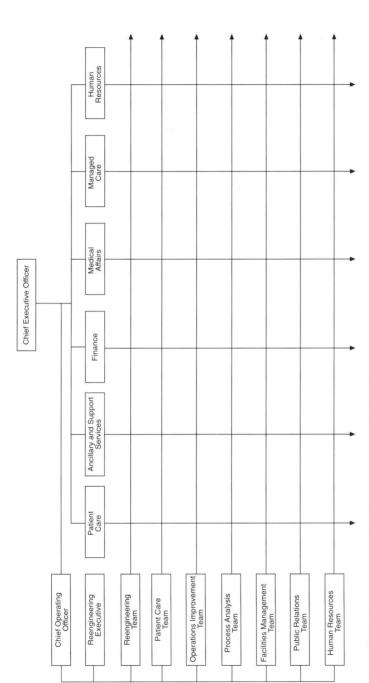

Figure 6–1 Matrix Structure for Reengineering in Health Care Organizations

disciplinary and focuses on patient care improvements and other operations improvements, such as maintenance services, business operations, and utilization management.

4. **Process analysis team**—This team is made up of members who, through education and experience, have developed an expertise in the analysis of existing processes, as well as process recreation. Their interaction will help all other teams to create value in the overall reengineering efforts.

5. **Facilities management team**—This team is charged with the responsibility for overseeing the maintenance and design of the physical plant. The team conducts plant inspections and makes recommendations for redesign based on government regulations as well as customer feedback. This team works with other reengineering teams to add value to the initiative where the physical plant is a component of a reengineering project.

6. **Employee relations team**—This team focuses on the critical issues around "people" in reengineering initiatives. It assists reengineering teams in developing and implementing a communications plan for the project. The team also works to reengineer performance evaluation systems, as well as recognition and reward systems for the newly created organization. Labor relations issues are also handled by the team.

7. **Public relations team**—This team works with all reengineering teams to develop public relations plans for the projects. It also focuses on the marketing of any new services that may have been created through reengineering. Another major focus of the team is to involve physicians, vendors, and other customers in the organization's reengineering efforts. The team also edits and produces an internal newsletter to keep everyone in the organization updated on the progress with reengineering.

Although this team structure is not all-inclusive, these seven teams will adequately serve most organizations in their reengineering efforts. However, organizations must develop teams based on their individual needs.

Regardless of the types of teams developed, the major imperative is that all of the teams are interactive with each other and within the vertical dimension of the matrix structure. This interaction will give maximum value to all reengineering efforts and will drive a fundamental change in the way health care organizations manage their business.

Our matrix model will assist health care organizations to dissolve boundaries and become more integrated. The need to integrate health care organizations more fully, both internally and externally, is a major imperative today in health care reform. "At the strategic level, boundaries are being redrawn as the outlines of integrated health care systems begin to emerge. Physicians, hospitals, payers, and insurers are reconfiguring their boundaries in ways that reflect changing conceptions of what business they are in."[8(p.68)] The future challenge of health care organizations will be to create a boundaryless system; one that is fully integrated and provides for a full continuum of health care services. A matrix organizational structure will facilitate that goal.

RETHINKING THE ORGANIZATION

Through reengineering, newer organizational structures will evolve. These newer structures will be focused on simplicity so that organizations can respond more quickly to rapid changes in both the internal and external environments. We envision the evolution of a new structure that depicts the newly created organization. Figure 6–2 is a representation of that vision.

To enhance the inherent simplicity and focus on the future imperative for health care organizations, this new structure is called the interactive model. This model depicts three core, structured elements of the new organization: (1) human resources, (2) finance and operations, and (3) clinical services. A circular structure is used for each element, to depict its high degree of interactiveness. Each of the core elements further interacts with each of the others. This integrated structure also demonstrates the further need to flatten the hierarchical structure of organizations.

Peter Drucker asserts, "The typical large organization, such as large businesses or a government agency, twenty years hence will have no more than half the levels of management of its counterpart today, and no more than a third the number of 'managers.'"[9(p.207)] This reality is evolving for health care organizations and will be realized in the near future. As Figure 6–2 demonstrates, only three executive positions besides the chief executive officer (CEO) will be needed in the newly integrated health care organization. All activities within the core elements of the new structure will be team based. Remaining managers will not function as they have traditionally. In the coming era, managers within the core elements will function as teachers, team coaches, and mentors. Traditional management duties and responsibilities will be incorporated into the established self-directed teams and will be accomplished by the teams.

This new structure will also drive changes in the redesign of senior management roles. "We must rethink what we want our senior managers to be accountable for. At the same time, we need to align authority and responsibility with that new notion of accountability."[10(p.103)] In the newly created organization, the core competencies of senior managers will be to:

- provide visionary leadership
- remove barriers of organizational transformation
- constantly drive the recreation of the organization

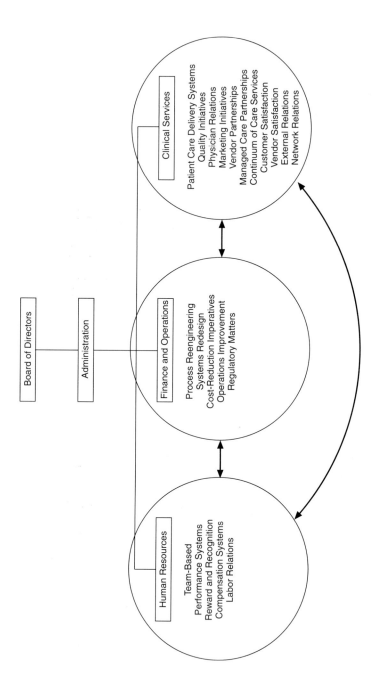

Figure 6–2 The Interactive Organization

- support organizational integration
- develop the continuum of care services
- establish partnerships with the organization's internal and external customers
- ensure that managers are accountable for moving the organization forward
- empower everyone in the organization
- create a knowledge-intense, learning organization
- constantly communicate with the members of the organization
- ensure decision making at the staff level

In creating the new integrated organization for the support of ongoing reengineering, Hammer and Champy[1] describe eight major shifts that need to occur throughout the entire organization:

1. a change from functional departments to teams
2. job change through redesign—from simple tasks to multidimensional tasks
3. a move from control to empowerment
4. a shift from training to ongoing education
5. a change from focus on the evaluation of activities to measurement of results
6. a change in management roles from that of supervisor to that of coach
7. organizational structure changes from hierarchical to flat
8. a transformation of executives into leaders

A health care organization that truly recreates itself through reengineering will experience these shifts, and these shifts will further support the environment necessary for ongoing reengineering. As the organization is recreated and a new structure emerges, some radical changes in reporting relationships will occur. "Executives must challenge the prevailing attitude that people in a particular occupation must report to individuals of a like occupation (accountant to an accountant, nurses to a nurse, pharmacist to a pharmacist)."[11(p.79)]

In a newly created organization, one founded on integration and a team-based structure, reporting relationships will need to change. Even with this inevitable change, the core element of patients' services in the new integrated structure (see Figure 6–2) should be under the leadership of a nurse executive—the one executive on the management team whose primary educational preparation was in patient care delivery. The nurse executive role will emerge as the pivotal role in the newly integrated system. It will be the nurse executive who will undoubtedly lead the reengineering of overall care delivery and who will sustain the organization and continue to move it forward in its overall transformation. Thus, it is imperative that nurse executives acquire new skill sets of transformational leadership, because they will be leading, not only the nursing practice environment, but in partnership with the CEO and a few other senior executives, an entire integrated system of care delivery.

CONCLUSION

To successfully reengineer and create an organizational culture that continually seeks ways to do things better through reengineering, organizations must be recreated. Essential to this transformation are (1) leaders who think and act in ways dramatically different from the past and (2) organizational structures that are simple, flexible, and adaptable to change. These two factors are critical if organizations are to be successful in the future.

REFERENCES

1. Hammer M, Champy J. *Reengineering the Corporation: A Manifesto for Business Revolution.* New York: Harper Business; 1993.
2. Stewart TA. Reengineering: The hot new management tool. *Fortune.* 1993;128(4):41–48.
3. Wachel W. Reengineering: Beyond incremental change. *Healthcare Executive.* 1994;9 (July/August):18–21.
4. Flarey D. The changing role of the nurse manager: Redesign for the 1990s and beyond. *Semin Nurse Managers.* 1993;1(1):41–48.
5. Flarey D. Redesigning management roles: The executive challenge. *J Nurs Adm.* 1991;21(2):40–45.
6. Helppie RD. A time for reengineering. *Comput Healthcare.* 1992;13(1):22–24.
7. Daft R. *Organizational Theory and Design.* 2nd ed. St. Paul, MN: West Publishing Co; 1986.
8. Gilmore T, Hirschhorn L, O'Connor M. The boundaryless organization. *Healthcare Forum J.* 1994;37(4):68–72.
9. Drucker P. *The New Realities.* New York: Harper & Row; 1989.
10. Lathrop J. *Restructuring Health Care: The Patient-Focused Paradigm.* San Francisco: Jossey-Bass, Inc, Publishers; 1993.
11. Shelley S, Jones L. The turnaround process: Management, board, and cultural changes. In: Baehr R, ed. *Engineering a Hospital Turnaround.* Chicago: American Hospital Publishing, Inc; 1993.

■ 7 ■

Teams: The Fundamental Reengineering Work Unit

Suzanne Smith Blancett, EdD, RN, FAAN
Dominick L. Flarey, PhD, MBA, RN, C, CNAA, CHE

Self-directed teams are an integral part of reengineering. From the reengineering team to the transition management team to the process teams, teams become the fundamental work unit in a reengineered organization. These cross-functional, interdisciplinary teams become cohesive groups of people working toward a common goal with a shared sense of purpose. They are distinguished from committees by the interdependence of their members: committee members are chosen specifically because they will represent and defend unique points of view, while team members are chosen because their unique talents will contribute to improving the whole. Only through team work can an organization focus on integrative work processes rather than fragmentation of work through tasks. Although building teams and realigning and allocating work through teams are time-consuming and cause some initial process delays, the lost time is minimal compared with delays from work allocated across functional departments and organizations. Typically a simple process done by one trained team member operates ten times faster than one completed piecemeal by members of individual departments.[1]

The traditional system of dividing work into tasks or functions often leads to employees of the same organization working at cross-purposes. What becomes most important is preserving the integrity of one's department or function rather than focusing on what is needed for the organization to meet its mission of service to the customer. This outlook promotes incongruent goals and encourages waste and inefficiency. The team approach in reengineering takes people, artificially separated by hierarchical organizational structures and reunites them, rearranging not what they do but how they do it.

There are many advantages to using teams to accomplish the work of integrated processes. As work units change from functional departments to process teams, less administration is needed; all team members assume responsibility for ensuring that customer requirements are met on time and with no defects. Empowered team workers find ways to reduce time and cost while continually improving the product or service. Control over the process also improves; since fewer people are involved in a reengineered process, it is easier to assign responsibility and monitor the results.

In addition to horizontal integration across functional lines, reengineered processes integrate the traditional vertical chain of command, eliminating hierarchy. Because the team is empowered to make its own decisions, decision making becomes part of its work. Compression of work both vertically and horizontally leads to fewer delays, lower overhead costs, better response to customers, and greater worker empowerment. Reengineered organizations will be structured around teams. "In fact, most models of the organization of the future that we have heard about, for example networked, clustered, nonhierarchial, horizontal, and so forth, are based on the premise that teams will surpass individuals as the primary unit of performance in the company."[2(p.19)]

THE REENGINEERING TEAM

Hammer and Champy[1] discuss several types of teams, from the primary reengineering team that reengineers the business processes, to the transition management team that oversees complex change, to the process teams that implement new work processes. The reengineering team is composed of the people who actually reinvent the business. Since the delivery of patient care is complex, involving more than one process, it is possible to have more than one reengineering team. The goal of the reengineering team is to improve the performance of the process. Team members are usually appointed by the chief executive officer (CEO) or the person or steering committee designated by the CEO to oversee the reengineering process.

A recommended team size is five to ten members, with representatives from functional areas that will be affected by the change, as well as outsiders. Team members from functional areas bring their knowledge and perceptions of how the organization operates currently, while the outsiders bring objectivity. A ratio of two or three insiders to every outsider is recommended. For example, in reengineering a core process such as patient admissions, organizational insiders might include representatives from finance and nursing, while an outsider might be a former patient or a consultant. Part-time specialists, such as technology or financial experts, can be temporary members of the team, as needed.

While department heads seem like the logical choice as the reengineering team insiders, care must be taken in making this choice. Department heads, as well as employees with seniority, may have a vested interest in maintaining the status quo instead of dramatically reinventing the business. Therefore, selection of the reengineering team members should be based largely on past demonstration of their ability to be good listeners and communicators, to be self-directed, imaginative, and visionary, and to raise questions and challenge assumptions. These traits can be found in employees at all levels.

Hammer and Champy[1] recommend that members of the reengineering team commit at least 75 percent of their time to the project, until at least the first pilot implementation—usually one year. Since the work of the reengineering team lays the foundation for the future and requires significant attitudinal and value shifts as well as knowledge acquisition, members should not be distracted by their old work. Team members should understand that they are on the team to pursue the collective interest of the organization, not the interests of their departments; ties should be severed. They also should not expect to go back to previous jobs, which probably will not exist after the reengineering.

In a complex reengineering project, the team may establish a variety of ad hoc groups to help with organizational and environmental data gathering. Although obtaining input from task forces is more cumbersome and time-consuming than doing the work alone, such input will broaden the base of support for the project, increase the staffs' feelings of ownership of the process, and increase the chances of finding truly creative and unique approaches to reengineering. For example, one hospital established ten "vision teams" to help establish institution-wide service standards in their respective areas and to help in streamlining processes.[3] Chapter 19 also presents discussion of different types of support teams established by a health care system to support the larger work of the reengineering team.

The reengineering team that is inventing new ways of doing work will be hard pressed to avoid the "endless planning, flawless executive model of problem solving,"[1(p.112)] which is a symptom of an organization mired in bureaucracy. To help avoid this problem, one role on the reengineering team is that of gatekeeper. Since the team will have to go through an iterative process of team development, the appointed gatekeeper will watch administrative details, such as moving the agenda, setting up the best meeting space, and monitoring team-developed governing rules. The primary role of gatekeeper, however, is always that of team member, suggesting that the role should probably be rotated among team members.

The greatest challenge the reengineering team will probably face is changing deeply held employee values and attitudes to match recreated vision, mission, goals, structure, and processes. To survive, workers in many traditional organizations have learned to cover up past mistakes and justify past decisions, to seek scapegoats, to make decisions on incomplete or inaccurate information, to avoid new challenges, and to be defensive and suspicious. An ongoing theme of the reengineering team must be to operationalize the traits on which trust is built—

integrity, doing the right thing, strength of conviction, confidence, safety, competence, fairness, reliability, openness, communication, constancy, and predictability.[4(p.26)] Establishing workers' trust in the organization is critical to the success of reengineering.

THE TRANSITION MANAGEMENT TEAM

When multiple reengineering projects affect every aspect of organizational life, the CEO most likely will appoint a transition management team (TMT).[5] Complementing the work of the reengineering team, the TMT is composed of senior managers and leaders, including but not limited to process owners. The TMT oversees the change process and is arbitrator for issues that transcend any given process. Representing the best interests of the entire corporation, the TMT has nine main functions:

1. communicate the mandate for change and the organization's new overall direction
2. stimulate interdisciplinary dialogue
3. decide how resources will be allocated and to stop nonuseful projects that are draining resources
4. coordinate and align projects
5. prioritize competing processes
6. monitor messages, policies, and behavior, especially those that are incongruous with the new direction
7. design, coordinate, and provide support for learning and creation
8. resolve conflicts
9. anticipate and address human relations problems.[5(pp.117–118), 1(p.114)]

The TMT is not solely accountable for all of these tasks; rather, the TMT monitors these areas and collaborates with the other teams, committees, and staff. The TMT should include a member of the reengineering team so that the requirements of reengineered work processes are coordinated with the management of change.

Another major function of the TMT is to assist middle-line and first-line managers in the overall transition to a team-based organization.

> This transition for managers is challenging for two primary reasons: they experience a perceived loss of power and control as they realize that their subordinates are to become their own managers, and they recognize that their repertoire of management skills, often developed over years of experience and struggle, will become somewhat obsolete.[6(p.37)]

PROCESS TEAMS

When people from several functional areas are joined, Hammer and Champy call them a process team, ". . . a unit that naturally falls together to complete a whole piece of work—a process."[1(p.66)] Process teams are a replacement for, not an addition to, departmental structure. Reengineered work processes are implemented, changed, further developed, and improved by process teams. Depending on the complexity and nature of the process, Hammer and Champy recommend different types of process teams. The simplest type of team is the caseworker, a process team of one. In this case, the process can be done by one person who is responsible for an end-to-end process.

A process for which a caseworker might be appropriate is related to sterile supply processing in the operating room. In this scenario, a surgical caseworker would be responsible for collecting instruments following a surgical procedure, cleaning, packing, and sterilizing the instruments, and then stocking them in the proper surgical suites on the basis of the next day's operating schedule. This type of caseworker exemplifies accountability for an end-to-end process.

When the complexity of the process makes it impossible for one person to handle, the process case team is needed. In this team, ". . . a number of people with different skills work together to complete routine, recurring work."[1(p.66)] Team members, among themselves, have the skills needed to handle the process. Because of the stability of the process, this day-to-day work team is usually permanently grouped together. Patient care for a particular type of patient, for example, requires a case team. This particular team concept is the foundation on which traditional case management has been developed.

Hammer and Champy recommend that a case manager be used when the steps of a process are extremely complex or dispersed in such a way that one person or a small team is impossible, as in the patient care delivery model.[1(p.62)] The case manager acts as a buffer between customer and team. In the customer's eyes, the case manager acts as though he or she were responsible for the whole process. To be successful, the case manager needs access to all people and information in the process. It is tempting to think that most hospitals already have the case manager described by Hammer and Champy in the form of the patient representative or the clinical case manager. However, this is not usually so. The patient representative and clinical case manager seldom have the responsibility and accountability to fully commit organizational resources, on the spot and as needed, to address problems.

Complementing the work of a process case team is the virtual team. This team is composed and stays together only to complete a particular, episodic task; for example, a virtual team could be formed to address a problem with quality, such as an unacceptable readmission rate following discharge from a particular unit.

Once the virtual process team has addressed the process problem, it disbands because the next issue or problem will require different team member expertise. See Chapter 17 for a discussion of one health care system's use of a variety of teams for reengineering.

TEAM TRAITS

Although a process team can be established in a day, the effective functioning of the team is an evolving process. The work of the team is to replace competitiveness, fragmentation, and territoriality with cooperation, integration, and collaboration—not an easy task for an organization making its way out of the morass of bureaucracy. The leader and team members have to learn how to share selected leadership and management functions, how to schedule work and staff, and how to monitor the group's productivity and ensure the team's ongoing development. The ultimate goal is a high-performing team that clearly understands its roles, activities, relationships, and environment and, most important, understands that it will be evaluated on these new working relationships.

What are some of the functions that might be taken on by a process team and shared by leader and team members? In describing a company with "very" self-managed teams, Peters lists ten shared activities:[7(p.238)]

1. recruit, hire, evaluate, and terminate employment (if necessary) on their own
2. regularly acquire new skills as they see fit, training one another as necessary
3. formulate, then track and amend, their own budget
4. make capital investment proposals as needed after appropriate study including such elements as supporting analyses and visits to vendors
5. handle quality control, inspection, subsequent troubleshooting, and problem solving
6. take on the task of constantly improving every process and product
7. develop quantitative standards for productivity and quality and then monitor them
8. suggest and then develop prototypes of possible new products and services
9. routinely work on teams fully integrated with counterparts from sales, marketing, and development
10. participate in corporate level strategic projects.

Peters' shared activities are all focused on the imperative of empowerment. These activities are essential to creating truly empowered teams. Empowerment is a function of four variables: authority, resources, information, and accountability.[8] To be fully empowered, teams must have the authority to make the right decisions for customers and the organization, the resources available to meet defined goals and objectives, the information necessary to reengineer work, and the accountability to feel ownership of the work to be accomplished. Of the four variables, accountability is the most important. "At its core, team accountability is about the sincere promises we make to ourselves and others, promises that underpin two critical aspects of teams: commitment and trust."[2(p.60)]

Blancett's survey of 20 nurse executives[9] showed that the most frequently shared work activities in patient services' teams were: interpersonal relations and conflict resolution; quality assurance and improvement; work quality issues; department-wide committee work; communication and coordination; purpose and scope of teams; unit policies, procedures, and standards; staff development and education; and decisions affecting patient care. Unlike the "very" self-managed teams of the organization described by Peters,[7] Blancett's survey[9(p.52)] showed that nurse managers retained responsibility for budgeting (94 percent), compensation (88 percent), hiring (76 percent), and discipline (71 percent). Blancett's findings suggest that we still have not truly tapped into the power and productivity potential of our teams. When an organization does not use the skills and talents it says it values, there is worker frustration, irritation, and often dysfunction.[10(p.3)] The organization actually produces just the type of worker it does not want.

LEADERSHIP AND MANAGERIAL TRAITS

In a reengineered environment that supports team ownership over work processes, management changes from supervisor to coach, from one who controls and directs to one who empowers, listens, and teaches. With empowered process teams, the manager is a mentor, facilitator, and resource who helps teams solve problems, provides advice, enables work processes, and develops people, taking pride in the accomplishments of others and their long-term career development.

Deciding who is right for this new role is critical to the success of process teams. One cannot automatically assume that current managers are capable team leaders. Potential team leaders should be chosen because they have demonstrated the ability to

. . . view change as an opportunity; are constantly pursuing new ideas; are confident and willing to venture into the unknown, to challenge traditional assumptions and rules; value diversity and [are] skillful in consensus-building among diverse groups; work well on a team with a shared vision; are inspiring and able to carry a message effectively to multiple audiences; and have a strong awareness of issues and trends affecting...practice.[11(p.5)]

Effective managers of process teams will have to be flexible. From the beginning of a team's life until its maturity, the manager's approach changes from "hands on" to "on hand." As team roles, relationships, and goals mature, the manager's role shifts from making decisions, to communicating tentative decisions for team input, to presenting information to the team before making a decision, to presenting a problem and asking for input, to defining parameters and letting the team decide, to acting as a resource as the team defines problems and makes decisions. As the team develops and the manager's role becomes more and more "on hand," the team will want to elect a team leader to act as coordinator of the group's work.

"Behavior of leaders accounts for about 13% of the variation in organizational effectiveness. This suggests that the behavior of leaders also has a major impact on the shift in the organization's culture."[12(p.44)] Thus, although new criteria become important in selecting team managers, ongoing education and support in new ways of thinking and doing things are essential to their success. Even the most facilitative managers need assistance in developing existing attributes and learning new approaches to collaboration, participation, and team decision making.

TEAM DEVELOPMENT

All teams, no matter what amount of preparatory education occurs, have to go through developmental phases—from the initial phase when an appointed manager is directing and developing the group to the final phase when the team is fully self-governing. These phases will occur at different rates based on the manager's team-building skills and the team members' receptivity and preparation. The goal is to go from a scenario in which upper management solves the problems to one in which everyone improves the whole system.

In a recent longitudinal study[13] of one organization's change from a bureaucratic structure to self-managing teams, the teams moved through three primary stages over a four-year period. First, each team developed collaborative relationships, establishing its values and program of work. In the second phase, the groups had well-established norms, which members enforced. Finally, group relationships, rules, regulations, and policies became stable and formalized. The authors make the point that the self-managed teams actually had more coercive control over their members than the original bureaucracy. The power of peer pressure to conform was demonstrated.

Several key factors facilitate the work of process teams.[7(pp.208–209)] To be effective, the team has to have space, equipment, and support for their activities.

Close geographical proximity of team members helps build team trust, loyalty, and commitment through social and work interaction. Accomplishing this end might necessitate renovation, relocation of people, and duplication of some equipment and support services. It is also important that team control, including evaluation of team members, be vested in the team leader and its members, rather than in the functional boss. Finally, the team should have the authority to deal with external vendors; commit its members' functional department resources, if there are still functional departments; and encourage contribution from outsiders.

As a new team starts its work, the manager's first goals are (1) to help it define its roles, matching member expertise and interest with the process tasks; (2) to develop the team's operating policies; and (3) to cross-train members in administrative and technical tasks. These activities merge into the problem-solving phase, where the focus shifts from tasks to process. The team will start to develop its unique mission and goals, which the manager will use to keep the team in focus and in action. Although problems and conflicts will occur throughout the life of a team, a manager's style of handling problems initially will be emulated and remembered by team members. If handled correctly, diversity and conflict can promote growth and encourage creativity. Whatever specific technique the manager uses, the overreaching problem-solving style should be to hear and appreciate differences, not try to reconcile them; to validate polarities, not try to reduce the distance between them; and to make it a practice not to avoid or confront extremes. The manager should put team energy into staking out the broadest common ground that all can stand on without compromise or force.

As trust builds and routine operations are understood, the team moves into its peak learning phase. It is motivated by achievement of short-term goals. Members teach other members, as well as being taught by others. The team has a unique sense of identity, learning from others' strengths and helping others improve weak areas. The team conducts most of the team's business. The manager serves primarily as consultant and advisor. Moving into the final stage of team development, members know how actions affect the whole and are fully capable of acting for the team. Informal leaders have emerged from the group. The appointed manager is now truly a resource, setting broad boundaries within which the team can function independently.

Meetings are a necessary part of the team's work. However, to be meaningful and as brief as possible, meetings should be called for three distinct purposes. The first type of meeting is a team process meeting, in which the agenda is group and work process issues. The second type is the problem-solving meeting, with the agenda focused solely on problems needing a team solution. The third type of meeting is the "no" meeting. This means no coffee, doughnuts, or chairs. It's a short gathering for ten minutes or less that is called when the team needs to have a quick huddle to communicate.

CONTRIBUTION AND PERFORMANCE

The shift to an organizational culture that values cooperation and teamwork mandates new approaches to promoting, rewarding, and compensating employees. The work of an employee in a reengineered environment changes from simple definable tasks to work that is substantive. The unproductive work of checking, reconciling, waiting, monitoring, and tracking is eliminated by reengineering—people spend more time doing the real work. In this type of environment, personal development occurs through expanding the breadth of one's work, learning more so one can encompass more of the process. Staff should be spending more time on work that adds value and less time on work that does not contribute to the value of the service or product.

This attitudinal and organizational shift in the nature of how work is done presents a significant challenge to administrators. While jobs are more satisfying, they are also more challenging and difficult. In a bureaucracy, there are plenty of simple, routine jobs that require no skill. In the reengineered organization, the norm is complex jobs for smart people; the criteria for entry into the work force have been significantly raised.[1(p.70)]

"Empowerment is an unavoidable consequence of reengineered process; processes can't be reengineered without empowering process workers."[7(p.71)] Roles are changed from controlled to empowered. Leaders do not want staff who follow rules but who will make their own rules. Teams invested with responsibility for an entire process must be given the authority to make the decisions needed to get it done. "As process team workers they are both permitted and required to think, interact, use judgment, and make decisions."[7(p.70)] Teams performing process-oriented work are inevitably self-directing. Within agreed upon boundaries of their obligations to the organization (e.g., deadlines, productivity goals, and quality standards), they decide how and when the work is going to be done. The real value in team development is when the goal is focused on self-direction. One study highlighting the outcomes from self-directed teams found that in the seven companies reporting, 93 percent of the teams reported improved productivity, 86 percent reported decreased operating costs, 86 percent demonstrated improved quality, and 70 percent reported better employee attitudes about their work and organizations.[8]

This move from individual to team competency shifts evaluation criteria to an emphasis on reward for team contribution. Hammer and Champy's list of beliefs they think all employees in a reengineered company must hold suggest areas in which employees can be evaluated and rewarded:[1(p.76)]

- Customers pay all our salaries; I must do what it takes to please them.
- Every job in this company is essential and important. I do make a difference.

- Showing up is no accomplishment; I get paid for the value I create.
- The buck stops here; I must accept ownership of problems and get them solved.
- I belong to a team; we fail or we succeed together.
- Nobody knows what tomorrow holds; constant learning is a part of my job.

Some possible evaluation criteria that arise from these beliefs are how well team members understand how their roles and responsibilities, their relationships with other staff and teams, and their personal characteristics and competencies affect superior team performance. They need to know the team will be evaluated on its outcomes—high-quality decisions; services and products made, produced, and delivered in a timely, cost-effective way; openness in team communication and conflict resolution; effectiveness in dealing with those outside the team; use of praise and recognition to support, develop, and encourage the team; and finally, the ability to articulate the team's goals.[14(p.96)]

Peters states that the average team member will be evaluated on contribution to the team, ability to manage external relationships, "ability to apply unique expertise, commitment to learning and improving that expertise, and becoming a teacher, passing lessons learned on to teammates and the broader network."[7(p.155)]

Having high-performance teams of empowered employees also mandates new approaches to hiring and developing employees. "Character" must be considered along with a potential team members' educational background, skills, experience, and training. Are they self-starting? Do they have self-discipline? Are they motivated to do what it takes to please a customer? Are they flexible? Do they enjoy work? Likewise, staff development programs shift from training (how to do the tasks of the job) to education (insight and understanding of the "why" of the work).[1(p.71)]

COMPENSATION

Another significant change that occurs with reengineering is that base salaries tend to remain relatively flat. Substantial rewards for performance take the form of bonuses, not raises. People can no longer be paid solely on job rank, seniority, or for just showing up. Contribution and performance are the primary bases for compensation; performance is measured by the value created, and compensation is set accordingly. Employers will start paying for performance and promote for ability.[1(p.74)]

When an organization values productivity over longevity, it is critical that management systems operationalize this value. ". . . the ways in which people are paid, the measures by which their performance is evaluated, and so forth, are the primary shapers of employees' values and beliefs."[1(p.75)] If all employees are not rewarded on the basis of contribution, particularly their contribution to the team's effort, it can have a demoralizing effect on the change process. This value extends to "perks" as well as compensation.

One executive, taking this belief to heart, realized during a reengineering project that his stated organization values did not match reality. He and other executives had large, windowed suites with their concomitant accessories. He realized the ambience of the executive offices sent two messages: "the wrong one and one that impedes communication."[15(p.9)] He pulled the plug on status symbols by creating an environment in which all offices were the same size, containing similar furnishings. His office was turned into an employee library. The executive stated, "If we are serious about teaming, then it is best to have executives in offices near other team members . . . we need to focus the company and the work environment around the people."[15(p.9)] This example illustrates how dramatic, radical, and far-reaching the implications of reengineering are.

CONCLUSION

With flattened hierarchies, increased managerial spans of control, and a more educated, versatile work force, self-directed teams are a necessity. It is through full empowerment of these teams that health care executives will realize maximum productivity and financial gains. Through these gains, the organization will unleash the creativity and commitment of its employees and be positioned to both survive and thrive in the years to come.

REFERENCES

1. Hammer M, Champy J. *Reengineering the Corporation: A Manifesto for Business Revolution.* New York: Harper Business; 1993.
2. Katzenbach J, Smith D. *The Wisdom of Teams: Creating the High-Performance Organization.* New York, Harper Business;1993.
3. Staff. Hospital hopes for $24 million savings by blending CQI with reengineering. *QI/TQM.* 1994;4(4):45–48.
4. Benson TE. Intangibles: The real bottom line. *Industry Week.* 1993;242(16):19–28.
5. Duck JD. Managing change: The art of balance. *Harvard Business Rev.* 1993;71(6):109–118.
6. Manz C, Sims H. *Business without Bosses: How Self-Managing Teams Are Building High-Performing Companies.* New York: John Wiley & Sons, Inc; 1993.
7. Peters T. *Liberation Management: Necessary Disorganization for the Nanosecond Nineties.* New York: Knopf; 1992.
8. Fisher K. *Leading Self-Directed Work Teams.* New York: McGraw-Hill Publishing Co., Inc; 1993.

9. Blancett SS. Self-managed teams: The sreality and the promise. *Health Care Supervisor.* 1994;12(4):48–55.

10. Eadie DC. Beyond inheritance: Developing a board leadership design. *Board Member.* 1994;3(2):3.

11. American Association of Critical Care Nurses. A call for transformational leaders. *AACN News.* 1994;May/June:5.

12. Sherer JL. Retooling leaders. *Hosp Health Networks.* 1994;68(1):42,44.

13. Barker J. Tightening the iron cage: Concertive control in self-managing teams. *Adm Sci Quart.* 1993;38(3):408–437.

14. Sovie MD. Care and service teams: A new imperative. *Nurs Economic$.* 1992;10(2):94–100,125.

15. Verespej MA. Goodbye, status—Hello, communication. *Industry Week.* 1994;243(6):9.

■ 8 ■

Creating an Environment for Reengineering

Gail A. Wolf, DNS, RN, FAAN

The purpose of the transformation of the American health care system is clear: to reduce health care costs while improving the quality and access to that care. What is not clear, however, is how this transformation is best achieved. Nurse executives face many uncertainties and challenges as they struggle to find creative solutions to dilemmas. We must change our outmoded practices and beliefs, develop strong and effective organizations, and yet protect those elements that are critical for quality patient care.

Many nursing leaders are turning to reengineering as a methodology for accomplishing these outcomes. For ultimate success, however, reengineering efforts need to be designed within two parameters. First, reengineering should not be done randomly, but in response to a shift in paradigms that needs to occur for future success. Second, the leader needs to develop the work environment to a level that will support the reengineering efforts.

In this chapter, the professional paradigm shifts that need to occur are discussed, and a model that can be used to accomplish this end is presented. Portions of this model—a transformational model for the practice of professional nursing[1,2]—can also be used to develop the appropriate workplace environment. Although this model was originally developed for nursing practice, the principles apply to any clinical discipline.

MODEL FOUNDATIONS: SHIFTING OUR PARADIGMS

A paradigm is a set of rules and regulations (written or unwritten) that does two things: (1) establishes or defines boundaries and (2) explains how to behave

Source: Adapted from Wolf G, Boland S, and Aukerman M, A Transformational Model for the Practice of Professional Nursing—Part I: The Model, *Journal of Nursing Administration*, Vol. 24, No. 4, pp. 51–57, with permission of J.B. Lippincott Company, © 1994.

inside the boundaries in order to be successful.[3] Within the profession of nursing, several values and assumptions must be reassessed to meet the future demands of our health care system. These values and assumptions are reflected in the following four paradigm shifts, which serve as a foundation for the model:

1. ***Professional nurses must evolve our practice from a "needs-driven" model of care to one that is sensitive to limited resources.***—Traditionally, nurses have been taught to identify and meet *all* patient needs. Professional nurses become frustrated when all needs can't be met, considering the result to be substandard care. Generally speaking, patients do not expect all of their health care needs to be met, only those they consider important. In the future, resources will be limited. Consequently, nurses must negotiate with patients to determine the critical needs and plan for the most effective use of resources to meet those needs.

2. ***Nurses commonly believe there is a direct correlation between manpower and quality. The true correlation is between critical thinking and quality.***—Nurses often think that "more is better" (i.e., more staffing results in better quality). In reality, less may actually be more effective, providing that resources are used appropriately. In many organizations, our human resources are not focused appropriately. Nurses are diverted and distracted from patient care in trying to cope with troublesome factors in the workplace environment. Broken or antiquated operating systems, interpersonal conflicts, lack of appropriate supplies, and lack of good collaboration are only a few of the many environmental factors that compete with patients for the nurse's attention. In the future, achieving quality must be accomplished through critical thinking focused on the unique needs of each patient, coupled with creative approaches for meeting those needs.

3. ***Standardization and routines for patient care will be replaced by individualization and creativity.***—In the past, routine practices (e.g., giving bed baths and obtaining vital signs) were implemented without analyzing whether they contributed to a quality outcome. Many of our standards of care are based on "the way we've always done it" rather than on the results of research. In the future, nurses must first define the outcomes they seek and only engage in work that aids in the accomplishment of those outcomes.

4. ***Accountability, responsibility, and authority for clinical decision making will evolve from the manager to the practitioner, in partnership with the patient.***—In the future, care needs to be exquisitely planned and managed. There is very little room for error, and no longer "one right way to do things." As the process of patient care incorporates

more critical thinking, negotiation, and creativity, authority for decision making must rest with the clinical practitioners in partnership with the patient. Ideally, this is a three-way partnership among the patient, attending physician, and responsible nurse. The partnership considers the unique requirements of each particular situation, develops an appropriate plan for accomplishing those requirements, and monitors outcomes.

Reengineering should not be done because it is "the latest trend and everyone is doing it." It should be a purposeful effort designed to support a change in belief. Such paradigm shifts can be used to guide reengineering efforts. For example, projects that improve operational systems and eliminate unnecessary work would support the second paradigm shift. Efforts that assign accountability and authority to a specific practitioner support the fourth paradigm shift.

TRANSFORMATIONAL MODEL: OVERVIEW

These paradigm shifts serve as the foundation for the transformational model. The model is divided into four components (Figure 8–1). In the *professional practice* component, assessment and activation of professional practice relationships and support occur. In the *process* component, there is engagement in purposeful and deliberate critical thinking, negotiation, and decision making, which brings together the unique needs of each patient, coupled with professional recommendations and a sensitivity for limited resources. This process results in the attainment of targeted goals—*primary outcomes*—which enhance quality care, patient satisfaction, and caregiver satisfaction, as well as *secondary outcomes,* which ultimately support consumer, organizational, and professional health.

TRANSFORMATIONAL MODEL: PROFESSIONAL PRACTICE COMPONENT

The inner core of the professional practice component contains the heart of the model (Figure 8–2). This core depicts the relationship between a nurse, patient, and physician plus, potentially, other members of the health care team. The remainder of the component is divided into four quadrants, which depict the relationships and supports necessary to support professional practice in a reformed health care system: transformational leadership, care delivery systems, professional growth, and collaborative practice. Each of these quadrants is further broken down into concepts that depict the ways each of the four quadrants can be operationalized in an organization.

Transformational Leadership

Transformational leadership is the type of leadership necessary to shift the organizational paradigms. It is viewed as an interactive relationship that is based on

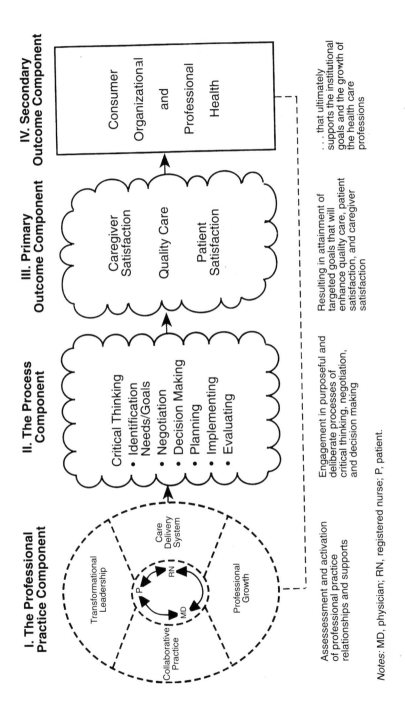

I. The Professional Practice Component

Transformational Leadership

Care Delivery System

Professional Growth

Collaborative Practice

P   RN   MD

Assessessment and activation of professional practice relationships and supports

II. The Process Component

Critical Thinking
- Identification Needs/Goals
- Negotiation
- Decision Making
- Planning
- Implementing
- Evaluating

Engagement in purposeful and deliberate processes of critical thinking, negotiation, and decision making

III. Primary Outcome Component

Caregiver Satisfaction

Quality Care

Patient Satisfaction

Resulting in attainment of targeted goals that will enhance quality care, patient satisfaction, and caregiver satisfaction

IV. Secondary Outcome Component

Consumer

Organizational and Professional

Health

. . . that ultimately supports the institutional goals and the growth of the health care professions

Notes: MD, physician; RN, registered nurse; P, patient.

Figure 8-1 A Transformational Model for the Practice of Professional Nursing. *Source: Copyright © 1993, Shadyside Hospital, Pittsburgh, Pennsylvania.*

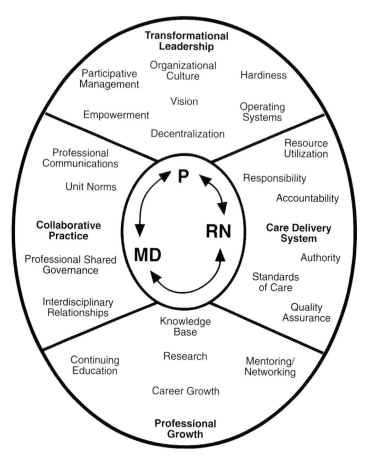

Notes: MD, physician; RN, registered nurse; P, patient.

Figure 8-2 The Professional Practice Component. *Source: Copyright © 1993, Shadyside Hospital, Pittsburgh, Pennsylvania.*

trust and has a positive impact on both the leader and the follower. It is a mutual responsibility of both, and, as leadership becomes more transforming, the purposes of the leader and follower become focused, creating unit, wholeness, and collective purpose.

There are seven concepts that collectively support transformational leadership within the model: hardiness, empowerment, vision, decentralization, participative management, organizational culture, and operating systems. Definitions for these concepts can be found in Exhibit 8–1.

Care Delivery System

Given the anticipated changes in health care, delivery systems that are efficient, nonfragmented, and focused on the patient must be developed. The care delivery system should allow for a significant amount of patient input and provide for the wise use of limited resources through partnership negotiation. To accomplish this, the care delivery system should be designed to give one nurse the responsibility, authority, and accountability for planning, organizing, and evaluating nursing care throughout the patient episode.

The six concepts that support this level of practice are defined in Exhibit 8–2: responsibility, authority, accountability, standards of care, quality assurance, and resource utilization.

Professional Growth

The profession of nursing, as an applied discipline, is evolving within a dynamic body of empirical, interpersonal, ethical, and aesthetic knowledge. The quality of nursing practice is contingent on the knowledge of individual practitioners and their willingness to engage in professional relationships and behaviors. Nurses need to have the requisite skills and knowledge to explore, validate, and direct the evolution of nursing practice.

Exhibit 8–3 defines the five concepts supporting this quadrant of professional practice: knowledge base, continuing education, mentoring/networking, research, and career growth.

Collaborative Practice

Collaborative practice encompasses the development and ongoing support of relationships between and among the professionals working within the health care environment. The framework for this element of professional practice is composed of the formal structures of the organization (such as policies, procedures, reporting relationships, and committee structures). More importantly, however, collaborative practice addresses key components of the "social architecture" of the work group, encompassing the expectations, personal values, and interpersonal relationships of the people who have aligned to achieve the vision of the organization.

The four concepts supporting collaborative practice are defined in Exhibit 8–4: professional communication, unit norms, professional shared governance, and interdisciplinary relationships.

Application to Reengineering

Each of these 22 concepts will be operationalized differently depending on the developmental level of the organization or work unit. A model developed by

Exhibit 8–1 Transformational Leadership

Health care is being transformed in a variety of ways including its scope, accessibility, and reimbursement. Accordingly, leaders of the clinical discipline of nursing must also transform that profession. Transformation leadership is an interactive relationship that is based on trust and that has positive impact on both the leader and the follower. The purposes of the leader and follower become focused, creating unity, wholeness, and collective purpose.

	Hardiness Personality factors reflecting an individual perception of commitment, challenge, and control	**Empowerment** An awareness of one's personal talents and power and how they contribute to the organization's goals	**Vision** Delineation of a possible and desirable future state
Reactive	Commitment to self or to select peers Problems seen as obstacles External attribution used for failure/ problems	Individual contributions diffuse, fragmented, controlled	No vision Focus on the past Efforts directed toward accomplishment of tasks
Responsive	Commitment to unit and majority of peers "First right answer" commonly used Beginning to use appropriate attributional processes	Value, talents, and abilities recognized by team members and applied in achieving organizational goals	Future state often identified as a correction of existing problems Focus on today and immediate future
Proactive	Commitment to nursing department beyond unit Issues seen as challenges Willing to assume responsibility for developing solutions	Work by individuals to develop skills that enable higher levels of performance for themselves and others Implementation of creativity and innovative approaches beginning	Anticipation of future and focus on achieving a "state of being" appropriate for that future Creativity and innovation seen as valued approaches for accomplishing vision
High-performance team	Strong commitment to profession and organization Willing to tackle major obstacles using group learning Strong sense of being in control	Members able to create a synergistic environment that enhances transformational change	Futuristic focus, continually evolving, and able to be translated into reality base

Source: Copyright © 1993, Shadyside Hospital, Pittsburgh, Pennsylvania.

Decentralization A management philosophy that allows decision making to occur at the lowest, most appropriate level	Participative Management Philosophy in which employee's input is an important contribution to the decision-making process	Organizational Culture Values and beliefs of the organization Trust, caring, mutual respect, and enthusiasm common	Operating Systems Systems and methodologies used to accomplish goals
Authority centralized Responsibility often delegated without corresponding authority	All key decision-making responsibilities held by leadership	Operating values often not visible, not present, or in conflict	Systems absent, defensive, dysfunctional, and resistive
Delegation of authority and responsibility to most appropriate level Accountability often not appropriately defined	Formal mechanisms for use by employees to contribute to decisions affecting their work	Key value expectations defined Shared values beginning to emerge in behaviors	Staff input incorporated to remove barriers First-order change through methods such as problem solving and TQM
Each unit autonomous in making decisions consistent with mission, vision, and values of organization	Involvement in all aspects of decision making, with input reflected in final outcomes for issues affecting work	Key values strongly embraced and demonstrated even in difficult situations	Purposeful redesign of systems to facilitate work Innovation and creativity valued and promoted
		Key values strongly embraced Staff able to perpetuate culture	Second-order change (major change in thinking) questioning value/intent of systems Creation of new synergistic systems and approaches

Exhibit 8–2 Care Delivery System

Given the anticipated changes in health care, delivery systems that are efficient, nonfragmented, and patient focused must be developed. The care delivery system should allow for a significant amount of patient input. The system must also provide for wise use of limited resources in order to position the organizational competitively in a managed care environment. In terms of nursing, this is best accomplished by giving one nurse the responsibility, authority, and accountability for planning, organizing, and evaluating nursing care throughout the patient episode.

	Responsibility Those things one is assigned and accepts the obligation of performing	**Authority** Power granted to fulfill a responsibility; the right to act
Reactive	Tasks performed as fragmented pieces of patient care	Unwillingness to make independent decisions Waits for direction
Responsive	Implementation of nursing process for assigned patients Autonomous and dependent scope of practice visible and balanced	Decisions made regarding activities with patient
Proactive	Ability to negotiate care with patients for mutually determined outcomes and to effectively plan for wise use of resources	Direction provided for others in plan of care Ability to hold others accountable
High-performance team	Critical thinking, integration, and synthesis in nursing process	Integration of nursing authority with other providers

Source: Copyright © 1993, Shadyside Hospital, Pittsburgh, Pennsylvania.

Accountability Formal obligation to be answerable for what one has done	Standards of Care Nursing processes used to achieve specific patient care outcomes	Quality Assurance Evaluation and oversight of nursing processes and relationship to outcomes	Resource Utilization The usage and control of organizational resources in meeting patient needs
Accountable for actual direct tasks performed	No systematic use of standards; task-focused, fragmented care	Evaluation of tasks	Perception of inadequate resources that may or may not be reality
Personal accountability accepted only for work done personally	Standards used as "rules" of practice	Primary focus on process Beginning focus on outcomes Unit specific	Use of resources in traditional ways
Accountability accepted for what occurs over entire patient care episode (self and others)	Standards used as "guidelines" of practice, with patient-specific modifications to achieve specific outcomes	Focus on anticipated outcomes More patient specific	Flexibility and innovative use of resources, which are adjusted to meet negotiated needs
Accountability for integration of other providers, management of case	Standards redesigned Innovative approaches to achieve outcomes	Evaluation of innovative approaches to achieve outcomes	Maximal efficient utilization of resources; decline in resource requirements

Exhibit 8–3 Professional Growth

The profession of nursing, as an applied discipline, is evolving within a dynamic body of empirical, interpersonal, ethical, and aesthetic knowledge. The quality of nursing practice is contingent on the knowledge of individual practitioners and the willingness of practitioners to engage in professional relationships and behaviors. The learning of professional behaviors is enhanced when desirable behaviors, skills, and attributes are defined, visible, promoted, and rewarded. Professional nurses acknowledge the dynamic nature of nursing through ongoing, diverse, and meaningful learning experiences in order to support, guide, and initiate changes in practice. Likewise, professional nurses utilize research findings and engage in research activities to explore, validate, and direct the evolution of nursing practice.

	Knowledge Base The grounding knowledge base of the practitioner	**Continuing Education** Learning activities beyond licensure requirements
Reactive	Individual practitioner's knowledge base unknown or assumed to be adequate based on general titles or degrees	Little or no engagement in formal educational activities Limited ability to extract or transfer practical knowledge from one situation to another
Responsive	Knowledge base levels are assumed except for obvious gaps or areas where problems arise Problem resolution usually based on prescriptive and group norms	Participation in required educational in-service and competency programs and activities Attendance of "corrective" support programming
Proactive	Knowledge base individually assessed Tailored learning activities targeted for maximum benefit Strategic matching of knowledge/skills to work opportunities	Participation in a wide variety of educational activities initiated Educational goals set consistent with organizational vision and in preparation for future work
High-performance team	Individualists lifelong learning approach adopted Perception of and engagement in wide variety of learning experiences and opportunities Open, creative, evolving attitude	Transformative learning approach created New learning opportunities created and initiated Focus on learning simply to learn

Source: Copyright © 1993, Shadyside Hospital, Pittsburgh, Pennsylvania.

Mentoring/Networking Relationships established with the intent of supportive growth for the individual and profession	**Research** Scientific inquiry into factors affecting professional nursing practice	**Career Growth** Purposeful, planned strategies to enhance long-range professional goals
Mentoring/networking experiences occurring rarely or by happenstance	Little or no research assumed	Little ownership for planning future activities and development Focus on day-to-day survival and tasks Motivation external
Mentoring occurring as "rescue" attempts to correct problems or deficiencies Prescriptive mentors (i.e., orientation preceptors)	Focused on problems Driven by needs	Many general competencies for safe practice consciously met Motivation external Accountability low
Mentoring opportunities built in, staged, or planned as essential developmental strategies for all levels of performances	Focused on model/outcome	Proficiency in practice area actively sought Professional community activities Motivation internal
Reciprocal dialogue among multiple experts	Focused on secondary outcomes Innovative, optimistic Potential driven	Self-mastery activities to become expert in chosen area initiated Optimistic future outlook demonstrated in leadership behaviors

Exhibit 8–4 Collaborative Practice

This section of the model highlights the framework for the development and ongoing support of relationships between and among the professionals working within the health care environment. This framework is composed of the formal structures of the organization (such as its policies, procedures, reporting relationships, and committee structures). More important, this section of the model addresses key components of the "social architecture" of the work group. It encompasses the expectations, personal values, and interpersonal relationships of the people who have aligned to achieve the vision of the organization.

	Professional Communication Verbal/nonverbal interactions that define relationships
Reactive	Communication is forced and "top down" only, with no established expectations for professional communication.
Responsive	The communication focus is on building conflict management skills, giving and receiving feedback, and building interpersonal relationships among unit members in the spirit of cooperation and respect for each other's rights as people. Expectations for interpersonal, professional communications consistent with the organization's values are established.
Proactive	Positive, professional communication is spontaneously initiated in an environment that fosters open dialogue between and among all levels of hospital personnel.
High-performance team	Communication is in a "state of flow," supporting the synergistic relationships between all members of the team.

Source: Copyright © 1993, Shadyside Hospital, Pittsburgh, Pennsylvania.

Unit Norms Generally accepted, formal and informal rules that govern interactions within a unit, which may or may not be consistent with the organization's culture	Professional Shared Governance Structure to support collaboration among professionals in determining standards for the professional practice of nursing	Interdisciplinary Relationships Interaction of the roles of the various members of the health care teams
Work practices are defensive, reflecting either a chaotic environment or strong, autocratic control.	Control of practice is authoritarian, rigidly enforced, or absent. The autonomous scope of practice is not formally recognized or incorporated into the environment.	Relationships are absent or ill-defined and may even have dysfunctional characteristics and hostile overtones.
Members of the unit participate in establishing expectations for practice. Formal mechanisms exist for incorporating staff input in an environment that offers formal and informal supports for the process.	Work is centralized to establish standards, as well as to evolve unit representatives into mentors who will facilitate the process of building consensus and commitment to the established standards within their unit.	Members of the teams have separate accountabilities; they operate in parallel, independent from one another.
Members of the unit can understand and articulate the relationship between their behaviors and successfully achieving the goals/vision of the organization.	Unit-based councils work as interactive teams to achieve consensus on decisions affecting their practice and incorporating a service or program perspective into the care provided to patients.	Peer interdependence characterizes the team, with a focus on consensus building and negotiation in the successful attainment of goals for all disciplines.
Members of the unit are self-directed in engaging in behaviors that define a unit-based vision and goals that are also consistent with the division's and organization's vision and goals.	The unit-based committee maintains an interactive, synergistic relationship with the shared governance activities on a divisional level.	The team operates within a learning environment that is able to critically evaluate its outcomes and modify or redesign its care delivery to better meet the needs of the patients it serves.

Nelson and Burns identifies four different levels at which an organization can operate: reactive, responsive, proactive, and high performance.[4]

The *reactive* level is not where an organization begins, but rather a state of disintegration that occurs when its leaders fail to maintain proper focus. Instead of planning for the future, leaders focus on the past or on dealing with one crisis after another. Nurses working in reactive nursing units have little enthusiasm for anything but survival. They are somewhat paranoid, pessimistic, and distrustful. The leadership style at this level is usually immature and frequently abusive. Because of the perceived risk, members of reactive units are the least willing to change, despite the need to do so.

At the *responsive* level, members are focused on achieving near-term goals. They work together well and are able to adapt as they identify and solve problems. There is a team perspective, and members look out for each other and for the good of the organization. Management keeps team efforts coordinated and responsive to changing needs and conditions.

The *proactive* level builds and expands on the responsive level, which requires looking to the future and taking the initiative. Members of a proactive unit see the future as a choice to be made, not as something with which one is required to cope. A strong shared vision that fits the values of the members and the organization serves as a compelling force for action. Strongly held values are a critical component at this level. These values and the norms of behavior that flow from them serve as the cultural "glue" for the organization. It is at this level that value-based transformational leadership begins to occur.

Continuing to build on the proactive level, the *high-performance* level emerges. This level is characterized by a high level of energy and spirit that results in markedly improved productivity. Leaders of high-performance teams find different ways to manage the flow of energy in their members. They also continually try to expand their own potential. High energy, creativity, and innovation are consciously built into the organization's operating values and cultural norms.

Using this framework, each concept within the professional practice component has been operationalized for a reactive, responsive, proactive, or high-performance organization or patient care unit (Exhibits 8–1 to 8–4). These matrixes can serve as an assessment guide, assisting the leader in determining readiness for reengineering.

In a reactive environment, reengineering is a futile effort. There is strong resistance to change and little trust between team members and the leader. Often, team members are unwilling or unable to visualize what "success" would look like and have little willingness to believe it possible. Staff members feel unempowered and usually do not feel a commitment to improving the organization unless it benefits them directly.

In a reactive environment, however, the ideas for reengineering can often be found. Operating systems are often dysfunctional, and a reactive staff is usually quite able to identify "everything" that is wrong. The key is truly listening to what the staff perceive is "broken," but listening can often be extremely difficult for the leader, who often feels either defensive or overwhelmed. However, the leadership is accountable for advancing a staff beyond a reactive level. The staff must play an active role in the progression, but they are dependent on effective leadership for the transition to occur.

One effective strategy is to use a modified nominal group technique to identify the issues. In this methodology, staff members are asked one critical question such as, What do you see as barriers to your effectiveness? Each person writes down five to ten responses, and sequentially, each person cites one factor until all are identified. These factors can then be grouped and prioritized, giving the reengineering team valuable data about the current system.

Using the matrixes in Exhibits 8–1 to 8–4, the leader can also use the identified problems from the nominal group technique to assess the developmental level for each of the concepts in the professional practice component of the model. Based on this assessment, plans for resolving the critical issues and developing to the next level can be established.

It has been our experience in implementing this model that most units begin to tackle the identified problems by examining unit norms and professional communications. As the staff begin to resolve issues, their sense of empowerment and commitment grows. The unit begins the transition from the reactive level to the responsive level.

In the responsive level, each member of the team starts to recognize personal values, talents, and abilities and begins to apply them in achieving organizational goals. As they contribute to decisions affecting their work, employees begin to feel more empowered. The tendency at first is to find the "first right answer," but gradually, thinking expands to include more creative options.

Reengineering efforts can begin at the responsive level, but they really blossom at the proactive level. In this phase, employees are able to see the future as something over which they have control. Strategies such as reengineering are embraced as a means for the empowered employee to create that future. What were formerly considered obstacles are now considered challenges. Creativity and innovation are seen as valued approaches for accomplishing the work of the organization.

Expansion of these efforts results in the formation of high-performance teams. Employees have a strong sense of being in control and are able to create a synergistic environment that enhances transformational change. The transformed organization is the true learning organization that continually expands, modifies, and redesigns systems to meet dynamic environmental changes.

TRANSFORMATIONAL MODEL: PROCESS COMPONENT

The process component is the "throughput" aspect of the model and addresses the nursing processes that will be used in planning, organizing, implementing, and evaluating nursing care delivered to patients. The underlying structure of the process component is recognizable as the traditional nursing process. However, this process has been reengineered to include an enhanced and deliberate emphasis on critical thinking and negotiation to meet the degree of individualization, creativity, and fluidity that the changing paradigms will require. The concept of negotiated care developed by Lyon[5] offers a methodology for accomplishing this and for pragmatically dealing with shrinking resources while preserving high-quality, individualized patient care.

TRANSFORMATIONAL MODEL: OUTCOMES

The primary outcomes of the model are three comprehensive and desirable outcomes of professional nursing practice: quality care, caregiver satisfaction, and patient satisfaction. The secondary outcomes of consumer, organizational, and professional health are the extended results of the primary outcomes. When patients are satisfied with their care, the reputation of the caregivers and the enabling institution increases, resulting in a more positive reputation and the likelihood for increased business. Similarly, caregivers who are satisfied with their work and their work environment are singularly the most influential factor in the recruitment of other professionals. The success of meeting the collective health needs of the community in a high-quality, cost-effective manner will determine the continued existence of the health care institution.

CONCLUSION

There is an old saying: "If you don't know where you're going, all roads will lead you there." As we prepare for changes in health care, we need a road map to guide us. We also need a conceptual framework outlining the necessary changes on which to focus our reengineering efforts. Finally, we need to create environments that will support those efforts. Hopefully, this model will provide some guidance as we bridge the gap between our current reality and future possibility.

REFERENCES

1. Wolf G, Boland S, Aukerman M. A transformational model for the practice of professional nursing—Part I: The model. *J Nurs Adm*. 1994;24(4):51–57.

2. Wolf G, Boland S, Aukerman M. A transformational model for the practice of professional nursing—Part II: Implementation of the model. *J Nurs Adm.* 1994;24(5):38–46.

3. Barker J. *Future Edge.* New York: William Morrow and Co; 1992:32.

4. Nelson L, Burns F. High performance programming: A framework for transforming organizations. In: Adams J, ed. *Transforming Work.* Alexandria, VA: Miles River Press; 1984:225–242.

5. Lyon B. Negotiated care: Nursing's product is patient outcomes not the nursing process. (Unpublished seminar material.) Ninevah, IN: Health Potentials Unlimited; 1989.

■ 9 ■

Executive Leadership Attributes for Reengineering

Leann Strasen DPA, RN, FACHE

Reengineering of health care organizations requires a fundamental shift in paradigms for the industry and professionals within the industry. It is an initiative that requires a different kind of leader than we have promoted in the past. The leader who can successfully reengineer organizations will have the personal attributes of respect, integrity, perseverance, self-control, and indomitable spirit. These attributes are crucial in the development of black belt martial artists or warrior leaders in environments of dramatic change and conflict. Development of these attributes is crucial for leaders who are responsible for reengineering their organizations for the 21st century.

This chapter outlines typical profiles of health care leaders, describes the challenges of reengineering in the health care setting, and goes on to describe how the development of these five executive leadership attributes assist leaders to successfully lead their organizations through reengineering.

WHAT DEFINES A LEADER?

Significant research and contemporary literature focus on the topic of leadership. Decades of leadership analysis provide us with over 350 definitions of leadership but little or no empirical understanding of what distinguishes leaders from nonleaders and effective leaders from noneffective leaders.[1-3] Some of the studies have focused on individual traits of leaders, some on the characteristics and accomplishments of organizations, and still others on the specific achievements of individuals. Kouzes and Posner believe leaders who get things done have the ability to challenge, inspire, enable, model, and encourage their followers.[3] Burns says that "The ultimate test of practical leadership is the realization of intended, real change that meets people's enduring needs."[4(p.461)]

Bennis and Nanus performed qualitative leadership research by interviewing 90 leaders for the purpose of identifying key common characteristics of leaders in successful organizations.[2] Their results identified four major competencies for the successful leaders they interviewed. These four major competencies are the following abilities:

1. to manage attention through vision
2. to manage meaning through communication
3. to develop trust through positioning
4. to deploy oneself through positive self-regard.

Some pertinent questions about leaders include the following:

- Are leaders defined by the eye of the beholder?
- Are leaders defined by how they think, what they think, or what they do?
- Are leaders defined by how they act?
- Are leaders defined by what they do or by what they get others to do?
- Is leadership defined as a function of the formal rank or position that someone holds?
- Must a leader be liked to be considered a leader?

After immersion in these concepts and theories of leadership, I choose to define leadership as the art of getting people to go places they would not go or do things they would not do by themselves. This definition contains a strong bias for action and acknowledges that something is measurably different as a result of the actions of a leader. A leader's influence results in people acting and/or thinking differently.

In a fairly static environment, leaders can rely on their expert knowledge to lead people effectively, because they have information others do not have. In an environment where the half-life of information is months to weeks versus years, however, it becomes more important for leaders to know how to think so they can apply proven principles to new and different situations on a daily basis. As a result of the magnitude of change anticipated in the 21st century, a leader's focus needs to shift from learning what to know to learning how to think and how to know, which represents a shift from a behavioral to a cognitive approach to leadership.[5]

Achievement motivation and attributional theory provide insights into this shift in leadership focus, which results in differences in the performance of leaders. According to Weiner's attributional theory, the way individuals explain past successes and failures to themselves affects their future performance.[6] Weiner described the concept that an individual's performance is a function of ability, effort, luck, and the difficulty of a task. Ability is an attribute that one is born with or without; it is not under a person's direct control. One can, however, control the level of effort expended, which can enhance or detract from performance.

Luck is generally considered out of one's control and a function of timing. The difficulty of the tasks undertaken, however, is under one's direct control. The way an individual explains past success or failure determines the activities and/or challenges chosen in the future. The challenges and/or activities one participates in will, in turn, determine future accomplishments. Based on Weiner's concept, effective leaders are individuals who perceive that they have ability, can expend the effort, can take advantage of luck and/or timing, and have the confidence to tackle tasks that are perceived as being very difficult.

The achievement motivation research also provides us insights into leadership by outlining two basic motivations for achievement: the performance motive and the mastery motive.[5] One who is motivated by performance wants to achieve in order to perform better than someone else. Our educational system has reinforced this motive to achieve with the preoccupation with grades. On the other hand, one who is motivated to constantly learn new things and master new skills is motivated by mastery. The mastery motive is a constant desire to improve oneself and develop new skills on an ongoing basis, irrespective of what others are doing. This background in attributional and achievement theory sets the stage for assessing the existing thinking patterns and behaviors of health care leaders. It allows us to then identify the specific thinking and behaviors required by leaders to successfully reengineer health care organizations.

Reengineering is an action word for responding to a rapidly changing environment and its associated shifting paradigm. To be successful in the 21st century, hospitals need leaders who can shift existing paradigms significantly on behalf of a changing external environment and changed customer expectations. Lao Tzu addressed this concept of shifting paradigms in the *Tao Te Ching* when he wrote: "When you have expectations, you will always perceive boundaries. When you eliminate your expectations, you can always perceive subtle opportunities you have ruled out with your expectations."[7(p.27)] Health care organizations are at the mercy of the artificial boundaries or paradigms that exist in the minds of their leaders. Successful leaders rid themselves of the influences of their past expectations and existing paradigms to reengineer their organizations to be successful in changing times. They bash the barriers that interfere with their organization's ability to be successful in the 21st century.

OBSERVATIONS OF CURRENT LEADERS

Over the past 12 years, I have worked with individuals occupying formal positions of authority on all levels of small, medium, and large organizations. I have worked closely with first-line managers, department directors, and executive level managers in organizations of all sizes, including the corporate setting. In this section, the term "leader" is used to mean individuals holding positions of formal authority in organizations. It will become evident that my description of existing leaders is not consistent with my previous description of a leader as a person who "gets people to go places they would not go or do things they would not do by themselves." I have observed a number of trends that represent an overview of the general thinking patterns and the resulting behaviors of existing leaders. These generalizations are not necessarily true about all leaders, nor are all of these observations applicable to any one leader. These trends reflect my perceptions of today's generic health care leader, and they dramatically affect an organization's ability to reengineer itself.

General behaviors I have observed in leaders include a short-term focus; a preference for maintaining the status quo; a desire to avoid innovative or high-risk interventions; a need to be liked by fellow employees; a preference for completing routine, well-defined work; an inclination for in-depth study and analysis of major issues; and a desire to avoid conflict situations at all costs. These behaviors have been fostered by decades of external reward systems. Based on an application of the achievement motivation concept, these behaviors appear to result from a strong performance motivation or a desire to perform favorably in comparison with peers, rather than from a desire to achieve one's ultimate potential. My observations are supported by Bennis' description of the behaviors of leaders.[1]

- Leaders tend to delay the tough decisions so they are not at risk of making mistakes.
- Leaders are so focused on managing things that take considerable time, they have little time or energy left to truly lead.
- The average organization is overmanaged and underled.
- Leaders pay too much attention and time doing things right versus doing the right things.
- Corporations spend increasing dollars on leadership courses, but there are fewer real leaders than ever before.
- The routine work of leaders crowds out the creative, innovative, nonroutine work.

Bardwick also supported these observations and described individuals living in the Age of Unreality as having the goal of being involved but not acting responsibly and generally trying to avoid reality.[8] She observed that too many individuals show up for work, do not accomplish much, and put in too much "face time." Absenteeism and sick time is 30 percent in the average company. Bardwick voiced the concern that leaders set up thousands of meetings; focus on doing things right versus doing the right things; write memos to everyone to cover themselves; to minimize their risk, never act without getting approval from their superiors; never disagree with the boss; avoid conflict at all costs; treat employees in a very paternalistic manner; and never contradict the majority. She goes on to describe leaders in very turbulent environments as being territorial; immobilized by fear; self-protective, with a narrow focus; rigidly following policies and procedures; and exhibiting dictatorial and inconsistent behavior. These observations paint a grim picture of the behaviors of many leaders and their lack of readiness and ability to reengineer their organizations.

EXECUTIVE LEADERSHIP ATTRIBUTES FOR REENGINEERING

Having assisted leaders in implementing reengineering projects in a number of organizations, I searched for a conceptual model of the leadership attributes that are key for leaders to effectively lead an organization through reengineering. This search, as well as my actual reengineering experiences, leads me to conclude that the key tenets and achievement motivation of a black belt warrior/leader in the martial arts outline best the traits that are crucial for effective reengineering leaders.

The black belt martial artist or warrior leader is motivated by mastery, that is, the constant and ongoing improvement of self. This mastery motivation or value significantly influences all the behaviors and actions of the martial artist. The black belt martial artist has a strong respect for all things in the universe, has the spirit and courage to die for personal belief, never gives up the quest for self-mastery, and is very self-controlled. The behaviors crucial for leaders of reengineering efforts include taking calculated risks, taking action that may be controversial, and the abilities to think strategically, to persevere, and to be a strong role model who communicates well and is very visible to employees. These behaviors originate from a mastery motivation or the desire to improve oneself and the organization on a continuous basis, regardless of external pressures.

On the other hand, the leader behaviors of maintaining the status quo, focusing on the short term, holding on to a need to be liked, and having a tendency to avoid unpleasant decisions and conflict situations create significant problems in an organization trying to reengineer its operations. These behaviors stem from the motivation to merely perform better than someone else and just to meet the expectations of others. This fundamental but very powerful achievement motivation perspective is one of the major differences between leaders who can and do successfully reengineer their organizations and those who never try, avoid the effort, or just go through the motions, with poor results.

The mastery motivated warrior/leader commits a significant amount of time and effort to developing the skills and attributes that allow success. That commitment of time and effort results in the internalization of the five tenets paramount in the successful mastery of the martial arts: respect, integrity, indomitable spirit, self-control, and perseverance. The mastery of these attitudes or traits allows the warrior/leader to effectively lead people through major battles in a rapidly changing world. The mastery of these attributes allows the health care leader to effectively lead employees through the major organizational reengineering efforts mandated by change in the 21st century.

The traits that are key for leaders in this context are really not skills, but attitudes or ways of responding to the world. This conclusion is in contrast to the fact that most articles on reengineering focus on the technical skills, abilities, or knowledge bases that leaders need to acquire. The key to successful leadership in the future is the personal development of the leader, rather than the development of technical skills. In chaotic environments steeped in conflict, the personal attributes of individuals become the difference between the leaders and the followers.

ATTRIBUTES OF LEADERS IN REENGINEERING EFFORTS

The five key attributes for executive leaders are respect, integrity, perseverance, self-control, and indomitable spirit. The importance and application of each of these attributes in the reengineering effort is described in detail.

Respect

Respect is the attribute that acknowledges the importance and interconnections of all parts of the whole, of all individuals in the organization, irrespective of their role or status, and of all entities in nature; it also recognizes the importance of their interdependence to the survival of the universe. The leader who has developed respect treats all employees like the leader wants to be treated and realizes the individual's importance and role in the overall functioning of the organization. In reengineering initiatives, respect motivates leaders to expect from employees only what they are willing to do themselves. When reengineering results in layoffs, this respect is translated into severance procedures that allow individuals to maintain their sense of self-worth and self-confidence, despite the changes occurring. In reengineering efforts, if employees are expected to accept salary or benefit reductions, the respected leader role models those expectations by first implementing changes in the executive ranks, such as reductions of senior managers and/or elimination of executive "perks." A basic principle of the universe is that you get back what you give to others. A leader who exhibits a lack of respect for employees as people usually gets back that same lack of respect. A leader who is not respected cannot be effective in leading a successful reengineering effort because employees focus their objections to reengineering changes on the leader as a person, rather than on the details of the specific changes that are taking place. Leaders who expect employees to accept signifi-cant changes while claiming exemption from the same changes create anger and resentment in employees and affect their perceptions of the real goal of the reengineering effort.

Integrity

Integrity is the attribute that drives leaders to make sure their words and ac-tions are always congruent. Congruency means that when leaders make prom-ises, they deliver, and that their actions always support what they say. In chaotic, changing times, it is important that employees can trust their leaders to be honest with them and know they are looking out for their best interests despite a hostile environment. This does not mean that the leader always has good news. It does mean that the leader is open and honest and communicates with them despite the nature of the message. Trust results from the presence of leadership integrity communicated to followers as a result of congruent verbal and nonverbal behav-iors. Integrity is a result of congruent verbal and nonverbal behaviors by the leader 100 percent of the time. Integrity is difficult to develop and easy to lose.

Perseverance

Perseverance is the attribute exemplified by the old adage, "Never, never, never give up!" Perseverance is the attribute that separates Olympic athletes from good athletes, marathon runners from ten-kilometer runners, and black belt warriors from white belt novices. Perseverance is what successful individuals at-tribute their successes to. Perseverance requires a strong positive self-image and confidence in one's abilities. Perseverance requires a belief that the effort put into a project influences the outcomes of the project. Perseverance can be developed by an individual by investing the time and energy to encourage a positive self-image, setting and writing annual goals, and making a personal commitment never to quit. Setting and writing down annual goals results in goal attainment. There is a commonly accepted statistic that 5 percent of the general population routinely writes down personal and professional goals on an annual basis. Of the 5 percent of people who set annual goals, 95 percent routinely accomplish their goals. Goal attainment results in increased self-confidence, which, in turn, en-hances perseverance in the attainment of future goals.

Perseverance is widely lacking in leaders because of our society's focus on per-forming only as well as others, our short-term focus, and the common belief that performance is a function of ability rather than effort. Perseverance is a manda-tory attribute for leaders attempting to reengineer their organizations, because major organizational changes require the overcoming of obstacles and hurdles.

Without strong perseverance, leaders become discouraged and do not forge on when faced with obstacles and hurdles.

Self-Control

Self-control is an important attribute for leaders in a chaotic environment of constant change. Chaos creates fear and uncertainty in the minds of employees. They expect their leaders to be "in control" in chaotic situations and to maintain an atmosphere of optimism. Leaders are supposed to communicate the message, "It's really OK. Don't worry; as the leader I have the skills and abilities to lead us through this chaos." To fulfill this expectation for followers, leaders need to be able to exhibit a strong sense of self-control by communicating optimism in the face of crisis and by coping appropriately and unemotionally in the face of crisis, instead of becoming impaired or immobilized by personal emotions in critical situations.

Self-control is directly related to a high level of self-discipline, which is essential to leading an organization through reengineering and which results in the leader's ability to role model the behaviors expected of followers. Role modeling is one of the most effective strategies of successful leaders, because actions speak louder than words. Employees typically believe most of what they see and little of what they hear from their leaders. Self-discipline is an essential attribute to ensure that one's actions are consistent with one's words 100 percent of the time. Self-discipline is inextricably linked to ensuring that actions are congruent with verbal communications, in order to establish the leader's integrity in the eyes of the followers.

Indomitable Spirit

Indomitable spirit is that intangible attribute in leaders that is easy to identify but hard to define concretely. It is the possession of the attitude or willingness to do whatever needs to be done to accomplish one's goals with enthusiasm and spirit. A prerequisite for indomitable spirit is the leader's identification of a commitment to accomplishing goals that are highly valued by the leader. The previously documented observations about leaders show that indomitable spirit is not a prevalent attribute in our society.

A second component of indomitable spirit is a high level of enthusiasm and excitement about one's goals that is clearly evident to others as a passion or obsession. This enthusiasm and spirit endure despite controversial, demanding, and/or conflicting external pressures. Indomitable spirit is linked with a high level of self-confidence and the belief that one's efforts will pay off in success in the long run. Indomitable spirit is sometimes defined as fighting spirit, which describes the tendency of a leader never to lose the enthusiasm to fight for important goals and values. This fight is continued to the "death" or worst-case scenario, if need be, because the leader values the goal above personal status. Indomitable spirit is the opposite of the apathy that has been described so frequently as the major disease affecting our society in the 1990s. Indomitable spirit results from a burning desire or passion to accomplish a goal and the willingness to pay the ultimate price to attain the valued goal.

A third component of indomitable spirit is the courage to do the difficult things needed for the long-term survival or success of the majority. Courage is key in leading a reengineering effort. Reengineering health care organizations involves bashing the professional paradigms of multiple professions. Reengineering challenges the professional paradigm that all nurses must report to a nurse and all pharmacists must report to a pharmacist. The reengineering process challenges the paradigm that registered nurses need to perform all direct patient care activities as described in the primary nursing model. Leading an organization through these challenges is very controversial, is counter to the socialization of most professionals, and requires significant courage in a health care setting.

Reengineering usually includes reductions in the number of traditional middle-manager roles and changes in the professional mix of staff in all professional departments. These are two very controversial aspects of reengineering that result in significant conflict within the organization. These conflicts may be accompanied by threats of unionization, legal action, and unneeded media attention, which require the leader to possess an adequate amount of courage to face the conflicts head-on without compromising the goal of reengineering by caving in to the self-interests of individual employees. The presence or lack of courage of the leader determines the level of perseverance.

CONCLUSION

The chaotic environment of the 21st century demands that leaders reengineer their organizations to position themselves to compete effectively in the marketplace. Reengineering demands that leaders develop the personal attributes of respect, integrity, perseverance, self-control, and indomitable spirit to be able to effectively lead their employees through a difficult and challenging process. Development of these attributes requires different interventions and approaches than those typically articulated in traditional leadership and management programs. Development of these attributes is accomplished by the individual leader who has a mastery orientation and commits significant time and energy to personal self-mastery. As a result of these insights, the author believes future management and leadership programs need to include simulations and case studies that have the goal of developing these personal attributes in leaders, so they can in turn effectively lead their organizations through the major organizational changes mandated for success in the future.

REFERENCES

1. Bennis W. *Why Leaders Can't Lead.* San Francisco: Jossey-Bass, Inc, Publishers; 1989.
2. Bennis W, Nanus B. *Leaders.* New York: Harper & Row; 1985.
3. Kouzes J, Posner B. *The Leadership Challenge.* San Francisco: Jossey-Bass, Inc, Publishers; 1987.
4. Burns JM. *Leadership.* New York: Harper & Row; 1978.
5. Covington M. *Making the Grade: A Self-Worth Perspective on Motivation and School Reform.* New York: Cambridge University Press; 1992.
6. Weiner B. *Achievement Motivation and Attributional Theory.* Morristown, NJ: General Learning Press; 1974.
7. Wing RL. *The Tao of Power: Lao Tzu's Classic Guide to Leadership, Influence, and Power.* New York: Doubleday & Co, Inc; 1986.
8. Bardwick JM. *Danger in the Comfort Zone.* New York: AMACOM; 1991.

■ 10 ■

An Update—
The Evolution of Reengineering

Mary Crabtree Tonges, MBA, MSN, RN

Reengineering can be described as a business revolution. Thus, it is not surprising that it is a dynamic phenomenon. This update highlights key aspects of the evolution of reengineering that have emerged since I coauthored the article that follows—*Reengineering: The Work Redesign-Technology Link.*

A MANIFESTO FOR RADICAL CHANGE: EVOLUTION OF THE REVOLUTION

The evolution and broadening of the reengineering concept is reflected in changes in its definition. Hammer[1(p.104)] initially employed the term reengineering to describe the radical redesign of work using the capacity for change created by new information technologies. In a more recent publication, Hammer and Champy define reengineering as "the fundamental rethinking and radical redesign of business processes to achieve dramatic improvements in critical contemporary measures of performance, such as cost, quality, service, and speed."[2(p.32)]

The term information technology no longer appears in the newer, more expansive definition, but the authors do describe it as an "essential enabler"[2(p.44)] and note that one of the hallmark characteristics of true reengineering is that the changes would not have been possible without modern information technology. Hammer and Champy's current conceptualization of reengineering encompasses more than the original definition, and they stress that process redesign triggers the need for changes in job designs, organizational structure, and compensation systems—in short, a whole network of new management systems to support the new process designs. In fact, they identify ignoring everything else except process redesign as one of the most common errors that result in reengineering failures.

Note: The author thanks Dr. Sidney I. Lirtzman, Baruch College, City University of New York, for his comments on an earlier version of the article that follows. She also thanks her colleagues, Joanne Ritter-Teitel and Maureen Bueno, for providing input on information systems issues from their practice settings.

128

Hammer and Champy[2] make a concerted effort to distinguish reengineering from other popular management techniques, including automation, downsizing, reorganizing, and total quality management/continuous quality improvement. There are a number of similarities, however, between reengineering and work redesign, particularly the sociotechnical systems (STS) approach to work redesign (Exhibit 10–1).

- Both techniques look at work from a systems perspective and recognize the interdependencies in processes that cross departmental boundaries.
- Both advocate starting from scratch, rather than tweaking current operations a little here and a little there.
- Both stress a "do—learn—do more," iterative approach.

The primary differences are in emphasis. Reengineering focuses heavily on business process and definitely incorporates information technology, while work redesign emphasizes the design of jobs. It makes sense to integrate these techniques by first creating new processes to accomplish the work and then designing the required jobs.

In summary, reengineering is still linked to work redesign, but the evolution of reengineering to a broader conceptualization appears to invert the relationship between these two approaches as originally described. Rather than being looked at as a way to incorporate technology within work redesign, reengineering now appears to be viewed as the more general, comprehensive technique. Process redesign comes first and is followed and supported by job redesign.

REENGINEERING THE PROCESS OF HEALTH CARE

While Hammer and Champy[2(p.35)] do not address the business of health care specifically, their concept of a business process as "a collection of activities that takes one or more kinds of inputs and creates an output that is of value to the customer" is certainly general enough to apply to health care. Discussions of

---

Exhibit 10–1 Reengineering versus Work Redesign

- **COMMONALITIES**
  Systems perspective
  Clean slate approach versus incremental fixing
  Iterative process
- **DIFFERENCES**
  Process and technology versus job design

reengineering health care are beginning to appear in the hospital administration literature.[3]

The output of health care is patient outcomes, but the process is so fragmented that care providers can easily become obsessed with tasks and activities as opposed to results. Patients need a coordinated, continuous process to get better and stay well, but what they frequently experience is a series of separate events. It is often difficult to identify one individual who is actually in charge of the whole process.

Reengineering in health care may occur in two waves. Initially, the focus may be on changing the infrastructure for care, that is, the core processes common to all patients (e.g., how entry into the system, diagnostic procedures, and therapeutic regimens are accomplished). With the development of a more efficient and effective framework for care, attention could be directed to further streamlining the specific processes for different case types through care and case management.

Breaking Rules in Health Care

Hammer and Champy[2] stress that reengineering involves breaking rules to create new ways of working, and they provide some thought-provoking examples. Several of their ideas have interesting implications for the delivery of health care. For example, these authors identify shared data bases as a disruptive technology that can break the old rule, "Information can appear only in one place at one time." They replace this rule with the new rule, "Information can appear simultaneously in as many places as it is needed."[2(p.92)]

Many operational processes in health care have been built around the limitation of pen and paper files, specifically, medical records. Hammer and Champy[2] point out that information on paper stored in a file can only be used by one person at a time, so work tends to be structured sequentially: one person completes a task and passes the file to the next person in line. The transmission of physicians' orders through the medical record, to the unit secretary, to the nurse is an obvious example of this situation in health care. The point is that data base technology makes this rule obsolete. Many people can use the same information simultaneously, so the process can be freed from the artificial limits created by sequencing.

Another of Hammer and Champy's rule-breaking examples involves the use of telecommunications networks to replace the old rule, "Businesses must choose between centralization and decentralization," with the new rule, "Businesses can simultaneously reap the benefits of centralization and decentralization."[2(p.93)] This change will become even more important as networks of providers develop across a wider continuum of care. Eventually, the hospital structure as we now know it may cease to exist. Today's hospitals may become intensive care centers with networks of relationships with multiple free-standing facilities, such as clinics, rehabilitation agencies, and hospices. As much as possible will be done outside of the traditional hospital in an effort to reduce costs.

Telecommunications will mean that clinical and financial information can be shared in real time among all the facilities in the integrated service network. Thus, central control can be balanced with responsiveness at the level of the individual agency, and beyond, as staff move in and out of clients' homes using notebook computers and wireless data communications.

Last on this list is the appealing idea that automatic identification and tracking technology, combined with wireless data communication, makes it possible to break the old rule, "You have to find out where things are," and replace it with the new rule, "Things tell you where they are."[2(p.98)] Not only do you not have to look for things, but when you want them to go somewhere else, they get the message right away. This has important implications for many aspects of health care (e.g., keeping track of wheelchairs, transporters, and even patients). This change could make it possible to finally resolve some of those seemingly simple, but ubiquitous, problems in hospital operations and remove them from the unsolved mystery list once and for all.

Hospital Health Care Assumptions and Rules

Breaking rules requires the explicit identification of assumptions that underlie them. Although such assumptions are rarely articulated and, therefore, frequently unrecognized, they guide our thinking and limit our creativity.

What are some of the assumptions or unwritten rules specific to the traditional hospital health care paradigm? Several examples are included in the display below. Although these statements are probably not cross-stitched on the office wall, most of us act as if they were true.

Hospital Health Care Assumptions and Rules

- Some nurses work in hospitals and some in home care, but the same nurse doesn't work in both.
- Patients have to come to us for care.
- We care for patients during discrete episodes of illness.

Why can't the same nurse care for a patient at home and in the hospital? Jeanne Donlevy has had such a program in place at Good Samaritan Hospital in Lebanon, Pennsylvania, since October 1992.[4] In the Connection Model she has developed, hospital nurses have the opportunity to extend the management of their patients' care across institutional boundaries and into the home. Consider the possibility of a nurse seeing an obstetrical patient at home antepartum, in the hospital, and again postpartum at home. This approach provides continuity for patients, a sense of completion for the nurse, and enhanced flexibility for hospitals that may be experiencing severe fluctuations in inpatient census but growth and better payment schedules in home care.

Who says patients have to come to us for care? The innovative team at Good Samaritan also makes preadmission testing and other services available to patients in their homes. There is a growing recognition that care delivery models that transcend hospital walls and episodic care are the direction of the future.[5,6]

Reengineering Oppurtunities in Health Care

Stewart[7] suggests that the best corporate candidates for reengineering are companies facing dramatic shifts in the nature of competition. That description seems particularly relevant to the health care industry, and it may be useful to examine some examples of opportunities for reengineering that are specific to health care.

Several potential applications of reengineering discussed in the article that follows are summarized in Exhibit 10–2. In addition to these possibilities, surgically implanted chips with embedded software or less invasive devices combined with telecommunications technology may create the potential to relocate much diagnostic testing and monitoring from the hospital to patients' homes. As new technological capabilities continue to develop, there will be other solutions looking for problems, and the nurse executive's challenge is to harness this potential to improve patient care.

CLOSING THOUGHTS

Few would disagree that these are trying times for health care clinicians and administrators. Yet the environment is also fraught with opportunity. If we can

---

Exhibit 10–2 Reengineering Opportunities in Health Care

- Electronic medical records with multimedia data
- Direct interfaces between monitoring devices and electronic records
- Voice-activated documentation
- Decision support for clinicians
- Electronic data interchange (EDI) among organizations
- Relocation of diagnostic testing and monitoring to home

stand the stresses and strains of change and recognize the opportunities available, there is enormous potential for progress in the delivery of health care services. Reengineering can help us to realize that potential to the mutual benefit of health care clients, clinicians, and organizations.

REFERENCES

1. Hammer M. Reengineering work: Don't automate, obliterate. *Harvard Business Rev.* 1990;68(4):104–112.
2. Hammer M, Champy J. *Reengineering the Corporation: A Manifesto for Business Revolution.* New York: Harper Business; 1993.
3. Bergman R. Reengineering health care. *Hosp Health Networks.* 1994;68(3):28–36.
4. Donlevy J. Responsive restructuring. I. Acute care nurses provide home visits. *New Definition.* 1993;8(3):1–3.
5. Bower K. Case management: Work redesign with patient outcomes in mind. In: McDonagh KJ, ed. *Patient-Centered Hospital Care: Reform from Within.* Ann Arbor, MI: Health Administration Press; 1993.
6. Miller N. An interview with Phyllis Ethridge. *Nurs Econ.* 1994;12(2):65–74.
7. Stewart TA. Reengineering: The hot new managing tool. *Fortune.*1993;128(4)41–48.

Reengineering:
The Work Redesign-Technology Link

Mary Crabtree Tonges, MBA, MSN, RN, and Eunice Lawrenz, RN

The nineties promise to be a decade of unprecedented technological progress and change. What contribution can these advances make to improving patient care and furthering the goals of nursing? The Secretary's Commission on Nursing recommended in 1988 that health care delivery organizations "develop and use automated information systems and other new labor-saving technologies as a means of better supporting nurses and other health professionals."[1] The use of information technology is in fact expanding rapidly in health care organizations, and these systems have the potential to change the work of patient care itself and the relationships among the people doing this work. Simply automating existing

Source: Reprinted from *Journal of Nursing Administration,* Vol. 23, No. 10, pp. 15–22, with permission of J.B Lippincott Company, © 1993.

operations, however, will not achieve information technology's full potential for increasing both the efficiency and effectiveness of patient care delivery.

The solution to achieving maximum benefit from incorporating these technologies in the redesign of work may lie in the concept known as reengineering. Reengineering is defined as "the power of modern information systems to radically redesign our business processes to achieve dramatic improvements in their performance."[2(p.104)] Information technology can create unique opportunities to do things in completely new and better ways. To capitalize on this potential, however, it is necessary to recognize and act on it by taking a "clean slate" approach to the development of new systems. Thus, the expert advice is "don't automate, obliterate."[2(p.104)]

INFORMATION TECHNOLOGY IN THE NINETIES

The introduction of computer-based information systems during the last few decades has profoundly changed the way data can be collected, stored, and disseminated. Advances in data processing technology have the potential to create significant changes within organizations in which communication of information plays an important role. Which specific information technologies will be dominant forces for change during the nineties?

Information technology researchers conducted a technological forecast to identify the information technologies that experts predict will have the greatest impact on organizations in this decade.[3] Respondents felt that "the business environment of the middle and late 1990s will be radically different from that of the 1980s."[3] A movement from "data dominance" to "knowledge dominance" was identified. Information will be made available in much more useful and immediately applicable forms to answer questions and support decisions. There was also agreement that "real gains in productivity will come from giving workers direct and immediate access to knowledge."[3(p.1333)]

More specifically, the respondents identified five groups of technologies, of which the most important two were human interface technologies (to improve the interface between people and machines) and communications technologies (to facilitate person-to-person and data communications). Each of these two critical information technology groups included several key items.

In group 1, human interface technologies, the key items were speech recognition, voice input-output interfaces, natural language interfaces, and high-end work stations. Important items included the mouse, touchscreens, light pens, windows, etc., and executive information systems. In group 2, communications technologies, the key items were voice-mail, e-mail, fax, VSAT (very small aperture terminal), EDI (electronic data interchange), and high-end work stations. Important items included ISDN (international standard data network), desktop publishing, and local area networks.[3(p.1334)]

These two groups were chosen as the most important, because the new interface technologies will enable knowledge workers (whose jobs require considerable learning and expertise) to easily access computerized information, and communications technologies will rapidly bring information from many sources to people and change "the way people interact, form teams, and pass knowledge back and forth."[3(p.1335)]

The most controversial finding was that artificial intelligence and expert systems will not be organizationally important. Artificial intelligence is "the effort to develop computer-based systems (both hardware and software) that behave as humans" in terms of such capabilities as language, visual and oral perception, and logical reasoning.[4(p.662)] Expert systems use artificial intelligence to automate decision-making processes and solve problems that usually require human thought.[4]

Information technology forecasting research helps managers understand the potential of available information technologies and the need to incorporate them into strategic planning. This type of information could be used to great advantage in health care.

THE IMPACT OF INFORMATION TECHNOLOGY IN HOSPITALS

Some experts believe that most implementation of information technology in health care to date has been restricted to entry-level applications. They predict, however, that the combined effects of the change to prospective payment and the accelerating pace of technological advancement will lead to very new areas of application for health care in the 1990s.[5] The fact that "clinically based management systems can give managers control over the patient care process (and related costs) in a real-time environment"[5(p.6)] will not be overlooked. Additionally, the simultaneous pressures for increased access to care and improved quality will drive the rapid growth of information technology implementation in hospitals.[6]

Contrary to the findings concerning the general organizational impact of artificial intelligence, authorities on information technology in health care forecast that expert systems will be incorporated in order entry, order communication, and results-reporting systems.[5] Examples of these applications include sophisticated allocation and scheduling systems, least-cost treatment protocols, and early warning diagnostic systems. In view of the intensifying pressure for cost control in health care and the natural fit of expert systems with supporting diagnostic and therapeutic decision making, they may well be right.

Health care institutions are understandably described as information inten-sive.[5–6] Martin states that most hospital activities "involve the processing of infor-mation at various levels of complexity"; moreover, he suggests that the "best, and probably the only, way to simultaneously achieve cost and quality improve-ments in our information-intensive organizations is to make substantial improve-ments in the way we handle information."[6(p.11)]

THE POTENTIAL OF REENGINEERING

The key to actualizing the full potential of computers to improve work flow and productivity may lie in resisting the natural inclination to simply automate existing systems. If the opportunity to design new approaches to sharing clinical informa-tion is recognized and acted upon, it could be an important step toward achiev-ing high-quality, less costly care through improved coordination, decision mak-ing, and control.

Hammer uses the term "reengineering" to describe using the capacity for change created by new information technologies to radically redesign work.[2(p.104)] For example, he describes a project in which an insurance company moved from handling customers' applications sequentially to empowering one employee, a case manager supported by an information system, to process an entire applica-tion.

Other authors describe this concept as "business process redesign."[7(p.11)] Re-gardless of the choice of terms, the point is the same. Many current business processes are based on decisions made by functional departments in an effort to optimize their own performance, with little attention to the impact on overall organizational effectiveness. Yet business systems are a configuration of coordi-nated services, not the sum of separate, unrelated parts. In health care, the best nursing division, medical staff, and pharmacy departments do not make the best hospital if they do not work together effectively as a system of patient care.[8] When existing departmental systems are automated in isolation, communication and coordination difficulties can actually be exacerbated. A broader reengineering approach can instead produce "boundary-crossing, customer-driven processes."[7(p.11)] Clearly, reengineering is highly applicable to the type of work process improvement that is central to total quality management and con-tinuous quality improvement.

The idea of changing procedures and processes because of the introduction of information technology may be difficult to accept initially, as it runs counter to the conventional wisdom concerning how to select and install a computer sys-tem. Rather than change tried and true approaches that have taken years to develop, most hospitals try to customize packages and integrate systems to cre-ate a fit with existing operations. Although reengineering may be a much more difficult and risky approach, the potential incremental gains are enormous. As Hammer so colorfully puts it, "it is time to stop paving the cow paths. Instead of embedding outdated processes in silicone and software, we should obliterate them and start over."[2(p.104)]

In discussing the identification of information technology levers, Davenport and Short[7] list nine information technology capabilities and their organizational impacts. Of these, four appear to have the most direct relationship to the key concepts of this discussion. The selected capabilities and their related impacts are summarized as follows:

1. Informational: brings vast amounts of detailed information into process.
2. Knowledge management: allows the capture and dissemination of knowledge and expertise to improve the process.
3. Analytical: brings complex analytical methods to bear on a process.
4. Geographical: transfers information with rapidity and ease across large distances, making processes independent of geography.[7(p.17)]

The process used by professionals to help clients in a service system, such as health care, can be conceptualized as a series of six cyclical steps: (1) information compilation; (2) information comparison; (3) information analysis; (4) selection of an intervention; (5) implementation; and (6) evaluation of the effect on the client. The information, knowledge management, and analytical capabilities of information technology can have an impact on this process at several points. Additionally, in a professional service system that involves multiple professionals working with one client (e.g., hospitals), the geographic capability is also important.

REENGINEERING IN HEALTH CARE

The potential benefits of reengineering in health care can be illustrated by a simple example. Consider the process used to order medication for a patient. In a traditional manual system, the following steps are usually involved:

1. The physician locates patient's chart and writes and flags orders for medication.
2. The unit secretary transcribes the order to medication Kardex and administration record and prepares the order for pharmacy via a carbonless copy of the order page or a requisition.
3. A registered professional nurse reviews appropriateness and completeness of the order and accuracy of transcription. If questions or problems exist, the nurse discusses them with the physician or unit secretary as appropriate.

4. The order is transported to the pharmacy by courier, a member of nursing staff, or pneumatic tube system.

5. The pharmacist reviews appropriateness and completeness of the order, contacts the physician if necessary, and then updates the patient's profile accordingly and initiates steps to fill the order.

This process is diagrammed in Figure 10–1.

A common approach to automating medication ordering is to leave most of the process the same, except have the unit secretary enter the orders into a data base. Unfortunately, this accomplishes very little, as the nurse must still verify the clerk's transcription after the order is entered, and the pharmacy cannot fill the order until it receives a hard copy. Yet available information technology creates the potential for many improvements in the traditional medication ordering process. Why not train residents and interested attending physicians to enter their own orders directly? Although some who are not comfortable with computers will resist, these objections will diminish as new physicians become increasingly computer literate. As illustrated in Figure 10–2, this approach could result in a process with the following steps:

1. The physician enters the medication order into the data base from whatever terminal is convenient, perhaps eventually from a hand-held device. At the time of entry, the system could check the order for appropriateness in terms of dosage, route, patient's allergies, incompatibilities with current drug regimen, and availability in hospital formulary. If there are any problems in these areas, the physician could be made aware of them immediately. The physician would also be informed through the ordering screens if any special information regarding documentation of required indications for use of a particular drug had to be provided.

2. Once the order was entered in the data base, other functions would be executed automatically, including alerting the nurse, printing a new medication Kardex and possibly an administration record (unless medications were documented via bedside terminals), and communicating the order to the pharmacy.

Such a process could reduce the risk of ordering problems and transcription errors, accelerate the communication of orders, increase physician convenience, and save nurses' and secretaries' time. The issue of physician convenience depends, of course, on the availability of a program with efficient screens and, perhaps optimally, other features to encourage physician usage. Physicians respond positively to the opportunity to create their own personal order sets. Many would also welcome the assistance of an expert system to support diagnosis and treatment decisions, but the use of such systems is currently still restricted to learning

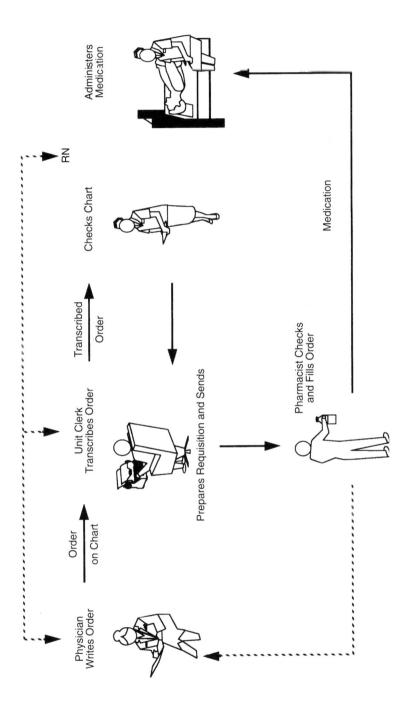

Figure 10–1 Traditional medication ordering process. The solid line indicates definite interaction, and the dotted line indicates routes of communication for clarification, if necessary.

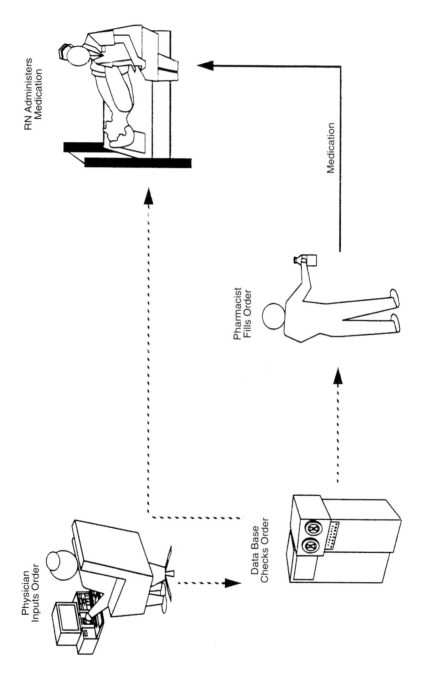

Figure 10–2 Reengineered medication ordering process. The dotted line indicates automated communication.

laboratories rather than actual clinical practice. As previously indicated, using information technology to radically redesign work processes and dramatically improve operations is the essence of reengineering.

Martin describes a possible structure for a fully integrated health care information system and applies the notion of reengineering specifically to the work of hospitals.[6] The structure proposed by Martin has six components: core, business/financial, communication/networking; medical support, departmental management, and medical documentation systems. The following four are most central to reengineering in the clinical area:

1. Core systems: involve common, centralized functions and the data bases related to these functions (e.g., registration, order entry, results reporting, and electronic mail).

2. Communications/networking systems: integrate stand-alone, special purpose systems, such as nursing acuity/scheduling and utilization review/quality assurance packages, into the information systems architecture of the institution.

3. Medical support: involves information systems that directly support and assist physicians and other health care professionals in caring for patients.

4. Medical documentation systems: involve the capture, storage, and use of data generated via the health care delivery process.

Martin also identifies the potential for a totally electronic medical record and describes the future medical documentation system and its relationships to other components as:

> A large "data base machine," with inputs received from departmental management systems as well as from "the information gathering and organization" components of the medical support systems . . . will electronically access the data base to provide active and ongoing support for the practice of medicine.[6(p.21)]

Many hospitals are upgrading their existing management information systems and considering the addition or expansion of clinical systems, but these activities are insufficient. Instead, hospitals must recognize that their product is patient care, rather than administrative functions, and completely rethink the way their information systems are conceptualized, designed, and managed.[6(p.24)]

INCREASED EFFICIENCY OR IMPROVED EFFECTIVENESS

Drucker makes the critical distinction that efficiency is doing things right, whereas effectiveness is doing the right things. He describes effectiveness as "the foundation of success" and efficiency as "a minimum condition for survival" after success has been achieved."[9(p.45)] What are the potential positive effects of reengineering in health care—increased efficiency or improved effectiveness?

Because of the intense pressure to decrease length of stay created by prospective payment, providing the same type of care more quickly has become a highly valued and sought-after goal. Faster is equated with better. Thus, the distinction between efficiency and effectiveness may easily have become blurred.

These two concepts are intertwined in health care, as they are in many endeavors. Having key pieces of information precisely when needed in the clinical decision-making process can make an important difference in both the timing of actions and the choices that are made. The speed of information technology can clearly increase efficiency by facilitating the attainment of the same outcome more quickly, but may also push clinical decision making further down the effectiveness continuum toward better outcomes. The use of artificial intelligence has the potential to lead to totally different decisions about treatment modalities, resulting in substantively better patient outcomes (i.e., improved effectiveness).

Health care professionals using expert systems to support their clinical decision making will have increased access to an expanded data base of the latest research findings. This information will provide a basis for designing treatment protocols involving choices that would not otherwise have even been considered. This is one example of the fact that our ability to generate information is outstripping our ability to process it without computer assistance. A second case in point is that the number of parameters currently monitored for many critical care patients exceeds the human capacity for simultaneous analysis and interpretation. As Knauss states, this work is "an information-based technological science," and has reached a point in its development where many decisions are too complicated for individual health professionals to make independently.[10]

WHAT LIES AHEAD?

All indications point to a great potential for growth in the use of information technology to improve the delivery of hospital care; however, there are at least three possible obstacles to the realization of this potential: (1) the development of information technology infrastructures to support the level of flexibility and integration required; (2) the conversion of large numbers of computer illiterate or computer phobic staff to skilled users of information technology in multiple aspects of their work; and (3) the costs and benefits of developing and implementing these systems in an environment of increasingly constrained resources. Ensuring the continued confidentiality of patient information is another important issue. Research on this subject is likely to be focused in these areas, and if the barriers can be overcome, myriad changes in hospital operations will occur in the next 5 to 10 years.

Information technology will have far-reaching effects encompassing the clinical, educational, and administrative arenas. Multimedia charts will enable clinicians to observe a patient's gait and listen to his speech, rather than just read another's description. Direct interfaces between sophisticated monitoring devices and electronic records are dramatically reducing the time spent recording various physiologic parameters, and voice recognition will facilitate documentation of all types.

Electronic medical records will streamline the collection and analysis of clinical information for quality improvement purposes, and extensive paper trails will give way to paperless reviews.[11] Libraries will be transformed from repositories of information to aggressive information service providers using electronic methods.[12]

Increased computerization of hospitals' clinical processes will improve the efficiency of communication between different professions and result in more interdisciplinary contacts. These changes could break down interdisciplinary barriers, facilitate collaboration, and strengthen working relationships. The context and characteristics of these interactions may not always be harmonious, however. The pressure to control cost could result in changes that lead to conflict and alterations in the power differences between professional groups. For example, the federal government is currently designing treatment guidelines for certain conditions. The original purpose of this work appeared to be that it would be used to improve quality, not to reduce costs.[13] Given the current economic environment and concern about health care costs, that outcome may be unlikely. Regardless, whether for purposes of quality or cost, such guidelines could be incorporated in computerized order entry systems and limit physicians' freedom to deviate from the approved plan of care for the patient's condition. Clearly this is one scenario in which there would be a great potential for conflict.

Administrative changes will be equally as significant as those in the clinical arena. Integrated communication systems will facilitate interorganizational exchanges. The electronic transfer of patient information among organizations has important implications for continuity of care and will radically alter communication between providers and payers. Integrated information systems will also promote the inclusion of nonfinancial measures in performance appraisal and incentive compensation systems.[14] At the highest levels of the organization, strategic planning and decision making will be supported by executive information systems. Finally, the information technology explosion will require the development of new roles and resources within institutions. Already, the roles and responsibilities of chief information officers are becoming broader, and numerous new informatics positions will follow.

This description of the office of the late 1990s appears to be equally applicable to the patient care unit of the not-so-distant future:

> Its staff of professionals and managers are surrounded by intelligent devices that speak, listen, or interact with them to determine what is to be accomplished and how it is to be done. Contacts with other departments, other divisions, customers, vendors and other organizations are made with little effort and without human intervention. Behind the scenes, systems are being developed by systems developers equipped with versatile and highly integrated software.[3(p.1338)]

IMPLICATIONS FOR NURSING AND NURSE EXECUTIVES

Decisions about information technology will significantly affect nursing practice and patient care delivery processes. It is unfortunate that the involvement of nurses in selecting patient care information systems may be novel enough to merit attention as a trend.[15] Yet a recent survey indicated that many nurse executives do not have the authority to make the final decision in purchasing a nursing information system.[16]

Nurse executives must prepare themselves and act on the opportunity to play a central role in the continuing automation of health care.[17] Of the nurse executive's information technology–related responsibilities and opportunities, the following are among the most important:

- Become knowledgeable about information technology and its potential, and keep well-informed about new developments.
- Advocate and negotiate wisely for nursing and patient care delivery when the organization is purchasing a hospital-wide information system.
- Strive to take full advantage of information technology's possibilities through reengineering.
- Take a leadership position within the institution in redesigning patient care delivery, including but not limited to nursing.
- Recognize that the impact of information technology on the social aspects of work, the interpersonal relationships, may be positive or negative. Information technology may enhance communication and collaboration or may lead to conflicts over alterations in the distribution of information and power. Be sensitive to the potential for conflict and deal with it proactively and skillfully.

To actualize information technology's full potential for improving health care delivery, nurse executives will need knowledge, vision, and courage, but the inherent benefits are well worth the effort and risk.

CONCLUSION

Knauss states that there is an "information revolution" occurring in health care, and the only thing getting cheaper is the quality of clinical information.[10] Thus, information can provide an avenue for dealing with the cost/quality dilemma. Because the health care system is driven by patient information, information technology will create major changes in the communication and integration of information, interprofessional relationships, and the delivery of care. Social issues related to health care access, cost, and quality are creating a pressing need for change in the way these services are delivered, and information technology offers potential mechanisms to effect the necessary changes.

The efficiency and effectiveness of a process are directly related to the quality and cost of its product. Regarding the management of quality, Gabor states, "the biggest payoff in healthcare may come from mastering the complex mix of processes that determine how quickly, how well, and at what cost individual patients are treated for myriad illnesses."[18(p.9)] Information technology can increase how quickly and well patients are cared for. Reengineering facilitates the realization of information technology's full potential for positive changes. Reengineering can be a critical factor in balancing the cost/quality equation in health care, and nurse executives must be in the vanguard of this effort.

REFERENCES

1. Secretary's Commission on Nursing. *Final Report, Volume 1.* Washington, DC: Department of Health and Human Services, 1988.
2. Hammer M. Reengineering work: Don't automate, obliterate. *Harvard Bus Rev.* 1990; 68(4):104–112.
3. Straub DW, Wetherbe JC. Information technologies for the 1990s: An organizational impact perspective. *Commun Assoc Comput Machinery.* 1989;32(11):1328–1339.
4. Laudon KC, Laudon JP. *Management Information Systems: A Contemporary Perspective.* New York: Macmillan, 1991.
5. Kerr JK, Jelinek R. The impact of information technology in healthcare. *J Health Admin Educ.* 1990;8(1):5–10.
6. Martin JB. The environment and future of health information systems. *J Health Admin Educ.* 1990;8(1):11–24.
7. Davenport TH, Short JE. The new industrial engineering: Information technology and business process redesign. *Sloan Manage Rev.* 1990;summer:11–27.
8. Ackoff R. The interactive planning model. Presented at the Conference on Strengthening Hospital Nursing: A Program to Improve Patient Care, Orlando, Florida, September 7-8, 1989.
9. Drucker P. *Management: Tasks, Responsibilities, Practices.* New York: Harper & Row, 1974.

10. Knauss W. National health care: political and economic prospects. Panel presentation at the Seventh Annual Commonwealth Fund Executive Nurse Fellows Conference, Leesburg, Virginia, August 14, 1992.

11. Wasden W. Quality assessment: From paper shuffle to paperless review. *Comp Healthcare.* 1991;12(9):29–30, 32.

12. Feng CC, Weise FO. Integrated academic information management systems: III. Implementation of integrated information systems. *J Am Soc Information Sci.* 1988;39(2):126–130.

13. Trends. *Hospitals.* 1993;67(1):46–47.

14. Eccles RG. The performance measurement manifesto. *Harvard Business Rev.* 1991; 69(1):131–137.

15. Trends. *Hospitals.* 1992;66(13):5.

16. Dunbar C. Nurses want information system selection power, but do they have it? *Comp Healthcare.* 1992;13(3):22–24.

17. Fralic MF. Into the future: Nurse executives and the world of information technology. *J Nurs Adm.* 1992;22(4):11–12.

18. Gabor A. When TQM doesn't succeed: Lessons from industry. *The Quality Letter.* 1992;4(6):9.

■ 11 ■

Reengineering in Health Care: Labor Relations Issues

Carol Boston, JD, MS, RN

Broadly defined, patient-focused care is the reengineering of patient care work so that hospital resources and personnel are organized around patients or customers rather than around specialized departments or functions. In a recent *Hospitals* magazine survey focusing on trends in patient-focused care projects, nearly one-half of all responding provider organizations reported major work redesign projects either under way or being planned. Survey results also reported the following services as being typically affected by a major work redesign initiative: nursing, housekeeping, laboratory and pharmacy services, respiratory therapy, physical therapy, food service, radiology, medical record keeping, central service, and materials management.[1] If this survey is any indication of the extent to which jobs are being changed in health care organizations, it is safe to assume that relatively few jobs in health care are *not* being affected somehow by hospital efforts to become "patient-focused."

The achievement of patient-focused care via work reengineering entails more than just the reorganization of reporting relationships and the rewriting of job descriptions for employees directly responsible for patient care. It involves strategic changes in the delivery of health care services, along with the identification and design of jobs needed throughout the organization to support the redesigned delivery system and the reengineering of organizational work processes to maximize the organization's infrastructure. Viewed from this perspective, work reengineering constitutes:

1. actual transformation of work by focusing on the design of organizational structures to reduce costs and to meet changing market needs
2. development of jobs that provide satisfied employees and customers
3. streamlining of work processes to improve services
4. enhancement of service value to improve outcomes

Health care organizations evaluating the feasibility of initiating work transformation projects to achieve patient-focused care are advised to fully recognize organizational implications from the standpoint of labor relations. Work transformation initiatives involve job redesign in the broadest context, including what types of jobs will exist, how many jobs, and the qualifications and responsibilities involved. Thus, labor relations implications *always* exist, whether or not the organization is unionized. This chapter provides an overview of labor relations law relevant to work transformation, key labor relations "hot spots" in the course of a work transformation initiative, and strategies to remain union free or avoid unfair labor practice challenges.

LABOR LAW AND LABOR RELATIONS OVERVIEW

The National Labor Relations Act (NLRA) has governed labor-management activity in proprietary and not-for-profit health care organizations in the United States since 1935. Between the years 1947 and 1974, nonprofit hospitals were excluded from NLRA jurisdiction. Jurisdiction was once again extended over the not-for-profit and other types of health care organizations via a congressional NLRA amendment in 1974 and has remained in place ever since. Prior to 1991, the National Labor Relations Board (NLRB) recognized three categories of bargaining units in hospitals: (1) all professionals, (2) all nonprofessionals, and (3) security guards. Since 1991, expanded NLRB rules affirmed by the U.S. Supreme Court allowed recognition of up to eight categories of bargaining units for hospitals: (1) registered nurses, (2) physicians, (3) health professionals other than registered nurses and physicians, (4) clerical workers, (5) technical employees, (6) skilled maintenance workers, (7) nonprofessional employees, and (8) security guards. In 1970, only 2.3 percent of all health care organizations were unionized; that figure climbed to nearly 20 percent in the late 1980s and remains at approximately 18 percent, despite the existence of over 1.5 million health care workers and 5,000 health care organizations.

Theories abound as to why employees seek union representation in health care settings. Historically, union-organizing activity has been linked to health care employee discontent with benefits, pay, promotional opportunities, supervisory practices, work climate, and recognition.[2] Additional issues surrounding union-organizing activity for registered nurses have related to professionalism and key elements of a professional practice environment.[3]

Within the past few years, significant numbers of hospitals have been forced to realign human resource utilization with shifts in patient volumes from inpatient to outpatient services. Such realignment has typically included restructuring of operations, elimination of management positions and/or layers, and decreased numbers of employees at the point of care or business encounter within the organization. These activities have frequently coincided with elements of work redesign: specifically, the identification of new roles within resized or restructured organizations to deliver patient care effectively and efficiently. For all health care workers, fear associated with job change or insecurity has heightened union awareness. For nursing professionals, labor organizations have stimulated interest in unions by suggesting potentially adverse effects of work redesign on the quality and safety of patient care.[4]

Section VII of the NLRA allows employees of an organization to band together in confronting an employer regarding the terms and conditions of employment. Employment terms and conditions can include the scope of one's job and responsibilities for job activities and for other employee activities. Because of the extent of work redesign currently occurring in health care organizations and the corresponding perceptions about job security and potential representations about quality of patient care, unions are being provided with fertile ground for employee consideration of union representation in health care organizations. In fact, the most recent statistics suggest a significantly higher success rate for elections to have unions in the health care industry, compared with rates in previous years and with those for all other industries combined.[5] Furthermore, numerous unions that focus on health care workers have pledged to step up organizing efforts.[6] These include the Service Employees International Union (SEIU); the Association of Federal, State, County, and Municipal Employees (AFSCME); and state nursing associations.

UNION "HOT SPOTS" IN WORK REDESIGN

Today's health care climate is driving the need for hospitals to organize operations as efficiently as possible to ensure the organization's economic viability. The unstable economy, growing concern over work reengineering in hospitals, and overall fear associated with job change contribute to uneasy labor relations between employees and management.[4] For this reason, in preparation for project initiation, leadership teams should conduct an analysis of features typically found in a work reengineering initiative that contribute to union awareness in health care organizations.

Downsizing

Nationwide health care reform endeavors, driven by political agendas and the private sector, have resulted in a tremendous shift in inpatient versus outpatient utilization of health care services within health care organizations and systems. Efforts to redesign clinical services that focus on health instead of illness and the need to deliver more cost-effective services in the wake of increased managed care/capitated payer arrangements have spearheaded substantial reductions in hospital inpatient utilization and the simultaneous need to adjust human resource utilization according to service needs.

Health care organizations embarking on a major work reengineering initiative may elect to resize the overall staff structure before the work reengineering initiative actually occurs and to align human resource utilization with specifically selected operating benchmark standards. Alternatively, the organization may defer resizing its staff structure until it is in the midst of the work reengineering process. Regardless of the point at which resizing occurs, this is a clear union hot spot for hospitals. Union experts agree that loss of position, pay, or job is ample incentive for health care workers to rebel and seek union representation for protection of their overall welfare.[4]

Skill Mix Changes

Human resources (wages and benefits) typically exceed 50 percent of a hospital's operating budget. Nurses are the largest group of employees; hence, nursing costs are the largest expenditure in the human resource budget. As a health care organization seeks opportunities for improving its overall cost structure to ensure financial viability in an increasingly competitive, managed care market, utilization of all resources comes under scrutiny, including the largest resource—human resources. In particular, how nursing professionals, specifically registered nurses, are being utilized in the care delivery setting has become a prime consideration as part of the major work reengineering projects. Customarily, an organization undergoing work redesign seeks to create jobs that call for all professionals, including registered nurses, to function at the upper limits of licensure. Such redesigning requires the simultaneous commitment to assign to an unlicensed worker patient care activities that could be performed by someone other than a licensed professional. Organizations that conduct work reengineering, depending on various internal factors, are demonstrating substantial changes in skill mix that comply with relevant state nurse practice acts and simultaneously yield substantive, annualized savings in labor costs. Two strategies for delivering this result are (1) the creation of roles for unlicensed caregivers to augment professional roles and (2) the cross-training of several individuals for appropriate activities within the delivery setting.

Skill mix changes within a health care organization as part of a work redesign initiative will undoubtedly result in decreased numbers of jobs for licensed professionals, including registered nurses. Two areas in which heightened sensitivity to the need for a union can be anticipated are (1) the loss of job availability for incumbents because of skill mix changes and (2) the delegation to unlicensed caregivers of tasks that have been historically assumed by licensed professionals.

The Process

The process or methodology a health care organization selects to guide its work reengineering design initiative can be a major determinant of union-organizing activity. Employees in contemporary health care organizations desire an active role in organizational decision making. When employee opinions are perceived as insignificant, serious employee discontent may develop.[3] Coercive approaches to achieve employee performance are becoming increasingly ineffective. In the mind of the employee, the employee is devalued, and discontent develops, creating an excellent opportunity for organizing efforts.[2] Hence, the more participative the process is for employees, the more likely it is that union sensitivity will be appropriately controlled during a work reengineering initiative.

STRATEGIES

Beyond participation in the process, the manner in which employees are treated during a work reengineering initiative is also a union hot spot.[4]

The need to develop a solid labor relations strategy as part of a work reengineering initiative exists when the commitment to work transformation occurs. Whether a health care organization is unionized or not is irrelevant. Non-union organizations will want to remain union free. Unionized organizations will desire union cooperation and the avoidance of any adversarial union-management relationships. The following labor relations strategies are applicable to all health care organizations—unionized or union free:

- *Communication*—Communicate openly, honestly, and frequently about the organization's commitment to work transformation.
- *Involvement*—Utilize a work reengineering process that provides for relevant and comprehensive involvement of employees and managers.
- *Recruitment and staff selection*—Design a solid human resources strategy for the recruitment and selection of staff into newly designed jobs.
- *Employee opportunity*—Provide relevant and sufficient opportunities for employee education and training.
- *Management education*—Provide management education for all managers and department heads regarding union prevention strategies and tips for detecting potential union activity.

Communication

As soon as the executive decision has been made to initiate a work reengineering project, a comprehensive communication strategy should be designed with the primary goal to demystify the work reengineering project for all employees. Key messages should be identified, along with key messengers. Critical messages include the organizational rationale for committing to work reengineering, what the organization hopes to accomplish with the reengineering efforts, how employees will be involved in discussions and decisions, and the time line for implementation. With job security a major concern for all employees, they will seek answers from management regarding potential layoffs, as well as change in actual job scope. If changes in the number of jobs are anticipated (i.e., change in skill mix of nursing professionals), management should provide employees with information regarding (1) how layoff decisions will be made and (2) organizational provisions for any employee who is displaced because of the work redesign initiative (e.g., job placement within the organization, outplacement services, and severance arrangements). Organizations with union contracts typically have contractual language stipulating how downsizing or layoff of unionized employees is to occur. In these cases, the contractual language needs to be closely followed to avoid any unfair labor practice charges.

In health care organizations, communication has historically followed hierarchical channels, with executive management providing some sort of regular communication to either department heads or employees, either in writing or verbally in structured management-employee meetings. Experts in organizational development have advocated the importance of solid communication strategies but such strategies to support major organizational change extend far beyond the relaying of information via appropriate, formal channels. They call for "dialogue" to encourage employees to raise questions, express concerns, and debate ideas.[7] Organizations committed to an effective communication strategy as part of work reengineering are urged to initiate new types of communication strategies that provide optimal two-way communication opportunities (e.g., round-the-clock town hall meetings, telephone hot lines, and question-and-answer columns in organizational newspapers). Two-way communication increases the probability that relevant employee concerns regarding the reengineering initiative will surface and will be addressed. Such efforts help to avoid any appearance of nonresponsiveness to employees. While the organization will not necessarily have the answers that employees wish to hear (i.e., a guarantee regarding continued employment) use of this strategy demonstrates significant responsiveness regarding the human impact of work reengineering.

Involvement

Involvement of people in a change process is viewed as a potent tool for overcoming resistance to change as well as for giving employees personal stakes in the change outcome.[7] Fears associated with job insecurity can be managed if employees believe that there is some opportunity or control over personal destiny. Hence, a participative process for discussions and decisions about the redesign of jobs and reengineering of work processes can foster positive employer-employee relationships during a highly stressful period for the organization as a whole. If management is perceived as providing opportunities for relevant input into work redesign and process reengineering decisions, then the perceived value of a union can be minimized.[2] Furthermore, the participative approach to work redesign and process reengineering decisions will provide employees with a sense of legitimate empowerment regarding significant organizational issues. Again, the need for a union is minimized in the eyes of the employee, because the employee's opinions are valued.[2]

Recruitment

Work redesign and process reengineering, if done appropriately, should result in the creation of new jobs or opportunities for the majority of employees in the organization. These new jobs and opportunities will include responsibility for specific technical activities, along with behaviors and competencies critical to the new delivery system model. As a health care organization proceeds with demonstrating or "piloting its new care delivery model," it will put into place new jobs for employees. The organization's leadership team has an important decision to make regarding these new jobs. Should incumbents from a demonstration or pilot unit or area automatically be placed in these new jobs, should the organization post new jobs so that employees from throughout the organization can apply, or should some other mechanism for external recruitment be used?

If new jobs for a particular unit or area are not automatically given to unit or area incumbents, selection criteria should be objective and valid for newly designed roles. Incumbents of a demonstration unit or area not hired for new jobs will expect objective rationale for not being hired. Any evidence of subjective hiring decisions or lack of fairness in terms of how hiring decisions are made could prompt disgruntled employees to seek union support for subsequent protection. Furthermore, if employee displacement is a possibility, then a fair severance program is essential, along with measures such as "outplacement support." While union contracts typically have language that provides for management decisions regarding human resource requirements, employees will evaluate the degree of assistance that the organization is willing to provide to displaced employees. What this assistance will be and how it will be provided is valuable information for the organization to communicate to employees prospectively in order to further minimize employee perception that a union is needed to negotiate such arrangements.

Employee Oppurtunity

Newly designed roles will undoubtedly call for new technical skills and behaviors. Typically, in work reengineering initiatives, the decision is made to create jobs that maximize professional licensure and simultaneously assign to nonlicensed personnel any type of activity that does not require licensure for performance. The cross-training of licensed and nonlicensed staff, along with the decentralization of services to the point of care or encounter, demands further skill enhancement of the involved employees. When employees are provided with comprehensive information about the scope and qualifications for newly created jobs, questions will be raised regarding the organization's commitment to assisting its employees for transition into these new jobs. Thorough planning for the education and training of employees is essential for effective reengineering outcomes, but availability of education and training for employees will also mitigate employee concerns that the organization is creating jobs for which the incumbent work force is not qualified.

Consideration must also be given to the types of team-based behaviors that the newly designed care delivery model will require. Education and development regarding behaviors essential to functioning in a high-performance, cross-disciplinary work team will be needed for all health care employees assuming new roles, including nursing professionals, who have probably been educated in the "primary care" model. Regardless of their jobs, team members in redesigned organizations will need to demonstrate effective interpersonal skills (e.g., group problem solving, negotiation, and conflict resolution). Team leaders will need to serve as coach, mentor, facilitator, and guide, instead of supervisor, director, or controller of responsibilities. When employees witness the gamut of educational opportunities made available by the organization to maximize employee chances of being successful in new jobs, they will be in a much better position to trust the organization, again minimizing the perception that a union is essential to the protection of employee interests in a changing organization.

Management Education

Even with a solid communication strategy, a work redesign process that provides for relevant employee involvement, and substantive education and training, groups of employees may still consider union representation as an alternative to current governance practices. For this reason, a preventive labor relations strategy at the start of a work reengineering initiative should always include a management education program that educates managers about various labor and employment laws and trains them in the skills necessary to manage, listen, and communicate with employees during a major organizational change initiative.[6] Because the first-line manager has day-to-day contact with employees and managers at the point of care or encounter within a health care organization, it is reasonable to assume that this manager is in an optimal position to detect and thwart union-organizing activity. In addition, a first-line manager, if not trained on management behaviors strictly prohibited during a union-organizing campaign, can further aggravate an already explosive situation.

The interpersonal relationships cultivated by front-line managers with employees—characterized by communication, understanding, trust, and responsiveness—are critical. Thus, management education on these types of management skills at the onset of work reengineering is extremely valuable to organizations attempting to mitigate union sensitivity. Furthermore, managers must be trained in activities strictly prohibited by NLRB during any union-organizing efforts, including prohibitions on threatening, interrogating, making promises to, or spying on employees in regard to union activity.[8]

For hospitals that are already unionized, additional strategies are suggested for early incorporation into the work reengineering initiative. Hospital administrators should work with labor relations personnel and counsel to accomplish the following:

- Identify specific labor relations issues relative to the scope of the hospital's project.
- Analyze the hospital's collective bargaining agreement provisions, work rules, and work practices.
- Review all relevant grievances and disciplinary actions.
- Compare current wages and benefits with those of similar employers.
- Create and facilitate the work of joint labor-management committees to ensure relevant input into the work redesign project.
- Negotiate with the union the specific opportunities for direct employee involvement in the work redesign process in order to avoid any impression of direct dealing with employees, which is expressly prohibited by the NLRA.

IN THE FUTURE

What lies ahead for hospitals faced with initiating a process to redesign work and reengineer processes in order to ensure quality, cost-effective service delivery in an increasingly competitive, resource-constrained environment? First, the need for organizations to deliver care differently will not abate. Thus, the shift in system focus from treating illness to managing health will continue, along with decreasing inpatient volumes and increasing outpatient services. While jobs in health care will be abundant, opportunities for jobs and career development will no longer be dominated by the acute care hospital. The work force that will be needed for the acute care hospital must be organized differently in order to deliver services differently; a systems approach to services and the utilization of high-performance, multidisciplinary work teams will be common features of new delivery systems. Jobs will change, as will processes, so that this organizational transformation can occur.

Second, organizing attempts in health care will continue. The most recent statistics demonstrate that unions have had the highest election victory rate since 1984. In the health care industry, 55.8 percent of union representative elections were won. In decertification elections, a greater percentage of health care workers voted to retain unions than to decertify them.[6]

Of interest to nursing professionals and health care providers is the recent U.S. Supreme Court decision ruling that nurses who direct the work of other employees could potentially be deemed supervisors according to federal labor law and, therefore, could be deprived of collective bargaining rights and NLRB workplace protections. In the wake of work redesign, nursing unions are criticizing the ruling, which suggests that front-line caregivers may be deprived of their ability to speak (vis-a-vis collective bargaining) regarding quality of care issues perceived as being affected by work redesign decisions.[9] Hospital administrators, on the other hand, may elect to test this ruling by deeming registered nurses ineligible for unions and furthering work reengineering efforts.

Developing an effective labor relations strategy as part of work reengineering is *not* an optional event. It is a mandatory component of the overall work reengineering plan in order to achieve organizational outcomes, mitigate union sensitivity, manage union relations, and avoid charges of unfair labor practice.

REFERENCES

1. Sherer J. Putting patients first. *Hospitals.* 1993;67(3):14–19.
2. McLaurin J, Berkely A, Taylor R. Perspectives on unions in hospitals. *J Health Hum Resources Adm.* 1992;27(4):267–275.
3. Flarey D, Yoder S, Barabas M. Collaboration in labor relations: A model for success. *J Nurs Adm.* 1992;22(9):15–22.
4. Sherer J. Can hospitals and organized labor be partners in redesign? *Hosp Health Networks.* 1994;68(6):58–59.
5. Becker W. Organized labor fights back. *Health Syst Rev.* 1993;27(5):30–32.
6. Vaccaro P, Bryant M. Proactive strategies may prevent union organizing efforts. *Provider.* 1993;29(11):49–51.
7. Kanter R, Stein B, Jick T. *The Challenge of Organizational Change.* New York: Macmillan; 1992.
8. American Organization of Nurse Executives. The role and functions of the hospital nurse manager. *Nurs Manage.* 1992;23(9):36–38.
9. RNs and Health Care Restructuring. *Calif Nurse.* 1994;9:6.

▪ 12 ▪

Facilities Considerations in Work Reengineering

Kerry A. Shannon, MS

As the reengineering of work processes has matured, a number of tenets have emerged, including

- the value of multidisciplinary teams
- the importance of managing change
- the need to include physicians
- the frustration with facilities

In comparison with the first three tenets, facilities issues have received little attention.

The leaders of many work reengineering projects in health care institutions would like to deny the importance of buildings. At one level, this seems to make sense. If one is attempting to foster creativity and excite employees about a new and improved care delivery system that will promote the hospital's future viability and image, it is not an advantage to highlight the fact that the environment will be the same long corridors with poor lighting and not enough storage space. This does not mean that reengineering is contingent on extensive construction. The issue is that the failure to appreciate the relationship between space and operations makes implementation of reengineered processes precarious. This chapter addresses critical issues related to facilities in work reengineering projects. A focused discussion on incorporating physical considerations into a reengineering project is also presented.

OPERATIONS AND FACILITIES

The relationship of spaces to processes is vastly different within, between, and among hospitals—an outgrowth of the fact that hospitals neither look nor act exactly alike. There are, however, certain characteristics of the relationship that are universal. The first is that space exists to support operations, and therein lies its value. The second is that space is the least flexible resource. While certain individuals might appear to be more rigid than bricks and mortar, it is still easier, with appropriate leadership and guidance, to change policies and procedures than to change physical conditions. There are obviously circumstances in which a building will not allow a method of care or a piece of equipment. In that case, changing the structure has to be evaluated, and if the buildings are considered to be a tool to support operations, the situations in which they require change are readily identified and evaluated. Ideally, this should be an integral part of the work reengineering process, but it often is not, for some very logical reasons.

One cause of this omission is that reengineering often focuses on reducing the operating budget, and buildings are traditionally thought of as being tied exclusively to the capital budget. Facilities are obviously part of the capital budget, but they also have tremendous ability to affect the operating budget. For example, it is becoming commonplace for inpatient nursing units to have one or more multitask, non-registered nurse job categories. Often, these positions are established to allow nurses to remain closer to the patient. Therefore, a significant amount of the multitask worker's time is spent in the movement of materials. In some institutions, an automated movement system, such as a pneumatic tube, would save significant time and money by reducing labor costs in addition to decreasing traffic in the hallways.

The increasing numbers of employee categories on inpatient units bring other space issues to the surface. There is often a net increase of people on the units, thereby increasing the need for areas in which to accommodate them. The assumption is that multiskilled workers will be either with patients, performing tasks on the unit, or transporting. The performance of certain tasks (e.g., any kind of documentation) consumes space. In addition, all employees will take advantage of staff support space such as locker rooms and lounges if they are made available. If the reengineered systems require frequent team conferences, meeting space may become increasingly less available. One solution is to reduce the number of beds on the units. In some cases, this solution makes sense, but in other instances, it will compromise the sought-after efficiency in nurse staffing and coverage.

A second, related reason that facilities implications are not well incorporated into reengineering projects is that hospitals that undertake work reengineering are often facing budget problems. This situation may cause administrators and board members to adopt the attitude that the building conditions are a given, as there is no money to be spent. The corollary is that the buildings must not be "that bad," because they are currently supporting activity. This corollary depicts a fascinating attitude and one which nurses and other care providers have unconsciously promoted by becoming extremely adept at working in less than ideal conditions. No industry has more examples of space innovation than health care, perhaps because in no other sector has the nature of the business been so drastically altered while the physical confines have been so stagnant. Countless hospitals are delivering high-quality, technology-intensive, acute care in buildings whose occupants are three generations removed from the planners. And yet, due to the ingenuity and willpower of dedicated caregivers and the perseverance of hospital engineers, the buildings continue to serve their purpose. The question is, at what cost? The answer comes through recognition of the maximum potential of the buildings and perception of the point at which continued investment for a given function from both the operating and capital sides exceed the opportunity cost of an available alternative.

Increasingly, there simply is no money to be spent on buildings, despite full recognition that it is desirable to do so. This situation does not diminish the need to incorporate physical conditions into the reengineering and probably enhances this need, because the mandate to quickly recover cost from the system is a condition of survival. In such a case, the care delivery system must take physical conditions as an assumption and design around existing constraints. For example, if the work reengineering seeks to decentralize clinical support services, there are likely to be space implications for supplies. If phlebotomists and respiratory therapists were formerly dispatched from a central area bringing supplies with them and those tasks will now be performed by unit-based personnel, the supplies must be stored somewhere other than in the hallway. It is now necessary to find space as well as to strike the appropriate balance between inventory levels and stocking frequency, which is challenging because materials management is probably being reengineered as well. Solutions to these problems should be created in the design phase of reengineering, when opportunities exist; if solutions to these problems are left until implementation, both the problems and attempts at solution can present unpleasant and expensive surprises.

Most health care providers are familiar with care delivery systems that are founded in proscribed physical conditions, for example, a satellite radiography room, pharmacy, and laboratory to serve patients in a given number of beds. Assuming that significant funding is available for new construction or renovation, such solutions may have intuitive appeal. They should be very closely scrutinized, however, because few institutions appear able to cause the rigid conditions imposed by such models to result in a desirable operating environment or positive impact to the bottom line. The philosophy of focusing work design on the patient, in which these programs have their roots, remains highly desirable and can be incorporated into work reengineering regardless of the physical conditions.

The reality that work reengineering can be intimidating and complex leads to the desire to have the process not overwhelm the institution. This phenomenon sometimes means that, while there is recognition that it might be nice to include the facilities as part of the process, it may "unnecessarily complicate" things. In addition, "we can always come back and do a physical plan later." Again, this mind-set is understandable but proven not to serve very well the organizations that adopt it. Essentially, if the reengineered work process is not compatible with the buildings, there can be both safety and cost-related consequences. Additionally, attempting to create a physical plan subsequent to reengineering, while certainly possible, is not ideal for several reasons, including the following:

- It would be necessary to find facility planners who can truly understand the operational implications and nuances of what may be a unique system without the benefit of having heard discussions related to its inception. Lacking this information, they will not have a basis for prioritization, which is typically required in physical planning.

- There may be enormous costs involved in changing the physical plant to support the processes resulting from the hard work of reengineering. Studying the effects concurrently can lead to a solution that is not capital intensive.

- Key players may have changed or consultants integral to the reengineering may no longer be around.

- All people have their limits in terms of the number of major processes they can engage in deeply. The law of diminishing returns is appropriately applied to major undertakings in close proximity. Therefore, considering facilities as part of the reengineering will take comparably fewer resources than will a separate, subsequent process.

- It is not uncommon for reengineering consultants to disregard facilities issues or to address them at shallow levels only. This omission is explained by the fact that the vast majority of individuals with expertise in reengineering do not have a background in functional physical planning. Therefore, many consultants, while able to recognize conflicts between care delivery systems and facilities, are not comfortable diagnosing or solving them. This is therefore an issue for consultant selection in addition to a consideration for allocating resources from the entity for which work processes are to be reengineered.

Once it has been determined that the work reengineering process should incorporate facilities considerations, the manner in which this incorporation will be achieved must be delineated. As with so many facets of this endeavor, the "how" is intimately tied to the "who." It is essential to identify individuals and teams (in-house or purchased resources) that can understand the intricacies of the relationship between operating conditions and buildings and can communicate them in a manner that heightens the awareness of all core team members. Similar to information systems and medical equipment, a working knowledge of physical resources during the design of future care delivery methods can significantly increase the effectiveness and efficiency of the process. In addition, space has an impact on everyone, and most employees experience some level of irritation or frustration with their work environments. Providing them with a basic understanding of facilities planning and management often reduces negativity and generates ideas for living more comfortably with constraints. It is therefore advisable to ensure that appropriate assistance, in the form of management time and/or consultants, will be available at least until the beginning of implementation.

INCLUSION OF FACILITIES CONSIDERATIONS

In terms of actual incorporation into a given process, a logical first step is to have someone take an objective look at those facilities that will be affected by the reengineered process(es). At a minimum, this evaluation should consider capacity, productivity, flexibility, proximity to key related functions, and image. This information becomes one portion of an education session for the core team members during evaluation of the current state and "visioning" of the future state. The attendees and timing for this activity will obviously vary, but it should occur early in the orientation and/or evaluation stage in order to contribute to setting the stage for the subsequent several months. Participants should include a significant number, if not all, of the individuals who will be detailing reengineered processes, so that at least one member of each work group has seen and can access the material. The session should be broad in nature, yet sufficiently practical and in-depth so that concepts can be readily applied. Exhibit 12–1 provides some potential topics and questions for the session.

This discussion is designed to make participants feel comfortable discussing issues related to the space in which they work. Having a basic understanding of why hospitals have evolved physically to what we have today and beginning to put relevant concepts in familiar terms has proven to be helpful for a number of groups. The "grass is always greener" idea runs rampant among hospital personnel. Nurses who must traverse long double-loaded corridors (hallways with rooms lining both sides) day after day commonly believe a triangular or radial nursing unit would be wonderful, but the noise and inflexibility of such units causes the nurses who work in them to wish for the "good old days" of double-loaded corridors. A similar issue arises in discussion of the recovery area and other diagnostic and therapeutic areas: there is a never-ending debate over private space versus open bays. The reality is that no one design is universally embraced and that employees' affinity for their physical work environment is rooted in the marriage of it to the operating systems, not to particular physical features. Arming

Exhibit 12–1 Topics and Questions for an Education Session

Topics for Consideration	Associated Questions
Categories of Space	What are the basic types of space? Are there relevant quantitative guidelines (e.g., allocations and ratios)?
Spatial Relationships	Are there key relationships within and between departments or functional areas? How have changes in patient care had an impact on spatial relationships? What is the impact on efficiency?
Way Finding and Traffic Flows	Can hospitals be user-friendly from a physical perspective? Are there operating systems that compensate for physical limitations?
Desirable Characteristics	What methods are working in transformed organizations?
Regulatory Issues	What are the standards imposed by governmental and accreditation agencies?

staff with basic information regarding health care facilities will assist in development of reengineered work processes that are responsive to this reality, thereby enhancing overall satisfaction upon implementation.

Cost is an important part of this discussion. It is advisable not only to share cost information, but to do so in a meaningful manner; cost should be appropriately addressed in the education session. For example, most people would guess, accurately, that hospital areas relating to surgery, critical care, radiology and imaging, and dietary services are generally the most expensive areas to construct or renovate. However, certain areas within these departments are less costly to change than others. The costs can easily range from $40 to $400 per square foot, depending on the magnitude and complexity of the change and the existing conditions. It is important to compare such numbers against cost and/or cost margin for performing a service in the space in question. If a work team reengineering a function has a basic understanding of such analytical tools, money and time can be saved throughout the system.

A relatively common illustration of this point concerns procedure rooms in intensive care units. Many hospitals built such rooms, particularly in the last 12 years, motivated by a desire for decreased patient movement and physician convenience. In general, these rooms cost approximately $500,000 dollars each to create, given the inclusion of appropriate equipment such as fluoroscopy and lighting. In most institutions, these rooms have witnessed infrequent, sporadic utilization, with an extremely high cost per procedure—both economically and functionally. Often, consideration to staffing, stocking, and cleaning was superficial. As staffing has become increasingly lean, the rooms are not practical. Health care employees involved in planning the units have indicated that they did not appreciate the significant costs associated with the space. Through reengineering, the basic desire to minimize patient transports has been achieved by creating ways to perform many procedures in the patient room, thus enhancing the patient experience and minimizing cost.

These examples of cost data relevant to facilities considerations in reengineering, represent the kind of information that will enhance a team's ability to move forward with sensitivity to the integration of operational and physical issues, whether the focus is on a single department, a multidepartmental function, or the entire hospital or institution. With most components of reengineering, it can be difficult to identify any single area of concentration, because the connections between entities are so strong and complex. With regard to facilities, the complexity is the primary source for both frustration and opportunity.

Consider the outpatient who will be in the hospital for several hours. These individuals, most of whom are former inpatients, can be found in cardiac catheterization, imaging, endoscopy, and chemotherapy. Although most of the needs of patients are similar, each of the different departments that "own" them often provide accommodations for preparatory procedures, recovery care, patient education, and family services, as well as all related support space. The departments are often inefficient due to a lack of critical mass of activity and crowded because technology and the number of patients receiving care were not anticipated at the time the area was planned.

One of the most exciting facets of work reengineering is the ability to rectify this type of situation. As we focus on process and patient needs and characteristics rather than on previously sacred departmental boundaries, we are in a position, not only to improve service, but also to reduce the cost of care delivery. Consider identifying a portion of the facility for recovery care of all outpatients. For most institutions, the creation of such an area reduces operating cost with minimal capital expenditure and ensures consistent quality of care. In addition, there is inherent uniformity in patient processing and the ability to accommodate future patient populations yet to be defined. The particulars of such an area vary widely by institution, involve relatively intricate planning, and are becoming a key issue for hospitals and ambulatory care centers involved in operational planning.

As outpatient encounters continue to replace inpatient admissions, facilities have excess inpatient capacity. Obviously, this is one motivation for reengineering, but it is also another rationale for making facilities part of the process and linking utilization projections with physical capacity and assignment. Historically, health care managers and administrators have spent an enormous amount of time and energy measuring and monitoring the productivity of the work force. Consequently, this industry is rich with knowledge that allows us to predict, adjust, and understand staffing and staff performance. As labor generally represents the single largest budget line item, such planning makes sense. The fact that we have not imposed similar expectations on space, typically the second largest budget line item, makes little sense in the present and future environments. The reimbursement patterns of the past, coupled with the concept that space is a "sunk cost," have bred the current situation, in which space productivity in a single hospital commonly ranges from 5 percent to 95 percent, with the majority being below both the estimates and the expectation of leadership.

Therefore, as part of the reengineering process, participants should become familiar with methods for measuring productivity and should develop productivity targets for key areas as well as for staff. Although this approach is relatively straightforward, it is time-consuming and is best used by smaller work groups who are concentrating on distinct areas as opposed to the entire hospital. Once this has been achieved, space productivity for the hospital as a whole, in the reengineered vision, should be examined with a focus on integration and consolidation opportunities. In some cases, it is possible to abandon huge areas or entire buildings simply by "working smarter." The advantages of emptying space range from eliminating all associated operating costs to considering an alternative use that would enhance the organization's cost position. There are hospitals operating today that if rebuilt using moderate productivity targets would occupy less than 70 percent of the current square footage. Cost savings for utilities, insurance, and security alone could represent millions of dollars.

Productivity of space can be measured independently of other performance indicators if there is an understanding of the relationship of activity to time. The value of the exercise, however, lies in the overall impact on the operating budget. Surgical services generally provide a good illustration and one that is commonly reviewed. In most hospitals, utilization of the operating room diminishes as the day progresses, resulting in space productivity of 70 percent to 80 percent, based on a 40-hour week. Merely expanding hours will often result in diminished productivity because the same amount of activity is now being spread over more hours, yet more payers and patients want the option of services on what are typically off hours.

In the case of operating rooms, the physician, who is the primary customer, would typically like to have many rooms functioning four to six hours per day—a condition that is not financially feasible for most institutions. Some providers are solving this problem by beginning with a space productivity target; for surgery, it is generally 80 percent to 90 percent. The rooms are staffed around this target in conjunction with a compromise of desirable hours for physicians and patients. The resulting hours differ by market area and individual hospital.

Such an exercise has tremendous economic potential but will reap desired rewards only as part of a comprehensive effort involving operational productivity and physician communication. For example, it may appear that the space is used for many hours per day, but if case times, turnaround times, and/or downtimes are unnecessarily long, space productivity may appear deceptively high as a direct result of low operational efficiency. The key is to understand each component of the evaluation and the manner in which the components relate to one another. If change is to be made, the physicians must be involved. Alterations in operating room assignments and schedules are often unwelcome. They can be successfully managed, however, if all constituencies are appropriately informed and consulted.

Similar to taking a macro view of the space implications, an independent review of the physical implications of all reengineered processes should occur once all operating details have been documented and prior to finalization. Ideally, such a review is performed by a highly cohesive team or one individual and is an extremely valuable exercise. The point was well illustrated by a hospital with multiple reengineering teams working, one of which was creating a new care delivery system for a major service line. One of the objectives was to enhance the image of the clinical quality; another was to increase accessibility. A feature designed and accepted to meet both objectives was to identify a unique entrance that would accept patients 24 hours per day. The entrance already existed and was staffed 14 hours per day. Another work team, committed to reengineering patient processing, decided to close the entrance in question entirely in order to simplify and clarify the manner in which patients physically accessed the institution. Both teams assumed their work was complete and were confident they had excelled. In fact, they had. The work of both teams was outstanding and had passed several levels of operational review. However, when implementation planning began, the problem surfaced, creating substantial conflict and requiring weeks of rework. Had there been a facilities-focused review, the implications would have surfaced earlier, and a solution could have been formulated within the confines and timing of the process.

Another hospital reengineered a process that would save hundreds of patient-days in critical care. The solution involved consolidation of beds in certain areas of the hospital; the team was delighted to accomplish its goal with little capital cost. The problem was that the solution located inpatient beds that have a code requirement for windows in internal space with no natural light. Again, had this issue been identified early in the process, a tremendous amount of time, energy, and hard feelings could have been avoided.

CONCLUSION

If the determination is made early to include facilities considerations in the process of reengineering work, it is not difficult to accomplish. Experience has indicated that both the outcomes and the processes are enriched by this integration. As all resources become increasingly scarce, it is incumbent on managers to understand the manner in which people and space can work most effectively together. Reengineering provides the perfect forum.

▪ 13 ▪

Chaos or Transformation? Managing Innovation

Jo Manion, MA, RN, CNAA

To successfully navigate the chaos of the '90s, the health care organization must be able to tap into the creative potential of its employees. Health care organizations today face a critical choice: innovate and change or expect to be replaced by organizations that do. It is the choice between chaos and transformation.

Creativity and innovation are hallmarks of the most successful health care organizations in the country today. Successful innovation is not magic or something that just happens when the synergy is right. Organizations with a track record of successful innovation have discovered that innovation must be managed. Innovation management is a developmental process, a process of becoming that does not happen overnight.

These successful organizations have established an internal climate that supports entrepreneurial activity and goes beyond paying lip service to the idea of innovation and employee intrapreneurship. They recognize that innovation must be systematic, organized, and managed rather than sporadic, incidental, and accidental. Innovation is expected and encouraged in the organization, and seen as part of the work to be done rather than something that happens in addition to the "real work" of the staff.[1]

Nurse innovation and empowerment are closely related. Individuals must be empowered before innovation will occur on a systematic basis. However, not all

Note: The author thanks Diane Miller, BSN, RN, and Sharon Cox, MSN, RN, consultants with Creative Nursing Management, for "sharing the light" and helping others understand a new framework for managing the process of change; and Nancy Post, of Post Enterprises in Philadelphia, Pennsylvania, for the tremendous work she has done in helping others understand the importance of balancing energy in their lives personally and professionally, and for the practical application of these principles to an organization.

Source: Reprinted from *Journal of Nursing Administration,* Vol. 23, No. 5, pp. 41–48, with permission of J.B. Lippincott Company, © 1993.

individuals who are empowered in their daily practice accept responsibility for innovation. In some cases, the individual may not have the specific skills needed, or the traditional, bureaucratic system they are in has too many barriers to innovation.

Some of the most effective innovations are developed by people who know the organization at its core. Nurses form the core of any health care organization and are in a position to be essential innovators. On the positive side, nurses are at the point of patient care delivery. Nurses have a generalist background that results in an understanding of the broad spectrum of needs exhibited by the client and family. On the other hand, creativity, the skills of intrapreneurship, and the management of change have not been part of the nurse's formal education, nor in many instances part of the socialization into the workplace. Most have been socialized to the nursing role in a bureaucratic, hierarchic organization whose structure alone intimidates the novice innovator.

Nurse innovation is the key to transformation of the health care organization and the health care system. While creativity is thinking up new ideas or putting things together in a new way, innovation is the implementation of the new or creative idea. Innovation implies that something has changed as a result of the creativity. The innovation may be a new product or service, or a new way of doing something. It may be as small as a simple change in the nursing unit or as major as the development of an entirely new service or the redesign of work flow within the department. Nurse managers and executives experience more success in their roles if their staff are skillful implementers of new ideas, and a specific process model can be helpful.

The five stages for managing innovation are based on an energy model adapted for organizations by Nancy Post, an organizational development consultant.[2,3] The framework has also been used for managing change in an organization.[4] The five stages or phases are preparation, movement, team creativity, new reality, and integration. During the preparation phase, major concerns to be managed are the mission or purpose and resource allocation issues. During the second phase, structural issues, such as decision making, authority levels, planning, and organizational structure, are considerations. Team creativity, the third phase, involves the issues of overall coordination and cooperation, priority setting, networking, climate setting, and internal communications. During the phase of the new reality, productivity and maintenance of the change are key considerations. Integration, the final phase, requires attention to quality control and evaluative efforts.

Assessing performance in managing these developmental phases is a critical first step for any organization or department seeking to improve its skill at innovation management. The assessment tool in Exhibit 13–1 can be completed and scored. The items are organized in groups of ten, with each group relating to one

Exhibit 13–1 What's Your IQ (Innovation Quotient)?

Directions: Answer with the same environment in mind for each question. For example, complete the questionnaire thinking of the entire organization, the department, or a unit work group. Don't answer one question thinking of the nursing department and the next item thinking of the entire organization. Answer by circling Y for yes, N for no, and S for sometimes to indicate the frequency.

Y   S   N   1. Does the mission statement or statement of purpose include any reference to employee creativity and innovation?

Y   S   N   2. Do job descriptions or role expectations include the expectation for individual innovation or support of innovation?

Y   S   N   3. Do the annual goals include implementation of innovative ideas or strategies that increase employee creativity or innovation?

Y   S   N   4. Are the people who are always questioning the status quo and looking for a better way encouraged and seen as "creative types?"

Y   S   N   5. Is there a lot of energy and enthusiasm for change?

Y   S   N   6. Does the clinical staff have ready access to funding for innovative projects?

Y   S   N   7. Are there mentors and sponsors available in the organization for the novice innovator?

Y   S   N   8. Do clinical staff and managers have time during their normal work week to work on innovations and creative projects?

Y   S   N   9. Are the boundaries and limits openly discussed with the innovator and clarified before problems occur?

Y   S   N   10. Are resources shared between departments and work groups?

Y   S   N   11. Is time taken to actually plan for innovation (as opposed to moving very quickly from identifying the need to actual implementation)?

Y   S   N   12. Is there an established process for managing change and innovation that internal leaders understand and are expected to utilize?

Y   S   N   13. Is a formal proposal format or business plan required before an innovative idea is considered for implementation? Do all members of the department know what the expected format is?

Y   S   N   14. Is there flexibility in how the plan unfolds, or are people held tightly to the specifics of the plan, i.e., the time frames, expenditures projected, process used?

Y   S   N   15. Does the clinical staff have easy access to the executive leadership team without having to go through multiple layers of management?

Y   S   N   16. Are plans developed before decisions are made?

Y   S   N   17. Do individual managers have control over funding so low-cost projects can be funded without a lot of rigamarole?

Y   S   N   18. Are there established, agreed-upon time frames for completion of projects?

Y   S   N   19. Are levels of authority clearly identified for project teams and committees?

continues

Exhibit 13–1 continued

Y S N 20. Do problems actually get solved in the organization so that you are not dealing with the same problems you were dealing with 3–5 years ago?

Y S N 21. Is there a spirit of cooperation in the organization? Can an innovator find others to cooperate in implementation?

Y S N 22. Do individual innovators retain control over their innovation as it is implemented rather than the idea being passed over to a manager or project director to actually implement?

Y S N 23. Is the general climate in the organization supportive, encouraging, and seeking of change and innovation?

Y S N 24. Is there a high level of trust in the organization between work groups, units, departments, managers, and clinical staff?

Y S N 25. Are the priorities established, resources assessed, and progress made on the important and major change projects under way rather than expending time and energy in an excessive number of projects at one time?

Y S N 26. Do managers and leaders act as catalysts for change and innovation?

Y S N 27. Is the majority of the management within the organization stable and effective rather than involved in crisis management, continually "putting out fires," feeling burned out?

Y S N 28. Are clinical staff members and managers skilled in creativity techniques such as story boards, attribute analysis, brainstorming, mind mapping?

Y S N 29. Can an individual innovator easily pull together a team of people from other departments and work groups to work together on a project?

Y S N 30. Are people comfortable with mistake making rather than seeing mistakes as something to be feared and avoided?

Y S N 31. Do people in the work group, department, organization support each other rather than engage in a significant amount of blaming, bickering, and backbiting?

Y S N 32. Are people in the organization encouraged to take care of themselves?

Y S N 33. Do people in the organization feel they can set limits, say no to assignments and requests, and not become involved in a particular change project?

Y S N 34. Are managers and leaders well centered, with a healthy balance of energy, rather than feeling burned out and out of balance?

Y S N 35. Are workaholic behavior and perfectionism discouraged?

Y S N 36. Are the organization basically stable and secure rather than an environment of great anxiety, high flux, and chaos?

Y S N 37. Are there mechanisms in place that give long-term support to changes and innovations that are implemented?

Y S N 38. Is there recognition and support that productivity increases occur only after the change is well established rather than immediately?

Y S N 39. Do people talk openly about their feelings related to change? Is it okay to express negative feelings about change, or is this seen and dealt with as resistance?

Y S N 40. Are there specific interventions planned and implemented to nurture people during change and major innovation?

continues

Exhibit 13–1 continued

Y S N 41. Are the values of the organization or work group clearly articulated with a clear connection between quality and innovation?

Y S N 42. Can the clinical staff articulate the values of the organization, and are the values articulated consistent with what is being practiced? (Example: while innovation and creativity may be articulated as important, in actual practice there is no allocation of resources to support it.)

Y S N 43. Are clinical staff and leaders in the organization inspired to become involved as innovators rather than being exhausted with the day-to-day work demands?

Y S N 44. When new responsibilities and tasks are accepted, are current responsibilities and tasks modified?

Y S N 45. Are managers and leaders skilled at managing change and the emotions involved to reduce the chaos and turmoil that typically occurs when something changes?

Y S N 46. Are people in the organization receptive to and excited about change rather than "fed up" with change, the "promise that things will be better after this, but they never are?"

Y S N 47. Is there a specific evaluation process to determine whether or not or in what ways the change has been beneficial?

Y S N 48. Are mistakes freely shared and seen as opportunities for everyone to learn?

Y S N 49. Do people feel comfortable about eliminating the unnecessary? Or is it difficult to let go of things from the past, including people or ways of doing things?

Y S N 50. Do people look forward to the future and change rather than continually lamenting over the "good old days," the way things were before the merger, before the change?

Scoring Directions: Each Y is 2 points, each S is 1 point, and each N is zero. Total the number of points.

phase of innovation management. Questions 1 through 10 relate to phase 1, questions 11 through 20 relate to phase 2, and so on. Scores of ten or less for each cluster of ten items indicate areas of needed concentration. Specific interventions will be discussed for each phase.

The five phases can be used as a balance model as well as a developmental model. The key elements in each phase must be considered fully. If any of the five phases are weak, there will be an imbalance in the system, which will impact the effectiveness of innovation management in the organization. Likewise, if there is an overemphasis on the characteristics of any phase, there will be imbalance and difficulties in the system. For instance, the mission of the department as it relates to innovation and expectations for innovation from staff must balance with the resources available, or there will be dissonance; similarly, a work group that is always planning but never reaches a decision is out of balance.

This model is also a developmental model and as such is sequential in nature (Figure 13–1).[5] Following these steps in sequence can help the leader manage the process of innovation. It is also an interactive and dynamic model. The primary issues of each phase are identified, and although it is recommended that they be considered sequentially, the issues of one phase can also appear and are appropriate to consider throughout the entire cycle. For example, although evaluation is a key element of the final phase, evaluation must also occur during the entire process, not just at the end.

PHASE 1: PREPARATION

In the first phase, preparation, the two major issues of purpose and allocation of resources must be considered and managed. This phase is the foundation of the process. It is primarily leader-driven and the responsibility of the nurse executive and the team of internal leaders. Clear lines of responsibility should be identified and decisions made about appropriate levels of authority.

Simply put, innovation must be an important element of the department's mission and a part of the everyday language before it will be accepted as a value. The leaders within the department need to have and share a clear picture of how the department will look and how the people within it will behave if innovation is a priority. The relationship of innovation to patient care and professional nursing practice must be clearly stated and demonstrated. Not only will it be important

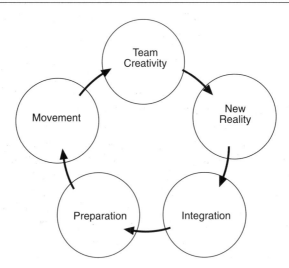

Figure 13–1 A Five-Phase Innovation Management Process

for members of the nursing leadership team to speak the language of innovation, they must communicate the expectation for innovation to the staff. This can be further emphasized by inclusion in the department's annual goals, performance appraisal process, and position descriptions.

The complementary issue of this first phase is the allocation of resources, including human and material resources. Adequate resources must be available if innovation is an expected part of the work of the organization. This includes time, access to other people, funding, and personal development time. It is difficult to expect people to work on innovative projects wholeheartedly in addition to carrying a full work schedule. Although an enthusiastic staff member will be committed enough to do so, it is an abuse of the human resources of the organization to expect this additional commitment on a long-term or continuing basis. People will be "used up" quickly. Mentors and sponsors must be available in the organization or department for the innovator. Resources openly shared between departments and work groups will increase the environmental support for innovation.

In some instances, the human resources of the department need further development. Leaders and clinical staff should be carefully assessed to determine the need for educational opportunities. Managers should be prepared for their roles as innovation managers. Individual innovators need programs or opportunities that focus on innovation and the skill development needed by a successful innovator. All members of the department benefit from general programs focusing on the need for innovation, essential skills, and their role in supporting fellow staff members who are innovators.

People in the department will need to hear the message repeatedly and observe actual behaviors and structural changes that support innovation before they will internalize the message that innovation is desirable and expected. The vision and day-to-day language must be congruent with the behavior of leaders. In some instances, changes in the structure of the organization will be needed. It will create dissonance if the nurse executive, managers, and leaders continually espouse the need for innovation and yet staff have no access to funding for innovative ideas, if new ideas can only be implemented after a tedious and difficult approval process, or if the creative individual who is always searching for a new and better way is seen and treated as a troublemaker and one to be controlled. Leadership behavior must be congruent with the message being delivered.

PHASE 2: MOVEMENT

Once the foundation is solidified, the leaders have a clear vision that has been consistently communicated and resources are in place, staff will begin to experience actual support for innovation. The second phase, movement, is next in sequence. During this phase, the structural elements supporting innovation throughout the department need to be established. If the vision is clear, the structure needed to support that vision will follow. The two aspects of this phase are planning and decision making.

Planning for a structure that will support innovation in the department is critical. The nurse executive facilitates this planning with participation and input from all levels within the department. A process for evaluating new ideas, gaining approval, and funding must be established. Two separate structures may be needed, one for larger projects that involve integral changes in the department and actual funding, and a simpler process for ideas with less impact and a lesser need for resource allocation. One approach being used today is the establishment of a center for innovation within the nursing department. This provides a structure for building a financial support base, generating revenue, and receiving gifts. Establishing a specific process for seeking innovative ideas from staff members and guidelines for approval and funding decisions is part of the work of a center and supports the work of innovation in the department.

Potential innovators often need skill development in the planning function. Some innovative projects are approved with very little planning, because they involve a small number of people and do not require additional funding. Formal business planning, however, may be necessary for larger projects that have significant ramifications in the department and organization or require extensive resource commitment. Innovators need support and encouragement in learning how to develop a business plan. Support from other departments, such as finance or marketing, may be needed. Planning for staff to have access to these resources will be important.

The complementary issue of this phase is decision making, and it is closely intertwined with planning. Once the planning is done, then decisions must be made. In some organizations, this is clearly out of balance. Much time is spent in planning, but the plans are never carried out because actual decisions are not made. Once innovation-supporting structural changes are determined, assignment of responsibility is necessary. How will the process be initiated? Who will be responsible? How will levels of authority be decided? Realistic time frames need to be established for each element of the plan and for communicating the plan to staff.

As the planning is completed, the need for further education and skill development for both managers and staff will become obvious. Planning skills often need to be developed or improved. In addition, there must be recognition that innovation planning is a process, not an end. By its very nature, innovation does not unfold as planned and there must be support, not just tolerance, for ambiguity, making mistakes, and plan revision. Visioning and strategizing are key skills for innovators in addition to the basic skills of leading groups, meeting effectiveness, and consensus decision making.

A potentially unexpected reaction from staff and managers that may surface during this phase is anger. Although it may not be significant or widespread, it may be present. In establishing a structure and process that support innovation in the department, the very creative individual may see it as stifling rather than liberating. Managers and leaders who have been supportive of the concept of innovation may feel irritated when they realize that successful management of innovation will take time and skill; it doesn't just happen. They may need to develop new and different skills. It will be important to see beyond initial resistance and evaluate whether the structure established supports innovators or stifles their work. Too much structure can inhibit creativity.

PHASE 3: TEAM CREATIVITY

After the foundation and structural issues have been dealt with, it is the third phase when results begin to appear. This phase is described as team creativity, or maturation, as the innovators within the department actually begin using the structure that has been established. The issues of priority setting, climate developing, coordination, cooperation, team building and networking, and internal communications must be considered. Each of these issues is an important key, and lack of attention to any one will result in a system out of balance.

Priority setting is easier if the structure for evaluating and approving projects is effective. A formal structure assists in identifying the projects that will be supported in the department during the year. In almost every nursing department, however, there will be many other changes and projects being implemented simultaneously. A major concern most nursing departments are experiencing is the need to fix everything yesterday. Unfortunately, when a department is engaged in too many projects, it reduces the likelihood that any are managed well. Determining the sequencing of major projects in the nursing department can be difficult, especially when other housewide projects are added because of external demands. Priority setting is the difficult task of determining what is most important to accomplish with the resources available. It does not mean doing everything that needs to be done, but making the difficult choices between those things that could be done. This requires extreme honesty by the nurse executive and leadership team and a willingness to refuse implementation of projects for which there are no resources to support.

Establishing a climate conducive to innovation is a key managerial role. Managers must be prepared and educated about the different elements of climate and work group culture and accept responsibility for the climate within their work group. Managers are needed who see their role as a catalyst: they release the energy of innovators within the staff. The response to mistakes made is a major element related to climate. If the system or the individuals within the system have a punitive or blaming response to mistakes made, the environment will impede and stifle innovation. Do staff members feel comfortable about making mistakes, and do they understand that the making of mistakes is inevitable? Or do staff members want an environment where they don't make mistakes? When mistakes are accepted as part of work life and as lessons to be learned, people are more likely to be risk takers and successful innovators.

During this phase, attention must be paid to the coordination of efforts to prevent duplication. Roles and responsibilities must be clearly identified and boundaries established. Levels of authority and access to resources must be discussed before the innovator receives approval and begins work on a project. Too often, the limits and boundaries aren't discussed until conflicts or problems occur. Cooperation must be obtained from coworkers, project team members, and potentially from other departments, depending on the project or innovation. The nurse executive and nurse managers may need to "pave the way" or "open the door" for the innovator to obtain needed cooperation from other departments in the organization. A nurse executive and managers who state expectations of cooperation and act as role models will help innovators work intradepartmentally in finding others to cooperate with the project.

Working effectively with a group or a project team is an important skill for many innovators. Although an individual innovator may need extensive coaching to be successful in this area, it is often more productive than pulling the project from the person who had the idea and assigning it to someone in the department with these already developed skills. Each situation will need to be evaluated separately. Staff members may need to learn how to lead meetings, manage group process, and use consensus decision making. Many project teams are more effective with members from other disciplines and support departments in the organization. Access to specialists in other departments is important. Members of the project team may need training in practical creativity techniques, such as game playing, brainstorming, mind mapping, story boards, and attribute analysis.

Communication is the last key issue of this phase. If effective innovation is to occur, staff members need access to information. This includes information about the organization and trends in health care and in their discipline. Truly amazing innovations can occur when members of the department understand the big picture and the major challenges the organization is facing. Open communication between all layers of the organization is critical. Key messages often need to be repeated as many as eight to ten times through a variety of methods. Usually, the fewer the layers of organizational structure, the more open the communication becomes.

Members of the department need to learn and use direct communication skills with each other. Negotiation skills are critical for innovators. People in the organization are expected to manage their relationships in a healthy and productive manner. This is not a typical pattern of behavior in most nursing departments, and many times it must first be shown by the leaders before it is used by staff members.

PHASE 4: NEW REALITY

The fourth phase is the new reality. The key issues relate to stabilizing the environment, maintaining the direction that has been set, and actually producing results from the innovative projects and changes that have occurred. A common error made in innovation management is expecting productivity improvements or gains, too early in the cycle. In projects where there are expected productivity gains, it may be months before the gains are realized, and productivity measures should not be prematurely used as a measure or indicator of success.

Stabilizing the change or innovation is an important step and should be considered carefully. Ways to anchor the change must be sought. This can be done by formalizing a structure or process that was used in trial, or by formally communicating the improvement or new service to the entire organization. Establish methods of rewarding and recognizing the innovator and project team. Rewards may come through increased learning and skill development, increased access to funding for future projects and educational support, or actual monetary rewards. Recognition can be through sharing of successes at staff meetings, through department or organization newsletters, or through specific celebration ceremonies. External opportunities for recognition and applause are wonderfully reinforcing for project team members. Support in publishing successes is another way of rewarding and recognizing innovators.

Productivity will be highest when managers and staff members are well centered, with a healthy balance of energy. During periods of intense change and innovation in a department, people can overexpend their reserves of energy, leading to overall decreases in productivity. Encouraging self-care and paying attention to the self-care needs of managers and staff are critical in an organization that innovates successfully. Although innovation is hard work, it can be energizing for many people. There is a tendency to not pay attention to replenishment needs. Successful innovation managers recognize that change work takes a great deal of energy, and sometimes time frames need to be modified, the frequency of meetings decreased, or extended periods away from the work encouraged. The end result will be increased productivity and creativity.

PHASE 5: INTEGRATION

The final phase of the developmental cycle is integration or closure. The key issues in this stage relate to evaluative functions and quality. This phase is often overlooked or undervalued, and yet it is critical for future successes in the department. Although evaluation is an important process throughout this developmental cycle, at this phase it is a key issue. The innovation should be measured for its beneficence and effectiveness. During the planning phase, key indicators of success were developed. The process used to develop or implement the innovation is evaluated. Key questions should include: what did we learn; what would we do differently; and is there anything we can stop doing? Cultivate an attitude within the department that these questions are a normal part of the process. Never let the evaluation process be construed as placing blame.

The quality of the innovation and the implementation process are critical issues at this stage. How would the process be changed the next time? What are the lessons learned? In addition, the relationship between the innovation and quality of patient care should be clear and used as an indicator of success. The innovation may only be indirectly related to patient care, but the implementation of creative ideas implies that something is better as a result of the new idea.

An important leadership function during this phase is to take the time to go through closure. Too often a project or innovation is completed without formal closure. Closure can occur in the form of celebrations or events. These can be held even if the project or intended innovation was a failure. There are lessons to be learned and successes in the most dismal of failures. In almost every instance, innovations occur as the result of the efforts of many people in the organization. It is important to focus on the success or the process rather than the individual whose idea it was in the beginning. Recognizing and rewarding team effort will communicate respect for everyone's efforts. Closure also implies letting go of things. There may be a need for grief work, the breaking up of a project team, letting go of the "old way," or releasing of an old mind-set. The need for grieving should not be underestimated during this phase. In dealing with these emotions, the individuals involved will be ready to move to the next project faster!

CONCLUSION

The challenges facing the health care industry in the 1990s are perhaps some of the toughest ever experienced. Meeting these challenges successfully will require every strength the organization and its people have to offer. Innovative, empowered employees will not be merely desirable, but absolutely essential for survival of the organization.

Creating a climate and structure within an organization that empowers clinical staff and managers alike takes a strong commitment and consistent effort on the part of the executive and leadership team. To make the leap from creative ideas to a new reality requires a process for managing innovation. It requires establishment of a supportive climate and individuals who have advanced skills in creativity, developing new ideas and plans, and the implementation of change. Transformation of the organization is the potential result.

REFERENCES

1. Manion J. *Change from Within: Nurse Intrapreneurs as Health Care Innovators.* Kansas City, MO: American Nurses Association, 1990;1–11.
2. Post N. Managing human energy: An ancient tool of change experts. *OD Practitioner.* 1989;21(4):14–16.
3. Post N. *Working Balance: Energy Management for Personal and Professional Well-Being.* Philadelphia: Post Enterprises, 1989.
4. Miller D. *Managing Change in Chaotic Times.* Minneapolis, MN: Kundschier-Manthey, June 1991. Satellite broadcast.
5. Post N. Systems energetics. Presented at the Creative Nursing Management meeting, Minneapolis, MN, August 1991.

■ 14 ■

Quality Improvement through Data Analysis: Concepts and Applications

Dominick L. Flarey, PhD, MBA, RNC, CNAA, CHE

"In God we trust. All others must use data."

W. E. Deming

According to Lawrence, "today, the principles of total quality management and continuous quality improvement are transforming the way American companies operate. Focusing on the customer and analyzing variations in outcomes and processes have become essential for survival in a competitive world."[1(p.33)] To provide leadership for quality improvement, nurse executives must understand and operationalize the concepts of process improvements. Essential to this is a working knowledge of customer expectations and needs, systems and processes, and variation analysis. Processes cannot be improved unless they are first prioritized, described, and broken down. Such a methodology facilitates their redesign, leading to demonstrable, measurable improvements focused on customer satisfaction and quality outcomes.

The first step in the improvement process is to carefully identify customers, both internal and external. The second is to determine their expectations and needs. It is essential to ask what quality means to them. Peter Senge[2] provides a simple, yet powerful definition of quality. He asserts that quality means "all things that matter to a customer."[2(p.124)] Determining what matters can be facilitated through surveys, both written and face-to-face, by convening focus groups of customers, and by measuring performance and outcomes.[3]

Once expectations and needs have been determined and performance and outcomes measured, step three, analyzing the data, begins. All the data need to

Note: The author thanks Jack Kenneson, BSME, Mechanical Engineer, for creating the graphs, and Hugh Owen, RPh, MS, for creating the flow charts.

Source: Reprinted from *Journal of Nursing Administration,* Vol. 23, No. 12, pp. 21–30, with permission of J.B. Lippincott Company, © 1993.

be analyzed for relevance and effects on existing processes. The most dramatic and long-lasting results occur when reliable data are measured and used to drive process improvements.[4] By measuring the process elements that lead to outcomes, such as patient satisfaction, and by using these measurements to manage patient care processes, health care organizations will realize continued favorable outcomes leading to greater successes.[5]

Dr. W. Edwards Deming,[6] the quality genius who revitalized Japanese industry, speaks of the absolute necessity to collect, measure, and analyze data to improve processes. He advocates statistical methods, which he asserts are essential for the transformation of business and for understanding processes, bringing them under control, and improving them.

According to Deming, statistical methods help zero in on variations and special causes of dysfunction in a process. He identifies two types of causality in variation, common and special:

> . . . common variation is inherent within the process or system; special variation is caused by a transient event. Common causes occur continuously and affect everyone working in the process. Special causes are unusual and may not affect everyone. Deming postulates that 94% of all variation is due to common causes which belong to the system, while only 6% of variation is the result of special causes.[7(p.78)]

The tools used by Dr. Deming have proven successful time after time in moving quality improvement programs forward and identifying common causes of variation. Most of these tools are simple; many are used specifically to organize and visually display collected data.[6] When used appropriately, they are powerful instruments for improving processes.

THE TOOLS OF QUALITY IMPROVEMENT

The tools for quality improvement are varied. Designed for different purposes, some provide meaningful classifications, identify causes of problems, and serve as a visual display of processes. Others display data, assess variability, enhance evaluation, and facilitate understanding of processes.[8] The tools are rarely used alone. Most often they are used in differing combinations based on the intent of the improvement team.

The following presentation highlights the most commonly used improvement tools. Concepts, uses, and applications are featured.

Flow Chart

A flow chart is a visual display of the steps in a process.[9,10] Developed in the 1950s, it provides a clear display in the actual "flow" of an activity or process.[11]

Common language symbols are used to draw attention to process steps. For example, arrows depict the sequential order of steps in a process; a diamond indicates that a decision is required in the process. Flow charts are invaluable for identifying problems, inefficiencies, and redundancies in a process.[10] Another important aspect of flow charts is that they promote understanding of how a process should be performed.[8] Such a realization helps identify the best opportunities for changes and improvements.[12] Flow charts are beneficial tools not only for examining processes where improvements are needed, but they can also be helpful when examining any process that seems workable but may contain redundancies and inefficiencies.[13]

A particularly useful method for using a flow chart in quality improvement projects is to first make a flow chart of how the process should work (the ideal), then make a flow chart of the current process (the real). This provides immediate realizations of inefficiencies, redundancies, and misunderstandings.[6]

Figure 14–1 show a flow chart of one hospital's scheduling process for surgical cases and preadmission evaluation and testing. A project improvement team convened to make improvements, as administration was receiving multiple complaints from customers about confusion and lack of time-schedule coordination with the process. Appointments for diagnostic testing, nursing evaluation, and teaching were not coordinated. This resulted in long delays between appointments and frustrated patients.

As Figure 14–1 demonstrates, there are many steps in the process that are redundant (i.e., the surgeon must make as many as three phone calls to schedule, and patients receive four phone calls from different departments). The process is disjointed, and communication between departments and with the patient is poorly coordinated.

After applying the principles of the quality improvement/problem-solving process, the project team redesigned the entire process, correcting all of the identified inadequate, redundant, and uncoordinated steps. Figure 14–2 shows the flow chart of the redesigned, improved process. The process was reduced from 14 steps to 8 steps. The new process allows for central scheduling and communications with the patient, with all departments involved in the process. Surgeons need only make one phone call to schedule the operative procedure and presurgical evaluation and testing. Patients receive only one phone call instead of four.

Other additions to this process improvement include sending all of the insurance forms and consents to the presurgical testing unit before the patient's arrival. Patients are instructed to report directly to the unit rather than to the patient registration area. When the patient arrives, the unit secretary works with the patient to complete the necessary forms. A satellite laboratory was placed on the unit so patients would not have to travel for diagnostic testing. The hospital is

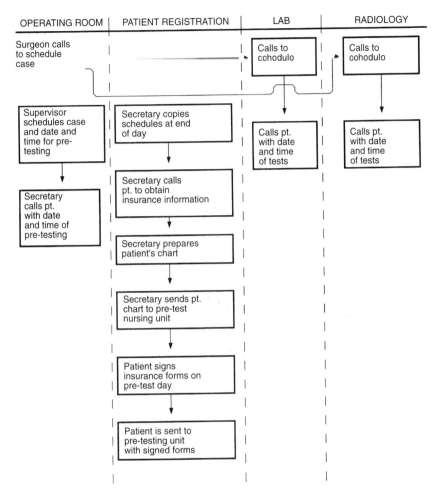

Figure 14–1 Flow Chart of Surgery Scheduling before Improvements

planning to add a satellite radiology unit, so that all services are centrally available to the patient. The goal is to maximize time and efficiency and decrease the need for transporting patients to several different areas, thus making the system user-friendly and decreasing the amount of time patients spend in the process.

This case depicts the use of a flow chart in driving multiple improvements in a process. The visual display of the process clearly reveals its inherent problems. When using a flow chart for process analysis and improvements, it is necessary that all members of the improvement team participate. Only in this way can

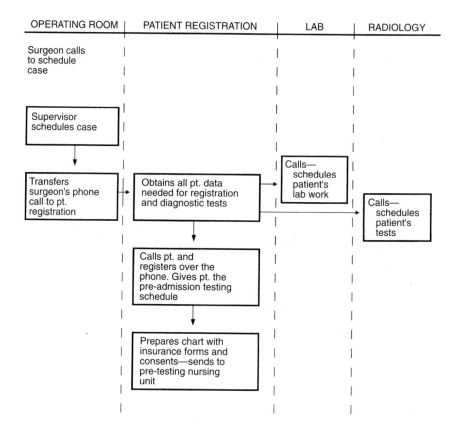

Figure 14–2 Flow Chart of Surgery Scheduling after Improvements

biases be dealt with and a common understanding across services and disciplines be reached. Flow charts are also very effective in pointing out where in the process it is necessary to collect data before redesigning steps.[9] This saves the team unnecessary frustrations and facilitates the overall improvement process.

Histogram

A histogram may be defined as a graphic summation of variations that may exist in a set of data, as well as the distribution of the variation.[10] "Histograms are perhaps one of the most misused statistical tools. They are effective only for data that come from a process that is in a state of statistical control."[14(p.106)] They are used to measure how frequently something occurs,[6] and whether the identified variation is normal or requires further attention and analysis.[10] In short, they per-

mit the improvement team to quickly determine how the data are distributed.[15]
Histograms are effective in the data analysis phase of the quality improvement
process. Events in a process will vary over time and thus produce varying results.
Leebov and Ersoz assert that:

> The degree and nature of this variation helps you to generate theories
> about problems in your process, the conditions under which your prob-
> lem is most severe, and how you might focus your efforts to improve
> the process. A histogram visually communicates information about
> variation in a process in a way that helps you to generate questions that
> focus your improvement efforts. After you create the histogram, you
> need to revisit your process to answer the questions the histogram
> raises.[3(p.125)]

To accurately construct a histogram, the following procedure is necessary: (1)
obtain a data set and determine the number of data points; (2) determine the
range of the data set by deducting the smallest value from the largest; (3) determine the number of classes in which the data set will be divided; (4) determine
the width of the classes by taking the range divided by the number of classes; (5)
determine class boundaries; (6) construct the histogram, placing values for classes
on the horizontal axis and the frequency on the vertical axis; (7) construct the
graph of the number of data points in each class; and (8) analyze your findings.[8,10]

To operationalize the concepts of a histogram, we will look at an actual quality
improvement case. This presentation focuses on process variations occurring
from the time an emergency room patient is admitted to inpatient status until the
patient arrives on a nursing unit. This study was conducted for the day shift. The
process was analyzed in response to patient and family complaints regarding long
waiting periods in the emergency room before transport to the nursing unit.

Using the procedure above, the team collected data and developed a histogram to assess variations in the process. The following highlights this development:

1. Data were collected related to the response time from the time an admission order was written in the emergency room until the time of the
   patient's arrival on a nursing unit. In this case, there were 100 data points.
2. The range was determined to be 50. This was found by deducting the
   smallest value (15 minutes was the shortest time in the admission process)
   from the largest value (65 minutes was the longest time in the process).
3. The number of classes (bars) that the data set will be divided into was 8.
4. The class width (the range divided by the number of classes) was 6
   (rounded off).
5. The class boundaries were calculated and are shown in Table 14–1.

Table 14–1 Histogram-Calculated Class Boundaries

Class	Data Set Values (mins)
1	15 to 21
2	22 to 27
3	28 to 33
4	35 to 40
5	41 to 47
6	48 to 54
7	55 to 61
8	62 to 68

Figure 14–3 shows the constructed histogram. In analysis, the variation is not within a normal range, but rather is skewed. Figure 14–3 shows that the skew is more positive than negative. This indicates that the process does require more in-depth attention and analysis.[8]

Leebov and Ersoz suggest that, when analyzing histograms, the following questions should be asked:

1. What is the current level of performance?
2. What is the pattern of variation around the current level?
3. What are the consequences of this variation?
4. What clues does this pattern of variation give you about the scope and nature of your problem?
5. What questions does it raise that you need to investigate?
6. What theories do you now need to test further?[3(p.127)]

In analysis, the quality improvement team discovered several reasons for the abnormal variation. Although the majority of the 100 patients in the data set were transported to the nursing unit within 20 to 40 minutes from the time the admission order was written, the team believed that this was an inappropriate length of time and could be improved on. The analysis that followed revealed two major causes for the delays. First, when it was determined that the patient was to be admitted, hospital policy required a family member to be present in the patient admissions area to provide secretaries with needed insurance information. This process was time consuming. Another long-standing policy prohibited the patient from being transported to the nursing unit until the secretary had received the needed information. Further analysis showed that the patient admissions area was busiest on the day shift (more patients were admitted during the day) and that family members frequently had to wait in long lines.

The second major cause identified was that the emergency room was not assigned its own transporter. Transporters were centralized and covered "call" for

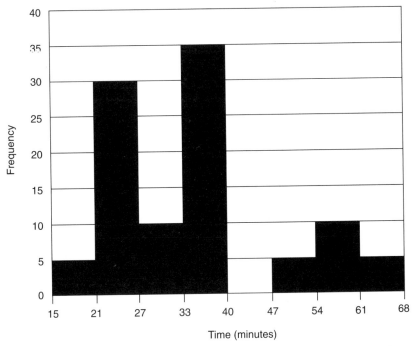

Figure 14–3 Histogram Showing Time from Admission Order for Emergency Room Patients to Arrival on an Inpatient Nursing Unit

the entire hospital. Frequently, when called to transport an emergency room patient to a nursing unit, they were busy with other transports and patients would have to wait. It was also discovered that a long-standing policy existed that provided that only one of the centralized transporters was assigned to respond to calls from the emergency room. If this transporter was busy, other transporters were not permitted to take the patient to the unit.

To improve the process, the nurse executive, at the recommendation of the quality improvement team, approved the following changes in the process: (1) when an emergency room patient was admitted to inpatient status a secretary from the admissions area came to the emergency room and obtained the needed information from the patient or family; and (2) one of the centralized transporter positions on the day shift was reallocated to the emergency room so that a transporter was always available.

After these changes were made in the process steps, the quality improvement team conducted a follow-up analysis. Using a histogram, they demonstrated that of a random sample of 100 patients evaluated after the changes were implemented, 75 were transported to the nursing unit within 18 to 28 minutes after the order was written.

Pareto Chart

A Pareto chart is a commonly used graphic tool for continuous quality improvement programs. It was originated by Vilfredo Pareto, a European economist in the 19th century. Using a graph, he showed that among the social class, 20 percent of the people had 80 percent of the wealth. This graph became famous, and from it emerged the Pareto principle, commonly known as the 80–20 rule.[3]

This rule is applicable in health care and can be simplified to infer that 80 percent of all problems result from 20 percent of the causes.[7] Accepting this, it might be said that 80 percent of all patient complaints arise from 20 percent of the system's or organization's problems, and 80 percent of all errors are made by 20 percent of the staff.[3] If the principle has merit, then, in application, if the small number of root causes were eliminated, 80 percent of the problems within the system or process could be eliminated. This principle is also frequently referred to as the phenomenon of the "vital few and useful many," as coined by Joseph Juran.[12]

The Pareto chart is actually a histogram visually displaying the few significant factors contributing most to the problem. In theory, it separates significant causes from insignificant ones.[13] Data displayed on a Pareto chart are arranged in descending order, with the major cause listed first. It is known as a cumulative, percentage histogram; causes are graphed as a percentage of the total and are arranged in descending order.[3]

In constructing a Pareto chart, the following steps should be followed: (1) select a topic of study (generally an outcome that may have many causes); (2) determine causes or conditions for comparison; (3) establish a standard for comparison (usually frequency); (4) collect the data; (5) compare the frequency of data; (6) on the vertical axis, indicate in increments the standard for comparison; (7) arrange each labeled factor on the horizontal axis in descending order; and (8) complete the bar graphs to indicate the frequency of factors.[8]

Figure 14–4 shows a Pareto chart detailing causative factors related to medication administration errors. A hospital had significantly high incidences of medication errors. A quality improvement team was formed to investigate the problem, analyze the process, establish causes, and redesign the process and system to reduce the number of errors.

The team collected data relevant to 50 medication errors occurring on six medical-surgical nursing units over a consecutive 3-month period. In establishing causes for each of the errors, it was found that 42 percent (21 occurrences) were related to the medication being discontinued but still administered to the patient;

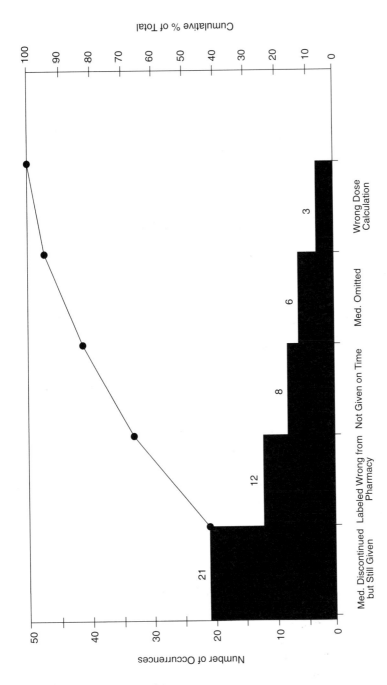

Figure 14–4 Pareto Chart

24 percent (12 occurrences) resulted from an error in labeling the medication by the pharmacy; 16 percent (8 occurrences) were due to the medication not being administered on time; 12 percent (6 occurrences) were due to the medication being omitted; and 6 percent (3 occurrences) were due to incorrect dosage calculations by the nurse.

The team took the results and further analyzed the reasons for occurrence using a cause-and-effect diagram. This allowed them to identify the root cause of the most frequently occurring errors. As such, the problems of administering discontinued medications and of errors in medication labeling were investigated.

It was found that the root cause related to discontinued medications was a lack of timely communication between the charge nurse and the nurses administering medications. The process was for the charge nurse to document on a log form at the nurses station when a patient's medication had been discontinued. In interviews with nurses regarding this process, they concurred that they were "too busy" to make frequent trips to the desk to check this particular form. Most frequently, they would administer the next scheduled dose without checking the discontinued medication log.

The root cause of the problem related to errors in the labeling of medications was also discovered. Analysis revealed that 90 percent of errors were made at the time information was entered into the automated pharmacy labeling system. It was found that a "check" process was not in place for information entered into the computer.

As a result of their efforts, the quality improvement team (which was made up of staff nurses, the nurse executive, and pharmacists) recommended and implemented changes to correct the root causes and reduce the incidence of errors.

The first change occurred on the nursing units. An additional carbon-contained copy was added to the physician's order sheet. When the physician wrote the order to discontinue the medication, a unit secretary would remove a carbon copy and hand it to the nurse administering the patient's medications. The nurse would then immediately verify the written order and document the discontinuation of the medication on the medication administration record located at the bedside.

The pharmacy department implemented a new "check" process for their automated medication labeling system. After the medication order was entered into the computer and labels were generated, pharmacy technicians were required to check the labels with copies of the original medication orders. A pharmacist then checked the labeled package and contents for accuracy.

After implementation of these changes, a retrospective 3-month study showed a 72 percent reduction in the number of medication errors occurring on the 6 medical-surgical nursing units. These examples are powerful displays of the effective use of Pareto charts and the Pareto principle in driving quality improvements. The Pareto chart is an excellent tool to use when cost constraints limit the ability to resolve all of the identified problems. Experimentation with Pareto charts has shown that the most effective interventions are those that correct the causes of greatest variation in a process or system.[7]

Cause-and-Effect Diagrams

Commonly known as a "fishbone" diagram, the cause-and-effect diagram is used in brainstorming sessions to identify a multiplicity of factors affecting a specific problem.[16] Often, this diagram is referred to as the Ishikawa diagram, named after its originator, Kaoru Ishikawa. Scherkenbach states that "cause-and-effect diagrams are extremely important because they force people to think explicitly about the specifics of their process as well as their suppliers and customers. Once this is done, problem solving and improvement is greatly facilitated."[14(p.105)]

The major benefits of cause-and-effect diagrams in quality improvement programs are: (1) they help identify and define a problem; (2) they assist in constructing a list of potential causes of a problem; (3) they help identify opportunities for improvements; (4) they identify the causes of variation within a process; and (5) they drive a team approach to problem solving.[8,14]

When the diagram is constructed, a basic fishbone structure is used. The problem or outcome is documented on the right side of the structure (horizontal line), providing focused attention. Diagonal lines are drawn above and below the central horizontal line and are used for defining major categories of causes. Four major categories are generally used—people, materials, methods, and machines—although other defined categories may be used. Major causes are identified and documented on horizontal lines connected to diagonal lines. Causes are elicited by asking "why" or "how."[8] Frequently, subcauses are documented below defined causes.[3]

Figure 14–5 presents a cause-and-effect diagram. In this case, nursing administration was confronted with many complaints of low levels of job satisfaction among the nursing staff. This was confirmed with a job satisfaction survey instrument. In response, the nurse executive held brainstorming sessions with the staff. Cause-and-effect diagrams were used to facilitate the sessions. Based on results, nursing administration developed and implemented a comprehensive 2-year plan to address the defined causes. Improvements were made in all defined areas. A follow-up job satisfaction survey revealed dramatic improvements in satisfaction levels. Other documented outcomes were a 20 percent reduction in turnover rates, fewer employee grievances, and marked reductions in employee absence.

OTHER USEFUL TOOLS

Although the above-detailed tools are the tools most frequently used in the quality improvement process, many other tools are available. Some of the other

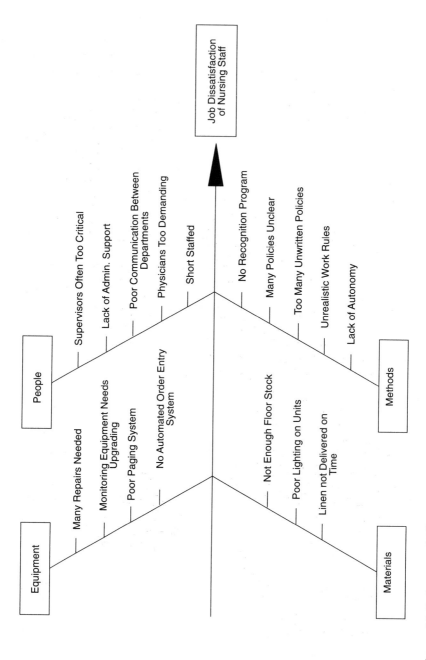

Figure 14–5 Cause-and-Effect Diagram

useful tools for use in process improvement follow. The reader is encouraged to use the references to learn more about these tools.

- *Scatter diagrams* are generally constructed with the aid of computer software. Used to pinpoint occurrences of a problem where two different variables are present,[7] they allow the study of relationships between variables when testing a cause-and-effect theory. They are also useful in analyzing raw data and to evaluate actions implemented to improve processes.[10]
- *Trend charts* "are performance plotters that can be used to monitor the movement in our long-range average and then draw conclusions about whether performance is moving up, down, or staying the same."[3(p.136)]
- *Control charts* are a more sophisticated trend chart. They are useful for distinguishing common and special cause variations. Data are plotted and assessed against three templates, a center line (the average), the upper control limit (UCL), and the lower control limit (LCL). Template values are defined based on the extremes of a bell-shaped curve used to assess common cause variations in a process.[17]
- *Run charts* display points on a graph to assess levels of performance over time. They are useful in identifying trends and analyzing and monitoring changes made to improve processes.[10]
- *Force field analysis* is a tool used to identify perceived driving and restraining forces that affect recommended changes.[13] It is useful in maximizing driving forces to improve a process.[3]
- *Selection grids* are used to help teams choose an option among many possibilities and provide validity for group decision-making processes.[10]
- *Affinity diagrams* are tools designed to help teams correctly organize large volumes of ideas and issues into major categories and provide structure and organization where there is confusion.[8]

CONCLUSION

Nurse executives must use the tools of quality improvement to guide process analysis and transformation. By incorporating these tools into our practice, we can be role models for our managers and staff members. Using these tools in practice will greatly enhance the success inherent in quality management.

REFERENCES

1. Lawrence D. Fulfilling the potential. *Healthcare Forum J.* 1992;35(2):31–37.

2. Senge P. *The Fifth Discipline: The Art and Practice of the Learning Organization.* New York: Doubleday, 1990.

3. Leebov W, Ersoz C. *The Health Care Manager's Guide to Continuous Quality Improvement.* Chicago: American Hospital Publishing, Inc., 1991.

4. Riley J, Heath S. Quality improvement means better productivity, *Healthcare Exec.* 1992;7(3):19–21.

5. Steiber S, Krowinski W. *Measuring and Managing Patient Satisfaction.* Chicago: American Hospital Publishing, Inc., 1990.

6. Walton M. *The Deming Management Method.* New York: Putnam, 1986.

7. White J, McLoughlin S. Measurement and standards in continuous quality improvement. In: Dienemann J, ed. *CQI: Continuous Quality Improvement in Nursing.* Washington, DC: American Nurses Publishing, 1992.

8. Joint Commission on Accreditation of Healthcare Organizations. *Using Quality Improvement Tools in a Health Care Setting.* Oakbrook Terrace, IL: Joint Commission on Accreditation of Healthcare Organizations, 1992.

9. Joint Commission on Accreditation of Healthcare Organizations. *Striving Toward Improvement: Six Hospitals in Search of Quality.* Oakbrook Terrace, IL: Joint Commission on Accreditation of Healthcare Organizations, 1992.

10. Joint Commission on Accreditation of Healthcare Organizations. *A Pocket Guide to Quality Improvement Tools.* Oakbrook Terrace, IL: Joint Commission on Accreditation of Healthcare Organizations, 1992.

11. Randolph W, Posner B. *Getting the Job Done: Managing Project Teams and Task Forces for Success.* Englewood Cliffs, NJ: Prentice Hall, 1992.

12. Juran J. *Juran on Leadership for Quality: An Executive Handbook.* New York: The Free Press, 1989.

13. Cornesky R, McCool S. *Total Quality Improvement Guide for Institutions of Higher Education.* Madison, WI: Magna Publications, 1992.

14. Scherkenbach W. *The Deming Route to Quality and Productivity.* Rockville, MD: Mercury Press, 1988.

15. Shott S. *Statistics for Health Professionals.* Philadelphia: WB Saunders, 1990.

16. Sorrentino E. Continuous quality improvement in nursing service. *Health Care Supervisor.* 1992;10(3):67–74.

17. Plsek P. Tutorial: Introduction to control charts. *Quality Manage Health Care.* 1992;1(1): 65–74.

■ 15 ■

Tools To Evaluate Reengineering Progress

Doris A. Milton, PhD, RN
Joyce A. Verran, PhD, RN, FAAN
Rose M. Gerber, PhD, RN
Julie Fleury, PhD, RN

The purpose of this chapter is to describe two scaling methods that can measure or monitor the degree of progress being made in any reengineering project. Both tools are helpful as well for measuring the strength of the independent variable in research projects designed to evaluate reengineering efforts.

One scaling method is designed to be used to determine the stage of implementation of a specific reengineering component. For example, an organization that is implementing case management can use the tool to determine the extent to which case management is implemented on each unit, in each service, or throughout the organization.

The second scaling method is helpful for organizations that are implementing more than one component at the same time. The tool can be used to determine the extent to which people view the different components as a unified reengineering effort. For example, if an organization is implementing case management, shared leadership, multipurpose workers, and employee empowerment all at the same time, the second tool can measure the extent to which all of these components are viewed as an integrated process.

IDENTIFYING THE NEED

Both scaling methods were created initially to measure the extent of progress in implementation of a professional nursing practice model. Differentiated group professional practice,[1] a five-year demonstration and research project, studied the effects of an innovative practice model on professional practice variables (group cohesion, organizational commitment, control over nursing practice, and autonomy), work satisfaction, nurse resources, quality outcomes, and fiscal outcomes. The demonstration model included the overall components of group governance, differentiated care delivery, and shared values in a culture of excellence and is described in detail elsewhere.[2] This model was implemented on nine demonstration units in three hospitals in both urban and rural settings.

In the early phases of model implementation, as with implementation of a reengineered process, it became clear that the nine units were unable to put the entire model in place at the same rate. This was due to many factors, but the primary one was the variance in individual unit readiness for specific changes. It was important from a research perspective to know the exact stage of implementation for each unit, since impact on outcomes logically depends on the degree to which change has occurred. It also became clear that some units would implement one component (e.g., case management) totally, while others would still be in the initial stages of implementing that component when the project finished. The investigators used Rogers' model[3] to delineate the stages that units would go through from the period before implementation to the time when few remembered that anything they were now doing was "different." The investigators developed the first tool, the level of implementation scaling method, to address that need.

It also became obvious that, since all units were not going to implement all components, they would be unable to view the model in its entirety. The investigators needed to know whether or not staff and managers on the units viewed the changes they were making as isolated efforts or as a total reengineering effort with several components. The investigators developed the second tool, the level of synthesis scaling method, to address that need.

ADVANTAGES OF MEASURING PROGRESS

Delineating steps in the reengineering process benefits administrators, managers, staff, and evaluators by helping them to decide whether or not the innovation has been implemented. If total implementation has not yet occurred, then all can participate in determining to what extent implementation has occurred and discuss ways of facilitating further progress. Also, since people who participate in the reengineering process commonly have differing perceptions of exactly how much change has occurred, it helps to have concrete steps outlined in a tool that can serve as the focus for discussion. Without distinct steps as a basis, it is difficult for those who are working very hard for reengineering to remain objective or, often, to realize that progress is actually being made.

Describing concrete steps in the reengineering process permits easier identification of markers for the planning process and time line. Reengineering innovations often are complex and require a long time frame for implementation. It is difficult to remain committed to major change without first outlining the steps in the process. For many, there is no sense of accomplishment or progress until the total project is integrated in the work setting. Tools that measure steps in the implementation process provide concrete milestones as markers of progress. It is important to celebrate at specific points in the change process, and the stages outlined in the scaling methods allow those times to be determined in a less than random fashion.

Reengineering the work environment is a process and not an event. Steps that are common to that process need to be outlined, regardless of what the specific changes are. Also, scaling methods that measure degree of implementation need to be "definition neutral." If the reengineering involves the implementation of case management, multipurpose workers, and peer review, for example, scales to measure the process of each change are needed. For either scaling method, the definition of each of those components and the relationships among them in a specific facility are irrelevant.

THEORETICAL BASIS FOR THE IMPLEMENTATION SCALING METHOD

The investigators used Rogers' theoretical process of the diffusion of innovations[3] for examining the process of implementation of the innovative model as it was occurring on each of the nine units. Rogers defines diffusion as the "process by which an innovation is communicated through certain channels over time among the members of a social system."[3(p.5)] He sees this process as occurring whenever an idea is new or is perceived as new.

Rogers describes the innovation-decision process in five stages: (1) knowledge, (2) persuasion, (3) decision, (4) implementation, and (5) confirmation. The investigators added an additional theoretical integration stage to describe the stage that follows confirmation in the work setting. Each unit needed to be aware of what the change would be and to be persuaded that it would make a difference; units needed to decide to make the change, implement it, confirm that a correct decision had been made, and then come to view the change as integral to "how things are done here." At that stage, the change can no longer be reversed by conflicting information, and in many cases, is indeed no longer viewed as a change.

DEGREE OF IMPLEMENTATION SCALING METHOD

The six stages of knowledge, persuasion, decision, implementation, confirmation, and integration were used as the theoretical foundation for a scaling method to measure or monitor the degree to which implementation of each component had occurred. The degree of implementation scaling method was developed to measure the extent of change with any innovation. It is sufficiently general to allow its use in a variety of settings.

The degree of model component implementation was viewed as occurring in discrete stages that could be measured on a scale of zero to nine (ten steps).

Scale	Steps
0	There is no current activity or planned action
1	The idea is being explored
2	There is an expressed commitment
3	Discussions regarding staff participation are taking place
4	A plan is developed
5	Initial processes are implemented or piloted
6	Processes are reviewed and refined
7	There is a core of support for the component
8	Most staff are implementing the component
9	The component is an integral aspect of unit functioning.

The implementation process occurs in ten identifiable steps from "no activity or planned action" to "total integration with unit functioning." The implementation scaling method is based on the assumption that any change that is totally integral with unit or total facility functioning is the desired end point. Each of the ten steps corresponds to one of the six theoretical stages described previously (Exhibit 15–1).

The ten steps of the implementation scaling method are used to measure the extent of progress of one overall change, such as shared governance. An overall process change that has several integrated subprocesses can have implementation scores for each subprocess component. If a measure of overall progress is needed, total scale points can be added to arrive at a composite score for the entire reengineering project.

Exhibit 15–2 shows an example of how the scaling method can be adapted for a specific reengineering component. The example is from use of the implementation scaling method in the differentiated group professional practice project to measure the extent of implementation of the group governance subcomponent of participative unit management. Each step of the scaling method can incorporate whatever change is being implemented. For example, if the reengineering process includes a change to using multipurpose workers, then step 4 of the implementation scaling method, "a plan is developed . . . ," becomes "a plan for using multipurpose workers is developed."

THEORETICAL BASIS FOR THE SYNTHESIS SCALING METHOD

In reengineering of a complex process, innovations are often viewed as separate changes and not as a part of the total process. Each component of the

Exhibit 15–1 Comparison of Innovation-Decision Process Stages with Corresponding Scaling Method Steps

Innovation-Decision Process Stage	*Scaling Method Steps*
1. Knowledge	1. There is no current activity or planned action (0).
	2. The idea is being explored (1).
2. Persuasion	3. There is an expressed commitment (2).
	4. Discussions regarding staff participation are taking place (3).
3. Decision	5. A plan is developed (4).
4. Implementation	6. Initial processes are implemented or piloted (5).
	7. Processes are reviewed and refined (6).
5. Confirmation	8. There is a core of support for the component (7).
	9. Most staff are implementing the component (8).
6. Integration	10. The component is an integral aspect of unit functioning (9).

reengineering effort, case management for example, is seen as completed whenever that individual change is implemented. However, an important part of the total change may be that several different changes, case management, multipurpose workers, and healing environment, for example, are seen as a blended package. This occurred in the differentiated group professional practice project when investigators wanted to determine whether people at each facility view the various demonstration model components as a synthesized totality. The investigators developed a different scaling method to measure the degree to which the separate components were seen as interrelated.

DEGREE OF SYNTHESIS SCALING METHOD

An additional scaling method was developed for use when a large change project has several components being implemented separately. For example, a professional practice model is typically viewed as a synthesis of components; however, components such as shared governance, peer review, and case management are commonly implemented separately. It is important that all the components be seen as a total package as implementation progresses.

The degree of synthesis of a total model was seen as occurring in discrete steps that could be measured on a scale from zero to five. The steps are:

Scale	Steps
1	There is commitment to a model
2	The model is described as separate components
3	Some of the model components are seen as interrelated
4	All of the model components are seen as interrelated
5	The model is described as a totality.

This scaling method can easily be adapted for use in any reengineering effort. Most reengineering efforts have a name such as patient-centered care or total healing environment. The name used at that institution is substituted for the word "model" in each of the six steps of the scaling method.

This scaling method assumes that the desired end point is the totally synthesized model. This scaling method provides a measure of the degree of synthesis of a reengineering project that is often difficult to quantify. Exhibit 15–3 provides an example of the degree of synthesis scaling methodology used in the differentiated group professional practice project. In that project, three major components were implemented separately, but all three needed to be viewed as interrelated in a unified model.

USE OF THE SCALING METHODS

In the differentiated group professional practice project, both scaling methods were used on an annual basis and were timed to coincide with collection of individual project participant data. In that way, the investigators could determine what effect the degree of implementation and synthesis—the independent variable—had on the outcome measures. Each model component received a score between 0 and 10, and the individual component scores were summed. That total was added to the level of synthesis score to arrive at a composite score. For research purposes, the composite score was used as a measure of the strength of the independent variable.

MEASURES TO INCREASE INTERRATER RELIABILITY

Scores on both scales were obtained through consensus among the co-principal investigators, the on-site program coordinator for each hospital, and the unit nurse manager and staff. It is helpful for administrators, managers, and staff to complete the scale at the same time and discuss their perceptions. An exchange

Exhibit 15–2 Degree of Implementation Scaling Method Example: Group Governance Subcomponent of Participative Unit Management

Scale Point	Step in Implementation
0	There is no current activity or planned action regarding staff participation in decisions related to patient care and unit management.
1	The idea of staff participation in decisions related to patient care and unit management is being explored.
2	There is an expressed commitment to staff participation in decisions related to patient care and unit management.
3	Discussions take place regarding staff participation in patient care and unit management decisions.
4	A plan is developed for staff to participate in patient care and unit management decisions.
5	Initial processes for staff participation in decisions related to patient care and unit management are being used.
6	Processes for staff participation in decisions related to patient care and unit management are being reviewed and refined.
7	A core group of staff participates in decisions related to patient care and unit management.
8	Most staff participate in decisions related to patient care and unit management.
9	Staff participation in decisions related to patient care and unit management decisions is an integral aspect of unit functioning.

Exhibit 15–3 Degree of Synthesis Scaling Method Example: Professional Practice Model

Scale Point	Step in Synthesis
0	None of the components of the professional practice model are discussed.
1	There is a commitment to a professional practice model.
2	The professional practice model components are viewed as separate.
3	Two of the three professional practice model components are viewed as interrelated.
4	All three components of the professional practice model are viewed as interrelated.
5	The professional practice model components are viewed as a totality.

of viewpoints, with documentation of behaviors related to the change, usually leads to a consensus score.

Steps were also required to ensure interrater reliability, not only among those at each demonstration site, but also among the co-principal investigators. The most effective way to increase interrater agreement was by reaching consensus on behaviors that would be considered to document achievement of a specific step on each scaling method. For example, step 4 of the implementation scale for participative unit management, as shown in Exhibit 15–2, states. "A plan is developed for staff to participate in patient care and unit management decisions." All those who participated in determining the last step on the scale that had been achieved by a particular unit agreed that, for step 4 to be considered accomplished, the unit would be required to have a written plan with a definite start date. Delineating specific behaviors helps to determine the appropriate step for change that is borderline between two steps. For research purposes, behaviors for each step provide the necessary documentation to ensure that step 4 at one facility is comparable to step 4 at another facility.

CONCLUSION

Two scaling methods for evaluating reengineering progress are presented here. One method measures or monitors steps in the implementation process; the other measures the extent to which several changes that are being implemented separately are viewed as a total package. Steps need to be taken to ensure that all who will be using each scaling method agree on behaviors that represent each step. In that way, users can be confident that the scaling methods are practical ways of measuring or monitoring reengineering progress. Quantifying progress is important for evaluative research purposes, as well as for establishing milestones for celebrating reengineering success.

REFERENCES

1. Verran J, Murdaugh C, Gerber R, Milton D. *Differentiated Group Professional Practice in Nursing.* Tucson, AZ: The University of Arizona College of Nursing. (A cooperative agreement award [U01-NR02153] funded by the National Institute of Nursing Research, National Institutes of Health, and the Division of Nursing, Department of Health and Human Services; 1988–1994.)
2. Milton D, Verran J, Murdaugh C, Gerber R. Differentiated group professional practice in nursing: A demonstration model. *Nurs Clin North Am.* 1992;27(1):23–30.
3. Rogers EM. *Diffusion of Innovations.* 3rd ed. New York: Free Press; 1983.

■ 16 ■

CareMap Systems and Case Management: Creating Waves of Restructured Care

Karen Zander, MS, RN, CS

Care delivery cannot be accurately or humanely restructured without being firmly grounded in the clinical content of the work itself. CareMap tools and case management models emanate from that clinical content and are thus a major component in the overall reengineering of the way care is delivered. In fact, as the profound knowledge held intuitively and formally by expert clinicians of every discipline comes to be discussed and then formalized on CareMap documents, that knowledge should actually drive all reengineering endeavors.

If the goal of restructuring is "to achieve quantum leaps in improvements in critical business indicators such as performance, costs, quality, service and speed,"[1] the methods of reengineering critical paths, their second-generation CareMap systems, and case management models have been extremely successful. In fact, they create at least three waves of restructuring, defined for CareMap evolution by Weilitz as (1) current practice, (2) best practice, and (3) ideal practice.[2] These waves are now occurring in a sea of massive change in which it is easy to lose one's bearings. This chapter will describe the three waves of restructuring health care, with an emphasis on key principles underlying CareMap tools and case management (see Exhibit 16–1) to ensure that care design and related changes will remain firmly grounded.

BACKGROUND

CareMap tools and case management were originated in the mid-1980s to lend structure where structure was potentially lacking or absent in light of case-type reimbursement by diagnosis-related groups (DRGs). These two methods of restructuring care arose as an answer to four main questions (Center for Case Management, South Natick, MA: 1992).

Exhibit 16–1 Principles To Help Ground Restructuring

1. Restructuring must emanate from new methods to achieve desired patient and family outcomes.
2. Optimal redesign should be planned in a budget-neutral framework.
3. All patients need well-managed care. Some need case managers as well.
   a. CareMap tools and unit-based care coordination or primary nursing for 100%.
   b. Case managers for 20%.
4. Restructuring should clarify and uphold the accountabilities of members in each involved professional discipline; outcome verification should not be delegated.
5. Always include physicians actively in the planning and implementation of methods to restructure, even if they have many concerns.
6. New models will have to provide both structure and flexibility simultaneously.
7. The health care transactions by clinicians should drive all other information, including cost data, and can do so in the future integrated automated systems.
8. "Key players must work on the premise that to win power absolutely is to lose performance ultimately."[8]

I. What is the work required to achieve desired outcomes in patients of certain case types or otherwise homogeneous populations?
II. What is the best way to produce the outcomes?
  A. Clinical decision making process
  B. Model
    1. people for care giving
    2. responsibilities
    3. relationships
    4. documentation
III. Who is accountable for outcomes?
IV. How do we restructure other systems to better support the work?

These questions, in the order given, represent a good approach to focusing on the nature of the work itself, followed by a logical transition to new structures. Reengineering in health care necessitates an evaluation of current structure, including financial efficiencies versus clinical effectiveness, which can also encompass patient and family satisfaction. The morale and commitment of the whole organization embarking on the evaluation must also be considered in reengineering efforts. It is assumed throughout this chapter that an executive level steering committee guides and integrates all reengineering projects.

The first principle of reengineering should be that the patient and family outcomes must remain the persistent and unifying force. Restructuring using

CareMap tools and/or case management can reinforce such a commitment. The principle of "patient centeredness" must be guarded with a vigilance previously unknown to many administrators or clinicians. It should become the overriding mission, not only of the care provider agencies, but of the payers as well. The following paragraphs are offered by Bower to further explain the important combination of patient centeredness and cost as goals of restructuring:[3]

> The patient must be the focal point of any redesign or restructuring efforts. The related goal becomes identifying and understanding the characteristics and needs of the patient populations served by the organization and restructuring the organization to meet these needs. Inherent in understanding the needs of the patient populations served is the notion of continuum. Establishing a focus on continuum means understanding patients' needs in all settings in which they receive or need care and understanding how all of the pieces fit together. Fragmentation of care negatively affects both quality and cost.

> Within nursing, a core consideration is that the most important relationship is that between the staff nurse and the patient. It is at the staff nurse level that most interaction takes place with the patient, the patient's family and significant others, and other disciplines. A basic goal, then, is to ensure that this relationship is supported and is maximally effective. In this context an effective nurse-patient relationship means that patient care is coordinated to ensure smooth progression toward desired physiological, psychosocial, emotional, spiritual, and financial outcomes in a manner that is satisfying to patients and their families. Organizational redesign must incorporate means of supporting that staff nurse-patient relationship at the unit and institutional levels.

In addition to patient centeredness, CareMap systems and case management help an organization to more tightly manage its variable budget. Although both methods have implications and ramifications for the fixed budget, these two methods *do not* directly change the fixed budget, as do some other reengineering endeavors. Rather, CareMap systems and case management should be viewed as occurring in a *budget-neutral* environment—the second principle of reengineering. Although the move to CareMap systems and case management may be motivated by financial concerns, the second principle of reengineering is that one should not assume or build in fixed budgetary changes during the initial planning and implementation of CareMap tools and case management. Budgetary changes should and will eventually emerge from the clinical groups working with administration, as the organization rides the waves of restructuring.

Keeping in mind the first two principles of reengineering—patient centeredness and budget neutrality—one can begin to objectively review CareMap systems and case management. Figure 16–1, "Reengineering from Current Practice to Ideal Practice," will assist the reader throughout in tracing the exciting and rapid evolution in health care.

FIRST WAVE: STRUCTURING CURRENT PRACTICE

CareMap tools structure current practice in the same way an orchestral score structures the efforts of all musicians. To continue the analogy, case managers structure care in the same way as an orchestra conductor pulls together the expertise of each instrument section (e.g., cellos and trumpets) to produce the desired musical effect.

To be more precise, a CareMap tool is a cause-and-effect grid that identifies expected patient-family and staff behaviors against a time line for a case type or otherwise defined homogenous population. The four essential parts of a CareMap tool are

1. a time line
2. an index of problems with intermediate and outcome criteria
3. a critical path
4. a variance record

A CareMap document reflects the best practice patterns of the clinicians of all key disciplines and departments who author the CareMap tool. It is used to coordinate, plan, deliver, monitor, document, and review care concurrently by individuals from all disciplines. Data from each variance record can be used retrospectively in aggregate form for continuous quality improvement (Center for Case Management, 1989).

A CareMap system (coordinated care) is a set of six components used around the clock to coordinate, organize, and sequence the care-giving process at the direct patient care level:

1. CareMap tools
2. variance analysis
3. communication
4. case consultation
5. health care team meetings
6. continuous quality improvement (CQI).

When all disciplines and departments actually use the CareMap tools as a system, *provider-controlled* care management is established.

Practice Level:	Current Practice ──→	Best Practice ──→	Ideal Practice ──→
CareMap Tool Development	Clinical testing, revisions by collaborative author teams, including • Keying which disciplines are authorized to verify which goals • Determining which tasks should require variance reports	Benchmarking between agencies	Patient-family community representation advisory to CareMap content Full CareMap system in place
Coverage by CareMap Tools	One map per care area per grossly defined patient population	Many types of maps to cover subsets of patient populations, variance analysis, and enhanced communication in place Companion physician order sets and patient education tools in place	Maps reconfigured to reflect changes in practice, technology, and services across the continuum
CareMap Tool Automation Status	Partial, fragmented, nonintegrated automation of cost and quality	Automated or scanned variance tracking	Integrated automation of cost and quality: • artificial intelligence • predictor modeling • group communication and conflict resolution software
Nursing Care Delivery	No or loose accountability model at shift and unit level for "mixed" or "modified" methods of care delivery	Primary nursing or care management at shift and unit level working with various staffing mixes and perhaps "multiskilled workers"	Physicians, nurse practitioners, and collaborative practice groups are "gatekeepers" of care Work force, ultraflexible, fluid between hospital and home
Case Management	Limited number of case managers to target high-cost case types Typically report to nursing or utilization review board	An array of clinical resource case manager pairs used at the episode level Careful definition of patient populations Case managers reporting to one or more of five or six possible departments	Clinical case managers "problem solve" care transitions with jurisdiction at the continuum level Report to centers of excellence
Payers	Largely mixed payers and DRGs		Predominantly capitated managed care

Note: DRG, diagnosis-related group.

Figure 16–1 Reengineering from Current Practice to Ideal Practice. *Source:* Copyright © 1994, The Center for Case Management, South Natick, Massachusetts

Exhibit 16–2 Congestive Heart Failure Care Map

	Day 1	Day 1	Day 2	Day 3	Day 4	Day 5	Day 6
	ER 1–4 hours	Floor Telemetry or CCU 6–24 hours	Floor	Floor	Floor	Floor	Floor
Location **Problem**				Benchmark Quality Criteria			
Alteration in gas exchange/profusion and fluid balance due to decreased cardiac output, excess fluid volume	Reduced pain from admission or pain free Uses pain scale O₂ saturation improved over admission base line on O₂ therapy	Respirations equal to or less than on admission	O₂ saturation 90% Resp 20–22 Vital signs stable Crackles at lung bases Mild shortness of breath with activity	Does not require O₂ Vital signs stable Crackles at base Respiration 20–22 Mild shortness of breath with activity	Does not require O₂ (O₂ saturation on room air 90%) Vital signs stable Crackles at base Resp 20–22 Completes activities with no increase in respirations No edema	Can lie in bed at base line position Chest x-ray clear or at base line	No dyspnea
Potential for shock	No signs/symptoms of shock	No signs/symptoms of shock	No signs/symptoms of shock	No signs/symptoms of shock Normal lab values	No signs/symptoms of shock	No signs/symptoms of shock	No signs/symptoms of shock
Potential for consequences of immobility and decreased activity: skin breakdown, DVT	No redness at pressure points No falls	No redness at pressure points No falls	Tolerates chair, washing, eating, and toileting	Has bowel movement Up in room and bathroom with assist	Up ad lib for short periods	Activity increased to level used at home without shortness of breath	Activity increased to level used at home without shortness of breath
Alteration in nutritional intake due to nausea and vomiting, labored		No c/o nausea No vomiting Taking liquids as offered	Eating solids Takes in 50% each meal	Taking 50% each meal	Taking 50% each meal Weight 2 lbs from patient's normal base line	Taking 75% each meal	Taking 75% each meal
Potential for arrhythmias due to decreased cardiac output, increased irritable foci; valve problems, decreased gas exchange	No evidence of life-threatening dysrhythmias	Normal sinus rhythm with benign ectopy	K(WNL) Benign or no arrhythmias	Digoxin level WNL Benign or no arrhythmias	Digoxin level WNL Benign or no arrhythmias	Digoxin level WNL Benign or no arrhythmias	Digoxin level WNL Benign or no arrhythmias

continues

	Day 1 ER 1–4 hours	Day 1 Floor Telemetry or CCU 6–24 hours	Day 2 Floor	Day 3 Floor	Day 4 Floor	Day 5 Floor	Day 6 Floor
Location				**Benchmark Quality Criteria**			
Problem							
Patient/family response to future treatment and hospitalization	Patient/family expressing concern Following directions of staff	Patient/family expressing concerns Following directions of staff	Patient/family expressing concerns Following directions of staff	States reasons for and cooperates with rest periods Patient begins to assess own knowledge and ability to care for CHF at home	Patient decides whether he or she wants discussion with physician about advanced directives	States plan for 1–2 days postdischarge as to meds, diet, activity, follow-up appointments Expresses reaction to having CHF	Repeats plans States signs and symptoms to notify physician or ER Signs discharge consent
Individual problem:							
Staff Tasks							
Assessments/Consults	Vital signs q 15 min Nursing assessments focus on lung sounds, edema, color, skin integrity, jugular vein distention Cardiac monitor Arterial line if needed Swan–Ganz Intake and output	Vital signs q 15 min to 1 h Repeat nursing assessments Cardiac monitor Arterial line Swan–Ganz Daily weight Intake and output	Vital signs q 4 h Repeat nursing assessments D/C cardiac monitor every 24 h D/C arterial and Swan–Ganz Daily weight Intake and output	Vital signs q 6 h Repeat nursing assessments Daily weight Intake and output	Vital signs q 6 h Repeat nursing assessments Daily weight Intake and output Nutrition consult	Vital signs q 6 h Repeat nursing assessments Daily weight Intake and output	Vital signs q 6 h Repeat nursing assessments Daily weight Intake and output
Specimens/Tests	Consider TSH studies Chest x-ray EKG CPK q 8 h× 3 ABG if pulse Ox: (range) Electrolytes: Na, K, Cl, CO_2 Glucose, BUN, creatinine Digoxin: (range)	B/G	Evaluate for ECHO Electrolytes, BUN, creatinine			Chest x-ray Electrolytes, BUN, creatinine	

continues

Exhibit 16–2 Continued

	Day 1	Day 1	Day 2	Day 3	Day 4	Day 5	Day 6
Location	ER 1–4 hours	Floor Telemetry or CCU 6–24 hours	Floor	Floor	Floor	Floor	Floor
Staff Tasks				Benchmark Quality Criteria			
Treatments	O₂ or intubate IV or heparin lock	O₂ IV or heparin lock	IV or heparin lock	DC pulse Ox if stable D/C IV or heparin lock			
Medications	Evaluate for digoxin Nitrodrip or paste Diuretics IV Evaluate for antiemetics Evaluate for antiarrhythmics	Evaluate for digoxin Nitrodrip or paste Diuretics IV Evaluate for pre-load/afterload reducers K supplements Stool softeners	D/C Nitrodrip or paste Diuretics IV or PO K supplements Stool softeners Evaluate for nicotine patch	Change to PO digoxin PO diuretics K supplements Stool softeners Nicotine patch if consent	PO diuretics K supplement Stool softeners Nicotine patch if consent	PO diuretics K supplement Stool softeners Nicotine patch if consent	PO diuretics K supplement Stool softeners Nicotine patch if consent
Nutrition	None	Clear liquids	Cardiac, low-salt diet	Cardiac, low-salt diet	Cardiac, low-salt diet	Cardiac, low-salt diet	Cardiac, low-salt diet
Safety/Activity	Commode Bedrest with head elevated Reposition patient q 2 h Bedrails up Call light available	Commode Bed rest with head elevated Dangle Reposition patient q 2 h Enforce rest periods Bedrails up Call light available	Commode Enforce rest periods Chair with assist 1/2 h with feet elevated Bedrails up Call light available	Bathroom privileges Chair × 3 Bedrails up Call light available	Ambulate in hall × 2 Up ad lib between rest periods Bedrails up Call light available	Encourage ADLs that approximate activities at home Bedrails up Call light available	Encourage ADLs that approximate activities at home Bedrails up Call light available
Teaching	Explain procedures Teach chest pain scale and importance of reporting	Explain course, need for energy conservation Orient to unit and routine	Clarify CHF Dx and future teaching needs Orient to unit and routine Schedule rest periods Begin medication teaching	Stress importance of weighing self every day Provide smoking cessation information Review energy conservation schedule	Cardiac rehab level as indicated by consult Provide smoking cessation support Dietary teaching	Review CHF education material with patient	Reinforce CHF teaching

continues

Exhibit 16–2 Continued

Location	Day 1	Day 1	Day 2	Day 3	Day 4	Day 5	Day 6
	ER 1–4 hours	Floor Telemetry or CCU 6–24 hours	Floor	Floor	Floor	Floor	Floor
				Benchmark Quality Criteria			
Staff Tasks							
Transfer/Discharge Coordination	Assess home situation: notify significant other If no arrhythmias or chest pain, transfer to floor Otherwise transfer to ICU	Screen for discharge needs Transfer to floor	Consider home health care referral		Evaluate needs for diet and antismoking classes Physician offers opportunities for discussion of advanced directives	Appointment and arrangement for follow-up care with home health care nurses Contact VNA	Reinforce follow-up appointment

Notes: ABG, arterial blood gas; B/G, blood gas; CPK, creatine phosphokinase; DVT, deep vein thrombosis; No c/o nausea, no complaints of nausea; OX, oximetry; TSH, thyroid stimulating hormone; WNL, within normal limits.

Source: The Center for Case Management, South Natick, Massachusetts. CareMap is a registered trademark of the Center for Case Management.

Case management is a clinical system that focuses on the accountability of an identified individual or group for the following tasks:

1. coordinating the care of a patient or group of patients across an episode or continuum of care
2. ensuring and facilitating the achievement of high-quality care and optimal clinical and cost outcomes
3. negotiating, procuring, and coordinating services and resources needed by the patient and family
4. intervening at key points and/or at times of significant variances from the plan of care for individual patients
5. working with others to address and resolve patterns in aggregate variances that have a negative quality-cost impact
6. creating opportunities and systems to enhance outcomes

Institutions are beginning to learn that a strategic application of either CareMap tools or case management or both is a powerful way to engage clinicians in producing changes. A third principle of reengineering they are using is (1) that all patients need managed care (via CareMap tools whenever possible, along with unit-based primary nurses or care coordinators) and (2) that about 20 percent of patients require episodic or continuum case managers, with or without CareMap tools.

A structure is the skeleton on which processes are attached by various kinds of connections. Structure gives consistency, predictability, and reliability to processes and roles. As can be seen in Exhibit 16–2, a congestive heart failure (CHF) CareMap document adds structure to the traditionally open-ended, rule-in/rule-out patient care process by incorporating agreed-upon patterns in care for a readmitted patient with CHF. This may not be the same pattern of care used for newly diagnosed or end-stage CHF. Through a guided process lasting about two to four hours, a multidisciplinary group graphs their current practice pattern against time. When a CareMap tool is used, the results are plotted on x and y axes, with time on one axis and a combination of staff interventions and anticipated patient-family responses on the other axis. Those responses define attainable, measurable intermediate and discharge goals or outcomes and represent the results of the contributions (tasks and interventions) of many disciplines and departments. In turn, the goals or outcomes are the ultimate measures of quality.

In classic project management or business terms, the CareMap tool describes a "production process," with the "product" conceptualized as outcomes rather than tasks. Unlike straightforward operations management in industry, the CareMap tool must reflect *and* enforce complex health care processes, which are based on such factors as strongly held traditions, knowledge, preferences, ethics, and values. A sound CareMap tool makes what clinicians refer to as "intuitive" more formal by encompassing the following components:

- a definition of norms for approximately 68 percent of a defined population, using a standard distribution bell curve
- relationships (loose or close) between tasks and outcomes, all with time frames
- accurate sequencing of outcomes as well as tasks
- interdependencies of the physiological body systems and of the professional disciplines and specialists that treat those systems
- a full scope of outcomes categorized long ago by the Joint Commission on Accreditation of Hospitals (Joint Commission)[4] and recently brought to light via the short form 36[5]

The four outcome categories of Joint Commission are:

1. Health— physiological status and mental status
2. Function—activities of daily living and role function
3. Knowledge—self-care, prevention, and detection
4. Absence of complications

Figure 16–2 shows pictorially how the CareMap tool "sits on top" of the algo-rithms, policies and procedures, standards, and "deep knowledge" of each disci-pline and department. However, each task and outcome in a CareMap tool is given equal weight, because each is critical to the patient or family being able to progress toward desired outcomes. For example, nutrition education by dietitians for patients with CHF is mapped on an equal plane with the timely processing of laboratory tests or physician consultation. Therefore, the authoring and use of the tool create a highly democratic, multidisciplinary environment from which the patient and family can only benefit.

Further structure is imposed by a CareMap tool in the way it is used clinically, because it builds on the scientific method with a heightened attention to evalua-tion. In addition, if a patient or family does not meet a specific intermediate goal or outcome criterion, as indicated on the map, the designated clinician must evaluate the reasons, "code" the variance, and initiate as well as document cor-rective action. For example, if a nurse's aide weighs a patient with CHF on day 3, the aide records the actual weight and reports it to a registered nurse, who will initiate corrective action because the actual weight is higher than the desired weight indicated for that day.

This example leads to a fourth important principle in reengineering: that re-structuring should clarify, not confuse, the accountabilities of each professional group involved in the model. In the CHF case, the registered nurse, not a licensed

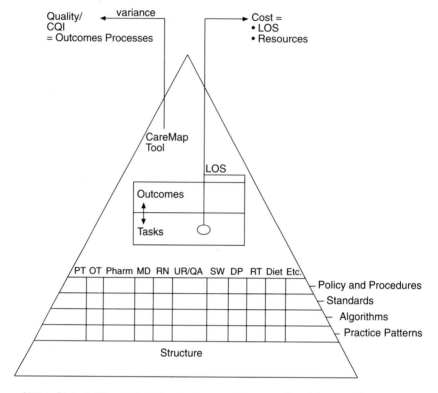

Notes: Diet, dietitian; DP, discharge planner; OT, occupational therapy; Pharm, pharmacist; PT, physical therapy; RT, respiratory therapy; UR/QA, utilization review; SW, social work quality assurance.

Figure 16–2 Anatomy and Physiology of a CareMap System. *Source:* Developed by K. Zander, 1993. Copyright 1993, The Center for Case Management, South Natick, Massachusetts. Updated 1994.

---

practical nurse or an aide, is accountable for the evaluation of the status of intermediate goals and outcomes. Although the aide can weigh the patient and record the weight, the registered nurse evaluates the data in light of everything known about CHF, this particular patient, and the system. It is imperative that each professional group not delegate verification of outcomes or recommendations for corrective actions to personnel at nonprofessional levels.

In the first wave shown in Figure 16–1, current practice nursing care delivery models, even with the use of CareMap tools, are somewhat loose in relation to accountability. A trend is emerging that organizations implementing CareMap tools eventually come face to face with any weaknesses in their nursing care delivery and begin to either revisit primary nursing care or establish care (not case) managers (coordinators). In primary nursing, the accountability for the outcomes of nursing care shifts from the head nurse to the designated shift nurses.

In addition, small numbers of case managers are generally used during the first wave to assist the organization in quickly gaining control of care for high-cost patient populations. Case managers are most often supplied by the nursing department or utilization review, depending on which department first saw the need and negotiated authority over it within the agency.

Case management models add structure to roles and relationships between direct caregivers and other expert resources such as continuing care and outpatient care services. Although case management models vary largely based on the locus of control or authority from which the case manager practices, they have more similarities than differences. Case managers manage a "closed loop process"[6] when they expedite all activities necessary to move or transition patients across care settings and/or maintain patients at their highest level of wellness in the community.

During the first wave of restructuring, patients with CHF are not usually selected for case management—not because they don't need it, but because CHF is often perceived as a ubiquitous but noncatastrophic condition. Because CHF is a high-volume case type, patients with CHF would have first priority for mapping, but populations with CHF are rarely chosen over surgical populations. Also, most physicians have patients with CHF in their practices, and most hospitals place them on several units. These characteristics and the others listed below make CHF a strategic population for case management, but case management won't be a reality for CHF patients in most organizations until the second wave of restructuring (i.e., best practice). Criteria indicating high priority for case management include

- high-cost populations
- predictably unpredictable or unpatternable conditions
- repeated hospital admissions
- significant variance from the anticipated plan of care
- high-risk socioeconomic factors
- involvement of multiple physicians or disciplines and/or agencies
- enhancement of strategic mission and/or market share for department or institution

SECOND WAVE: RESTRUCTURING CURRENT PRACTICE TO BEST PRACTICE

The second wave of restructuring using CareMap tools and/or case management models generally occurs within 3 to 12 months after completion of the first wave. It does not often occur all at once throughout the entire organization, however, but rather within one specialty or service in its own developmental process. Certainly by this stage, the executive level steering committee is well into supporting the movement to best practice by

- determining the nature and use of variance in single and aggregate form
- supporting use of CareMap tools and selected case management by allotting a budget for education of all involved departments
- actively clarifying how CareMap tools and/or case management supports the organization's mission to key groups (e.g., board and physicians)

Moving to best practice entails the organization's commitment to developing a system instead of tentative projects. To create a system, many traditions and long-standing policies must be exposed and evaluated in the light of their contributing or detracting from efficiencies and effectiveness. The common stimulus for moving from a project orientation to structuring a whole system is, for good or bad, a financial one. Certainly, the penetration of managed care and contracting into a state or region creates the greatest financial pressure for restructuring. Managed care and contracting also dictate the timetable for restructuring.

CQI seems to serve as an organization's conscience when it ponders and initiates restructuring. The variance data, especially in the clinician and system categories of the CareMap method, became fertile ground for CQI endeavors. But more important, the culture created by CQI is crucial to and enhanced by restructuring work processes and roles.

In the best practice model described in Figure 16–1, CareMap tools have undergone clinical testing and revision by author teams. Also in place are variance analyses (sometimes automated) and enhanced communication channels such as nurses' shift reports centering on length of stay and clinical outcomes or daily instead of weekly discharge planning rounds. Best practice reflects an institutional movement toward the rigorous monitoring of and responsiveness to patient and family needs.

Toward that end, nursing finally tightens up or establishes a primary nursing system or determines it will develop *unit-based* care managers. Care managers may or may not take direct care assignments, and they function as team leaders, facilitating smooth transitions for patients as they problem solve issues that affect quality, resources, or length of stay. To accomplish their coordination, they work closely with those involved in utilization review and discharge planning and with social workers, physicians, nursing staff at all levels, secretaries, laboratory staff, and admissions department personnel. The expectations of unit-based care coordinators are the same as those of primary nurses in this new era. However, units and organizations having primary nursing hold these high expectations for the majority of registered nurse staff, while those using care coordinators hold these high expectations for a minority of staff registered nurses.

Either primary nurses or care coordinators may have "targeted" populations such as patients with CHF within their assignments. By the time they are in a best practice wave, they will have CHF CareMap tools for all three tracks: newly diagnosed, readmission, and end stage. These documents will include items that focus on Lasix, angiotensin converting enzyme (ACE), inhibitors, body weight, and self-care knowledge about diet and home medications. The clinicians will know how to adapt CareMap tools for individual patients with several comorbidities, and they may be able to anticipate problems almost before they occur. Better yet, primary nurses or care coordinators will be members of a collaborative practice that, every three months, reviews the care and variances from the plan of care for patients with CHF and constantly revises CHF care management tools to make them more precise. In addition, they will create companion physician order sets by the day, when possible, as well as improved educational information for patients and families. Most important, they will have incorporated the knowledge of home care and primary care experts in their best practice design.

By this point in restructuring, the organization may begin to institute case managers; the CHF case manager would facilitate care across care areas throughout an episode of exacerbation of the condition. For this to occur, physicians need to accept case management as a system that has merit for their patients and even for themselves. A fifth principle in restructuring is that restructuring will be more accurate and ultimately proceed faster if physicians are involved every step of the way.

Attaining a comprehensive CareMap and case management system entails the criteria listed in Exhibit 16–3. By the time all criteria are met, an organization would be well into a third wave of restructuring.

THIRD WAVE: IDEAL PRACTICE

Ideal practice, in a snapshot, is a point at which the best practice defined by clinical experts is totally reinforced by every administrative, management, and clinical action. Ideal practice is replicable patient after patient, any day of the week, any time of the day! In ideal practice, patients and their families feel control in their health care while receiving it, and some are actively included in continuous planning and quality improvement.

The goal of ideal practice is accountability and conversion to a matrix structure. Ideal practice is made possible by three main changes, as yet incomplete in the real world:

1. automation of a CareMap system
2. direct patient care always managed and frequently given by a registered nurse accountable for outcomes that nurses can bring about in their specific care areas

Exhibit 16–3 Characteristics of a Fully Integrated CareMap and/or Case Management System

	No Action	Somewhat	Mostly	Fully
1. CareMap system and/or case management named specifically in institution's mission statement and year's goals?				
2. Infrastructure for CareMap system—Do you have				
* Executive steering committee that meets at least quarterly?				
Full-time project manager?				
* Relationships clarified between CQI, UM, UR, QA, etc.?				
Regular review and feedback by collaborative clinician groups?				
Initial education of all staff and managers?				
* Comfort level and participation of department heads?				
Ongoing education of all staff and managers?				
3. CareMap as core of medical record				
* Legal issues resolved?				
Multidisciplinary in content?				
* Multidisciplinary in care management and variance recording?				
* Streamlined permanent documentation?				
A patient/family version of CareMap tool?				
* Clarification of volume and type of variance data desired?				
4. Episodic-based care, beyond acute setting				
CareMaps describe care beyond traditional acute care boundaries where appropriate?				
People connected formally across boundaries?				
5. Accountability for outcomes formalized and clarified within each department				
* Nursing determines its infrastructure for case accountability.				
Physicians determine an infrastructure for continuity.				
Primary nursing?				
Case managers utilized?				
Collaborative practice group established?				
Other formal mechanisms?				
6. Program evaluation of cost and quality				
Variance data about interventions				
* Variance data about outcomes				
* Data about cost, not charge per case				
Research				
Patient/family satisfaction data				
7. Operational restructuring				

Note: *Critical challanges;CQI, continuous quality improvement; QA, quality assurance; UM, utilization management; UR, utilization review.

Source: Copyright © 1993. The Center for Case Management, Inc. South Natick, Massachussetts.

3. episode- and/or continuum-based case managers who report to centers for excellence or formal collaborative practices, whichever group is accountable for the capitation budget.

There are some precedents for each of these three changes required to get to an ideal practice level. When reviewing the following descriptions, a sixth principle should be remembered; paradoxically, new models will have to provide structure and flexibility. They will need to remain relatively fluid to be adaptive to external pressures unanticipated at the time the models are initiated.

Automated CareMap Systems

Currently, portions of a CareMap system are being automated on mainframe computers and personal computers. The seventh principle—the main principle offered here—is that, ultimately, all information (data) can be driven by the clinical interactions set up on the CareMap tool and variance records. Some vendors do not yet realize this principle. This information includes

- costs
- acuity
- scheduling of patients
- research findings and other background information
- policies and procedures
- documentation by norms and exceptions

In the aggregate form, patient data from CareMap tools, including the variance record, can be sorted by any element. When CareMap tools are applied as standardized documentation for a majority of patients as well as a template for those for whom no preset criteria or plan is useful, variance data for the majority can replace or greatly augment current CQI techniques. CQI itself will not be a separate entity but rather an organizational mandate of centers of excellence.

Nursing Accountability at Unit or Area Level

In ideal practice, nursing will have fully engaged in models that require accountability for nursing-related outcomes achievable within that unit or area. The greatest challenge will be to the role of unit (nurse) manager, unless that role becomes one of care coordination instead of budget and crisis management. If unit managers continue to be removed from the detailed clinical action of their staffs, however, by having to "cover" larger number of units, as is currently the case, they will not be able to be care coordinators.

More likely, the third wave will be characterized by two roles in each discipline: management of staff and management of patients. Although it is possible to manage patients through staff, such management requires a management style different from that of most unit managers and department heads. However, the definition of a unit may change with the emergence of fluid work forces giving care in the hospital, in the home, and in outpatient services. There may eventually be continuum managers of multidisciplinary staffs, each staff professional having "dotted lines" to his or her own discipline.

Continuum Case Managers and Centers of Excellence

Ultimately, a smooth flow of services to the patient and family will be expedited by case managers operating out of the hospital and outpatient arenas.[7] They will most likely be nurses and will create an individualized network of services to assist recuperation and wellness.

CareMap systems and case management models can be the bridge that connects administrative product lines to clinicians and their patients. Patients with CHF will be cared for by clinicians who work with and even "use" the case manager to influence care decisions. The case manager will have a "dotted line" relationship to his or her discipline but an operational reporting relationship to the cardiology (or medical) center of excellence. There may be more than one case manager, depending on the volume of patients with CHF and other cardiovascular conditions. The center of excellence would be co-directed and would manage the capitation budget.

Matrix Design

Figure 16–3 shows a rudimentary organizational chart with a simple matrix design. Matrix is a "multiple command" system in which people have at least a dual reporting structure. Although a matrix structure is best for keeping an organization informed, responsive, and flexible to external forces, it is also a complex one in which to work. A high percentage of employees who can handle and negotiate within a somewhat ambiguous network is necessary to the success of matrix structures.

Health care is already predominantly a matrix, but the industry is not using inherent or formal matrix principles well. Getting to and through the third wave of restructuring requires the involvement of administrators, managers, and clinicians who understand matrix concepts. They will need to maximize the potential of matrix structures and learn how to avoid "matrix pathologies." The eighth and last principle of reengineering is a quote about life in a matrix structure: "Key players must work on the premise that to win power absolutely is to lose performance ultimately."[8]

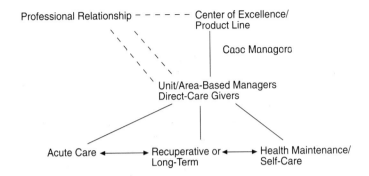

Figure 16–3 A Matrix Structure for the Continuum

CONCLUSION

Reengineering implies an orderly sequencing of changes, with a clear view of how the end condition should look, feel, and behave. Rather than a finite end condition, the health care industry may actually never quite crystallize into a "steady state" again, any more than a sea remains the same. There will constantly be waves, which are a natural part of the sea. Perhaps the best one can do in restructuring health care is to be part of the sea, knowing wave characteristics, and knowing how to produce new waves. Three waves of restructuring from current practice to best practice and ideal practice have been described, along with eight principles to guide and ground the decisions.

Paradoxically, when it comes to reengineering nursing, CareMap systems and case management, specifically, help nursing become what it does best, by better defining nursing's skilled contributions to clinical outcomes, including nurses' abilities to coordinate and expedite care delivery throughout complex organizations. Models of care coordination and case management, although highly collaborative, establish accountabilities more clearly than ever before. In nursing, there will be clearer choices than were previously available as to the level of accountability one is willing to commit to *and* the kind of structure in which one is willing to work. And when our society is ready for it, CareMap systems and case management will be creating a fourth wave called healing.

REFERENCES

1. Hammer M, Champy J. *Reengineering the Corporation: Manifesto for Business Revolution.* New York: HarperBusiness; 1993.

2. Weilitz P. Presented at the meeting on Fast-Tracking CareMap Systems and Case Management Implementation; August 1, 1993; St. Louis, MO.

3. Bower K. Case management: Work redesign with outcomes in mind. In: McDonagh K. *Patient-Centered Hospital Care*. Ann Arbor, MI: Health Administration Press; 1993:49.

4. Joint Commission on Accreditation of Hospitals. *PEP Retrospective Audit*. Chicago, IL: Joint Commission on Accreditation of Hospitals; 1974.

5. Geehr E. The search for what works. *Healthcare Forum J.* 1992;35:28–33.

6. Davenport T, Nohria N. Case management and the integration of labor. *Sloan Manage Rev.* 1994;35:14.

7. Donovan M; Matson T, ed. *Outpatient Case Management*. Chicago, IL: American Hospital; 1994.

8. Davis S, Lawrence P. *Matrix*. Reading, MA: Addison-Wesley; 1977.

■ 17 ■

Reengineering Patient Care in a Multi-Institutional System

Marjorie Beyers, PhD, RN, FAAN

Reengineering patient care delivery takes many forms and may settle in either broadly at the organizational level or narrowly at the task level. It may focus on a whole new way of delivering care. This chapter provides (1) an overview of ways in which multi-institutional systems can approach the redesign of patient care, (2) a perspective on the potential for redesigning health care, and (3) considerations and approaches to reengineering patient care delivery.

In today's practice, the broadest approach to reengineering patient care is found in the development of networks and new types of systems. This formation of health care networks and community care systems emphasizes patient care services from wellness to death. Nursing's knowledge base is being tapped in this reengineering. Nursing care knowledge and competence, which are demonstrated in patient assessment, care planning, and continuity of care, are highly valued. Other health professions and the public are picking up and using nursing's language. The language once formerly heard in nursing circles now appears in the *Wall Street Journal.* Nursing has a good opportunity to reposition patient care in the broader arena by claiming its own work and building on it.

Health care networks of different types are being formed as part of health care reform. These emerging types of health care networks are reflected in new types of corporate structures—arrangements and alignments between and among hospitals, long-term care facilities, and other health care institutions. Emphasis on physician-hospital bonding prevails. The general environment offers untapped possibilities for nursing that can be nurtured.[1] Nursing's capability to provide care along the entire spectrum of care for communities is an asset that nurses must claim and use, or else others will adapt and adopt it. Nurses now have an opportunity to shape and define clinical nursing roles that contribute significantly to health care in ways that realize the potential to serve and contribute to the nation's health.

REENGINEERING: THE IMPORTANCE OF LANGUAGE

Cycles of change are very short in today's world, and the words used to de-scribe the phenomena are being developed quickly and used loosely. Today's language lacks precision sufficient to describe reengineering, multi-institutional systems, and other key concepts. Although reengineering, restructuring, rede-signing, and reform have been differentiated, they are more alike than different in that they mean change. It is quite possible to have a lengthy discussion of reengineering among experts without a significant meeting of the minds. The importance of a common language to describe the emerging patient care sys-tems and networks cannot be overemphasized as an imperative in reengineering initiatives. A multi-institutional system has an advantage because it can create its own glossary of terms for system-wide communication, which is a powerful tool in creating both vision and common understanding in redesign initiatives. Elec-tronic mail and agile minds are both needed to keep up with the short change cycles in the evolution of health care.

REENGINEERING IN A CORPORATE STRUCTURE

Multi-Institutional Systems As Corporate Structures

For simplicity, multi-institutional systems are referred to as corporations in this chapter. A multi-institutional system is a corporate body with health care services provided in multiple settings. The term corporate in health care has been associ-ated with multi-institutional systems, even though free-standing hospitals may be corporations. The multi-institutional systems may comprise different types of services. For example, a multihospital system is defined as two or more hospitals or a horizontally organized system. A multi-institutional system includes hospitals, long-term care facilities, home care, and ambulatory care. These systems are re-ferred to as vertically integrated systems, meaning that they have comprehensive service capability for the continuum of care. For purposes of this chapter, the loosely applied term corporation is used to refer to the multi-institutional system.

Focus on Nursing Services

Although this article focuses on nursing services, it is unlikely that reengi-neering initiatives will concentrate solely on nursing services. Because nursing care is so integrated in the total care the patient receives, reengineering nursing services naturally implies a more broadly based approach: patient care. It also naturally implies involvement of physicians, pharmacists, and other health care professionals in the reengineering process.[2] Nurses in a multi-institutional system have a distinct advantage by working together to define and position clinical nursing care in the broad arena of health care systems. Another advantage to nurses who participate in reengineering nursing services in a multi-institutional system is the energy and growth for nurses, physicians, administrators, and others involved.

The Design of Reengineering

Reengineering is simply changing what is to what could be. In a corporation, the initiative may involve reengineering the corporation.[3] Examples are formation of a system or network of care—a specific type of service or job category within the corporation. Health care corporations have been influenced just as other businesses, by futurists. Visions of the future conjure up images of a world in which electronic communication prevails and one in which data and information are available to anyone who has access to a computer and software.[4] This world is very different from the one we have known. An outcome of this information age is that the traditional power structures of organization give way to more fluid forms of decision making and participation. Health care is as influenced by these changes as other businesses. The economic constraints in health care, however, tend to mask the widespread societal and technological changes. Even so, hospitals, like businesses, are being reshaped, refinanced, realigned, and reformed.[5]

One can conclude that radical change in all types of organizations is inevitable and that one of health care's general precepts is that the changes must effectively address economic constraints. Health care is subject to societal changes influencing business in general. Power in the future lies not in traditional structures but in designing the reengineered organization. Being in control is of the essence.

After Accepting the Need To Change

The inevitability of change is an underlying assumption that significantly influences decisions about redesigning. What to reengineer, which methodology for redesign to use, and how to implement the change process are the important questions. How to evaluate the outcomes of change is the greatest challenge. In a sense, formation of the multi-institutional system—a different type of corporate structure for most health care entitities—is a "redesign." It is also an example of how change that focuses on one aspect of the organization eventually influences all other parts. Only recently has nursing service in a corporation been significantly influenced by reengineered corporate structures. The emergence of clinical services as the reason for being, which has been made clear in health care reform debates, has opened up avenues for increasing the visibility of clinical services.[6]

Needless to say, nursing is a major clinical service, recognized by many as one of the significant, fundamental services for which health care corporations exist.

Clinical services are rising to the front lines now because more care is being delivered in ambulatory, home, and nontraditional settings. These services delivered in multiple sites are seen without the mantle of the hospital or the service infrastructure the hospital conveys. The captive hospitalized patient with a captive staff is giving way to an informed participative client who expects excellent, competent, quality care. This imposing list of adjectives is used to indicate that clinical services may be provided in a variety of settings with equally good results if the caregivers are competent and have the appropriate resources. The increasing mobility of clinical health professionals supported by mobile technology allows many new approaches to care delivery.

Another indication that clinical services have been discovered by the public and by payers is the attention being given to methodologies in care delivery. Care planning, for example, in the form of clinical pathways, is now used as a way to define clinical services, control the cost, promote understanding of health care in the business world, and ensure a measure for utilization of health care resources and productivity. The public is hungry for something tangible to use in managing health care. The expert judgment and clinical knowledge that have been the health professionals' commodities continue to be poorly understood because the outcomes of decision making are more measurable and visible than the decision-making process. Defining health care outcomes continues to be an area of discovery that has yet to fulfill the public expectation of a tangible, visible expression of professional clinical care.[7] This matter remains fundamental in any redesign initiative.

The Scope of Reengineering

Reengineering has to start somewhere. Choices have to be made about the best way to introduce reengineering in a corporation or any of its organizations. Consider the range of possibilities for where to start redesigning:

- the organizational structure
- leadership
- access to care
- the system for care delivery in a region or community
- the way clinical care is delivered within a system
- the work of the organization: patient care delivery
- the way clinical care is delivered in any given entity (e.g., in a long-term care facility or on a patient care unit)

- the way nurses work with other health care professionals
- the way patients access and use the health care system
- ways patients and families participate in the care of patients
- an information system that supports patient care delivery
- admitting and discharge processes for care episodes
- staffing to include multicompetent workers
- services to provide comprehensive care
- care planning to provide continuity of care

This list of possibilities provides a brief view of the complexity of decision making regarding reengineering. It is neither inclusive nor proven. Reengineering initiatives in health care as well as in business have not been tested or verified through research.[8] The culture of reengineering is emerging from the lore of anecdotal information, expert observations, and the natural order of adaptation to a changing world. Storytelling has become an important way of transmitting information about reengineering, the methods and processes used, and the barriers to change. The question of where to start with redesigning initiatives is thus open to debate and influenced by business imperatives, patient or community priorities, and the talents and predilections of the grass roots and leaders who are redesigning organizations.

INITIATING REENGINEERING EFFORTS

Reengineering is initiated as soon as the decision is made to think about and plan for the change. Reengineering is all about change. The literature offers contrasting viewpoints about the optimum way to initiate change. Terms such as reengineering, restructuring, redesigning, and reform are used. Definition of the meaning of each of these terms is a moot point when people are experiencing change. Some argue for a top-down approach, whereas others believe in a grass roots approach.[9] The fact is that reengineering, redesigning, restructuring, or reforming initiatives will not be effective unless the whole organization is engaged in meaningful ways. The approach to restructuring in a corporation is more complex than in a single organization. If the change is to be corporate-wide, should the change be designed at the corporate office level and then implemented in each organization?

Another view of how to initiate and implement change within a corporation is to introduce the change in one or more of the corporation's organizations and then spread to the remainder, over time. This approach allows testing of the reengineering initiative and an opportunity to learn from the pioneer implementers. The possible pitfall is that the redesign initiative will be tailored to a given organization. The question of replicability must be addressed in this approach. Resistance from other corporate sites can stem from the question of whether the same reengineering design will work in every organization in the corporation. One organization within the corporation can reengineer effectively without significantly changing the corporation as a whole.

BUILDING ON STRENGTHS

Multi-institutional systems have an advantage of system-wide sponsorship, mission, values, and usually, a vision of the current state as well as the future. Consistency in these important elements provides a unifying thread that expands the perspective of restructuring. One can depersonalize change in a corporation by transcending any one organization's response to change. When all organizations within the corporation are experiencing similar change effects, the perspective of organizational change as a global phenomenon can override the tendency to be paranoid about local power and motivational issues. The perspective of change rather than interpersonal or departmental conflict changes the playing field. A corporation also has the advantage of networking and sharing among peers in a noncompetitive environment to promote understanding of change and acceptance. When managed well, the strength of shared experiences can become stimulating and supportive. One can share in a group in which all are members of the same corporation more easily than with those eyeing one's market share. Competition to perform does exist in corporations, which can facilitate good performance.

THE CRITICAL ELEMENT IN REENGINEERING: THE WORKER

In either multi-institutional corporations or single organizations, successful reengineering is dependent on recognizing that the worker is critical to the organization's success. Consequently, change has to involve the workers to gain commitment and participation. Change processes grounded in enhancing, improving, or strengthening the relationships between and among people at all levels in the organization are more likely to be successful. Early restructuring initiatives tended to follow more traditional change processes that began with creating readiness to change before implementing great change. In today's world, this approach is referred to as incremental change, which may not be bold enough or fast enough to keep up with the times. Any initiative or process that provides a pathway to restructure by making people more comfortable with their own decisions, with change, and with team approaches to problem solving and decision making is useful.[10]

Truly radical change engages people in fundamental ways. Radical change implies a new reality. The world as we know it no longer exists and new ways must be found. Such change involves not only the workers but also their workplace, the materials and technology they use to perform work, and their communication. Technology is the operative word in radical change.[11] The point is that change is inevitable; there are different avenues for initiating change, and the approach to change must be as carefully designed as the desired change.

A CORPORATE APPROACH TO CHANGE

Entry points to reengineering by corporations may range from a broad approach, such as changing the corporate organizational structure, to a very specific approach, such as a task analysis and work reengineering initiative. Some highlights of change particular to corporations deserve consideration:

- reengineering organizational structures
- centralization versus decentralization
- the centralized, decentralized, and combined reengineering models
- common themes in reengineering processes.

Reengineerng Organizational Structures

In the broadest sense, multi-institutional systems are the result of a form of organizational reengineering. Establishment of a health corporation with multiple entities unites them in a corporate body that may achieve both economy of scale and economy of scope.[12] Shared financing, purchasing, and policies and procedures improve efficiency if applied appropriately. Corporations, because of the variety of entities that make up the whole, may also develop a broader perspective of health care. Formation of health care networks to provide care throughout the life span—the continuum of care—is an example of a broader perspective, allowing not only shared resources but also more comprehensive services.

The corporate structure reengineering focuses on the function of the corporate office in relation to the entities. Commonly centralized functions are finance, purchasing contracts, human resource policies, and quality management.

Should executive management and operational aspects of the services be centralized? If the answer to this question is yes, then the corporate structure reflects centralized policy and decision making, with model management structures put in place in each of the corporate entities. For example, chief executive officers are generally employed by the corporation. In centralized corporations, finance officers and human resource executives are also corporate employees. A reporting line authority is typical of centralization.

If the answer to the question is no, corporate office functions may focus on administrative matters involving the corporation as a whole, with each entity managing its own business. In this case, it is typical to establish management goals and objectives that local managers must meet.

Centralization versus Decentralization

Reengineering the corporation may involve changing from a centralized to a decentralized structure or vice versa. Centralized structures allow more control and a sense of "systemness," whereas decentralized structures provide for shared governance models with local decision making. Health care services by nature tend to be local, owing to the unique relationship between the services and persons who use them. A community hospital, home care agency, or ambulatory service is locally based in relation to the persons served. Corporations, to be successful, attend to the local nature of health care when designing the structure. Even academic health science centers, which serve a wider range of persons from geographically distant locations, are community and culturally based.

The two key questions are:

1. Which health care services and/or management structures should be centralized to achieve an advantage in the marketplace and which should be decentralized?
2. Which functions are best provided centrally and which are best provided locally?

Corporations with organizations in different geographic locations must be sensitive to local culture. A health care organization, to be effective, must provide services commensurate with local expectations. The strength of local influence on the organization may override corporate influence on some matters. Meeting local expectations is important. Corporations may have designed image, approach, and service structures sufficiently unique and replicable to be implemented in different settings. Psychiatric services of the 1980s were organized and implemented in such a way. General medical-surgical services generally have not been designed for such generalized application.

Three Models

Three models of corporate reengineering can be applied to nursing services.

1. *Centralized model*—In a centralized model, which is compatible with a centralized system, change is planned for system-wide implementation.

2. *Decentralized model*—In a decentralized model, corporate entities may be unified by mission, values, and financing, but the management and operations of health care delivery are locally defined and controlled.
3. *Combined model*—In combined models, functions that affect all entities equally, such as human resources, purchasing, or quality management, are centralized; the other functions are not centralized.

Health care corporations that include a number of hospitals and perhaps a long-term care facility and home care services may be centralized, decentralized, or a combination of both.

Centralized Reengineering Model

Reengineering in a centralized model is accomplished by deciding what the redesigned structure should look like, planning the process to accomplish the redesigned structure, and implementing the change. The decision-making process can be approached in several ways. Consultants may be engaged to design the model. The consultants usually work with selected corporate staff in this design and may also implement the model. In some cases, the corporate staff, working with representatives of each entity, may implement the redesigning. A centralized approach is advantageous because it allows for one plan, one design team, a common implementation strategy, and objectives. Disadvantages include the local nature of health care, with variety in culture, patient population, and staff expertise in each of the corporate entities. All of these factors must be considered when planning the most appropriate redesign initiatives.

In general, either very specific or very general approaches to reengineering work best with the centralized model.

Assessing readiness for change in each setting is basic to implementation. When the restructuring has to do with work redesign or changing staff tasks, the temptation to implement the "boilerplate" can be very strong. Centralized reengineering works best if staff employees are included in planning and implementation and if the initiatives are kept in perspective to the whole.

Decentralized Reengineering Model

In an effort led by corporate staff with or without consultants, decentralized reengineering models are planned and implemented in the local organization. In the decentralized approach, the corporate entities may share educational programs and visioning sessions to determine what the future should look like, and they may agree on major themes and concepts integral to redesign. Each entity then takes its learning and works out the redesign plan and implementation locally. The advantage of this approach is that people in each location are empowered to think through the reengineering process and to structure the plan and implementation in ways that suit the local institution, while also meeting the corporate objectives for redesign.

The result is an approach compatible with local culture and resources. Disadvantages include costly repeated discovery of what works and what does not, uneven change due to different resources and leadership, and less consistent results. Decentralized reengineering requires development of clear performance outcomes that serve as guidelines or outcomes to be achieved in order to minimize the effects of each organization finding its own level of performance.

Combination Reengineering Model

Both centralized and decentralized aspects of reengineering are included in the combination reengineering model. The centralized model features include visioning of the future, consideration of possibilities, and agreement on priorities by all participating entities in the corporation. Commonly shared materials and resources may then be developed to save time and money in the development process. Local autonomy is respected, in that each entity selects its own plan to implement the changes, but with commonly held corporate objectives for change. Some aspects of change, such as a task analysis, a job or work redesign process, or a service line plan may be implemented in all settings. The way in which more specific change is implemented and related to the whole is designed locally.

Advantages of this model include savings from selected planned interventions or changes, while local needs and control issues are accommodated. Disadvantages of this combined model relate to the difficulty in selecting change initiatives and plans that can be used with equal results by each entity and that fit into each different structure. More process is required to retain the focus on objectives for redesigning. Local events may distract from the reengineering, yielding uneven results and intervening factors that may be interpreted as negative to the desired change.

The models for reengineering fit different types of corporations. In all three, the decision must be made about what to reengineer. Consider the possibilities: the list of where to begin reengineering offers a brief glance at the complexity of reengineering.

In addition, corporations may consider reengineering to be a way to form alliances with physician groups or to acquire new entities to expand markets. The range of possibilities is usually translated to "opportunities" to improve, enhance, or streamline the organization.

Common Themes in Reengineering Processes

Corporations have an advantage in reengineering afforded by the networking and sharing that go beyond one setting. Within a corporation, peers may work together and share ideas without the constraints of competition. In today's health care environment, changes are inevitable. The emphasis on health care reform has accelerated redesign initiatives. Now, leaders of these initiatives must decide whether to redesign from the inside out to create integrated networks for care. This inside-out approach fundamentally changes the relationship among entities providing patient care such as home care, long-term care, and acute care. Another option is to focus on the arrangements between and among the various settings where health care is delivered, without significantly changing each setting. In light of today's challenges, some of the redesigning initiatives that seemed bold, now fade in comparison with the new care networks being formed.

Reengineering patient care delivery in the corporate structure allows a broad view of the delivery system. If the corporation includes primary care, acute care, long-term care, and home care entities, the broad view leads to reengineering to provide the continuum of care in ways that change each entity.

All entities must have representation in planning and development to foster successful reengineering attributes, which are as follows:

1. Commitment
2. Common vision
   - organization of services around patients
   - premise of optimized resources: higher quality and lower costs
   - optimal use of resources
   - increased flexibility, increased responsiveness to patients
   - continuity of care
     — in-hospital component
     — for episode of care (time limited and across settings) and managed care (continuum from wellness to illness care, over time, and across settings)
   - multiskilled staff
   - expanded roles and functions (cross-training and new education)
   - integrated teams
   - a key role of registered nurse as patient care coordinator

SPECIAL CONSIDERATIONS FOR REENGINEERING CLINICAL SERVICES

Some reengineering initiatives focus directly on clinical services. These initiatives must be sensitive to the fact that clinical services are embedded in professional disciplines and organizational habit. In many reengineering efforts, formation of clinical care teams causes much soul searching, and in some cases, an identity crisis.[13] In some reengineering initiatives, issues to be addressed must be considered throughout the redesign process.

Most clinicians will be concerned about the following three issues:

1. Who is accountable for care outcomes?
   - physician
   - nurse
   - team
2. How can staff be motivated to accept accountability?
3. Which clinical services and management structures should be consolidated? What criteria should be used for consolidation?

MANAGING THE ISSUES

Assessment

Reengineering is facilitated by assessment of patient care and nursing services in the corporation. This assessment provides insights about initiation, implementation, and evaluation from the outset. The assessment includes eight key aspects as follows:

1. determination of what should be the same and what should be differentiated
2. framework for patient care delivery
3. principles for application to patient care
4. guidelines for patient services delivery in the continuum
5. clarification of roles and functions of nurses and other clinicians
6. definition of relationships and decision-making process
7. community involvement
8. proposal for system of care delivery

Participation

Leaders from the many organizations within a corporation gain by sharing and learning to work with each other's cultures.[14] For example, some may sense that their hospital is very open and people oriented. Others may perceive that differences in employee satisfaction and involvement are significant and may serve as barriers. They feel that "mixing cultures" will result in some lost identity.

Risk Taking

Formal and informal leaders emerge in reengineering efforts. These persons are risk takers who take the lead in supporting and shaping a different model for patient care delivery. In the early stages of reengineering, understanding and awareness may be provided for key staff by having them read and research reengineering and by having them talk to others who have experienced similar changes. These methods help prepare people for change. Risk takers usually emerge in this awareness-heightening stage of the process.

Consultants

Whether to use and how to use consultants in the redesign process are important considerations. Are consultants needed to help prepare a design team? To design the change? To provide for cultural team building? Often, consultants are engaged to lead key staff in the thinking and visioning phases, to ensure consistency in expectations and goals for the change process. This shared visioning also begins the processes of building implementation teams, to draw people into doing the work of reengineering. Inclusion of appropriate groups—care providers, ancillary staff, and support workers on the team in training—is necessary for effective change.

Assessment of readiness for change may be helpful to put the process on a fast track. One common approach is to deal with attitudes about patient care and services provided for clinical and nonclinical aspects of care. How does a patient perceive the care provided? If the readiness for change must be developed and if the staff is not prepared for empowerment and leadership, the reengineering may be initiated in discrete ways. An example is work reengineering analysis in which all work is examined, tasks are differentiated, and staff is assigned to perform them. One pitfall in this approach is that almost anyone can perform one or two tasks. Unless decision making is provided for, and unless oversight is provided to ensure that tasks are performed correctly and appropriately, the discrete task analysis approach can reduce the success of the outcome in the long term and the credibility of the change process in the short term.

Incentives for Reengineering

One of the challenges of reengineering is gaining the support of employees and retaining it through the change process. Initiatives such as gain-sharing programs, which develop responsible teams whose performance is measured against organization-wide targets for financial and clinical outcomes, serve to help team members perceive the team as a part of the organization as a whole. To be effective, team goals must be quantifiable, attainable, and relate to the whole institution. Evaluation of outcomes is used as a performance measure for salary increases, gain sharing, or other financial rewards. The best incentive is involving staff in the study of what and how to reengineer.

Retaining the Commitment

The downside of reengineering is that, if it is not managed appropriately, staff may suffer loss of identity, alienation, loss of pride, nonconstructive competition, and loss of commitment.

Reengineering that starts with or that involves nursing services is best fostered when the following features are attended to:

- common philosophy to determine the model
- model to try out what works best
- common decision regarding framework and attributes of change
- linkages with centralized functions, such as accounting
- patient-centered value system
- team skill—a specialized task or skill efficiency
- sense of oneness
- commitment to patient
- commitment to improvement

CONCLUSION

It is easier to put a model on paper than to figure out how it works. Often, the desired impact on patient care is different from what is expected. Questions of accountability are inevitable. Can several people on a team be accountable for coordinated effort or does there need to be a standard-bearer for key aspects?

The code words for reengineering, restructuring, redesign, and reforming are similar: work "smarter," consolidate, avoid duplication, eliminate unnecessary processes or steps, and look for ways to improve outcomes without using more resources. For nurses responsible for patient care delivery, these code words continue to be compelling. Nurses, perhaps because of gender characteristics, education, or sheer practicality, are by nature resource conservationists. In fact, this tendency of nurses may be the greatest barrier to nursing's capability to effectively reposition itself in the future.

The approaches to reengineering may be global or very specific. Reengineering activities become increasingly more defined as the process flows from conceptualization to application. Initial design is more abstract and allows room for brainstorming and creativity. Implementation plans become more specific and less open to discussion and debate. Application to practice becomes even more defined and specific. It is easy to flow with the reengineering movement and to become focused on "the project" or the redesign activities. It is important to view these focused activities as means to an end. The opportunity to enhance nursing's future capability to serve communities, patients, and families lies in keeping the global view alive. Most reengineering initiatives decrease layers in organizations, disperse decision making, and expand the scope of employees. Nursing must retain a perspective of global redesign, in which nursing care is a major component of health care in the continuum. Real change lies in this global perspective.

REFERENCES

1. Sovie M. Exceptional executive leadership shapes nursing's future. *Nurs Econ.* 1987;5(1): 13–20.
2. Keeney R. Creativity in decision making with value-focused thinking. *Sloan Manage Rev.* 1994;35(4):33–44.
3. Hammer M, Champy J. *Reengineering the Corporation: Manifesto for Business Revolution.* New York; HarperBusiness; 1993.
4. Tonges MC, Lawrenz E. Reengineering, the work redesign-technology link. *J Nsg Admin.* 1993;23(10):15–22.
5. Krepinevich A. Keeping pace with military-technological revolution. *Issues Sci Technol.* 1994;10(4):23–29.
6. Madden MJ, Ponte P. Advanced practice roles in the managed care environment. *J Nsg Admin.* 1994;24(1):56–62.
7. Bandeian SH, Lewin L. What we don't know about health care reform. *Issues Sci Technol.* 1994;10(3):52–59.
8. Caldwell B. Special report: Missteps, miscues. *Information Week.* June 20, 1994:50–60.
9. Jansen E, Eccles D, Changler G. Innovation and restrictive conformity among hospital employees: Individual outcomes and organizational considerations. *Hosp Health Services Adm.* 1994;39(1):63–80.
10. Wilson B, Laschinger S. Staff nurse perception of job empowerment and organizational commitment: A test of Kanter's theory of structural power in organizations. *J Nsg Admin.* 1994;24(45)(suppl):39–47.
11. Sewer A. Lessons from America's fastest-growing companies. *Fortune.* August 8, 1994: 42–60.
12. Stuckey J, White D. When and when not to vertically integrate. *Sloan Manage Rev.* 1993;34(3):71–83.
13. Velianoff G, Neely C, Hall S. Developmental levels of interdisciplinary collaborative practice committees. *J Nsg Admin.* 1993;23(7,8):26–29.
14. Sandrick KM. Prepare for change. *Trustee.* 1994;47(7):6–9.

▪ Part II ▪

Reengineering in Action: Case Studies

■ 18 ■

Developing Team-Based
Patient Care through Reengineering

Jo Manion, MA, RN, CNAA
Phyllis M. Watson, PhD, MEd, RN

Never has the health care environment changed at such a rapid pace. A key to dealing effectively with change is development of resiliency, flexibility, and adaptability within our organizations. The dangers of entering a new millennium with an organizational structure that is a relic of the past are becoming increasingly obvious. In 1987, during the strategic planning process at Lakeland Regional Medical Center (LRMC) it became clear that traditional productivity improvements and downsizing strategies were only short-lived solutions to the key issues the organization was facing. The executive team agreed to take a proactive stance. Examining all processes and rethinking the way patient care and services are delivered were the first steps. In effect, a complete restructuring, or reengineering, of the organization was planned.

HISTORY

The process began in January 1988, when LRMC and the consulting firm of Booz-Allen & Hamilton, Inc., initiated jointly funded diagnostic analyses of how LRMC provided patient care. The 1988 results of these data-based analyses included several startling findings:

- Only 16 percent of the hospital's structure was spent delivering medical, technical, or clinical care.
- Documenting, scheduling, and coordinating were the primary operating functions of the hospital.
- "Ready-for-action" (structural idle time, waiting for something to happen) was the largest single consumer of hospital resources.
- As much time was spent on coordinating and scheduling activities and procedures as was spent in providing medical, technical, and clinical services.

241

Conclusions based on these analyses were that the true drivers of performance and cost included the organization's operating structure and approach, management processes, and deployment strategies.[1] Significant structural redesign was undertaken to position the organization for the future. In April 1989, the patient-focused model was initiated as a pilot project.

Intense scrutiny of all processes contributing to the delivery of patient care resulted in several new operating imperatives:[1]

- The patient care unit would be "decompartmentalized" to ensure that staff resources were better utilized and patient focused.
- Jobs on the unit would be structured for the greatest possible continuity of patient care, creating the need for employees to be cross-trained to perform work outside their usual areas of functioning.
- Restructured jobs would increase the quality of work life and job satisfaction for health care workers and support staff.
- Patient outcomes (quality of care and satisfaction with care) would be measured at the staff level, and teams would be held accountable for these outcomes.
- The unit's operating approach would stress responsiveness to enhance quality of care for patients and support for physicians.
- The hospital would be separated into five operating centers, each managed as a unique entity with a patient-driven operations approach that emphasized accountability for the quality and cost of services provided.

The success of this pilot unit has been reported in many forums. Since that time, reengineering of the organization has continued at a steady and incremental pace. The senior and middle management at LRMC now recognizes that reengineering is a journey with no end, a continuous performance improvement process to be embedded in the organizational culture, rather than a one-time event.

As the journey toward continual improvement through reengineering has progressed, the process has been guided by four principles:

1. Resources must be patient focused and fully utilized.
2. All operations must be responsive to patient and physician needs.
3. Individuals at all levels must be accountable and satisfied.
4. Patients must readily perceive value in their care.

These principles gradually evolved and are now used daily in problem solving and in planning solutions to the challenges faced in redefining what we do, how we do it, and how well we do it.

This chapter explores one aspect of the reengineering work accomplished by LRMC: the development of a multidisciplinary team-based structure. The original pilot unit established a team-based structure to assure continuity and accountability. However, the needs of the teams were not well understood and teams were not proactively developed after they were established. Like all aspects of Lakeland's evolution, teams were on a journey. Thus began the evolution to a team-based structure and eventually to self-directed work teams.

Historically, the use of patient care teams in health care was significantly different from this current evolutionary step. Many people hear "teams" and think the concept of patient care teams is a reversion to a form of "team nursing," when in fact it is truly the next step in the evolution from primary nursing. The team, rather than an individual nurse, is fully accountable for the care of patients for whom they have accepted responsibility. The team assesses needs and plans, implements, and evaluates their patient's care. This model is based on the recognition that the work of patient care is dependent on the contributions of more than one individual from one discipline.

At LRMC we have adapted the definition of teams used by Katzenbach and Smith.[2] A team is a small, *consistent* group of people with a relevant shared purpose, common performance goals, complementary skills, and a common approach to its work. Team members hold themselves *mutually* accountable for the team's results and outcomes.

The goal at LRMC is for processes in the organization to be restructured so that the team caring for the patient provides 85 percent of all services and care required—a "whole piece of work" to the extent that is feasible in a complex institution driven by high-level technology. Consequently, cross-training and redeployment of key services to the patient care unit are essential for the model to work effectively. Caregivers gather laboratory specimens, transport patients, and prepare food, rather than delegating such responsibilities to other health care workers. For "the team" to be accountable for the full scope of services required by the patient and family, they must have the responsibility, knowledge, skills, and clear authority with which to carry out the services.

All professionals from radiology, laboratory, nursing, and support staff must report to the patient care department leader and not to a central (tribal) leader. Ownership for the "full piece of work" includes full accountability for personnel, leadership, management, quality of work, expense, revenue, and costs. This concept alone may seem contradictory to the conventional wisdom that the professional nurse should be fully utilized for the advanced professional skills he or she brings to the patient and should not be "bogged" down in responsibilities that can be delegated to other, less professionally prepared workers. However, from the patient's perspective, that conventional wisdom results in more and more "faces in the parade" and increased fragmentation of care. Fragmentation of care reduces the quality of care, because it is in the transfer of responsibility between caregivers and between departments that errors are more likely made. Recent approaches to patient care delivery, such as the partnership model, are based on the recognition that in today's complex environment it takes more than one person to be effectively accountable for patient care; it takes a team.

At Lakeland, we quickly learned that there are at least two major aspects to building effective patient care teams. The first is designing the structure. How many team members are needed for this patient population? What complementary skills need to be represented? The second aspect is the cultural change needed, not only by team members, but throughout the entire organization. How will the team share the work? How will they accomplish the work? How do they make the transition from an individual-based practice to a team-based practice?

TEAM STRUCTURAL DESIGN

A successful team design depends on the careful analysis of patient care needs. If people are arbitrarily placed together on a team because of previous assignment patterns or schedules, the model is not "patient focused" but instead is determined by convenience or by existing patterns and structures. Analysis of patient care needs is based on review of historical data that reflect the full spectrum of self-care assistance (patterns of care) and services needed by the patient. Services include the assessment, diagnosis, and prescription expertise of each professional, in addition to testing and treatment services, which include laboratory and radiological examinations and treatments and procedures ordered, as well as the pharmacological needs and the workload required for care of the patients. At LRMC, decisions are always based on data, not intuition or perception of past experience.

Patients are regrouped (or reaggregated) on the basis of analyses of similarity of the patterns of care and services required. Team structures are then designed specifically to meet the needs of the patient in each of the populations. The workload requirements of the patient population drives the team structure. In addition, team structures may be different based on the length of stay of the patient population. For example, in the emergency room care team design (see Figure 18–1), the length of stay of patients is in minutes or hours, not days. Consequently, care team designs are specific to shift and the needs of the patient population. Teams never "pass off" their patients to another team.

The care team designs for the adult and geriatric patients are different from those for the pediatric patients. Furthermore, care team design is affected by the level of acuity of the patients within those groups. For example, as depicted in Figure 18–1, pediatric type 1 and 2 patients (e.g., a child with acute respiratory

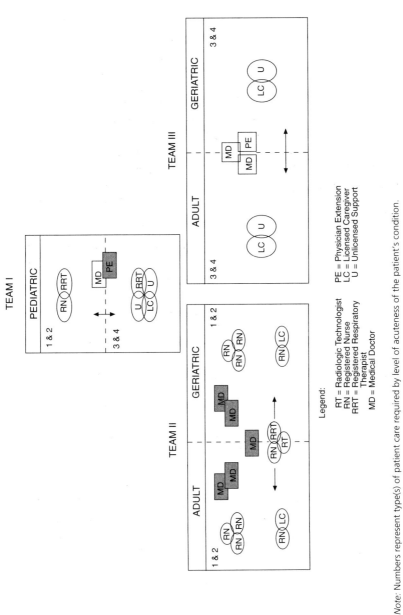

Legend:

RT = Radiologic Technologist
RN = Registered Nurse
RRT = Registered Respiratory
Therapist
MD = Medical Doctor

PE = Physician Extension
LC = Licensed Caregiver
U = Unlicensed Support

Note: Numbers represent type(s) of patient care required by level of acuteness of the patient's condition.

Figure 18–1 Care Team Design for Emergency Services for the Day Shift

distress) would be cared for by a registered nurse and a registered respiratory therapist who are working in a pair on that shift. Patients would be assigned to the pair on the pediatric team by the gatekeeper (a person expert in both triage and resource management) on the basis of the patient's identified needs at triage. The quad team (four individuals—two unlicensed, one registered respiratory therapist, and one licensed caregiver, probably a licensed practical nurse), would receive pediatric patients in less acute, stable condition, with no medical complications (types 3 and 4). Other members of team I are the physician and physician extender who work with both the quad and the pair to meet the needs of pediatric patients in either highly acute or less acute conditions.

In contrast, team II would receive adult and geriatric patients in highly acute condition. For example, one triad of registered nurses in team II would receive adult patients experiencing mild cardiac infarction, while the other triad of registered nurses would receive geriatric patients experiencing mild cardiac infarction. Subteams of team II are composed of a greater number of licensed individuals, and team II is designed specifically to meet the needs of the adult or geriatric patient in highly acute condition. Team III is specifically designed to meet the needs of the adult or geriatric patient in less acute condition. These team designs were the product of 16 months of work by staff and physician project team members—expert emergency room practitioners—in cooperation with our consultants from the Patient-Focused Care Association. The team composition and work capacity was designed so that patients in highly acute condition never wait for care and patients in less acute condition seldom experience a wait for care. Consequently, resources were shifted to professional personnel to meet the medical, technical, and clinical needs of our patients as they became well understood after the months of workload quantification and data analysis.

In contrast, in a patient population like the mother-baby population, the length of stay is 24 hours to several days. Therefore, teams surround patients and cross shifts so that the total patient continuity can be attained. Examples of the care teams and support teams designed for the mother-baby unit are depicted in Figure 18–2.

As illustrated in Figure 18–2, the teams in our mother-baby population were designed to meet all of the needs of the mother-baby populace and their extended families, including prenatal education, labor, delivery (including caesarean section), postpartum care of the mother, bonding of the mother and the infant, and infant care. Consequently, these teams contain registered nurses and operating room technicians for 24 hours a day, seven days a week.

Individual care teams, such as care team I and care team III, care for their patients from admission through discharge and never pass them off to another team. Care team III has more personnel on the day shift, because they will be assigned the patient population with elective caesarean section. Consequently,

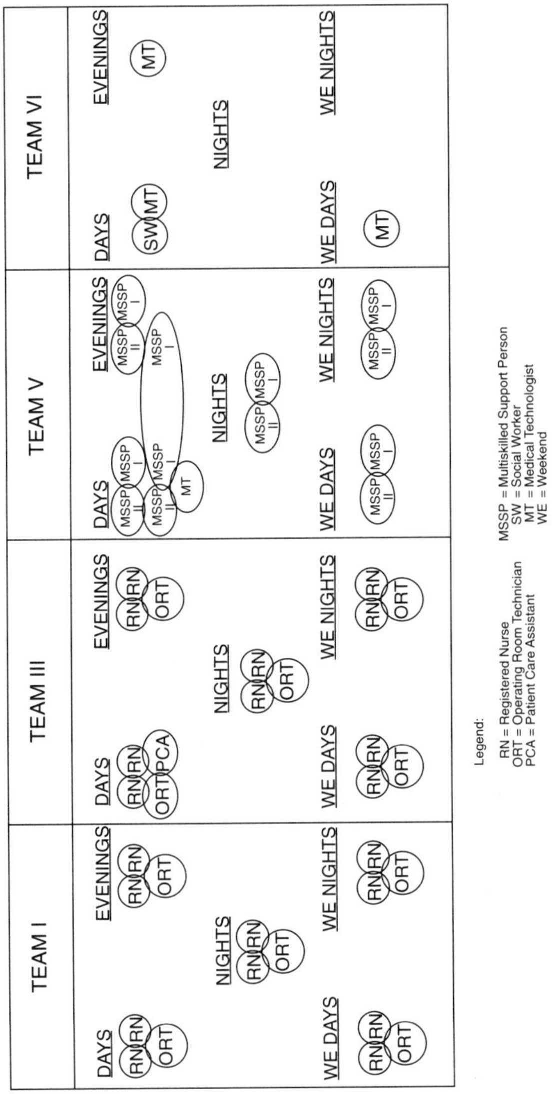

Figure 18–2 Care Team Design for Mother-Baby Services

Legend:

RN = Registered Nurse
ORT = Operating Room Technician
PCA = Patient Care Assistant

MSSP = Multiskilled Support Person
SW = Social Worker
MT = Medical Technologist
WE = Weekend

this team's workload will be higher on the day shift than on other shifts. Team V is a team consisting of staff who support admitting functions, the clerical functions tied to unit leadership, and continuous improvement activities and other unit support activities including environmental cleaning. Team VI is a team of focused practitioners who support the four care teams in the delivery of care to the patients, including laboratory testing and complex discharge planning. Again, staff and physician teams worked for over one year to analyze the needs of our patient population, including their admission patterns by hour and day, predictability and variability in workload, and variations and complexity of patient needs. Eleven separate patient types were identified, and the workload of each patient type was quantified. Teams were designed so that patient needs could be met during both high- and low-workload periods. The patient-focused development team at LRMC provided the analytic support to the project team's workload quantification and care team design.

In the past, many health care organizations used shift-based patient care teams. In such teams, caregivers on one shift form a team and assume responsibility for certain patients. Membership of the team may or may not be consistent from day to day. There were teams on each shift, and patients could be assigned to two or three different teams during a 24-hour day and even to teams with different members the following day. In the patient-focused care team, the team consists of the caregivers across all shifts. The members of the team are consistent from day to day and even on weekends, using weekend staff. Figure 18–3 visually depicts these differences. At Lakeland, this consistency of assignment of a patient to a care team has been maintained at a 94 percent rate or better since implementation.

ASSIGNMENT OF PATIENTS TO TEAMS

With a fixed-team organizational structure, patients are assigned to teams, rather than staff being assigned to patients. This is a very different concept from determining the patient's needs and then assigning the patient to a staff member or partners on a shift-by-shift basis. Traditionally, data on the acuteness of the patient's condition are obtained and then used to quantify workload and the number of caregivers needed, whether the caregivers work individually, in partnerships, or as teams. In the patient-focused approach at LRMC, the fixed-team structure is designed around the predetermined and predicted needs of the patient population. Teams are established, and patients are then assigned ("put into" teams), like adding a cup of water to a pitcher. When the pitcher is full, the next cup is put in another pitcher. Thus, patients are assigned to a team for their full length of stay. Teams are fully utilized but not overloaded.

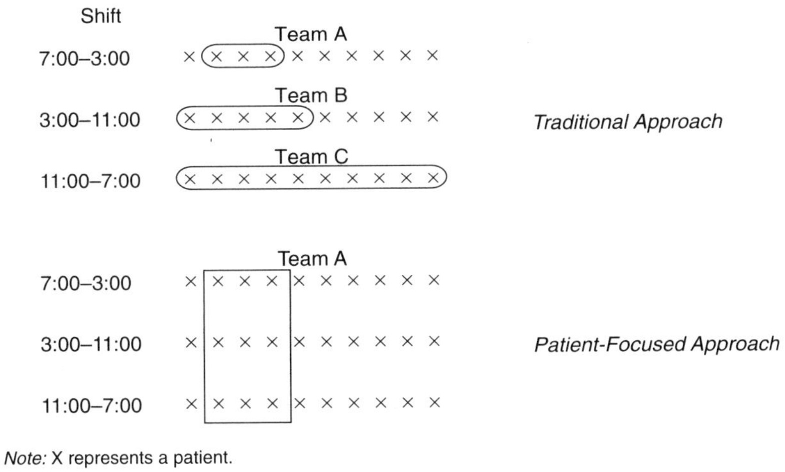

Shift

Team A
7:00–3:00 × ⊂× × ×⊃ × × × × × ×

Team B
3:00–11:00 ⊂× × × × × ×⊃ × × × × ×   *Traditional Approach*

Team C
11:00–7:00 ⊂× × × × × × × × × ×⊃

Team A
7:00–3:00 × | × × × | × × × × × ×

3:00–11:00 × | × × × | × × × × × ×   *Patient-Focused Approach*

11:00–7:00 × | × × × | × × × × × ×

Note: X represents a patient.

Figure 18–3 Team Approaches

DEVELOPING "TEAMNESS"—THE CULTURAL CHANGE

Simply structuring people into teams was not enough to ensure that they would provide patient care as a team at LRMC. Few of us have had experience truly working as a team in the workplace. We may have been a part of an effective work group in which we coordinated our efforts and communicated to others what we had done. Being part of a team, however, implies joint problem solving and planning and working at all times to improve the results of the team. There is a process to building effective teams, and if the teams are not committed to the process, they will not become high-performing teams capable of self-direction.

Teams were not part of the original design for the patient-focused model, but in fact, developed on the basis of evaluation of the operational effectiveness of the model. For caregivers to be accountable as fully as possible for patient care outcomes, their span of responsibility needed to be increased, as well as their level of control over as many aspects of the patient's care as possible. A consistent team of caregivers can be empowered at a higher level and for more responsibility than can an individual. Thus, it became clear that a team-based structure was necessary to meet the intent of the third principle of reengineering (individuals at all levels must be accountable and satisfied); therefore, the evolution of our early teams to truly functioning teams was slow. In the beginning, the teams were responsible for patient care outcomes and self-scheduling. Assumption of additional traditional managerial responsibilities did not come until much later.

After several years' experience, it became clear that teams would not evolve without expert leadership and a specific approach or discipline to assist their development. Recently, this approach has been formalized and is used for groups coming together as teams. The major components of this process—team purpose, roles and responsibilities, and performance goals—are discussed in the following sections.

Team Purpose

A group of individuals will not form a team unless they have a clear, identified purpose that is relevant to the members. For patient care teams, the purpose may appear very clear. However, the team must do the work of identifying their purpose or there will not be the same commitment as when the purpose is established by a higher authority. An example of a team purpose statement is the following:

> Together with your physician, we pledge to provide quality and continuity of services to the patients and families entrusted to our care by meeting their physical, emotional, educational, and spiritual needs. We strive to support and help each other, learn from each other, and be a role model for others.

The team does not develop this purpose in isolation. In the early stages of team formation, strong and supportive outside leadership is critical. Identifying individual and team values is an important part of this work. The team discusses their stated values and what they mean. They also evaluate gaps between their desired values and their daily experience as a team. The team's values can be included in their purpose statement. An example of an actual team's value statement is the following:

As a Team We Value:

Teamwork—working synergistically together and cooperatively working with others toward a common goal

Competence—being good at what we do and being capable and effective

Integrity and honesty—acting in line with our beliefs, "walking our talk," and being sincere and truthful with ourselves and others

Communication—communicating through open dialogue and the exchange of views and by open and honest dealings with each other and those with whom we come in contact

Creativity—finding new ways to do things and developing innovative solutions to issues and problems

During their discussion of gaps between values and experience, this team identified competence, integrity, and honesty as essential values they had to live by. They also discovered that during times of stress, their value of creativity was the first to go.

Each patient care team works on its purpose and values during a team retreat day. Some teams even develop descriptive slogans, a coat of arms, and stationery. When new teams form now, this is the first work they do together as a team.

Team Roles and Responsibilities

Empowerment and acceptance of responsibility cannot occur if there is confusion about roles and responsibilities. This major issue arises early in the formation of multidisciplinary teams. Team members work together and gradually reach agreement on how they will deliver patient care. Sharing responsibilities begins to occur in their daily practice.

However, the team must consider not only its functional work (patient care) but also its operational work (becoming a team and accomplishing team roles). Who will be responsible for collecting quality data, for scheduling, for education, and for coordination with other teams? At LRMC, an approach was adapted from Wellins and his colleagues[3]—the team 101 concept (Figure 18–4). Basically, the team decides what responsibilities it has for team operations and how to share the responsibilities. Team members accept these responsibilities for varying periods of time. Team members also agree on a common approach for the team's work. How will team members communicate with each other? When and where will team meetings be held? Will an agenda be used, and who will prepare it? These are some of the areas in which agreement is needed. Team consideration of these questions helps to clarify team roles and structure and helps teams to function more effectively.

In the original design of the patient care team, the need for complementary professional skills is considered. As the team comes together and begins their work, the emphasis switches to the interpersonal skills of the team members. During the team's development, there are cases in which additional skills are needed within the team, and arrangements are made to obtain those skills. For example, during the early formative stages of a team, a member may leave and need to be replaced. The team may not have been taught interviewing and selection skills. For the team to accept the responsibility of selecting a new team member, they will need to develop these additional skills.

Performance Goals

Specific performance goals are needed for the team to continually improve and develop. Goals are developed and shared with the department manager. The

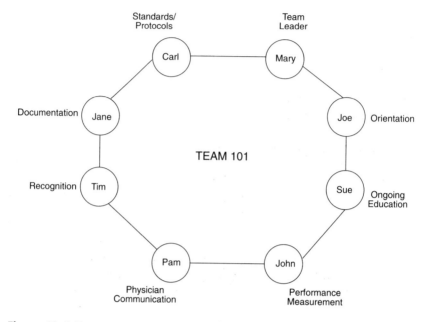

Figure 18–4 Team 101—Assignment of Responsibility within the Team

team is responsible for developing action plans to implement and reach the goals. Well-written performance goals that challenge the team result in a sense of synergy that is extremely powerful. Typically, it has taken much longer for teams to gain skill and competence in writing and achieving their performance goals than might be expected. The explanation for this phenomenon may be that goal setting is a higher-level skill than simply writing the goal correctly in an appropriate format. This skill also includes being future-oriented and proactive, as well as having the ability to sort through a variety of possible actions and using judgment to choose a specific action. Well-delineated performance goals and quality measurements are essential for team accountability. The following example illustrates a specific team goal and appropriate action steps:

1. Identify the education needs of the team by June 15, 1995.
   a. Draft a needs assessment survey by March 15, 1995.
   b. All team members complete the survey by April 15, 1995.
   c. Tabulate results and discuss at the May team meeting.
   d. Identify the three top team priorities and develop action plans for meeting these educational needs by June 15, 1995.

    e. Individual team members will have identified a personal educational action plan by June 15, 1995.

Working to clarify these issues of purposes, roles, and responsibilities and a common approach to their work form the foundation for good team development. Other issues also arise and must be addressed, but if the team has done this work, it is more likely to evolve successfully. Other key issues that must be considered are the role of organizational leadership in relation to the team, the need for team education, and how to maintain the link to the caregiver's professional discipline.

ADDITIONAL KEY ISSUES

Leadership

The nature of reengineering teams, especially self-directed work teams, implies a very different relationship to management and leadership than that in traditional structuring. Responsibility, power, and decision-making authority must be transferred to the team; otherwise, the group does not evolve and develop as a team. Managers must become coaches and leaders. In the beginning, coaching the team takes a significant portion of the manager's time. In fact, simple managerial tasks that previously were accomplished in very little time can take two or three times longer during transition. Time is involved as the manager teaches the team to take on new responsibilities. In addition, tasks completed by the team members require more time in the beginning because they are at the novice skill level.

The role of leadership for teams is paradoxical and difficult for many managers to grasp. It can be frightening for a manager to teach the team to do things for which the manager has been responsible in the past. Managers gradually begin to see that they now are expected to use their time differently. They begin to focus on coordinative efforts within the organization as a whole—strategic planning, coaching, and developing the team.

Managers need to learn the process of coaching and appropriate ways to develop the teams. Some managers will simply turn responsibilities over to the team with little or no guidance—a "sink-or-swim" approach. Others will provide resources such as educational opportunities but will relinquish their responsibility for team development to the educator or consultant. Managers must feel ownership of the process of team development or progress will be slow or nonexistent.

Managing teams is very different from managing individuals and is a difficult distinction for many managers to make. If there are 70 employees and 7 teams within the department, the manager will often focus on managing the 70 employees. In a team-based approach, the manager focuses on the seven teams, perhaps developing a department "leadership team" consisting of the manager and the "in-team" leaders. The manager coaches the in-team leader, who then coaches the team. At times, the manager may be involved in coaching the entire team.

Other issues faced by the manager in a team-based patient care unit include the following:

- how to build and maintain the vision of the unit as a whole
- how to prevent teams from becoming isolated
- how to help teams to work together
- how to recognize when teams are dysfunctional and intervention is needed
- how to recognize when teams are exceptional
- how to assess the teams accurately and determine their level of development
- how to avoid holding back exceptional teams because not all teams are at the same degree of development
- how to coach teams for continual development and improvement

Another dilemma for the manager stems from the growing competence of teams. As teams grow and become more competent in their roles, they take on some of the most satisfying management functions. For example, as teams solve and/or prevent problems, the manager has to give up the role of "unit/department savior." The tricks of salvation previously gave traditional managers a great deal of recognition and satisfaction. An example relates to clinical leadership and relationships with physicians. In a fixed-team structure with the manager as leader, physicians should relate primarily to the teams and not expect managers to solve problems. This transition is difficult for both the manager, who previously received a great deal of recognition from the physician and satisfaction from that recognition, and for the physician, who begins to question, "Who's in charge? Who's the captain of the ship?" Some physicians feel that their authority is diminished in this flattened structure, because they relate directly with "staff level" personnel rather than management and administration. It takes time for the physicians to see that their bonding and input to the team structure is actually much greater and has a more significant impact on patient care than it did in a traditional structure.

In the same way, the manager/leader has to give up the role of "clinical expert" and "patient savior." Over time, as managers change roles and become leaders, their satisfaction comes from seeing the staff become clinical leaders who make a major difference in patient outcomes by teaming with the physicians and really focusing on changing practices that can have a dramatic effect on patient outcomes. The managers realize satisfaction by developing people and leading teams of people.

Education

The transition from working independently to working as part of a consistent team is significant for health care employees. At LRMC, patient care teams require not only increased technical competency in a wider range of skills, but also greater ability to facilitate interpersonal relationships than before. Developing competency in multiple clinical skills was a key focus in the early years of this conversion, and this requirement remains a primary focus for new teams as they form. There was also an appreciation of the need for interpersonal and team-building skills. However, in more recent years, we have realized the critical need for an educational process that teaches team members how to do the work of becoming a team. This education must be ongoing for each team and must occur "just in time" for movement to higher levels of development. The formal education must be followed at each step with new expectations, mentoring, and support. The provision of education is a shared responsibility of team members, the manager, and the central education department.

Education is like planting a seed. If the ground is not watered and fertilized, the flower will never bloom. This describes the nature of the relationship between education and leadership. Education can plant the seeds, but they will not bear fruit unless coaches and leaders are there to nurture and nourish the team and provide competent, caring, and consistent guidance as the team accomplishes its work.

Governance Structure

The impact of tribal behavior on multidisciplinary team formation is significant. Peg Neuhauser,[4] describing tribal life in our organizations, points out that we are all members of a tribe. Some of us belong to a professional tribe, and others belong to a departmental tribe. At issue is how to move the organization from being tribal within single disciplines to being tribal as teams, without losing the value of the professional tribe.

Tribal barriers are broken when multidisciplinary teams begin to form. Members of the different disciplines get to know each other and learn each other's language and values. As the team goes through its early formation and attachments, it becomes important for team members to focus on their similarities rather than their differences. Consequently, they may choose to ignore their differences. As an example, during the first year of multidisciplinary patient care teams at LRMC, the nurses in the teams decided they did not want to celebrate national Nurses Week unless "everyone" could celebrate Nurses Week. They were deemphasizing their uniqueness. This issue was confronted immediately as being potentially destructive in the long run. It is the very differences and pride in the uniqueness of each person and profession that makes the team effective. The differences are to be recognized and celebrated rather than deemphasized.

The redeployment of professionals from the pharmacy, laboratory, social services, dietary services, and physical therapy, as well as the integration of radiology technologists and respiratory therapists into the care teams raised the need for a structure that keeps professionals closely connected to their specific discipline. A governance structure for each profession has evolved to ensure continued involvement in professional standard setting and issues relating to quality of care.

A professional governance structure is far more than a committee structure for participative management. It is the discipline that assumes responsibility for determining appropriate professional standards and practices. The practice councils also represent the important values of the profession and may set actual performance standards for professional practice.

BARRIERS TO TEAM-BASED STRUCTURE

There are significant barriers to implementation of a team-based structure. Culturally, we are inclined to value independence and individualistic thinking and behavior. Working in partnerships and on teams requires us to function differently, and this can be difficult. In addition, there is a tendency to return to previous and comfortable ways of working together, as well as a tendency to confuse team structure with a bureaucratic structure. The continual evolution of teams is a challenge to our need for stability and closure. In addition, there are many system issues that create difficulties for teams.

System Issues

The typical bureaucratic organization is full of barriers and roadblocks to the implementation of a team-based structure. Three of the most common issues have to do with team-based information reports, reward and recognition systems, and performance appraisal. These three examples are closely interrelated. Teams accepting additional responsibility such as controlling expenses or maintaining a high level of patient satisfaction need information to be reported on a team basis. In most organizations, patient satisfaction survey results and budgetary variance reporting is usually accomplished by a department rather than a team. Changing these traditional systems can take years in an organization.

Most reward and recognition systems are individually based rather than team based. Employee of the month programs allow no recommendations for teams. It takes a conscious effort to build in ways to recognize team achievements. The performance appraisal system is one possible way to do this. Organizations committed to recognizing and rewarding team performance have started basing a team member's annual salary increase, at least in part, on the performance of the team. To do this effectively, however, all team members must be evaluated at the same time and outcome measures for evaluation of the team's performance must be developed.

Our individualistic approach to performance evaluation was another barrier to team effectiveness. Individuals were evaluated based on the anniversary of their date of hire. Consequently, even if team outcomes were a part of the individual's performance standards, team members received different scores on the same standards because they were evaluated at different points in time. It was clear that this did not reinforce team behavior and/or team accountability. Consequently, Lakeland is in the process of converting its entire performance evaluation structure so that entire teams can be evaluated at the same time. This means evaluation dates will be staggered across teams within units to keep the overall workload of the evaluations balanced, by not evaluating all teams at the same time. When this is accomplished, every team member will receive the same score on all team accountability items on an individual performance evaluation. We believe that this approach will have a significant impact on reinforcing team authority, responsibility, and accountability.

Structure

When managers or teams are faced with difficulties or challenges, they tend to revert to previous structures with which they are familiar. Often, superimposing a bureaucratic structure on a team structure will stifle the resilience and flexibility that is a prime benefit of the team structure. Consider, for example, the team 101 concept previously described. It is an excellent method for clarifying and defining responsibility within the team. It provides much-needed structure for individuals who require structure to function comfortably. One consequence experienced, however, was that this then defined the committee structure within the unit. In other words, the team members from each team who were responsible for education became the department education committee. The same was true for areas such as performance measurement, standards/protocols, and recognition. Soon, important decisions on these elements were being made in the unit-based committees, in essence, replacing team-based decision making with a bureaucratic model. Some decisions are appropriate for a unit-based committee, but many need to be made within the teams. Guarding against this tendency to use structure to solve operational problems requires continual vigilance on the part of leadership in a team-based organization.

Reteaming

Another issue surfaces when there is a need to reform teams or to intervene when a team is dysfunctional. Once teams form, they tend to want to remain as

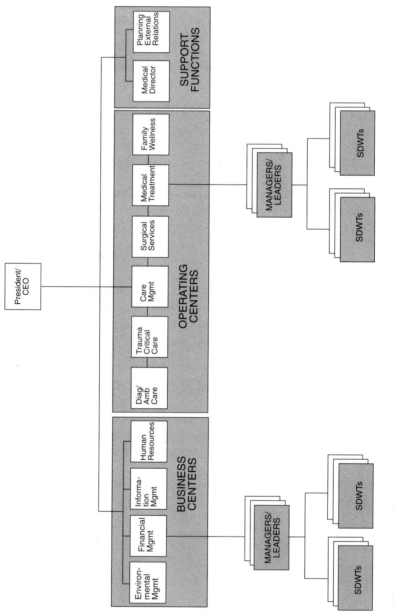

Notes: Mgmt, management; Diag, diagnostic; Amb, ambulatory; SDWTs, self-directed work teams.

Figure 18–5 Organizational Chart—Lakeland Regional Medical Center

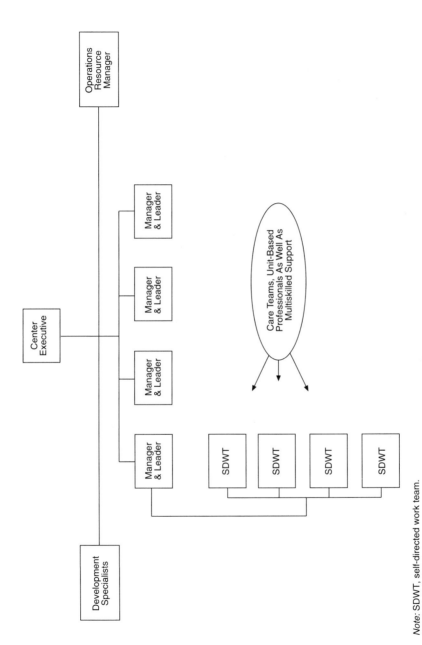

Note: SDWT, self-directed work team.

Figure 18–6 Organizational Structure of a Business Center

teams. This tendency is in opposition to the philosophy of continual improvement. In some cases, teams are no longer appropriate, or the original design is not as effective as anticipated, and reteaming is necessary. An early example at LRMC was the original decision to pair caregivers. These caregivers formed extremely close partnerships but provided care on only one shift. When the need to enlarge the team to include caregivers across all shifts was identified, it was a struggle for these partnerships to become part of the larger team.

MOVING BEYOND PATIENT CARE TEAMS

Implementation of a team-based structure proceeds differently in every organization. In some instances, teams may be implemented throughout the organization, not just in the patient care units. At LRMC, the team-based structure began with patient care teams. Soon, it was obvious that this structure left out the support staff and the focused professionals (e.g., pharmacist, laboratory technician, social worker, and physical therapist) on the unit. A parallel structure has been developed, and these employees have since begun the process of team formation. In addition, we have used the team process to implement leadership and project teams within the organization. Figure 18–5 shows the current organizational chart. Figure 18–6 depicts the structure of a business center. Both structures are based on self-directed work teams functioning as the structural component of the centers.

CONCLUSION

The implementation of team-based patient care through reengineering has improved the quality of patient care significantly at LRMC. In addition, staff and physician satisfaction is high. The process continues to unfold, with new lessons learned daily. The journey has been eventful. The experiences of the past years will be useful, as the remainder of the organization is reengineered.

REFERENCES

1. Watson PM, Shortridge DL, Jr, Jones DT, Rees RT, Stephens JT. Operational restructuring: A patient-focused approach. *Nurs Adm Quart.* 1991;16: (45–52).
2. Katzenbach JR, Smith DK. *The Wisdom of Teams: Creating the High-Performance Organization.* Boston: Harvard Business School Press; 1993.
3. Wellins RS, Byham WC, Wilson JM. *Empowered Teams: Creating Self-Directed Work Groups That Improve Quality, Productivity, and Participation.* San Francisco: Jossey-Bass; 1991.
4. Neuhauser P. *Tribal Warfare in Organizations.* Cambridge, MA: Ballinger; 1988.

■ 19 ■

Advancing the Continuum of Care: The Lutheran General HealthSystem Experience

Stephen L. Ummel, MA
Julie W. Schaffner, MSN, RN
Bruce D. Smith, MBA
Patti Ludwig-Beymer, PhD, RN, CTN

This is the story of transforming a vertical system, begun in the 1980s, into a continuum of care for a different time and a different consumer under a new set of rules. Lutheran General HealthSystem (LGHS), in Park Ridge, Illinois, is an instructive model of a vertical health system consciously transforming itself into a continuum of care. Seamless networks are now seen as an ultimate business model for effectively linking the delivery and financing of health care across a continuum, within which all providers are aligned under a common set of incentives, to manage care in a highly cost-effective fashion. Such a model is attracting national acclaim for both reducing costs and improving care. The experiences described here often occurred in the face of staff indifference and internal competition with other priorities.

LAYING THE GROUNDWORK FOR A CONTINUUM OF CARE

LGHS was an industry pioneer in the 1980s with system development through corporate reorganization and diversification. Like other larger systems at the time, LGHS diversified its core business to replace the anticipated demise of acute care hospitals. Unlike most hospitals, however, Lutheran General took a highly vertical route with a physician-hospital organization (PHO), a medical group, and managed care development.

LGHS began its seamless network development in 1990 with some organizational challenges and risks. Its national health focus, largely an expression of mission, was a distraction. It also contradicted the popular notion that health care is a local phenomenon. Furthermore, inherent complexities of Lutheran General's polycorporate organization—a confederation of quasi-independent subsidiaries with redundant governing bodies and management functions—were the antithesis of "integrated" and "seamless." LGHS also experienced, as many systems still do today, a tension between the flagship hospital stakeholders and new system leaders. In addition, LGHS welcomed a new chief executive officer (CEO) in late 1989 and experienced the normal increase in staff apprehension about leadership style and vision.

Since 1990, LGHS has been aggressively parlaying its strong corporate culture, long-standing vertical structure, and sophisticated physician/managed care infrastructure into a seamless network or continuum of care. Seven leading-edge breakthroughs have been realized, allowing LGHS to transform into a continuum of care:

1. vision
2. continuous quality improvement
3. internal integration
4. organizational reengineering and identity
5. information systems
6. physician alignment and leadership
7. managed care

Vision

A key bridge between the 1980s and 1990s, between succeeding CEOs and the move from a system to a seamless network, was the development of a new vision. Adopted in late 1990, its primary thrust was broad stakeholder ownership and conversion of a loose national health enterprise into a continuum of care for Chicagoland. Fortunately, the system's work was facilitated by a 93-year history with multiple continuum-like resources:

- a 149-person multispecialty medical group
- a 7-year-old health plan (a PHO) with exploding care management know-how
- primary care physician leadership and size
- long-standing primary care medical education programs
- over 70 Chicagoland sites and virtually all levels of care
- a large cost-effective suburban teaching hospital
- a reputation for quality and innovation

Continuous Quality Improvement

With a new vision, the transformation process at LGHS unfolded under the new CEO, who personally sponsored continuous quality improvement (CQI) as the hospital's central operating philosophy. Among health care systems, LGHS was an early adopter of the continuous quality improvement philosophy. Beginning in 1989, key LGHS executives, physicians, and associates began CQI training by immersing themselves in a four-day conference sponsored by the Harvard Community Health Plan. LGHS quickly embraced the Deming theory of quality management as the one best suited to its values and, more important, one necessitating a complete cultural transformation. Management dismissed the option of creating a hybrid quality management approach, because it felt that such an action would only protect the old rules and slow the process of change.

In place for five years, CQI has facilitated the expected level and pace of change. Its most welcomed impact, however, has been the gradual conversion of LGHS associates from their bent toward professional identity and work site attachment to broader system thinking. The aim of LGHS as a whole is beginning to supplant the traditional obsession of only that subsystem with which associates are connected. Furthermore, CQI has redirected the organization's physician culture from a purely hospital focus to a system vision and connection. Early in the transformation, physicians were attracted to and productive within the CQI framework, given its scientific approach, use of data, and newfound sense of empowerment to finally improve dysfunctional operating systems of which the physicians had long been so critical.

CQI has given LGHS a more unified focus and a noticeable self-confidence to routinely collaborate to reach the aim. CQI emphasizes an interdisciplinary team approach to problem solving, and such an approach was enthusiastically embraced at LGHS. The commitment to interdisciplinary teams has provided a strong foundation for teamwork to implement a continuum of care, which calls for reengineering rather than improving health care. Quite apparently, most if not all of the institution's other integration breakthroughs would have either failed or been suboptimized had it not been for the ever-increasing penetration of CQI.

Internal Integration

LGHS administrators knew in the period of early transformation planning that cultural and clinical results would follow other simpler integration measures. To generate some early successes, the system launched a two-year process of internal governance and management integration. Since it implicated the board and senior management so symbolically, this action sent a message of intent as to the larger system transformation ahead. Equally compelling was the goal of senior management to earn credibility from skeptical physician and hospital stakeholders.

In late 1989, to coincide with the appointment of the new system CEO, LGHS administrators took it upon themselves to collapse a vast network of separate boards into one system board. Board committees were similarly consolidated and focused on a new agenda for the 1990s. By 1991, LGHS management began reengineering a legion of separate quasi-independent subsidiaries with their own corporate cultures and strategic directions into a totally integrated network with one management team, consolidated corporate functions, one vision and mission, and one set of core values.

As a first phase of any network transformation plan, it is vital for health systems to erase the complexities of a first-generation organization—vestiges of rampant corporate diversification in the 1980s. Quite simply, it is unrealistic to ask clinicians and hospital leaders to do what corporate and system leaders are unwilling to address in the form of organizational renewal.

Finally, LGHS came to grips with the increasing difficulty of managing national health businesses in addictions and senior services while striving to better serve the Chicagoland health market. Starting in mid-1993, LGHS undertook the admittedly painful process of divesting all of the out-of-state assets to local institutions and strategic partners.

Organizational Reengineering and Identity

One of the least cited dimensions of seamless network development is organizational reengineering. It is not equivalent to reorganization or restructuring, both of which are typically occasioned by financial recovery plans. Organizational reengineering, at least at LGHS, was an open, creative effort at further integration by simplification and alteration. In June 1993, this reengineering took LGHS from a traditional hierarchical organization to a structure that could be represented by just six connected circles (see Figure 19–1). Highly CQI-oriented, the new contemporary structure has eliminated or lowered organizational barriers, achieving change through teamwork. It has focused and simplified the system organization in much the same way that CQI empowers staff at the working level.

The groundwork for the structural reengineering began with a corporate identity program in 1992–1993. Faced with dissimilar and often confusing subsidiary names, marks, and other corporate identifiers—still another byproduct of the 1980s corporate diversification—LGHS sought to totally overhaul and unify its identity. The goal was to create a clear, consistent image in marks, logos, and nomenclature, in everything written and spoken about the system, its products and services.

Information Systems

Leadership recognized in 1990 that information technology would play an indispensable role as a major integrator of system operation and newly re-

Hospital & Acute Care

Continuum Support

Office of the President
Foundation
Ethics
Mission/Church Rel.
Design Team/ IS
Research

Managed Care & Networking

Primary & Ambulatory Care

Quality & Care Management

Notes: Rel., relations; IS, Information Systems.

Figure 19–1 Organizational Structure. *Source:* Courtesy of Lutheran General HealthSystem, Park Ridge, Illinois.

engineered processes. At the time, the hospital's information system consisted of a large mainframe computer operated largely for the benefit of Lutheran General Hospital. To transform LGHS from a system to a Chicagoland continuum would require a major infusion of capital and leadership into new computer architecture. To tightly link network development with information technology, the division of information systems was realigned, from system finance to the system CEO. In addition, a new Information Technology Advisory Committee, comprised of system-wide leaders, was appointed and chartered. It was assigned to reposition information systems as a key resource to and integrative agent for the planned network transformation.

In 1991, a five-year strategic information systems development plan was approved. It detailed an aggressive plan for investing over $20 million to implement a Chicagoland-wide area computer network. Still in process, this network will link all of the organization's more than 70 sites of care in Chicagoland and other strategic partners, including physicians and payers. Already, nearly 500 LGHS physicians are tied into its Physician Information Network, one of the many nodes on the larger network. Ultimately, under open-system architecture, the network will effectively integrate all of LGHS' clinical, financial, and administrative data into a real-time computer system. See Chapter 21 for a further discussion of reengineering information systems.

Physician Alignment and Leadership

LGHS has always counted medicine as one of its principle assets. The physician culture at LGHS is comparatively advanced in both structure and alignment with the system. The foremost medical challenge to the hospital's leadership at the outset of this transformation was persuading and motivating its physicians to further align themselves with the system. A schism had inevitably emerged in the 1980s because of too few common interests. Hospital physicians felt the system's national business agenda was inconsistent with the local one. The complex polycorporate structure at LGHS also precluded necessary management-physician synergies.

LGHS has gradually but tenaciously begun to optimize its physician resources through ten strategies:

1. a new vision emphasizing physician partnering
2. joint physician and manager learning on and off campus
3. involvement of physicians in CQI through direct teaching, internal consultation, and practice as team leaders and members
4. increased number and proportion of physicians in governance
5. increased number and proportion of physicians in full-time, salaried senior management roles
6. increased involvement of both group- and community-based physicians in major system projects and strategic initiatives
7. improved two-way communication practices
8. access to state-of-the-art information technology
9. strengthening of the Lutheran General Health Plan (PHO)
10. expansion of the hospital-based medical group

LGHS sees its large and growing multispecialty medical group, formed in 1980 with 43 teaching physicians, as a major resource for network positioning and long-term success. Since 1990, the Lutheran General Medical Group has grown from 149 to 223 physicians, with 40 percent in primary care disciplines. Its sites of care now number 26. Moreover, it has been more fully integrated into LGHS in terms of information systems, quality and care management, management support, and strategic direction. The medical group continues to supply an inordinate amount of LGHS leaders, CQI champions, and Lutheran General Health Plan medical directors.

The "tension" that universally prevails between group-practice and community-based physicians has been contained at LGHS by commingling them in its PHO. With 530 physicians in the Independent Practice Association, 223 of whom are aligned with the medical group, the PHO is demonstrating that both group and community medical practice styles can be aligned in a common managed care contracting unit. It is important to note, however, that despite a conscious effort to foster a pluralistic medical environment, unfulfilled expectations of community-based physicians persist.

Managed Care

Managed care is central to the organization's network operations and ultimate performance. LGHS entered the retail side of managed care in 1980 with the creation of Parkside Health Management Corporation. Now named HEALTH DIRECT, Inc., and operated as a 50/50 joint venture with EHS Health Care, HEALTH DIRECT, Inc., is a full-service managed care company doing business directly with Chicagoland employers. Its preferred provider organization network serves more than 240,000 people. New health maintenance organization (HMO) and point of service products are actively enrolling members. Co-owned by two large Chicagoland health systems, the network includes over 35 hospitals and 4,000 physicians. LGHS' management has acquired invaluable knowledge and technologies from HEALTH DIRECT, Inc., to apply internally to the Lutheran General Health Plan.

The Lutheran General Health Plan, created in 1983 as one of the country's first PHOs, is LGHS' wholesale managed care enterprise. Under the medical leadership of primary care physicians, it serves approximately 44,000 people through 5 major HMO and 14 PPO contracts. While the Independent Practice Association is largely capitated, the practices of individual primary care physicians and some specialists are subcapitated. Accordingly, there are sophisticated practices with credentialing, care and utilization management, physician office audits, and clinical guideline development.

LGHS and its health plan have become further aligned over the past few years by co-appointing a new senior managed care executive as both president of the health plan and chief managed care officer of the system. Strategic business planning is also being integrated along with information systems, quality and care management, and other core functions. In retrospect, what has ensured the organization's success in managed care is having only one fully integrated contracting unit embracing all system facilities, 223 group physicians, and 307 community physicians. This unified structure has ensured leverage with buyers and insurers.

PLANNING FOR A CONTINUUM OF CARE

The ultimate expression of reengineering a vertical system into a continuum of care is fully integrating its multiple levels and sites of care into a seamless network. LGHS administrators believe a continuum of care, properly designed and operated, will soon become the "health product of the future." As such, it will replace the full-service hospital. A local continuum has the following characteristics:

- replaces a fragmented delivery system
- reduces cost, clinical overuse, and waste
- enhances quality of care and service
- stimulates reengineering of clinical processes
- activates health care reform
- aligns physicians and other partners

It is a formidable undertaking. LGHS is unaware of a single, authentic continuum of care that exists in the United States today—one that embraces all the classical levels of care and is totally integrated from the customers' point of view. A continuum was envisioned by LGHS as early as 1990 and were featured prominently in its new vision. However, its research and development were deferred for two years to allow CQI to penetrate the culture and to coincide with the planned completion of management and clinical integration across the system.

In 1992, a task force of senior executives was named to develop a continuum of care. Responsibility for operations and limited meeting times forced the realization that additional resources must be devoted to the task of planning and implementing a continuum. The sheer complexity and enormity of integrating 70 quasi-independent sites of care into a continuum prompted senior management in January 1993 to consider a bold vehicle for design and project management. Consequently, a continuum of care design team of 15 associates, comprised of 4 physicians, 2 nurses, and 9 additional executives, managers, and professionals was appointed. The design team leader, the vice-president of information systems, had a voice in team selection but did not select members independently. Instead, each team member was selected by the task force on the basis of predetermined criteria that included CQI literacy, strong content knowledge, ability to be a team player, creativity, and respect throughout the system.

It was a curious and delicate process to ask some of Lutheran General's most talented and secure associates to drop everything they were doing to work on something as abstract and risky as a continuum. Of note, each design team candidate accepted the invitation. Over the ensuing 12-month period, they first became a bonded team and then successfully discharged their assignment of designing and recommending a massive implementation approach for the continuum.

The team spent 20 hours in initial team formation, including an 8-hour outdoor team building experience provided by the POWER Program, a part of LGHS. These team experiences helped members to shed their individual corporate and department identities and begin, together as one voice, to plan organizational transformation.

In collaboration with many other groups across the system, the design team set about planning a methodology to implement a continuum of care. The team recognized the enormity of their task and realized that a radical redesign[1] of LGHS was required. While the team used CQI tools, they realized that their task was to reengineer the organization rather than merely improve the processes.

The first task was to embrace an overall aim or organizational direction. The original continuum task force had developed a strong aim that was based on the work of Connie Evashwick.[2] The design team examined that aim and revised it slightly to the aim as stated in Exhibit 19–1.

As the design team began to meet with groups of system associates, it became obvious that this lofty and worthy aim was difficult to communicate. For many, it was too abstract and theoretical to have meaning in their daily work. Thus, the design team clarified key aspects of the aim, as listed in Exhibit 19–2. Even with the clarifications, however, the aim needed additional description to make it meaningful. The design team identified six areas integral to the accomplishment of a continuum of care:

1. care management
2. finance
3. information systems
4. administrative structure
5. physicians
6. sites and services

Care management, finance, information systems, and administrative structure were identified as key structures for integrating care. Physicians and sites and services were viewed as essential aspects of planning the continuum.

To assist in describing the end state, the design team identified specific design characteristics. The team used the six key areas above as a framework to help in

Exhibit 19–1 Aim of the Continuum

A customer-oriented seamless system, composed of services and integrating mechanisms, that guides and tracks individuals over time through a comprehensive network of health, medical, and social services, spanning all levels and sites of care, improving the health status of target populations.

Source: Courtesy of Lutheran General HealthSystem, Park Ridge, Illinois.

Exhibit 19–2 Clarification of the Aim

Aim—CHICAGOLAND CONTINUUM OF CARE

A customer-oriented seamless system, composed of services and integrating mechanisms, that guides and tracks individuals over time through a comprehensive network of health, medical, and social services, spanning all levels and sites of care, improving the health status of target populations.

Clarification

Being **"customer oriented"** means knowing who our customers are, finding out what they expect, putting them first, and exceeding their needs and expectations.

"Seamless" refers to integration so that individuals do not inadvertently leave the continuum for services. For example, a system that is seamless may have one registration, one common information set that flows with the individual, and one care plan that extends across sites and episodes.

A **"system"** is a network of interdependent components that work together to accomplish a common aim: improved health status for the people we serve.

"Integrating mechanisms" are structures and processes that assist in care for individuals over time and place. They may include care management, administrative structure, information systems, and finance.

A **"comprehensive network"** implies that the individual will have access to the type of services needed. While LGHS will not necessarily offer all types of care, we will link with other health care and social service agencies to ensure that individuals receive the care they need.

Our focus on **"improving health status"** means that while continuing to care for the ill, we will also increase our focus on health promotion and disease prevention. This will involve collaborating with many agencies in the community, such as schools and churches.

"Target populations" are groups of individuals served by the system on the basis of the continuum's ability and/or responsibility to meet their health needs. The groups may be defined by geography, disease, ethnicity, age, employer, congregation, or enrollment in health plans.

Source: Courtesy of Lutheran General HealthSystem, Park Ridge, Illinois.

the development of these specific design characteristics. A total of 61 design characteristics were identified. These characteristics specified what the continuum would look like when it was in place.

At each step in this process, the work of the design team was shared with the original task force and with other groups throughout the system. The design team established a communication subgroup. An elaborate communication plan was put in place, using existing meetings and internal publications. Early in the project, the team recognized the necessity of communicating the need for the radical reengineered process being proposed. To vividly describe the need for change, a case study was used, first in slide form and then as a videotape. The case study sends a strong message to associates during this time of radical system change.

As part of the communication plan, team members served as liaisons to specific standing meetings, making numerous presentations to a variety of groups. When necessary, meetings were held to supplement content presented at standing meetings. For example, characteristics related to physicians were shared with six physician reactor panels. Over 60 physicians attended these meetings and provided their perspective on what the continuum should look like in the future. On the basis of input from within and outside the system, the design team revised and clarified the design characteristics.

Even with the aim, clarification, and design characteristics identified, the design team was left with the question, "What needs to be done to make the continuum of care happen?" To answer the question, the design team considered the overall aim and each design characteristic and identified major tasks that needed to be accomplished to reach the aim. As tasks were identified, they were subjected to three tests:

1. Could the task be done?
2. If the task were done, would the design characteristics be in place?
3. Was there another way to accomplish the aim?

With this framework, the design team identified key tasks—critical success factors—that were required to ensure the creation of a continuum of care. The critical success factors were revised and refined on the basis of input from the task force and other groups and individuals. Recognizing that the critical success factors would not be accomplished through routine operational departments, the design team recommended the formation of a nonhierarchical, interdisciplinary team composed of associates, physicians, and community partners to address each factor (Exhibit 19–3). Each team would be responsible for aligning existing resources related to their charge and authorizing additional implementation teams as necessary.

In addition, the plans called for a continuum council to implement the continuum of care. The council, composed of the leader of each continuum team, as

Exhibit 19–3 Continuum Teams and Their Critical Success Factors

Team	Purpose
Strategy and Sponsorship—	To expand the LGHS network and implement a continuum of care
Target Populations—	To identify, develop, and maintain relationships with continuum target populations
Providers and Facilities—	To determine the adequate number and appropriate mix of providers, facilities, and sites to achieve that mix
Service Linkages—	To establish and maintain a network of services linked by integrating mechanisms
Promotion and Prevention—	To implement a plan for target populations that assesses needs and base line health status and employees health promotion and disease prevention strategies
Care Management—	To establish and use a system of care management over time and across appropriate levels, sites, and providers
Internal Incentives—	To develop and use internal incentives that encourage alignment and optimize system performance
Physician Alignment—	To link physician compensation to the success of the continuum
Information Systems—	To implement an aligned and coordinated information system plan
Risk/Capitation—	To manage health care services under systems of risk/capitation
LGHS Performance—	To develop and use measures of system performance

Source: Courtesy of Lutheran General HealthSystem, Park Ridge, Illinois.

well as several additional senior executives, was to be led by the chief operating officer of the system. The continuum of care and the organizational structure are presented in Figure 19–2. The council's charge included the following responsibilities:

- provide overall guidance and direction to continuum teams
- approve continuum team implementation plans
- monitor progress of continuum teams
- coordinate, align, and integrate continuum team efforts and results
- identify and resolve issues that are barriers to continuum implementation
- authorize resources to support continuum teams
- share knowledge, experience, successes, and learning regarding continuum of care

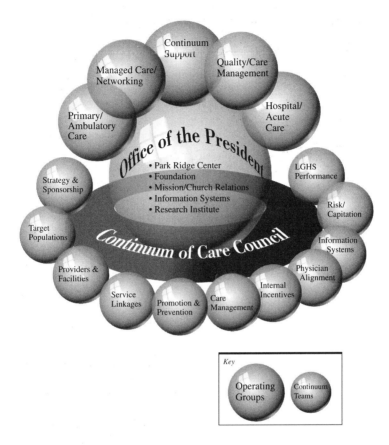

Figure 19–2 Organizational Structure with Continuum Teams. *Source:* Courtesy of Lutheran General HealthSystem, Park Ridge, Illinois.

Changes were also planned for the work of the design team. The design team transitioned from 15 part-time individuals to 5 full-time and 5 part-time individuals. Two design team members left LGHS to assume vice-president positions elsewhere; three were selected as leaders for individual continuum teams. The remaining design team members were placed on a continuum team to assist team leaders in establishing the teams, particularly through start up. They were to provide content knowledge and project management to each team. In addition, they were to function as an integrating mechanism between teams, ensure continued alignment of the teams, and maintain the overall integrity of the continuum of care design.

IMPLEMENTING A CONTINUUM OF CARE

After the team structure was endorsed by the task force and executive council, the task force was disbanded. The executive council was faced with selecting team membership. The council decided to name a leader for each team and then bring all leaders together as the continuum council, with that body selecting team membership. Criteria for selecting team leaders were established by the executive council. Criteria included the following qualifications:

- demonstrated ability to lead and manage change
- demonstrated leadership skills
- ability to oversee all aspects of the process
- ability to implement the critical success factor plan
- knowledge of the critical success factor plan
- commitment to Chicago continuum of care
- training as CQI team leader
- demonstrated "systems" thinking

Executive council members then used brainstorming to identify possible team leaders. Following structured discussion, the members reached consensus on the individual who best met the criteria. That individual was then offered the opportunity to lead a team. As with the creation of the design team, all those who were approached agreed to serve in the leader role. Selection of leaders for the ten teams took approximately eight hours. The executive council, headed by the president and CEO, agreed to function as the strategy and sponsorship continuum team.

Roles and responsibilities of the team leader included sponsorship for the initiative, team facilitation, ensuring implementation of the critical success factor, and coordination and communication with other teams and the continuum council. Team leaders are "champions" of the continuum of care.

The first task of the continuum team was to select the membership of each continuum subteam. In selecting members, the council used a generic set of overall criteria, including the following:

- demonstrated ability to lead and manage change
- knowledge of critical success factor content
- ability to implement critical success factor and design characteristics
- ability to coordinate resources as necessary
- demonstrated leadership ability
- experience in working on a team

- basic working knowledge of CQI
- demonstrated "systems" thinking

A crucial restriction was that individuals could only participate on one team. To avoid limiting the selection to a relatively small number of people who usually served on teams, this approach allowed talented associates from throughout the system to be considered and selected. In addition, specific criteria were established for each team. Brainstorming was used to identify names that met the criteria. "Multivoting" was then utilized to select individuals for each team from throughout the system. Council members were initially skeptical of the process. After the first team was selected, however, the general consensus was that the team had the potential to be effective. Thus, the council grew comfortable with the process. The process of selecting members of the care management continuum team is presented in Exhibit 19–4, to provide an example of the selection process.

After all team members had been identified, the council reviewed all teams. In several cases, individuals had been placed on multiple teams. The council used structured discussion and then resolved the issues of duplication by consensus. Identifying team members took approximately 16 hours of council meeting time. Responsibilities for team members included the following:

- achieving a common understanding of the critical success factors
- reviewing resources and current efforts within the system
- developing a work plan for achievement of critical success factors
- obtaining approval for team work plan from the continuum council
- identifying needed resources for implementing the work plan
- reporting progress to the continuum council
- implementing the work plan
- coordinating and communicating inter-team issues
- establishing implementation teams and appointing a team leader
- authorizing necessary resources for implementation teams
- approving implementation team plans
- monitoring the progress of implementation teams

Team membership was communicated in writing to LGHS associates and their immediate supervisors. Of the 116 associates who were asked to participate, only one individual declined. Membership was also extended to two corporate partners: Abbott Laboratories and Johnson & Johnson. In addition, several community members, including a dentist and a faculty member from a nearby university, were asked to participate. A special "kickoff" breakfast was held to launch the

Exhibit 19–4 Care Management Selection Example

The Care Management Continuum Team is responsible for ensuring that LGHS establishes and uses a system of care management over time and across appropriate levels, sites, and providers. When care management is defined and in place, care will be managed to provide "best practice" to all individuals—the right care at the right time using the appropriate resource. Individuals will become members of the LGHS family when they first interact with the system, whether that encounter takes place in the doctor's office, an adult day health care program, the hospital, or a congregationally-based health promotion activity. Individuals will not be frustrated by answering the same questions as they move to additional providers at different sites.

As with the selection of team members for all continuum teams, selection of members for the care management continuum team began by reviewing the general selection criteria. In addition, team-specific criteria were identified. For the care management team, all team members were expected to have demonstrated their commitment to the philosophy of care management. Team composition was expected to include members with the following qualifications:

1. clinical department chairperson(s)
2. primary care physician
3. managed care experience
4. registered nurse with care/case management experience at the administrative level
5. accomplishments in improving processes
6. non-acute care experience
7. operations experience
8. physicians from diverse specialties
9. link between acute care and outpatient and community settings (e.g., social service and allied health services)
10. behavioral health background
11. medical staff officer

A talented group of individuals was selected, based on the two sets of criteria, with some team members meeting multiple criteria. As part of their start up, all currently operating initiatives, task forces, and committees related to care management were profiled, and many of these will become implementation teams. All existing efforts will be under the umbrella of the continuum of care structure.

Additionally, newly formed implementation teams will be necessary. For example, an implementation team may be charged with operationalizing the Agency on Policy Research guidelines for clinical practice improvement.

implementation phase. Continuum team formation was announced, with all team members introduced to consistent information in a festive atmosphere.

Team members were very enthusiastic about their selection. Some associates who had not been selected were disappointed, prompting implementation of a special communication plan to assure all associates of the role they would play in implementing the continuum of care.

During the start up of the continuum council and continuum teams, team formation and intensive learning occurred. Start up included learning modules and an outdoor team building and training experience. It was believed that the front-end work was critical to the team-building process for new groups who had not previously worked together.

Because many group members have completed a basic level of CQI training, CQI tools, such as the seven-step meeting process, are utilized and a meeting record is maintained. Ground rules have been established and used by the team. Facilitation is provided by a design team member, a member of the CQI staff, or by self-facilitation. An early and essential task for the continuum teams has been identifying and aligning resources devoted to the team's critical task. As seen in Figure 19–3, many resources exist, but they need to be aligned for the most effective outcome. In addition, continuum teams will authorize additional resources when necessary to accomplish their purpose.

EVALUATION

The difficulties encountered in changing organizations have been discussed at length in the business literature. Yet this remains a perplexing issue to organizations as they struggle to adjust to new market requirements in order to continue to prosper or even to survive.

The current line organization renders the day-to-day service and operational activities that provide care for the patients and customers. By its very nature, the line organization strives for conformity, consistency, and stability. Although changes are made to improve the performance, these changes are usually very incremental and safe. They rarely are of a significant magnitude. The line organization staff certainly are not capable of responding to the strong market changes that are currently occurring in health care delivery.

The concept of the design team was to create a group outside the line organization that could put together a process to create the exponential change required to respond to the new market demands. Learning from past experiences, LGHS realized that expecting line managers to plan and accomplish organizational reengineering in addition to their regular workload would not work. The day-to-day work would consume the time and mental capacity of the members, leaving little energy for creative design of change. Additionally, the organization had learned that outside consultants can compose excellent plans but have great difficulty getting the staff to buy in or adopt the recommendations.

The design team was an interdisciplinary team of individuals who were a part of the organization. In addition, the design process utilized was inclusive, with

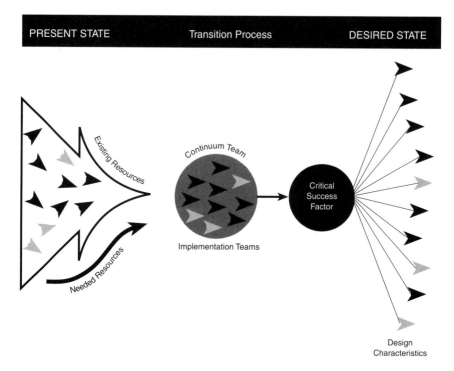

Figure 19–3 Alignment Diagram. *Source:* Courtesy of Lutheran General HealthSystem, Park Ridge, Illinois.

input coming from many members of the organization itself. Thus, use of an internal design team had three advantages:

1. The team was comprised of members of the organization, many of whom had been with the organization for many years.
2. The members were given the time necessary to invest in an effort of this magnitude.
3. The team was selected and supported by the task force, which was composed of executive leadership of the organization.

Organizationally, the design team concept was very attractive. First, it initially removed from the executive group the pressure to come up with a specific plan for the continuum. It was convenient to say, "The design team is working on it." Second, the design team actually started producing some output that appeared to have value and demonstrated some progress, reinforcing the feeling that this was a good idea.

This honeymoon continued until the first checkpoint occurred, approximately five months into the project. The design team had established specific deliverables for the first project checkpoint. This was done to give the team purpose, direction, and a specific target to shoot for. It also provided a strong incentive to produce valid output to direct change rather than merely state concepts and ideas. The deliverables consisted of the aim, design, characteristics, critical success factors, and proposed implementation and communication plans. These elements have been described earlier in the chapter.

At this first checkpoint, the task force realized that the design team was advocating a specific strategy that would require major changes in the way things were being done. Prior to this point, the preliminary output of the design team had been enthusiastically embraced. When the magnitude of change was acknowledged, the reaction became more cautious, representing the initial manifestation of resistance. Progress slowed as the task force engaged in word-smithing and conceptual debate. For the most part, the core design stood up very well to the extended scrutiny.

The time between the first and second checkpoints was spent in communicating the design to organizational groups, receiving input and feedback, and incorporating more ideas into the refinement process. The products for the second checkpoint, four months later, were clearer and more specific and had better definition. The presentation format, which incorporated tangible examples, became more effective as a communication tool. The design team responded to the feedback from the organization, resulting in a much better product. However, the core design remained intact. At this juncture, there was moderate resistance from the line management leadership, but the process continued, although at a slower pace than was recommended.

The next potential barrier was the appointment of teams and team leaders to implement the design. The process to overcome this barrier was to establish an organized methodology for the executive council and continuum council to follow when selecting individuals for each of the teams, as described earlier in this chapter.

Currently the 11 teams are completing their planned start up, training, and learning phase. Each team experience has been unique. Barriers encountered, however, have been minor rather than major. There are the constant questions of how the continuum teams fit with the current organizational structure and how to find the time for implementation given the current heavy workload.

Many of the perceived barriers are created or imposed by the teams themselves. For example, the teams are questioning their charter and are trying to define their scope of responsibility and authority. Teams are exhibiting much concern over the boundaries of their activities. These perceived barriers can be resolved within the team framework itself, as the teams begin to view themselves as empowered to make decisions and move the process forward. The teams are beginning to show some signs of maturing to this point, where they will consider resolving rather than raising these issues. The team efforts will then begin to move forward rapidly. A series of checkpoints in the coming months provides the teams with both targets and incentives to produce activities and results that will further advance the development of a continuum of care.

The key question for the strategy and sponsorship team is the focus for the organization. The design team has long stressed the importance of one system aim that everyone strives to achieve. Organizations trying to do too much in too many areas tend to fail. There is a need to set a specific aim and focus on making it happen. Accomplishing an aim requires constant attention and is critical to eventual success.

The extensive communication plan developed by the design team has been well received. An employee survey completed in March 1994 showed that a large number of staff were aware and knowledgeable about the continuum and that even more felt it would improve the quality of care available (Exhibit 19–5). Of the 5,491 employees at LGHS identified as potential respondents, 4,091 (75 percent) completed the survey. These results suggest that the continuum is taking hold and being internalized by the organization. The continuum as a reengineered LGHS is establishing a momentum at all levels that will hasten its implementation.

A major caution comes from Stephen Shortell, who has done an extensive study on health care systems and continuity of care.[3] We are at a critical stage, as the design team, which has the passion for the vision, passes the continuum reengineering project to many other associates for implementation. It is safe to assume that the staff may not initially have the same level of passion. Leadership and care must be exercised at this stage to ensure a smooth handoff, so that the process moves forward. This will remain an issue as the work cascades to additional implementation and work groups.

Health care in the United States is undergoing a systemic restructuring. Private sector capitation is one of the driving forces. Health policy will only hasten that process. Such basic restructuring has already affected other business segments in the United States and elsewhere in the world. When such a paradigm shifts, everyone goes back to zero. Not surprisingly, then, what worked for management in the past may not work as a resource or strategy under a new set of rules.

To thrive within capitation and to fulfill new social contracts with communities, health providers are uniting themselves to improve handoffs, minimize inappropriate utilization, reduce operating costs, and demonstrate quality. Integrating what are now highly independent providers will yield new networks capable of accepting and managing risk. Aside from aligning provider incentives for the first time in history, they create a large and diverse enterprise to reengineer the total health care process and better serve the entire local health market, thus creating

Exhibit 19–5 Employee Survey on Continuum of Care

Item	Percentage of Employees Agreeing or Strongly Agreeing with Statement
1. Developing a continuum of care will improve our services and benefit the community	94%
2. I understand the importance of developing a seamless continuum of care	91%
3. I am aware of LGHS' strategy to develop a continuum of care	89%

an altogether new health care system more in keeping with society's needs today. LGHS has envisioned this paradigm shift and has committed itself to a full corporate transformation through reengineering. Time will judge whether or not it has altered its business enough to be valued by an increasingly discriminating health care consumer.

REFERENCES

1. Hammer M, Champy J. *Reengineering the Corporation: Manifesto for Business Revolution.* New York: HarperBusiness; 1993.

2. Evashwick CJ. Definition of the continuum of care. In: Evashwick CJ, Weiss LJ. *Managing the Continuum of Care.* Gaithersburg, MD: Aspen Publishers, Inc; 1987:23–43.

3. Shortell SM, Gillies RR, Anderson DA, Mitchell JB, Morgan KL. Creating delivery systems: The barriers and facilitators. *Hosp Health Service Adm.* 1993;38(4):447–466.

■ 20 ■

Business Process Reengineering: One Health Care System's Experience

Carol A. Veihmeyer, MBA, RN, CNAA

REENGINEERING—GETTING STARTED

This case study focuses on how one health care system made the decision to reengineer itself and the process they pursued. Fairmount (a pseudonym for the real client) is a three-hospital system on the East Coast. The hospitals consist of one teaching facility with more than 500 beds and two 200-bed community hospitals. The system includes a full continuum of care, including urgent care centers, clinics, a few primary care practices, an ambulatory care center, home care services, and a long-term care facility. Although the pieces of an integrated health care delivery system are in place, the parts function independently and competitively with each other. Currently, there is very little managed care penetration, approximately 10 percent, although fixed payers (Medicare, Medicaid, and managed care) represent 40 percent of all payers. Within the state's boundaries are two other systems of equal size. One of those systems has initiated acquisitions within Fairmount's market. Additionally, Columbia/HCA (Hospital Corporation of America) owns one local market competitor and is reportedly in discussions with a closely located academic medical center. Fairmount's operating budget for fiscal year 1993 was approximately $300 million, with profits exceeding $30 million.

Obstetrics, cardiology, and orthopedics are lead product lines. Fairmount enjoys a regional, and in some cases national, reputation as a market leader. Why change this success story? The wake-up call for this organization came during payer contract negotiations. Despite years of continuous improvement efforts focused on cost and quality outcomes, Fairmount was surprised to find their pricing 30 percent above the market. Given Fairmount's current environment and industry reforms, expectations for increased managed care penetration and subsequent lower hospital utilization and lower reimbursement for hospital services as well as years of experience with continuous quality improvement, and a culture of proactively addressing market challenges, Fairmount leadership looked to California-based models for future cost-restructuring scenarios. The model assumed 50/50 profit sharing between physicians and hospitals. Given the number of beds at Fairmount, the model's projections, and the current environment, Fairmount's leadership decided to undertake cost restructuring targeted to achieve a $70 million cost reduction over five years. This target set the stage for the reengineering initiative.

What is reengineering? Hammer and Champy define reengineering as the fundamental rethinking and radical redesign of the organization and its operating systems to achieve dramatic improvements in operating effectiveness by focusing on a set of related customer-oriented business processes.[1] The reengineering methodology of Coopers & Lybrand Consulting (C&L) is BreakPoint business process reengineering (BPR).

BreakPoint is defined as the transformation in customer-perceived performance that is so marked as to produce a significant and sustained increase in market share. BreakPoint occurs when one or more of the value parameters of time, quality, cost, or service builds on or enhances the organization's capabilities, transforming them into competencies (Figure 20–1). Competencies create competitive market advantages. BreakPoint BPR seeks to radically change core business processes to achieve dramatic performance breakthroughs, while managing business risk and cultural change. BreakPoint achieves these outcomes through integration of the business process reengineering across functional boundaries while incorporating business strategy, customer value, change management, and information technology.

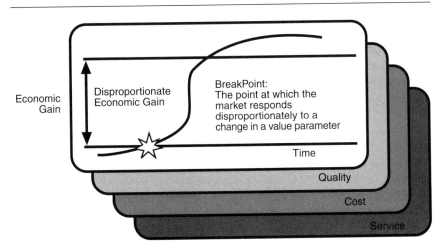

Figure 20–1 BreakPoint Definition

Why reengineer? History has taught us the following:

- Downsizing alone does not improve competitive performance.
- The return on investment in technology has been limited because the approach has been to automate existing functions.
- The work force has not been fully involved, constraining their contribution.
- Programs have been sponsored at the functional rather than the chief executive officer (CEO) level.

Organizations have attempted to change through a variety of methods (Figure 20–2). The major differences between the various change methods are the type of change required (strategic versus tactical) and the timing of results required (fast versus measured) (Figure 20–3).

The major differences between BPR and continuous quality improvement are the selection of core processes in BPR, rather than any process; the use of technology and human resource enablers; the challenging of process fundamentals; and the expectation of two to three times the level of improvement, versus 10 percent to 30 percent improvement.

The major issue facing most health care organizations is how to simultaneously reduce costs, increase productivity, and provide higher levels of service and responsiveness to customers. C&L's experience in BPR has produced the simultaneous results of 90 percent reduction in cycle time, 100 percent improvement in customer service, and 50 percent improvement in productivity, within a two-year framework. Searching for these types of results, many organizations are finding their way to reengineering as a change option.

There is much discussion in the literature regarding how radical is radical, or how much of the current state needs to be "blown up" for the approach to be considered reengineering. This consideration is of obvious importance in the health care system, because the processes of health care provider are influenced by regulations that have impact on the degree of change potential, although experience has proven resistance to change and to risk management to have greater influence.

What is radical is defined in the perceptual framework of the organization and of individuals experiencing the change. However, the radicalness of reengineering exists in the degree of change in the performance outcomes, not necessarily in the processes used to achieve those outcomes. Our experience has typically found a basic foundation of people, leadership, organizational culture, functional expertise, and/or information systems that can be recombined and redirected to achieve a competitive advantage. By nature, however, reengineering requires managers to move beyond current levels of performance by moving away from traditional ways of thinking and behaving.

	Process Improvement	Process Reengineering	Process Innovation
	Streamline Existing Process	Create New Process	
	Any Process		Strategic Process
	Enhances VA Activities and Removes Non-VA Activities		Creates New VA Activities
	Systems Modified	Systems Replaced	Systems Created
	Technology Assessed	Technology Drives	Technology Enables
	Meet Customer Expectations		Lead Customer Expectations
	Designs from Current Process		Designs from Clean Sheet of Paper
	10%–30% Improvement	30%–50% Improvement	
		3 to 5 × Return	>5 × Return
	3–6-Month Cycle	9–12-Month Cycle	2 to 3 Years To Realize Results

Note: VA, value-added

Figure 20–2 Comparison of Change Methods, Expected Results, and Timing

Nature of Change

	Strategic	Tactical
Fast	Resizing	Process Improvement (CQI)
Measured	Reengineering	Redesign

Speed of Results Desired

Figure 20–3 Comparison of Change Methods by Nature and Speed of Change

What to reengineer? BPR concentrates on a few core processes. A core process is a linked set of activities that crosses functional boundaries, addresses the needs and expectations of the marketplace, builds on the organization's capabilities, and is an inherent basis of the organization's competitive position. Core processes represent significant resource investment, are tied to the strategy of the organization, and are critical to the ability to excel in order to match or beat the competition.

Core processes vary by industry and are influenced by the particular market. Regardless of the market, however, certain core processes are common to all health care provider organizations. Figure 20–4 provides examples of health care provider core processes. Fairmount developed the following criteria for selecting core processes for evaluation:

1. strategic relevance
2. resource investment
3. importance to customers
4. cash flow impact
5. likelihood for success.

Using these criteria, Fairmount selected care and therapeutics, access, and materials management for reengineering. Information management, physician and community relations, and network development were not selected because of existing initiatives within those processes. Using these criteria or others, it is difficult to imagine any health care provider not choosing the care and therapeutic process as one to evaluate for reengineering opportunities, since all providers

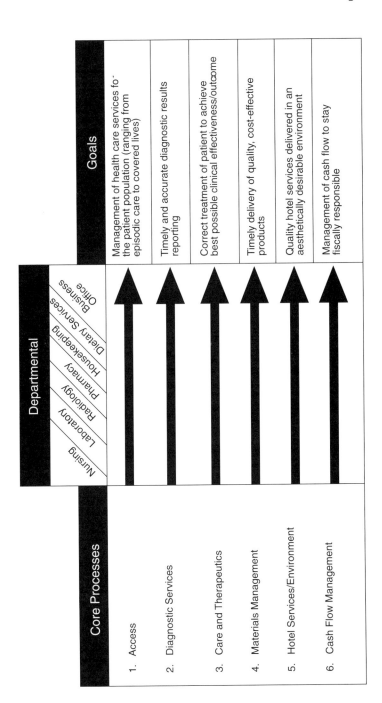

Figure 20–4 Examples of Health Care Provider Core Processes

are in the business of care delivery to patients. Many nonprovider organizations, such as pharmaceutical and insurance companies, have focused on claims or order management, materials management and billing, or financial management as processes to reengineer. Likewise, some health care providers have built on these experiences and chosen these same processes as the first to reengineer. The rationale that weighs in favor of selecting these processes is the high likelihood for success, positive cash flow impact, and developed linkages to an insurer or vendor as a key customer.

How to reengineer? Before moving into the process of reengineering, some key issues should be assessed: sponsor commitment, change management, technology enablement, and human resource enablement.

Sponsor Commitment

Sponsor commitment is the degree to which the person who allocates the resources required to make the change maintains focused commitment to the change. Typically, this person is the CEO. Unlike continuous quality improvement (CQI), a process based on grass roots involvement, BPR is a top-down process. Figure 20–5 provides an example of how various levels of the organization become involved in the BPR process. Because of the top-down nature of BPR, sponsor commitment is essential to the process. Senior-level involvement can be ensured by various means. At Fairmount, the chief operating officer led the initiative.

The steering committee included representatives from the system and each operating unit and physician leadership. The steering committee met every week

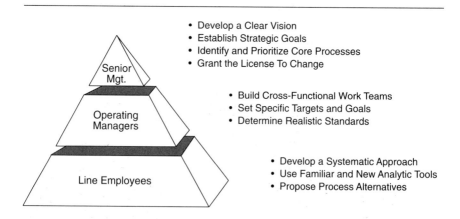

Figure 20–5 Proposed Staff Involvement in BPR Process

during the initial phase and confirmed the commitment of the system chief financial officer to one of the core process teams. Maintaining sponsor commitment needs to be an ongoing focus throughout the process.

Change Management

Change management is the method used to manage the human and technical aspects of the change process. Most change processes fail because the need to manage the human aspects of change is underestimated. The human aspects of change include everything from changing organizational culture to changing individual behaviors and attitudes. Initially, change management focuses on evaluating the organization's cultural enablers, barriers to change, and capacity for change, given prior change efforts and existing change initiatives. These issues become more focused as the change becomes more defined. The barriers must be managed in order to successfully implement and realize the anticipated results. The enablers can be built on to support the change process. The success or failure of prior change initiatives will influence the degree of change resistance. Since very few health care organizations have successfully implemented change to completion, resistance to change tends to be high. It feels like just another "solution of the week." In addition, the coordination of ongoing initiatives with the reengineering project must be managed in order to reduce the overall amount of change experienced, while both short-term and long-term realization of opportunities are supported. Eventually, the culture and the BPR work must be mutually reinforcing to succeed.

After sponsor commitment is confirmed, the change management focus should elicit sponsorship from all senior managers. In Fairmount's case, the focus became building sponsorship within the steering committee, which was an essential foundation for moving the project forward to the next level of involvement. The initial change management plan also focused on communicating to all constituencies and receiving feedback from them regarding the change process.

Technology Enablers

Traditionally, health care technology investment has been in diagnostic equipment because hospitals were reimbursed for it, physicians have requested it, and patients have defined quality by the presence of it. Although some hospitals have made investments in robotic applications and automatic teller machines in distribution functions such as pharmacy and suppliers, most hospital technology investments are limited to diagnostics and financial information systems. It is not unusual to find sophisticated systems with very manual information systems or a high degree of stand-alone functionality. What truly differentiates reengineering from other change methods is the use of technology as a "driver" of the future state and an enabler of the new process.

The use of technology as an enabler allows new organizational paradigms to be developed. Hammer and Champy[1] describe the new paradigms possible in health care through technology enablement (see Exhibit 20–1). The difference between health care technology and technology used as an enabler in other industries is that health care technology is typically a packaged software solution, and reliance on such solutions does influence process design possibilities. Thus, it is even more critical that operations and technology personnel work together throughout the BPR process. Since most of Fairmount's existing systems are financial systems, the organization had information and financial systems personnel dedicated to each core process team. In addition, prior to starting the core process evaluation, the information strategic plan was evaluated for fit with the overall strategic plan, and planned future IS initiatives were included in the visioning of the future state. The application of new technology provides new opportunities for process design. It also tends to prevent the backward slide toward current state, since the current state ceases to exist with technology enablers. It is the combination of both human and technology enablers that create the new future state behaviors. For example, cross-functional teams are enabled by training and team structures and are then rewarded by team-based compensation, but the underlying decision support system actually enables the team empowerment to happen. Without technology enablement, the human resource enablement costs become prohibitive.

Human Resource Enablers

In order to achieve the results of reengineering, the organization must achieve a lasting change in people's attitudes and behaviors. What does it take to change behaviors or attitudes? Compliance change strategies focus on changing behaviors. Commitment change strategies focus on changing attitudes. Compliance and commitment strategies involve realignment of the human aspects of change, such as training, education, compensation, organizational structure, management philosophy, decision making, communication, and performance management. Since health care is a service-based industry, the human aspects of enablement have received more attention than the technological aspects. As noted earlier, however, unless emphasis is placed on human and technological components, it is very difficult to truly change an organization to the degree necessary to achieve the results expected in reengineering (two to three times the investment).

Staff can be cross-trained and rewarded to encourage performance in expanded roles, but without computerized clinical decision support systems to enhance skills training, the degree of role expansion is limited. However, there is still

Exhibit 20–1 Technology Enablement Rules

Rule 1: *Old Rule:* Information can appear in only one place at one time.
Disruptive Technology: Shared data bases
New Rule: Information can appear simultaneously in as many places as it is needed.

Rule 2: *Old Rule:* Only experts can perform complex work.
Disruptive Technology: Expert systems
New Rule: A generalist can do the work of an expert.

Rule 3: *Old Rule:* Businesses must choose between centralization and decentralization.
Disruptive Technology: Telecommunications networks
New Rule: Businesses can simultaneously reap the benefits of centralization and decentralization.

Rule 4: *Old Rule:* Managers make all decisions.
Disruptive Technology: Decision support tools (data base access, modeling software)
New Rule: Decision making is part of everyone's job.

Rule 5: *Old Rule:* Field personnel need offices where they can receive, store, retrieve, and transmit information.
Disruptive Technology: Wireless data communication and portable computers
New Rule: Field personnel can send and receive information wherever they are.

Rule 6: *Old Rule:* The best contact with a potential buyer is personal contact.
Disruptive Technology: Interactive videodisk
New Rule: The best contact with a potential buyer is effective contact.

Rule 7: *Old Rule:* You have to find out where things are.
Disruptive Technology: Automatic identification and tracking technology
New Rule: Things tell you where they are.

Rule 8: *Old Rule:* Plans get revised periodically.
Disruptive Technology: High-performance computing
New Rule: Plans get revised instantaneously.

---

great opportunity for human resource enablement in the adoption of team-based financial compensation structures for nonmanagement personnel.

GETTING STARTED—THE OVERALL PROJECT

With the target set, Fairmount decided that consulting assistance would be necessary and hired C&L. The initiative called "improving value through design" was defined as a system-wide, long-term, customer-focused approach. The initiative sought to measurably improve Fairmount's value to its priority customers through improving customer-defined service, quality, and cost-effectiveness. To attain this goal, the focus of effort was placed on improving clinical and operational efficiencies. The initial phase of the work focused on identifying, quantifying, and prioritizing all performance improvement opportunities that could assist with meeting the $70 million target of cost reduction while improving service and enhancing clinical outcomes. In addition, because the concept for moving forward was a working partnership between C&L and Fairmount, responsibility was jointly shared between C&L and Fairmount personnel for all aspects of the work.

Since Fairmount currently had ongoing CQI efforts in all of the hospitals, ranging from redesigning nursing care, to critical path development, to improvement of the admission, discharge, and transfer processes, the fit of ongoing initiatives with new initiatives had to be sorted out. Fairmount's CQI approach had been very successful in building grass roots support for change and in building process team skills throughout the organization. The organization was proud and supportive of its CQI efforts and results. However, with a $70 million target, a different approach would be required.

The goal-setting phase was designed to identify, quantify, and prioritize all opportunities and to focus the remaining effort. The approach was organized into the following components:

- organizational effectiveness
- operational effectiveness
- clinical effectiveness
- core process evaluation
- technology evaluation
- change management

The components and their goals are detailed in Exhibit 20–2. The organizational and operational effectiveness and change management components were initiated first, with core process, technology, and clinical effectiveness elements staggered to start within two months.

GETTING STARTED—CORE PROCESS REENGINEERING

The core process evaluation started with a BPR seminar for the steering committee. The steering committee was introduced to reengineering concepts and C&L's BreakPoint BPR methodology. Given the CQI environment, focus was placed on differentiating BPR and CQI. Expectations for results, timing, and the magnitude of change were established. Because Fairmount had recently completed a strategic planning initiative, the strategy was confirmed, and the steering committee defined Fairmount's core business processes. Fairmount selected care and therapeutics, access, and materials for reengineering. Since CQI teams at the various hospitals were involved with at least two of the three processes, meetings

Exhibit 20–2 Improving Value through Design's Components

Initiative	Goal
Organizational Effectiveness:	Assess the degree of alignment of the organizational structure with the strategic plan, and identify opportunities to realign the organizational structure to achieve a more efficient and effective patient care delivery system.
Operational Effectiveness:	Compare operational performance to national benchmarks, and quantify and identify operational improvement opportunities.
Clinical Effectiveness:	Use clinical resource management opportunities to achieve benchmarks in length of stay, ancillary utilization and outcome improvements related to DRGs.
Core Process Evaluation:	Identify and quantify core process improvement opportunities.
Technology Evaluation:	Evaluate current and planned future technology capabilities to meet financial, operational, and clinical information requirements.
Change Management Evaluation:	Identify cultural enablers and barriers to change, and develop an effective communication plan.

were arranged between the core process facilitator and the process team members to understand how the current initiatives and future direction might fit together. Since only one or two core processes would be selected for reengineering, the current process teams continued their efforts during the six-week evaluation phase.

Membership of the core process teams included a representative from each operating unit and a representative from any related existing process teams. Membership ranged from five to eight. The teams received the same BreakPoint BPR orientation as the steering committee. Their orientation session included team-building exercises and discussions of team ground rules, charters, and meeting schedules. Each team met weekly for six weeks in a four-hour meeting. Their objectives for those six weeks included: evaluation of the core process value and resource utilization from a system perspective; quantification and prioritization of short-term and long-term opportunities; and development of consensus regarding the fit between the system mission and the strategic plan and the stakeholder requirements that lead to the new process vision. The objectives of the sessions were as follows:

- *Session 1*—Define process mission, stakeholders, boundaries, and macro flow (or overview).
- *Session 2*—Translate key stakeholder requirements into performance indicators. Measure current performance.
- *Sessions 3 and 4*—Confirm strategic fit. Analyze current process performance (financial and operational).
- *Session 5*—Idealize the future state process. Define future state performance measures. Measure gap between current and future state.
- *Session 6*—Prioritize recommendations. Assess the change management issues.

PROCESS, MISSION, STAKEHOLDERS, BOUNDARIES, AND MACRO FLOW

The care and therapeutics team defined the mission of their process to be fully integrated care delivery across all disciplines, in which the patient and community coordinate the care process through two-way communication of accurate and appropriate information, in order to achieve optimal outcomes at the lowest possible cost across a seamless continuum of care. Stakeholders included patients, payers and purchasers, care providers, and regulatory agencies.

Patients, defined as including individuals, population groups, and the community, were prioritized as the primary stakeholders of the care and therapeutics process. The care process began with awareness of a need, including the organization's active involvement in the preventive aspects of care: health fairs, outreach programs, and education sessions. The process ended with cessation of service, which included medical information transfer to other providers, grief and grieving support to survivors, and referral to other providers and/or services. The care process included all preventive inpatient and outpatient aspects of care, since the process for all three types of care is the same, even though currently they operate independently. The care and therapeutics macro flow is shown in Figure 20–6.

STAKEHOLDER REQUIREMENTS AND PERFORMANCE MEASURES

Although requirements were defined for all stakeholders, the team focused on patient requirements. Based on the process mission and validated by feedback from the customers, resulting from work completed by the process improvement teams, the core process team defined the following requirements, which are based on the four value parameters—time, quality, cost, and service:

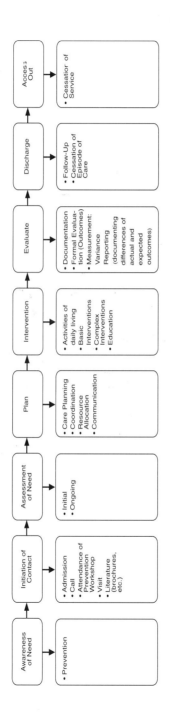

Figure 20–6 Care and Therapeutics—Current Macro-Flow

- cycle time—efficient processes
- quality—right outcomes
- cost—low cost
- service—accurate and timely information

Due to the six-week time frames and the high level (or broad overview) of this evaluation, the teams decided to limit performance indicators to available information. One indicator was selected for each requirement, but since the process included preventive and inpatient and outpatient aspects, the team tried to define a measure of preventive inpatient and outpatient services for each indicator. For example, cost was measured from an inpatient perspective (total cost per day), an outpatient perspective (total cost per visit), and a preventive aspect (total cost per workshop or seminar). The team was amazed at the amount of data available but frustrated by the lack of good information.

ANALYSIS OF STRATEGIC FIT AND CURRENT STATE

Care and therapeutics was categorized as an "identity" process for the organization. An identity process is closely linked to the organization's strategic intent, business vision, and core competencies. The team evaluated each strategic and operating goal for fit with the care and therapeutics process.

The current state was evaluated by organization, resource consumption, and technology investment. The labor resources invested in the care and therapeutics process far exceeded those for other processes, supporting, beyond strategic fit, the case for selecting care and therapeutics as the process for reengineering. The technology investment of patient accounting and order entry alone, at every hospital, indicated significant opportunity for technology enablement, but issues related to technology investment and timing were also raised.

FUTURE STATE

The team refocused on its process mission statement and brainstormed to determine what Fairmount would have to do to meet that mission and fulfill defined patient requirements. An orientation to potential technology and human resource enablers was presented, and the team visioned possibilities, given various combinations of technology and human resources. The future state macro flow was visioned to be much more focused on prevention and outpatient processes than currently; to have a great reduction in coordination, communication, documentation, and supportive care aspects; and to be integrated among all care providers as in one assessment, plan, and outcome evaluation, implemented by a coordinated team of caregivers. A graphic example of the future state is shown in

Figure 20–7. The impact on both the current performance indicators and new performance indicators was assessed.

CHANGE IMPLICATIONS

After the gap between current state and future state was assessed by comparing current to future state in terms of labor savings and technology, and the opportunity was estimated in terms of the degree of human resource investment. Change management implications were then evaluated. Figure 20–8 is an example of the evaluation form. Although an obvious case for the reengineering of care and therapeutics can be made by strategic fit, importance to customers, resource investment, and long-term cash flow, care and therapeutics often fails selection because of a reduced likelihood of success and low short-term return on investment. This phenomenon is in large part due to the boundary issues between all of the professional disciplines and to the high degree of sponsor commitment required to change this process. The reengineering of care is simply not a task that can be delegated away from top management, and there are many competing priorities for most executives. On the other hand, if health care providers are primarily in the business of patient care and most of their business is patient care, then it makes sense that the care and therapeutics process be the first process selected for reengineering.

When care is reengineered first, the other core and noncore processes can be subsequently redesigned to meet the new requirements of the reengineered care process, and health care providers can become truly patient-centered organizations.

PROJECT OUTCOMES

Sources for the $70 million cost-reduction target were identified, quantified, and prioritized through a combination of organizational structural changes, departmental improvements, nonsalary cost reductions, improved clinical efficiencies, and core process reengineering opportunities. The core process opportunities alone represented over $50 million of the total quantified opportunities.

The majority of the core process reengineering opportunity rested within the care and therapeutics process. Five factors supported the reengineering of this process.

1. Two of the three hospitals had already identified or started some type of patient-centered care initiative.
2. Any other process selected first would then have to be reengineered after the care and therapeutics process was changed.

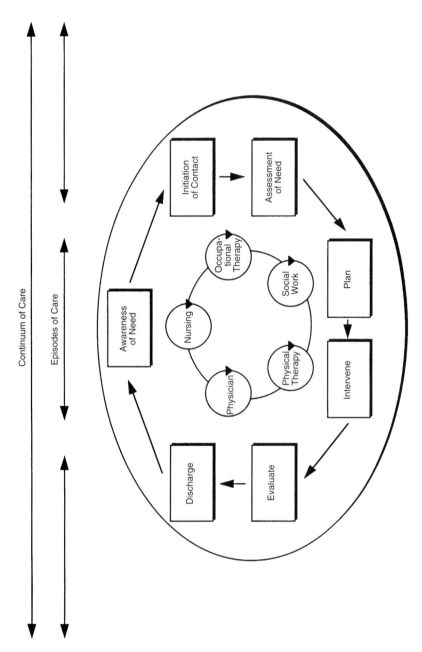

Figure 20–7 Care and Therapeutics—Future State

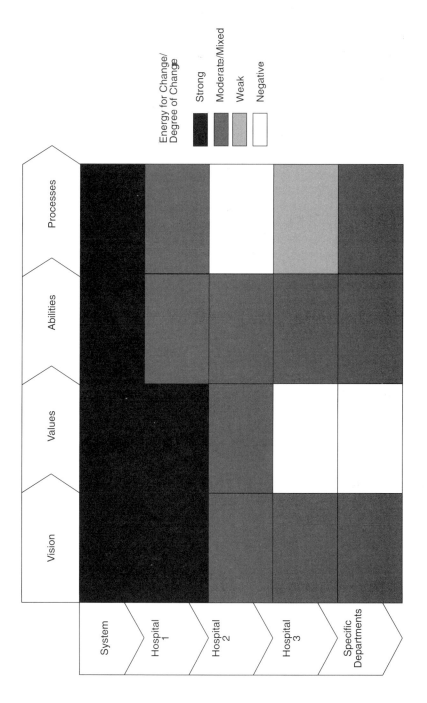

Figure 20–8 Change Implications

3. The resource investment in the process exceeded that in any other process.
4. The process was strategically significant and important to customers.
5. It was important to reengineer the care and therapeutics process prior to starting implementation of new patient care systems. The organization was involved in a system-wide information systems implementation anticipated to start with patient care systems in 1995.

The negative considerations were (1) perceived change management risks, (2) the significant investment in both human resources (training and incentives) and technology (new information and communication systems), and (3) low short-term return on investment. The care and therapeutics process was selected as the first process to be reengineered, and the reengineering phase started within the first year.

The first year's targets were addressed through a combination of organizational restructuring, selected departmental improvements, and nonsalary cost reductions. The first year's targets were set at a 15 percent total cost reduction. The remaining opportunity was spread over a four-year horizon, with $30 million to be realized within the first two years and the remaining $40 million over the following three years. The $40 million savings was focused (1) on two sequenced core process reengineering initiatives, the first started in the first year and the second in year three and (2) on redesign of the highest volume diagnosis-related groups' (DRGs) clinical processes in the three major service lines (obstetrics, cardiology, and orthopedics). The results from care and therapeutics reengineering are not anticipated to be realized until year three.

The overlap between the core process and departmental opportunities was managed by mapping departmental costs to core process reengineering opportunities. Once the targets were set for organizational changes and departmental changes, those opportunities were backed out of the core process opportunities and the process opportunities were restated.

Fairmount is currently in the reengineering phase.

CONCLUSION

BPR is a change methodology that can address the complex and contradictory problems faced by most health care organizations—improving services and quality while reducing overall cost significantly. It is a change methodology that can be used in a stand-alone reengineering project or as part of a comprehensive cost restructuring, as with Fairmount. This methodology is appropriate for organizations that have a two- to three-year horizon for return on investment and are willing to invest the resources in terms of time, people, and technology to realize the benefits. In other words, it is not for organizations in crisis. Such an approach will only provide the documented results of two to five times the investment if the recommended criteria for core process selection are applied. Any large process can be reengineered to reduce costs and cycle time. However, the benefits cited from our experience can only be realized through core process reengineering. Therefore, it is important to spend the time up front to reasonably "discover" all of the core process reengineering opportunities and to make the right selection(s).

It is anticipated that most health care organizations will have to reduce operating expenses by 10 percent to 20 percent as a result of market reform. The current thinking, given the experience of highly managed care markets such as those in Minneapolis or California, is that it will take 10 percent to 15 percent expense reduction in the next two years to remain competitive, then an additional 10 percent to 15 percent the following two years, and so on until the market stabilizes. Given this consideration, most health care organizations will only be able to meet the first two years' targets by incremental change strategies such as organizational downsizing, compensation and benefit restructuring, nonsalary cost restructuring, and cash flow management. The remaining cost restructuring will have to fundamentally change the processes within our organizations, the related work, and roles and management structures. BPR, through human resource and technology enablement and change management, offers the best known methodology to accomplish this magnitude of change and expected results within a two- to three-year horizon.

REFERENCE

1. Hammer M, Champy J. *Reengineering the Corporation: Manifesto for Business Revolution.* New York: HarperBusiness; 1993.

■ 21 ■

Reengineering Information Management To Support Clinical Function

Rella Adams, PhD, RN, CNAA
Lisa E. Gray, MSHA, RN,
Eric Six, MD, FACS, ABQAURP
Thomas H. Watkins

Health care reform is driving the entire industry to reexamine how it does business. Economic and political forces are tearing apart a structure that has been thoughtfully built over the past century. Traditional ways of doing business no longer work, because the economy will not support them. Health care administrators, physicians, and insurance companies are desperately seeking ways to survive without losing their financial security and ability to administer to society's health care needs.

The challenge in the business of health care is to find innovative ways to reduce costs while maintaining quality. Advances in computer technology are one building block that has considerable impact on the economic future of health care. New technologies that lend themselves to this include digital electronics, optical disk storage, advanced video displays, advanced computers, artificial intelligence, fiber optics, distributed computing, lasers, and microwaves.

Medical information system design must focus on patients and user-friendliness. It must follow the patient from the point of entry throughout the entire system, tracking services, costs, and outcomes. It must be dependable and must adapt to system changes rapidly. Information systems must also interface easily and economically with medical devices and other information systems that support patient care.

Patient care data such as orders, results, patient scheduling, critical paths, acuity, outcomes, and the cost (centralized billing) of patient care should be immediately available for analysis and team planning. This information must be stored with the capability for review whenever and wherever the patient reenters the system. Physicians must have this information in their offices, homes, hospitals, and clinics, so there is no delay in patient care or disposition. Only then can the system become seamless and cost-effective and the electronic patient record become a reality. A national network of information can then be achieved. The utilization of nationwide data lends itself to limitless possibilities for education and research. Patients, families, and health care professionals will then be able to work more effectively on areas of prevention and compliance, which ultimately relate to a healthy, productive society.

If managed care is the future, then patient identification and data retrieval at any location within a network of providers must be accomplished with speed and accuracy. The information system becomes the link between physicians' offices, outpatient clinics, hospitals, and third-party payers. Efficiencies in diagnoses, treatment, and follow-up allow providers delivering care the ability to bid more effectively for managed care contracts. Information technology is the key to the future of health care's economic survival in the managed care arena, and reengineering is the strategy that allows health care providers to turn that key.

PLANNING THE PROJECT

Our information system reengineering project took place at Valley Baptist Medical Center (VBMC), a 456-bed tertiary care, nonprofit hospital located in the Rio Grande Valley of Texas. A broad spectrum of health care services are provided, ranging from acute care to skilled care to community health. In 1989, a decision was made by key stakeholders to start with "a clean sheet of paper" and invest people and finances in order to build a totally comprehensive information systems network over a five-year period. This decision was considered to be a very aggressive, strategic move, and the project was given to a team of professionals who were not only dedicated and knowledgeable but had a track record of success in the world of information technology.

Two components necessary for a reengineering project to materialize are financial support and the commitment of key stakeholders. Also, pivotal to the success of a project of this magnitude is planning. The analysis, contract, and planning phases of the project encompassed a $2^1/2$-year time frame. It was during this time that four critical elements were defined to begin the reengineering project:

1. analysis of information systems being marketed
2. identification of the Medical Center's unmet informational needs
3. projection of the future needs of the Medical Center's information system
4. establishment of a design for a total information system serving the Medical Center

To accomplish these tasks, several important questions had to be answered.

• What information systems are currently in place?

- Do these systems meet the users' expectations?
- What roles are information systems envisioned to play in the future?

As part of the information-gathering process, a two-member team of facilitators was formed. The facilitators consisted of a computer consultant representing information services and a medical information liaison person representing clinical services. This team was charged with the responsibility of meeting with key management personnel to map the strengths and weaknesses of current information systems in the hospital and to identify opportunities for improvement in future systems.

We soon discovered that many of our individual departments had begun to realize the importance of information management. The systems that were in place, however, were either specialized or departmentalized. These systems fulfilled a need in a department, but they had not been purchased with the goal of integration in mind. While some departments had departmental systems in place, other departments still operated on a manual basis with no support from a computer system.

Because the hospital information system had become inadequate and antiquated and was composed of a series of fragmented departmental systems, there was clearly a need for a strategic plan for information management that crossed all departmental lines, integrating horizontal and vertical components of our system. The facilitators began by identifying the unmet needs of the users and the anticipated needs for the future. Initially, meetings were scheduled with each department manager, who identified staff members to discuss the current systems in place as well as future needs. Next, department managers were given information on the newest technology and functionality available and were invited to participate in scheduled demonstrations of different clinical information systems. Feedback was gathered from managers and staff as to which features were needed and which system best met their individual needs.

Clinicians felt it was imperative to be able to follow the patient from the point of entry throughout the entire system, including multiple stays as well as inpatient stays versus outpatient visits. Information accessibility was the key. Outside pressures from reimbursement mechanisms were forcing us to decrease the length of hospital stay and associated costs, while still maintaining quality. Information on orders, results, critical paths, outcomes, and cost had to be integrated into a system that was easy to use and readily accessible. It was decided that this new system had to be all encompassing if the clinician was to render care effectively and demonstrate performance improvement. The outcome for system selection and design must result in a total electronic record.

After the initial needs assessment was done and system previews were completed, personnel from administration, clinical areas, and medical staff formed a strategic plan for information systems called the strategic health care information resource initiative (SHIRI). A chronological presentation of the components of SHIRI is shown in Table 21–1.

HISTORICAL REVIEW OF SYSTEMS

During the 1970s, as information technology became commonly available and affordable to the American hospital, VBMC implemented a shared financial system. This system made use of a regional data center to process patient accounting transactions and the hospital's financial applications. Similar to procedures at most comparable institutions, VBMC data were manually gathered from charge tickets and admission slips, key entered during the evening shift, and transmitted in a batch to a central site. Processing took place during the late night hours. The information processed consisted of patient bills and reports, patient census, and departmental utilization information predicated on charges. This information was returned electronically and printed by the hospital's financial department the following day. Although major medical centers in urban areas began in the 1960s to adopt more advanced capabilities based on in-house, second-generation mainframe computers, the typical community hospital possessed neither the internal resources nor the funding for such projects. The advent of remote computing, using a method referred to as remote job entry (RJE) made financial health care computing available to the average institution. Financial applications and patient accounting moved from the posting machine era to a true data processing facility. Considering the volume of information managed by hospitals, this first step was somewhat rudimentary, although it served to reduce labor and improve the accuracy of information that was processed.

In the late 1970s, hospitals in the United States were investigating ways to prevent lost revenue through mismanagement of paper records. Charge tickets for services rendered either did not reach the business office, were illegible, or were delayed past the time when the patient's bill was produced. This scenario led health care system developers to produce a new family of products, entitled order communication systems, for general acute care hospitals. These systems processed admissions and registrations, provided an on-line patient census, maintained a simple master patient index, accepted orders for patient services, and delivered requisitions to ancillary departments. A hospital could readily justify the cost of such a system through realization of lost revenue within a few short years. Increased speed of requesting services and supplies for patients, accuracy of accounting information, and elimination of the key-entry function were also important benefits gained through use of order communication systems.

During the latter 1970s, VBMC engaged a major consulting firm to study the hospital's information-processing needs and develop a plan for the coming de-

Table 21-1 The Components of the Strategic Healthcare Information Resource Initiative (SHIRI)

Systems and Facilities Successes	Date of Installation	Platform	Functionality
Medical Information, Inc. (eventually McDonnell Douglas, then First Data—a subsidiary of Federal Express)	1970s	Four phase (local) IBM mainframe (remote)	Shared financial system
Nursing Management and Staffing System: ANSOS	1984	PC-based, stand-alone system	Automated nurse staffing office system
Hospital Information System (HIS): GTE	1988	Midrange	Orders communication/laboratory results reporting; patient accounting and financial applications
Laboratory Information System (LIS): SUNQUEST	1988 Upgrade, 1991	Risc-based	Full laboratory information system
Time and Attendance System: Denniston & Denniston	1991	Unix/Intel and Microsoft Intel	Employee time transactions tracking system
Hospital Information Network (HIN), Stage I	1991	Copper 10-base-5 and 10-base-T, Ethernet 802.3 implementation utilizing IPX/SPX and TCP/IP protocols	PC-based applications on hospital-wide network Standardization of word processing, spreadsheet, and graphical applications
Electronic Claims Management Applications: CIS Technologies	1991	Microsoft/Novell/Intel platform via the integrated HIN and interfaced to patient accounting applications	Electronic billing for business services
Interface Engine (Ingine)	1992	Microsoft/Novell/Intel platform integrated via HIN and direct connectivity	Platform for integration
Home Health and Hospice Management Applications: Provider Solutions	1992	Unix/Intel platform, utilizing shared HIN workstations	Billing and management for hospital-based home health and hospice agencies

Surgery Scheduling and Management Applications: ORSOS	1992	Microsoft/Novell/Intel platform integrated via HIN	Management and scheduling of the OR
Risk Management Applications: Risk Alert	1992/1993	Microsoft/Novell/Intel platform integrated via HIN	Risk management tracking and management system
Revenue Management and Cost Accounting Applications: Medicus	1993	Microsoft/Novell/Intel platform integrated via HIN	Revenue management and cost accounting
Remote Server Facility	1993	N/A	Nonstaffed physical facility located within the main hospital building with a controlled environment and redundant and conditioned utilities; high-security, housing-specific hardware platforms; and the subordinate network cross-connect facility for the main building
Critical Care System, Stage I (adult areas only): CareVue 9000	1993	Unix/Risc and Microsoft/Intel platforms	Flow sheet charting and bedside device interfaces
Environmental Services Management System: Huntington Labs	1993	Microsoft/Novell/Intel platform integrated via HIN	Environmental services monitoring and tracking management system
Clinical Codification System: Medicus	1994	Microsoft/Novell/Intel platform integrated via HIN	Clinical codification system for medical records
Information Services Pavilion	1994	N/A	Two-story physical facility with controlled environment and redundant and conditioned utilities; high-security housing; central server facility staffed 24 hours; and master network cross-connect facility

continues

Table 21-1 continued

Systems and Facilities Successes	Date of Installation	Platform	Functionality
Hospital Information Network (HIN), Stage II	1994	Optical fiber Ethernet 802.3 implementation utilizing IPX/SPX and TCP/IP protocols with expansion of existing copper 10-base-T facilities	Housing for administrative support unit, central operations unit, clinical support unit, education and standards unit, software management units, user-relations unit, training facility, library, media fire vault, and paper-storage facility; Link for interconnectivity with fiber optics
Tandem Fault-Tolerant Platform (for Clinical Information System: PHAMIS-Lastword)	1994*	N/A	Multiple processor server platform with very high fault-tolerant rating as base for clinical information system integrated via HIN
Critical Care System, Stage II (OR/Recovery-CareVue 9000)	1994*	Unix/Risc and Microsoft/Intel platforms	Flow sheet documentation and bedside device interfaces
Clinical Information System, Stage I: PHAMIS-Lastword	1994*	Tandem	Order communications, census, registration, result reporting, medical records, and patient billing applications to replace existing HIS applications
Critical Care System, Stage III (High-Risk L&D, Neonatal ICU and Pediatric ICU)	1995**	Unix/Risc and Microsoft/Intel platforms	Flow sheet documentation and bedside device interfaces
Clinical Information System, Stage III: PHAMIS-Lastword	1995**	Tandem	Pharmacy, ancillary management, advanced nursing, and physician access applications

*Installations in progress.
**Planned installations.
Note: N/A, not applicable; L&D, labor and delivery; ICU, intensive care unit.

cade. A major study of the flow and management of information within the hospital was undertaken. The recommendation resulting from the study was to acquire and implement a proven order communication system and, in parallel, to replace the shared financial system with a similar system from a vendor. This financial system provided additional functionality and support for financial applications. Following the study, a formal search was conducted to determine the most suitable and economically beneficial products available. Subsequent to the search, the consultants negotiated contracts with the vendors of both systems, and implementation was targeted for the beginning of VBMC's 1981 to 1982 fiscal year. VBMC's board of trustees was heavily involved with all aspects of the decision and contract process.

The hospital realized that the implementation experience of their data processing department staff was minimal. Therefore, resources would be required to effect optimal system implementation and adoption by users. VBMC engaged a fledgling consulting business that had the appropriate focus and experience with similar activities to manage the project. Planning for the parallel implementation of the computerized order communication and financial systems began in the middle of the hospital fiscal year 1980. VBMC dedicated one full-time financial staff member and one full-time clinical person to the project. The consultant also dedicated a senior staff member for the project's duration on an as-needed basis. Although the project staff was small and augmented by vendor resources, the resulting implementations occurred on time and within budget. Adoption of the system's total components was successful, and all anticipated benefits were realized beyond expectation. The hospital had truly moved into the age of automation current for 1980.

The state of computerized support remained static at VBMC for the next five years, and by the mid-1980s, several factors caused the hospital to consider expansion of its computing facilities. The advent of diagnosis-related groups (DRG) reimbursement required additional processing capability for patient accounts. Medical records required functionality beyond current capability. The clinical laboratory was sorely in need of automation that would connect data on discrete diagnostic instrumentation. The order communication system was at its physical limits with regard to terminals. The need for additional information by which ancillary and supporting departments could better manage their services was evident. The clinical departments of the hospital were also in desperate need of support through application of information technology.

In response to these requirements, the hospital conducted a needs analysis and an informal search for replacement systems. The decision was made to move financial processing in-house and combine the functions of order communications and finance on one platform. Due to the experience of the director of data processing, midrange platforms from a major hardware manufacturer were preferred. Three vendors of software systems thought to be suitable were identified and negotiations followed. Systems with capability to support clinical delivery were still in their infancy. However, the clinical administrators of the hospital had substantial authority in the decision process.

The successful bid came from the vendor who committed to delivery of a beta arrangement for its planned system for advanced nursing functionality, in addition to financial and order communication functions. The outcome of this decision process was to begin implementation of a replacement hospital information system (HIS). In 1987, an automated system for the clinical laboratory was installed, with implementation planned for the 1988 fiscal year.

The laboratory information system (LIS) implementation went well because it was encapsulated in the clinical laboratory and minimally interfaced to the new HIS. However, almost every hospital has experienced a disaster with a computer system implementation. VBMC's first negative experience was with its project to go in-house with an HIS. Fortunately, the most major problem was that of an undersized hardware platform. Terminal response time was measured in minutes, not seconds. The easy remedy was to add more processing power. With double platforms, however, the response time never reached anticipated levels. Downtime for day-end processing required almost the entire eight hours of the third shift. Because VBMC was, at the time, a 456-bed facility with very active critical care units and an emergency department, the impact was severe. A number of user terminals had to be shut down during peak times to keep the processor from failing. Users of the system were inconsolable.

The system's hardware platform was obsolete before the implementation was complete. The commitment to a beta arrangement for advanced nursing functionality was dropped by the software vendor since VBMC had now become a poor demonstration site. The hospital struggled with an inadequate computing environment for three years before coming to the conclusion that a replacement was absolutely necessary. The benefit of this predicament was a major opportunity for change. It had become possible to reengineer information management to support clinical function.

REENGINEERING INFORMATION MANAGEMENT

Reengineering means starting all over again, starting from scratch. How things were done yesterday doesn't matter. What does matter is being able to put aside the conventional wisdom of getting a job done and taking time to decide the best way to accomplish it. In reengineering, old job titles and organizational arrangements are artifacts of the past.[1] We knew what we needed and that was to investigate how we wanted to organize now, after analyzing today's markets and technologies.

The small consultant business used for earlier implementations at the hospital was called in late 1990 to assist with the planning for a new information management initiative. More than a year was spent developing the master plan. Figure 21–1 is a schematic diagram of integration of information systems at VBMC. Once again, the board of trustees became involved in the planning process in full support of the hospital's administration and physician staff. Initially, a large committee representing all interests in the hospital was selected primarily for political reasons. Once the hospital users saw action forthcoming, a number of working task forces were appointed to address specific areas of automation need. The large committee was then disbanded in favor of the smaller, more-focused groups. The complexity of the project and the multidisciplinary, hospital-wide approach necessary for reengineering demanded that the groups be composed of experts in selected areas. The reports and recommendations from these groups were then integrated through the health care informatics committee. Figure 21–2 represents the groups in the organization for information management.

In addition, department-specific task forces were empowered to set standards and policies. A series of information security policies eventually came from this process. These policies proved vital to the integrity of the institution. Exhibit 21–1 is an example of a security policy. More recently, task forces have provided standards for bar coding and have requested that imaging scans and x-rays be integrated within the system and available to all hospital departments.

In parallel with the planning process, a full-time network engineer designed the most important component of information integration, interconnectivity. No matter what the plan defined, all components had to be linked together. Many advancements in network design were just being developed. For the purpose of expediting establishment of a hospital-wide network, early decisions were made on the most readily available products and standards. This approach allowed the network to develop while discrete systems were being acquired and required system vendors to comply with the hospital's scheme of interconnectivity. Trying to randomly interface disparate systems ends with frustration, noninterfaced functions, and expensive data storage.

As the plan evolved, several major challenges faced the hospital. The most significant was size of capital investment. Historically, VBMC had allocated less than 1 percent of its revenue for data processing. Now it was looking at budgeting in excess of 3 percent for operations, as well as setting aside a major block of capital funds. As the hospital grew, it became evident to the board of trustees and administrators that more modern methods to manage the hospital's information must be made available. Only with a comprehensive information system would more beds and diagnostic facilities allow competition in managed care environments. The commitment was made and funding was now available for the reengineering project. The consultant's project manager was charged with obtaining maximum functionality at minimal cost. More important, the board of trustees mandated clinical functions as the highest priority for information management.

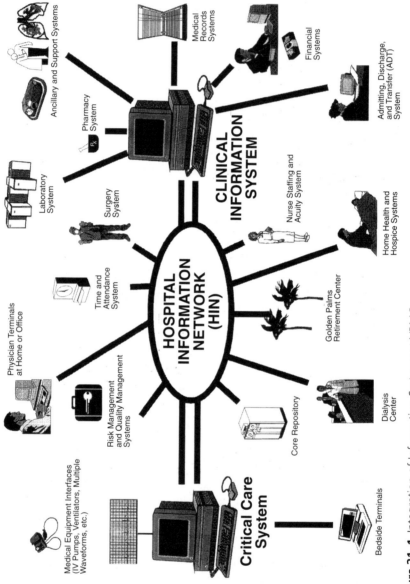

Figure 21–1 Integration of Information Systems at VBMC

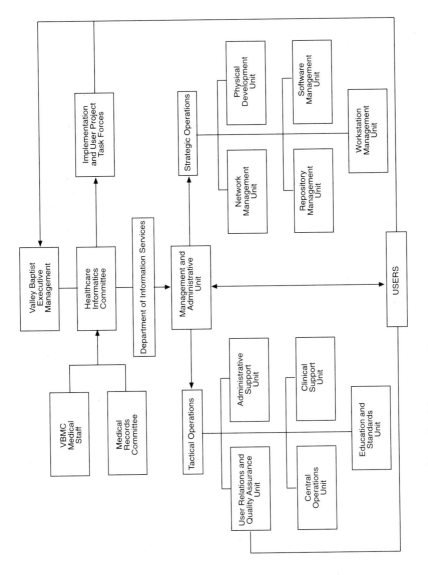

Figure 21–2 Organization for Information Management

Exhibit 21–1 Policy for Information Security—New Equipment Acquisitions

Definitions:

Connectivity Features—the software and hardware that enable communications between computer systems

Hospital Information Network (HIN)—the electronic computer network that interconnects the various computer/electronic systems at VBMC

Information Security—the assurance that all prudent and necessary measures have been implemented to guard against unauthorized disclosure of hospital information

Project Managers—Individuals or committees with the responsibility for overseeing the acquisition of computers, systems, or electronic equipment for use at VBMC

Purpose:

Retrofitting information security and connectivity features into computer and electronic equipment is expensive. By having such features installed into equipment during or prior to acquisition and installation, connectivity and information security concerns can be guaranteed. Prudent decisions during the equipment acquisition cycle can translate into substantial savings for VBMC. Consequently, a careful appraisal of the connectivity and information security features of equipment should be addressed prior to negotiation of a final purchase agreement.

Policy:

Project managers will coordinate all purchases of computer systems, electronic equipment, and software with information services to ensure that all information security and connectivity issues are addressed in the purchase agreement and to ensure that equipment and/or software purchased conforms to existing VBMC information services department standards and the VBMC long-range information management plan.

Procedure: Coordination of Computer Purchases

1. **Project Managers will:**
   - Address information security and connectivity issues in negotiations for equipment and software that will need to interface or transfer data to HIN or any other VBMC information system during the evaluation phase of equipment acquisition.
   - Ensure that equipment being considered for purchase conforms to existing VBMC information service department standards and to the VBMC information management plan.
   - Involve information services in the equipment acquisition cycle in an effort to address the technical aspects of issues concerning information security and connectivity.
   - Attach a completed addendum for confidentiality, integrity, and security form (VBMC form 1902ECA1) to the purchase agreement or contract for all equipment that will interface with HIN or that will be used to hold, process, or transfer hospital information.

2. **Information Services will:**
   - Serve as a technical resource for project managers regarding information security and connectivity issues.
   - Determine whether systems being considered for purchase meet the information security and connectivity requirements specified in VBMC policies and/or required for VBMC systems.
   - Serve as a technical liaison between VBMC project managers and vendors when technical issues concerning connectivity or information security are involved.
   - Make recommendations concerning the purchase of systems after a thorough review of the equipment's capability to meet VBMC connectivity and information security requirements.

The second major challenge was human resources. Since there were no significant computer facilities in the Rio Grande Valley, there were few people to recruit for implementation and operation of such a vast computer project. Importing persons with the necessary skills and knowledge would be too costly and could not guarantee success. The decision was made to develop the expertise of people living in the Harlingen area. Liaisons were put in place with the local technical college. An internship program was established, and several key senior people were recruited to furnish the core personnel necessary for systems development. Approximately two years were necessary to develop staff. People who were previously oil roughnecks, shoe salesmen, and waitresses received education as technicians, programmers, cable pullers, network engineers, and user support specialists.

In reengineering, the emphasis shifts from training to education. Training teaches employees the "how" of a job, whereas education teaches them the "why." It is necessary to educate new employees in order to increase their insight and understanding. Then these employees are empowered to break existing rules and given the authority to make the decisions that are necessary to get the work done.[1(pp.71–72)] We needed people who could create the job, not make a fit into an existing job.

The third major challenge was to find physical space for both people and equipment. The hospital's capacity to house anything additional had disappeared some years before. Many departments were using off-site locations. VBMC already had a building that had accommodated a school of vocational nursing for the past 40 years. The two-story dormitory built in the 1950s was being used as an archive for old records and film. Since VBMC is located in a hurricane prone area, the dormitory's shell was constructed from poured concrete. This became a perfect computer services building with a second floor out of water's reach.

The fourth challenge was the development of a standard agreement for use with information system vendors. This challenge required dedicated time and effort by a few individuals who serve on the health care informatics committee. The institution needed a contractual framework that would set forth the criteria to effectively interface systems, capture data for the long term, manage implementations, and ensure policies on security. The conditions and terms under which systems would be acquired had to be a standard format. The outcome was the development of VBMC's agreement for an "information management solution." Although prior implementations had been made with other agreements, this agreement was built as a bilateral contract that described a system procurement in terms of objective and mission rather than hardware and/or software commodity. Exhibit 21–2 lists the standard elements of the agreement for an information management solution. This contract format has now been used successfully with all acquisitions since 1993 and continues to be referred to as the Information Management Solution.

Exhibit 21–2 Agreement for an Information Management Solution Document

Structure of the Agreement
Definitions
The VBMC Operating Environment
Mission of the Solution
Statement of Common Objective
Scope of Solution Components
    Hardware Platform Components
    Terminal and Workstation Components
    Standard Software Components
    Custom Software Components
    Standard Interface Components
    Custom Interface Components
    Schemes of Interconnectivity
    Documentation Components
    Professional Services
    Training and Education Components
    Ongoing Support Services
Functional Specifications of the Solution
Logical Implementation Phases
Component Implementation Cycles
Integration of the Solution
Implementation Management
    Implementation Period
    Implementation Manager
    Qualification of Staff Resources
    Secure Access by Staff Resources
    Staff Resource Experience Levels
    Monthly Progress Reporting
    Interim Progress Reporting
    Automated Project Scheduler
    Implementation Plan
    Absolute Milestone Events
    Communication Contact Channels
    Problem Escalation
Specific Responsibilities
Compliance with Policies and Standards
Certificates of Software Quality
    Grades of Software Experience
    Severities of Software Anomaly
Acceptance of the Solution
    Phase Acceptance
    Final Acceptance
Period of Solution Effectively
Minimum Performance of the Solution

Maintenance and Support of the Solution
Licensure of Proprietary Software
    Proprietary Software
    Master Licensed Software
    Third-Party Licensed Software
Rights to Custom-Developed Software
Cost Capitation
    Capitation of Minimum Cost
    Capitation of Maximum Cost
Accrual of Capital Asset
Reimbursement for Professional Resources
Reimbursement of Travel Expenses
Terms of Payment
    Payment upon Invoice
    Payment upon Completion and
    Delivery
    Payment upon Milestone Achievement
    Method of Invoicing
    Retirement of Invoices
    Retainer
    Payment of Retainage
    Interest
Tax Liability, Exemption, and Identification
    Tax Liability
    Tax Exemption
    Tax Identification
Advance Payment Surety
Cost of Payment Surety
Cost of Money
Economic Destabilization
Audit of Contract Records
Breach of the Agreement
Remedy for Breach of the Agreement
Waiver of Breach
Termination of the Agreement
Limitation of Liability
Management Activities
Rights and Access to Design and Source
    Code
Business Reporting
Performance Bond
Performance Penalties
Insurance and Indemnity
    Comprehensive General Liability

continues

Exhibit 21–2 continued

Professional and/or Product Liability
Workers' Compensation
Comprehensive Automobile Liability
Indemnification
Relationship of the Parties
Infringement on Proprietary Software
  Rights
Ownership and Confidentiality of
  Information
Proprietary and Confidential Agreement
Proselytization of Employees
Mutual Representations
Compensation for Procurement
Venue and Jurisdiction
Legal Fees and Costs

Force Majeure Event
Assignment
  Assignment of the Agreement
  Assignment of Software Licenses
  Assignment of Benefits and Proceeds
Article, Schedule, Exhibit, and Annex
  Headings
Provisional Invalidation
Excessive Scope
Amendment of the Agreement
Formal Notice
Additional Provisions
Authority of Signatories
Signatory

The final challenge was to implement an overall initiative that would satisfy all reasonable user demands and give the users access to information systems with current technology. This initiative would serve the clinicians with accurate and accessible information to optimize their time and ensure quality of health care. It would also support the institution for upcoming operational requirements in a managed care era and provide a flexible mechanism for growth and change.

During 1991, the first year of the hospital's information management initiative, a major amount of work had been accomplished in planning and budgeting. In 1992, the first components of the initiative were put in place and staff development was initiated. The ten key second-year components of the initiative were

1. Complete implementation of the time and attendance system, which used voice telephones for input and interfaced to the HIS.

2. Install six major network backbone cables within the main hospital building in a manner to reach all locations through closeted network distribution equipment using twisted-pair phone cables.

3. Implement an electronic claims submission system interfaced to the HIS.

4. Begin development of an interface engine to be the ultimate device of interface resolution for all new systems.

5. Begin development of a standard agreement for an information management solution to be used for all new system acquisitions.

6. Establish standards for equipment, technology, and networks.

7. Establish policies for information security and integrity.

8. Informally begin a search for a major clinical information system and re-

placement system(s) for order communications; admission, discharge, and transfer; and finance.

9. Implement a surgery scheduling and inventory system.
10. Implement a clinical and administrative management system for the home health and hospice departments.

The third year of the initiative, 1993, saw an explosion of user workstations. The current HIS used only terminals. No more than two dozen personal computers were in use at the time the initiative began. As users saw the power and utility available with a networked personal workstation, the demand far exceeded budget, physical space, and available power outlets! This trend continues.

The major components of the initiative in the third calendar year were

1. Physically develop the planned information services pavilion.
2. Physically develop connectivity between the main hospital building and the campus external to it.
3. Physically develop an unstaffed server facility within the main hospital building.
4. Implement the first phase of a critical care system in four units.
5. Select and negotiate an agreement for a new clinical information system.
6. Begin implementation of a series of functional data base modules for the risk management and medical staff offices.
7. Implement a cost accounting system and revenue management system.
8. Implement a clinical codification system to replace the HIS function no longer supported.
9. Implement a management system for the environmental services department.
10. Expand both the information services staff and the base user network (HIN).
11. Initiate plans for interconnectivity by trenching for 16 four-inch conduits with manways on the hospital's immediate campus, with plans to convert all backbone cables from copper wire to fiber-optic cable.

All 1993 objectives were met, except for the selection and implementation of the clinical codification system, which was delayed until early 1994.

CONCLUSION

Reengineering the information system network was an enormous project, but it was necessary for the hospital's survival because of the demands of the new health care environment. Within the whole process, there was change—change in the way the work was accomplished, change in the jobs and structure, change in the management and measurement systems, and change in our culture, beliefs, and values.

We looked at what we had accomplished. We agreed we were not experts in the redesign process; we brought in an outsider to be the director. We threw away our preconceived ideas about information systems, and we worked in teams that always placed the needs of the customer first. We congratulated ourselves for our great ideas. Most of all, we enjoyed the challenge. What major goals have been accomplished by this reengineering project? We have the newest, user-friendly technology that not only enhances communication throughout the medical center but satisfies the needs of our customers by giving them the data to get their jobs done in the most efficient, effective way now and for the future.

REFERENCE

1. Hammer M, Champy J. *Reengineering the Corporation: Manifesto for Business Revolution.* New York: HarperBusiness; 1993.

■ 22 ■

Process, Results, Implementation: One Hospital's Reengineering Experience

Carolyn Hope Smeltzer, EdD, MSN, RN, FAAN
Nancy Mansheim Formella, MSN, RN
Heather Beebe, MBA

To be successful, reengineering requires administrative leadership and interdisciplinary, multifaceted worker participation. Most institutions have placed great emphasis on a disciplined process for making decisions regarding work restructuring. The same amount of attention and resources needs to be devoted to the institution's commitment and the process required to successfully implement the approved changes or ideas that were reengineered.

This chapter focuses on the redesign of a 289-bed teaching hospital and how the changes were implemented and evaluated. A very disciplined structure extremely similar to that for the design process was set up for the implementation process. Managers who designed the changes were also the champions for planning and executing the changes. In addition, the process included special attention to planned integration of interdepartmental changes, detailed planning for isolated changes that enabled the new model for patient care to be realized, and a time line that was sensitive to a domino effect of all the changes. Human resources, organizational development, communication, and education were all underpinnings of this hospital's successful implementation of a reengineered work process. Education encompassed role changes, skill changes, management of the change process, and team-building skills. This chapter focuses on results two years after implementation. The results demonstrate the achievements of meeting the hospital's targeted 15 percent budget reduction, improvements in patient and nurse satisfaction, and selected improvements in quality of care.

INSTITUTION

St. Luke's Hospital, a Mayo-affiliated hospital in Jacksonville, Florida, embarked on a nine-month reengineering process for patient care and with an additional 18 months planned for the implementation process in order to realize a 15 percent budgetary reduction while maintaining or enhancing the quality of care. The hospital is unique in the sense that, for a hospital of its size, it has numerous specialties. The hospital, which is in a growth phase, wanted to ensure a continued healthy financial margin of operations and improve the coordination of services among the departments, as well as maintain the quality of care. The institution, although one of the most historic hospitals in the South, had recently moved into the newly designed Friezen Hospital. Consequently, the institution introduced its old system and methods for delivering care in a newly designed hospital, thus creating numerous inefficiencies and systems issues.

Hospital leaders had a vision and motivation to change. They were committed to be prepared financially for managed care, wanted to improve services, and also felt they had a commitment to improve staff satisfaction and decision-making ability and to empower the work force to initiate cross-departmental problem solving.

THE PROCESS

The reengineering was a three-phase process (Figure 22–1). The first phase was a set-up and preparing the organization for changes that included analyzing financial opportunity for improvement and developing a clearer vision for the future of patient care. The second phase consisted of designing how the patient care process was going to be delivered, and the last phase encompassed planning the implementation steps to achieve change and implementing the rollout to all units, to provide the new model of patient care. A main thrust of the last phase was constant evaluation of the effectiveness of the changed practice. At base line and two years after reengineering, data were gathered regarding patient satisfaction, quality of care indicators, and nurse and physician satisfaction. These data were compared and analyzed to determine the effectiveness of the new delivery process.

Set-Up Phase

The purpose of the set-up phase was

1. to determine the actual dollar savings opportunities in the operating budget
2. to help provide the motivation to change
3. to listen to individual and departmental concerns
4. to teach basic principles of analysis and work restructuring

In addition, the staff offered input into designing a new, efficient, and effective model of patient care.

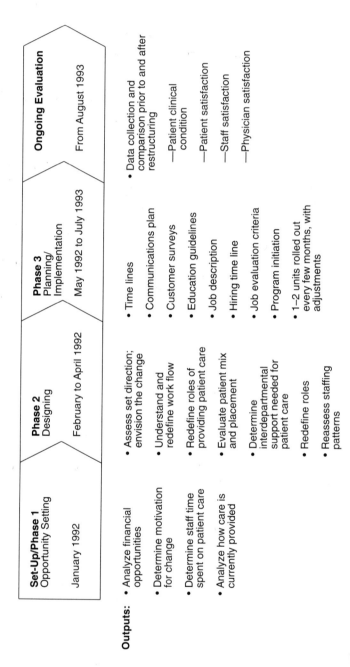

	Set-Up/Phase 1 Opportunity Setting January 1992	Phase 2 Designing February to April 1992	Phase 3 Planning/ Implementation May 1992 to July 1993	Ongoing Evaluation From August 1993
Outputs:	• Analyze financial opportunities	• Assess set direction; envision the change	• Time lines	• Data collection and comparison prior to and after restructuring
	• Determine motivation for change	• Understand and redefine work flow	• Communications plan	—Patient clinical condition
	• Determine staff time spent on patient care	• Redefine roles of providing patient care	• Customer surveys	—Patient satisfaction
	• Analyze how care is currently provided	• Evaluate patient mix and placement	• Education guidelines	—Staff satisfaction
		• Determine interdepartmental support needed for patient care	• Job description	—Physician satisfaction
		• Redefine roles	• Hiring time line	
		• Reassess staffing patterns	• Job evaluation criteria	
			• Program initiation	
			• 1–2 units rolled out every few months, with adjustments	

Figure 22–1 Process and Timing

During the two-month set-up phase, the institution was analyzed financially by comparing its performance to that of other institutions and to its own perform-ance over time. Also, during this time, numerous interviews were conducted with individuals at all levels in the institution to determine their motivation for wanting change.

Several observations were made during this time. One of the most significant was a commitment to facilitate a change in nursing practices. There was opportu-nity to reduce the nursing department's operating budget by 12 percent. Sacred cows, such as the patient classification system, were challenged within the first two weeks of the project.

In addition, during the set-up phase, a staff questionnaire was distributed to multidisciplinary workers. The purpose was to elicit information regarding the amount of time, ideally, they would like to spend on direct patient care activities and how much time, ideally, they would like to spend on direct and nondirect patient care activities. The survey also requested staff to identify the values in patient care they desired, as well as to identify what had already been changed in the environment to enhance patient care. Two years after design, the same sur-vey was given to staff to elicit how they were spending their time when delivering care in the new model.

Staff also presented a seminar after analyzing how they historically had pro-vided patient care. They followed a surgical patient through the first 24 hours of a hospital stay. A slide presentation illustrated the number of interactions patients had with different workers and the inefficiencies of delivering patient care. In addition, staff reported on models of care that are currently used in the community.[1(p.216)]

Design Phase

The design phase consisted of analysis and answering numerous questions re-garding development of a patient care model. Six major areas of emphasis for delivering the model were addressed.

1. Assess and set direction.
2. Understand work flow and the patient's needs.
3. Redefine roles.
4. Evaluate patient mix and location.
5. Evaluate the enabling ideas in terms of interdepartmental support needed for patient care.
6. Reassess the staffing patterns relative to meeting the financial targets.

In addition, part of the process was to define what administrative structure could best support the new patient care model. Key questions were identified under each phase and answered during the model development. This process took approximately six months. The key questions during the assessment and the process of setting direction included the following:

- What is the current situation in providing care?
- What guiding principles must be considered in order to make coherent decisions during the process?
- What needs to be achieved for the caregiver and for the patient?

The exercise on clarification of values that was completed by numerous disciplines indicated the institution's value system and helped the patient process team identify principles for both the patient and the caregiver. In terms of patients, the following principles were agreed on:

1. Provide continuity in care.
2. Provide care via a qualified caregiver.
3. Provide all the care that a patient requires.
4. Create a written plan of care, with consistent education for patients.
5. Provide mutual discharge planning with the patient.
6. Provide an understandable explanation of what happens to the patient throughout the hospital stay.

For the caregiver, the following guiding principles were developed:

1. Create continuity in scheduling.
2. Devise a model in which caregivers have the knowledge needed to care for patients.
3. Make resources needed for patient care readily available.
4. Facilitate the creation of fair, manageable assignments.
5. Create a collaborative team-oriented environment.
6. Achieve an appropriate nurse-patient ratio.
7. Establish professional nursing practices with knowledgeable caregivers.
8. Create a feeling of job satisfaction with respect for and pride in all professionals who contribute to the care of patients.
9. Develop the ability to delegate tasks to those who can best do the job.

After developing these guiding principles, the patient care team determined their goals. The main goal was to increase the time nurses spent on direct patient care. The staff reported spending 54 percent of their time in activities that contributed to direct patient care. In addition, the group identified the following goals for the new process:

1. Maintain the quality of care.
2. Leverage the registered nurse's time based on increasing the ability to delegate.
3. Decrease documentation and patient classification paperwork.
4. Improve interaction and services between nursing and pharmacy.

Understanding Patient Needs and Work Flow

To develop an understanding of the work flow, each head nurse was asked to answer the following questions for staff input:

- What do patients need?
- What do patients receive?
- When can only registered nurses provide care?
- Who is best suited to provide certain types of care?

These answers facilitated the patient care team's categorization of the type of work performed by the worker. For example, the nurse would do patient assessment, titratable drips, and sterile dressings; floor hosts would clean rooms and pass trays. After the tasks were categorized, key questions were then asked about each task. These questions included the following:

- Which tasks could be delegated to a patient care technician?
- Which tasks could be eliminated?
- Which tasks could be modified?

Redefining Roles

Redefining roles was a major focus of the patient care team. Key questions for redefining roles and developing new roles to provide efficient patient care were the following:

- What tasks can be delegated?
- What functions should be decentralized?
- What functions should report to nursing?
- How should the span of control change?

All roles within patient care changed through the process of redefining roles, with the goal of increasing the time spent by the nurse on direct care activities. Leveraging the skills of the nurse and realigning all patient care workers to be team members reporting to someone where the work actually occurs were major foci. A patient care technician role was also developed; the patient care technicians have expanded skill training for a set of patient care tasks delegated by the registered nurse. A decentralized housekeeping role was also created; yet a centralized function would be responsible for training the housekeepers, ordering the environmental supplies and equipment, and cleaning outside of the nursing service areas. Nurse managers, however, would hire, direct, supervise, discipline, and evaluate their housekeepers.

In terms of administrative support to the nursing units, the role of the head nurse was changed to nurse manager, with major changes in accountabilities for unit-based administrative support. In addition, the role of the clinical coordinator was developed to manage unit-based clinical protocols.[1(p.218)]

Evaluating the Patient Mix

During numerous discussions on how to efficiently provide quality care, it became obvious that the patient care team needed to challenge assumptions about the location of patients in the hospital. Key questions during this phase of work reengineering were as follows:

- How should the location of patients be organized to provide for the most efficient care?
- Are three intermediate care units necessary?

After analysis of patient placement, the patients were aggregated into different services. During the process, the surgical intensive care unit and cardiac care unit were consolidated under one clinical manager, one progressive care unit was created with a clinical manager, and a 15-bed hematology-oncology bone marrow transplant service was created. In addition, four 40-bed services were created, as opposed to the former 20-bed units. The advantages of creating enlarged services included an increased span of control for the clinical manager, resulting in 7 clinical managers rather than 12; fewer transfers of patients; fewer patients off service; and the ability to increase the size of the units with a fluctuating census, as opposed to having to close units. These services also allowed for more flexibility in staffing and scheduling, in addition to decreasing the amount of resources used.

Evaluating Enabling Ideas

While much of the time of work restructuring was focused on developing new processes for care delivery, a number of individuals worked on enabling ideas for efficiencies that would affect the model of care. Key questions asked during this phase included the following:

- What do patients and nurses need from other departments?
- What processes can be simplified or eliminated?

• How will these changes enhance the model of patient care?

The enabling ideas agreed on were divided into the categories of documentation, communication, scheduling and assignment practices, pharmacy service enhancement, and a miscellaneous category.

Reassessing Staffing Patterns

The last phase of the model development process consisted of examining all the changes described and answering the following questions:

• How much of each type of resource is needed per staff member for staff to provide care?
• How much will it cost?

Total full-time equivalents (FTEs) increased by five, and the skill mix of registered nurses was reduced from 87 percent to 62 percent. The resulting annual dollar savings was $1,856,454, or 15 percent of the nursing operating budget.[1(p.222)]

The next phase of the work focused on how to organize the magnitude of change that was envisioned. The challenge was how to operationalize all of what was reengineered.

IMPLEMENTATION PLANNING

Implementation is hard work. Just as the visioning and designing processes test the stamina of the organization, figuring out all the "hows" of implementation required continuous evolution of the organizational culture and tested management capability. Detailed plans were developed for the more complex processes. Interdependencies between processes were identified and coordinated. Employees were educated for new roles with new technical skills. There was a need for new schedules, new job descriptions, new policies, and new aptitudes, as well as new attitudes. Furthermore, everyone within the organization had to become comfortable with the paradigm of a new patient care model. Constant and consistent communication was a priority during the actual initiation of patient care units, with workers actually providing care in a different manner. Due to the significant amount of change, certain issues took on new importance—education, communication, organizational development, and human resources policies regarding layoffs, hiring, or placement of employees. Resolution of these issues was basic to a successful implementation process.

Successful implementation is characterized as much by the results and evaluation of those changes as by the journey. The journey involves minimizing the impact to the labor force; investment in human capital relative to education; organizational development; and institutional attention to the cultural byproducts of the changes. St. Luke's Hospital planned a process for implementation that had the basic underpinnings mentioned above. There was a substantial reduction (15 percent savings in the operating budget and a shift from a registered nursing staff of 87 percent to 62 percent without any layoffs)—all achieved within a one-year period.

In recognition that implementation is a journey as well as a destination, key success factors were integrated into St. Luke's implementation plan, including the following:

- being prepared to commit the level of time, effort, and resources required
- providing clear structure, accountabilities, and tightly managed time frames
- keeping the vision alive

Leadership remained visible and committed to the process of change and expressed that commitment by the following actions:

- communicating among staff, physicians, and departments
- communicating with various forums and audiences to encourage sharing of information
- reenergizing staff through public recognition of success along the way
- nurturing the seed of cultural change
- resisting the temptation to revert to old ways of thinking
- addressing concerns of key constituents (physician and staff) at the institutional level
- not allowing individuals to disrupt progress
- incorporating paradigm shifts into measurement and evaluation systems
- investing in St. Luke's employees
- providing the technical and managerial tool kits needed to succeed in the new model of care
- integrating implementation into a continuous quality improvement effort
- incorporating the new work concepts into meeting the requirements for the Joint Commission
- acknowledging and facilitating transition through the grieving process associated with change

PROCESS AND STRUCTURE FOR IMPLEMENTATION PLANNING

St. Luke's Hospital embarked on a five-month planning process for implementation. The planning process was complete prior to "rollout" of the first unit of the new model of care. The first step was to have a disciplined process and structure developed that would provide for smooth implementation. A disciplined structure was set up for the implementation process of reengineering. Managers in the reengineered divisions and individuals who helped design the new process of delivering care were involved with implementation. In addition, the process created a planned integration of all the changes, oversaw the details of isolated changes, and developed a time line that was sensitive to the domino effect of all the changes.

The structure that St. Luke's Hospital developed to ensure proper planning for implementation is illustrated in Figure 22–2. Similar to Hammer and Champy's transition management team,[2–4] a steering committee guided implementation and provided a link to hospital administration regarding the process toward change. Membership included the nursing administrators, key interdisciplinary managers, some staff nurses, physicians, and leaders in the human resources and financial management departments.

In addition, two other roles or functions provided support to the implementation planning steering committee: coordination and communication. These support roles were created to coordinate the execution of all processes implemented, to track the progress toward implementation goals, and to communicate with all departments and staff regarding changes as they were occurring. The steering committee also created two ad hoc work teams: one for documentation and one for service area patient placement. The documentation group was responsible for education and implementation of the exception-based charting system—problem, intervention, and evaluation (PIE). Prior to implementation of any model changes of patient care, the unit needed to integrate a streamlined approach to documentation.

The service area and patient placement group needed to determine new admission policies for patient placement and transfer within the hospital, as well as determining what structural changes were required. In addition, secretarial changes were needed to effectively change a 20-bed unit so that it would become an effective 40-bed unit. This ad hoc team determined the timing and order in which units would become a new service. Both documentation and service changes had to be completed prior to rollout of the first new patient care unit.

Other work teams that were formed to ensure a smooth and successful implementation addressed housekeeping, job descriptions, the clinical coordinator position, and administration changes, education and role of the registered nurse, and staffing and scheduling. Each work group developed time lines and work plans. The total implementation planning time line was five months and was composed of over 500 steps that needed to be accomplished.

Each work team had a specific charge. The charge of the work team on housekeeping was to develop a housekeeper job description; establish systems for hir-

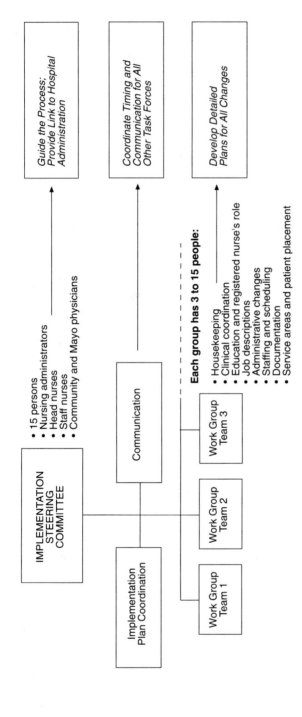

Figure 22–2 Structure for Implementation

ing, supervision, and training; develop a daily staffing system; and define the relationship with central housekeeping. The mission of the work team on job descriptions was to complete all job descriptions, coordinate job analysis with compensation and benefits, cross-reference new job descriptions with policies and procedures, and determine the evaluation criteria for the new jobs. The work team on the clinical coordinator position was charged with the following accountabilities: identify qualifications for this position, identify selection criteria, develop a job description, and identify the role orientation needed. The work team on administrative changes developed criteria as well as a process for nurse manager selection, for revision of the nurse manager job description, and for decisions on the number and placement of nurse manager positions and the role orientation and training required. The working team on the education and role of the registered nurse developed a curriculum for nurses as well as one for patient care technicians. The work team for staffing and scheduling built staffing bases to meet the financial targets reductions, implemented scheduling system changes, scheduled orientation of staff, established centralized and decentralized roles and functions, and implemented an automated scheduling system. In addition, this work group was accountable for deciding on the time line for all new and revised roles, planning classes in conjunction with the service development team, and revising all registered nurse job descriptions to reflect changes.

Once these groups were under way, two other work groups were formed. One group was formed for all the isolated enabling processes that needed to be implemented, e.g., a new patient classification system, an automated patient Kardex, and a different method of dispatching and distributing pharmaceutical agents. This group was additionally charged with prioritizing the enabling processes that had to be implemented prior to changing the skill mix of caregivers and deciding which processes could be deferred until after major change had occurred. The human resources work team developed a plan for attrition, hiring practice, and transfer policy, with the main goal of being sensitive to avoidance of layoffs.

The other additional process team was the evaluation work group. This group was responsible for creating a system to evaluate all the changes in relation to staff, patient and physician satisfaction, patient satisfaction, and quality of care. This work group developed the methods of evaluation and designed tools to measure the effects of model changes. It collected base line data to enable meaningful comparison after implementation. The process of change implementation was also evaluated. This evaluation provides a basis for modification of specific aspects of the design if objectives are not being achieved.

Overall activities during this three- to five-month period included the following:

- identifying critical path activities and interdependencies of processes
- formalizing communication efforts

- identifying personnel impact and timing
- developing job descriptions, a recruiting plan, and salary and wage changes
- identifying evaluation criteria for success (cost, quality, and service)
- planning for implementation of enabling processes and rollout
- identifying which units and services would be initiated first
- developing implementation of patient aggregation by placement in service areas
- reviewing and revising policies, procedures, and descriptions
- assessing strengths and weaknesses of implementation leadership
- developing curricula

Outcomes from these work teams included the following:

- summarizing all changes to date
- educating the steering committee regarding level of implementation complexity
- positioning nursing executive for ongoing physician and administration support
- maintaining continuity of the current process
- ensuring broad-based understanding of desired results
- "recharging batteries" when a service was initiated
- focusing work group efforts
- maintaining continuity of process
- developing a comprehensive work plan for all aspects of implementation rollout and a clear understanding of commitment to achieving results throughout the organization
- pursuing constant communication with staff regarding the progress of change
- developing strategies to overcome the obstacles to successful implementation

IMPLEMENTATION ROLLOUT

Determining which unit will be the first to implement a new process is an important decision. The "initiation unit" selection was based on the following criteria:

1. clinical leaders' strength
2. political visibility
3. stable staff

4. minimal attrition
5. vacancy rates for registered nurses
6. attending physician support
7. a stable unit patient population

A conscious decision was made not to call the first unit rollout a "pilot," because this was not a unit test. The first unit's success was not going to determine whether to continue or discontinue the model on other units. Rather, the first implementation would be a learning experience that would help to identify issues that could be improved or avoided when the rest of the hospital's units were rolled out.

All patient care units were delivering the new model of patient care within 11 months. The plan called for the entire rollout to be completed within 12 to 18 months. The staff, in fact, exceeded the plan's requirements because of their enthusiasm to be delivering a different model of care. In addition, the hospital functioned on two systems of providing care during the transition period. Central departments, in particular, were taxed during rollout, thus a speedier rollout of all units was desired.

In the rollout phase, it was extremely important to have institutional commitment and visibility. Leadership was consistently challenged as to whether the changes were or would be effective in relation to all the efforts invested. These challenges came from staff, physicians, and some administrators.

During the units' actual change, there is no such thing as communicating too much or to too many audiences. It is safe to assume that anyone who is remotely affected by the change has a need for special communication. It was recognized that even though physicians had been told about the imminent change in delivering patient care, they required special communication prior to each unit rollout.

Education was a key factor in the success of changes in the patient care areas. The education was not focused only on technical skills or role changes but encompassed the value system of providing patient care. Creativity was demonstrated in the design and implementation of education programs for new, changing roles. Competency was taught and tested by creating games like "Jeopardy." Learning was fun and attending the game session gave assurance of competency.

Team building concepts were also incorporated to ensure teamwork rather than simple mastery of task delegation. Accountability was demonstrated in determination of the site of the education as either a classroom or the unit base. Nurse managers and clinical coordinators were also held accountable for ensuring that the new workers were integrated on the unit, that their competencies were being utilized, and that they showed promise of being successful.

Actual change does not have the same impact as planning or making decisions regarding change. During the planning stage, there was still an element of "it may not affect me." Individuals initially may not have fully realized exactly how the change would affect them or their departments, but it became more clear during implementation. Anxiety over the change became more evident, and communication during this time was vital.

Communication was also used to minimize rumor and misconception about the change. In addition, active communication elicited a feeling of participation in the change process. Communication about the change also helped individuals to prepare for specific education and skill training.[5(p.374)]

During the rollout of patient care units, a Gantt chart was used to track the implementation of all processes (Figure 22–3). Time lines were adhered to because of the domino effect the majority of ideas had on the rest of the work reengineering plans and changes. At every point prior to the change, there was anxiety in the environment, and individuals used numerous reasons to ask permission not to initiate the change. Issues of vacations, regulatory site visits, and routine organizational tasks all became reasons why individuals asked for extensions on the implementation date of various changes. By avoiding change of one date, which would most likely have affected other components of the plan, the goal of minimal slippage in time lines was achieved.

EVALUATION AND RESULTS

The new model of care was evaluated in terms of achievement of skill mix changes, financial target reduction, and quality of care (medication errors and falls), as well as how staff spends their time. In addition, staff, physician, and patient satisfaction was measured prior to and one to two years after the model was initiated. The time frame of two years after implementation was thought appropriate because it allowed individuals affected by the changes a chance to adapt to the changes prior to the evaluation. In addition, a planned time frame for evaluation prevented department managers, staff, or physicians from requesting evaluation data before staff had a chance to adapt to the changes.

A financial target reduction of 15 percent was achieved through work process reengineering. These reductions do not include the one-time training cost, and all the numbers were adjusted for inflation and patient volume changes. Prior to reengineering, the nursing staff actually spent $14 million in delivering care; two years after reengineering, the cost was $11 million. In addition, nursing administration reduced its operating budget by $300,000 (5 percent). In general, the skill mix was reduced from 87 percent to 62 percent registered nurse staff without laying off one nurse.

Staff time after reengineering was analyzed with the same tool used prior to reengineering. Staff were asked specifically to answer questions about how they spend their time in five categories of work: (1) providing direct patient care,

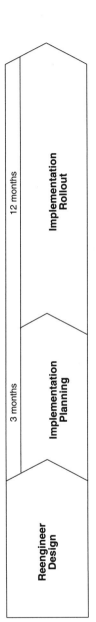

3 months | Implementation Planning | 12 months | Implementation Rollout

Reengineer Design

Implementation Planning

Activities
• Identify critical path activities, interdependencies
• Formalize communication efforts
• Identify personnel impact and timing
• Develop job descriptions, salary and wage changes, recruiting plan
• Recruit for new positions
• Identify evaluation criteria for success
• Plan for implementation of enabling ideas
• Identify initiation units
• Develop patient aggregation implementation
• Review and revise policies and procedures
• Assess strengths and weaknesses of implementation leadership
• Develop curriculum

Desired Outcomes
• Comprehensive work plan for all aspects of implementation rollout
• Clear understanding of and commitment to results throughout organization

Implementation Rollout

Activities
• Conduct hiring of new workers
• Train and orient new and existing workers
• Maintain formal communication efforts
• Stagger change across units
• Evaluate success against predetermined criteria
• Modify as necessary
• Gradually disband work groups as responsibility for change is fully integrated into daily life

Desired Outcomes
• Achieve cost, quality, and service targets

Figure 22–3 Patient Care Implementation Planning and Rollout

(2) providing support to ancillary workers, (3) conducting clerical work, (4) participating in unit support activities including team meetings and orientation of new staff members, and (5) attending educational inservice programs. In addition, prior to reengineering, they were requested to determine how much of their time they would like to allocate to those activities. The results are displayed in Figure 22–4. Although all their goals of how much time they would like to spend on specific activities were not achieved, the results show progress in the right direction. More time was being spent with patients, less time was spent on ancillary and clerical support, and more time was devoted to unit support and educational inservice programs.

The quality of clinical care was evaluated in terms of the number of falls and medication errors; both decreased after the reengineering process (Figure 22–5). In addition, patient satisfaction was measured through a survey tool prior, during, and after implementation. Patient satisfaction during this substantial change process did not decrease and slightly improved (Figure 22–6).

Perhaps some of the most telling results are not recognized from survey tools, but rather from the interview process and individual testimony. A cardiovascular nurse stated, "Now I'm assigned care of seven patients versus five, but I have a patient care technical (PCT) [aide] working with me. I have more time to assess and respond to clinical issues now; I have more time to talk with my patients, improving their patient teaching and discharge planning."

Another nurse stated, "This is just a short note to let you know what a great job our 11 to 7 PCT is doing. Now that I work with a PCT, I can't imagine how we ever survived before. Work is usually done without being asked. We have a great bunch and I hope they keep up the great work."

Another nurse stated, "By having a PCT, I'm able to spend more time and really get to know my patients and their diagnoses and look into their histories. I'm able to see the total picture . . . where the patient was and why they're here."

Comments from patients included the following:

- "Patient care technician Beth is such a sincere, kind person who seems to know instinctively that some patients need a little emotional boost along with their physical care."

- "I was especially impressed . . . by the cooperation that was evident between the nurses and the PCTs with them."

- "PCTs Erica and Tom were exceptional in the many small ways that are important to a patient—encouraging, humorous, and calm."

- "I've had surgery at St. Luke's before—approximately two years ago—and everything has changed! Everything and everyone has improved on excellence!"

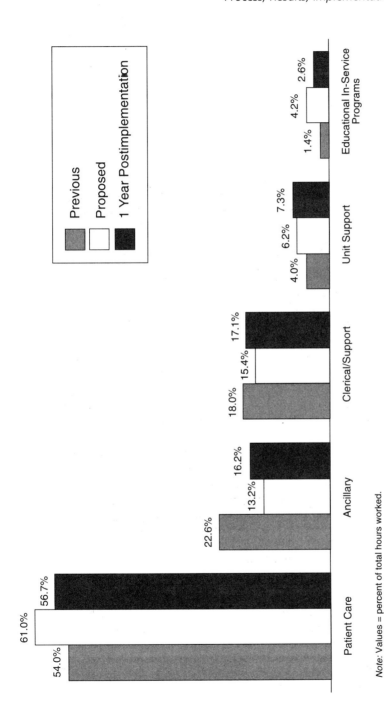

Note: Values = percent of total hours worked.

Figure 22–4 Staff Satisfaction: Patient Care Staff Time Distribution

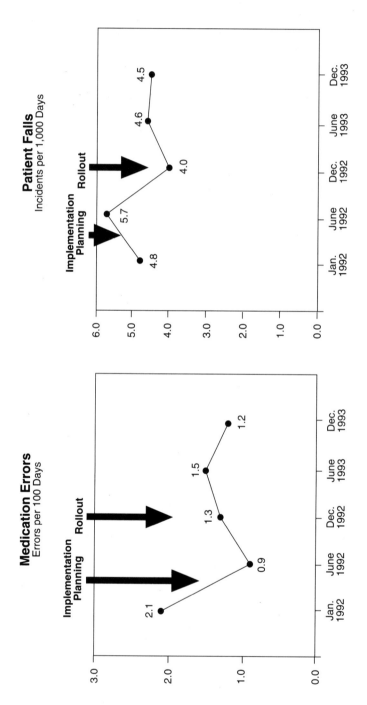

Figure 22–5 Clinical Quality Indicators. Courtesy of the Quality Assurance Department, St. Luke's Hospital, Jacksonville, FL.

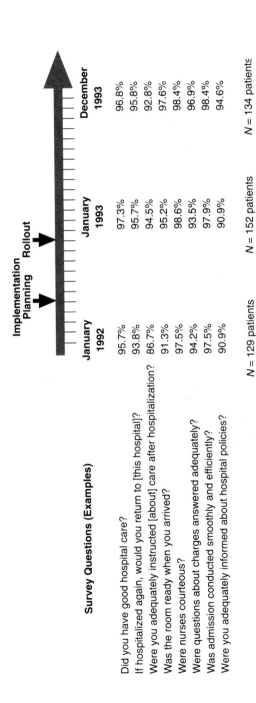

Survey Questions (Examples)	January 1992	January 1993	December 1993
Did you have good hospital care?	95.7%	97.3%	96.8%
If hospitalized again, would you return to [this hospital]?	93.8%	95.7%	95.8%
Were you adequately instructed [about] care after hospitalization?	86.7%	94.5%	92.8%
Was the room ready when you arrived?	91.3%	95.2%	97.6%
Were nurses courteous?	97.5%	98.6%	98.4%
Were questions about charges answered adequately?	94.2%	93.5%	96.9%
Was admission conducted smoothly and efficiently?	97.5%	97.9%	98.4%
Were you adequately informed about hospital policies?	90.9%	90.9%	94.6%
	N = 129 patients	N = 152 patients	N = 134 patients

Note: Satisfaction was measured as percentage of patients responding "Yes" to survey questions.

Figure 22–6 Patient Satisfaction. Courtesy of the Quality Assurance Department, St. Luke's Hospital, Jacksonville, FL.

CONCLUSION

Successful implementation of a work reengineering project needs to be planned and have active leadership, a committed institution, education to reinvest in the worker, and honest, open communication. It is difficult to address all the challenges that major change will create, but a system, structure, and process need to be in place to address the obstacles to change and the strategy for success.

Objectively, evaluating the successes and failures of reengineering implementation provides a basis for creating a list of lessons learned. These important lessons of St. Luke's Hospital are listed in Exhibit 22–1.

Results of our work reengineering process are directly proportional to the time invested in the process of making decisions regarding changes in patient care. The amount of change that is achievable and successful is directly related to the amount of time invested in detailed planning for the change.

Exhibit 22–1 Lessons Learned from Implementation

LEADERSHIP	• Identify champions for change • Enable decision making at the line level • Make institutional level commitment visible to all workers • Demonstrate that ownership and accountability rest with the client • Provide extra support for the last steps; prevent stalling
PLANNING	• Minimize downtime between design and implementation • Identify critical paths, interdependencies, to avoid delays • Provide clear structure and accountabilities, tightly managed time frames • Focus on desired outcome of change rather than feelings about change • Be prepared to speed up implementation when change is successful • Be prepared to redirect efforts as indicated by monitoring tools
EDUCATION	• Prepare as carefully for role changes as for technical skill enhancements • Ensure standard skill set for common groups of workers
COMMUNICATION	• Communicate, communicate, communicate • Actively pursue physician involvement and understanding • Pay attention to semantics: "initiation units" more appropriate than "pilots"

REFERENCES

1. Smeltzer C, Formella N, Beebe H. Work restructuring: The process of decision making. *Nurs Econ.* 1993;11(6):215–258.
2. Bolton L, Aydin C, Popolow G, Ramseyer J. Organizational change. *J Nurs Adm.* 1992; 22(6):14–20.
3. Lawson K, Formella N, Smeltzer C, Walters R. Redefining the purpose of patient classification. *Nurs Econ.* 1993;11(5):298–302.
4. Malley J, Serpico-Thompson D. Redesigning roles for patient-centered care: The hospital representative. *J Nurs Adm.* 1992;22(7/8):30.
5. Smeltzer C. Lessons learned: Implementing cost reductions and enhancing quality. *Nurs Econ.* 1993;11(6):373–375.

SUGGESTED READING

Spitzer-Lehmann R, Yohn K. Patient needs driven integrated approach to care. *Nurs Managers.* 1992;23(8):30.
Zelaukas B, Hower D. The effects of implementing a professional practice model. *J Nurs Adm.* 1992;22(7,8):18.

■ 23 ■

Systematic Layout Planning for Facility Design of an Imaging Services Department

Dawn P. Rinehart, MN, MBA, FACHE
Diane Shindoll, BSIE

Sarasota Memorial Hospital (SMH) began its journey into quality management in March 1993. At that time, a nine-step problem-solving model was adopted for all teams that had been formed to improve systems with direct impact on patient care. The teams consisted of staff who were experts in the specific processes to be improved.

In October 1993, SMH opened a new critical care center, which allowed for the relocation of the emergency department, laboratory, operating rooms, and all critical care beds. With the relocation of the emergency department, the imaging services department, located adjacent to both the old and new emergency departments, was identified for expansion. Traditionally, when departments were scheduled for expansion, the management team met with the architects to design the new area, and medical and hospital staff were consulted when appropriate. This process led to the creation of a layout designed to meet projected needs on the basis of current practices and systems.

During a recent department's expansion, the hospital learned a very important lesson. In 1992, the admitting department was renovated. Immediately after the new area was opened, patients were waiting in long lines outside the admitting department, much like a line waiting to see a box office hit at the movies. Management's first assumption was that the amount of waiting space was not adequate. Therefore, immediate attention was focused on identifying additional waiting space. However, the administrator of admitting decided first to elicit input from all admitting department staff. Meetings were held around the clock to incorporate their ideas. By the third meeting, an employee spoke up and said, "This isn't a space problem, but an admitting process problem. The admission process takes too long. If that problem was resolved, the space might be ad-

Note: The authors wish to acknowledge their team members: Robert Stouffer (Team Leader), Dr. Hal Ackerstein, Ellen Barnes, Nydia Gosicki, Robert Hayes, Melissa Hill, Dot Jones, Rick Lopez, Janet Moshier, Barbara Pittenger, Shirley Robertson, Vicky Stidham, Dale Thomson, and Barbara Twohie.

equate." Attention immediately was focused on improving the admitting system rather than increasing the waiting space. Employees determined that over 60 percent of the patients could be pre-admitted over the telephone and would, therefore, require only a signature when they came into the hospital. When this change was implemented, waiting lines were eliminated. We learned a big lesson: *what appears to be obvious may not be the problem.* Therefore, solving the obvious may not improve the service and can be very costly. If the admitting area had been expanded, the cost would have been significant and the waiting times would not have been improved.

PREVENTING FIRES VERSUS PUTTING OUT FIRES

Many organizations suffer from the syndrome of "crisis management" and never have time for proactive strategic management. SMH is no exception. When the time came to renovate the imaging services area, the vice-president and the director responsible for the imaging services department proposed that a redesign team be formed to help in the layout design process. Since the new imaging services space would be available in one month for renovation, the administration's initial reaction was that there was not enough time to incorporate the team process.

However, in light of the hospital's new strategic focus on becoming a quality managed institution, the decision was made to postpone the renovation and to invest the time to incorporate staff input into the redesign project. A team was formed to identify the most efficient use of the dedicated space.

THE REDESIGN

The team began redesign by following SMH's nine-step quality improvement process. The team quickly realized, however, that the nine-step process for solving problems was not an ideal approach for the facility redesign process. Modifications were made to the process improvement model, and the team proceeded to follow a hybrid of the revised nine-step process (see Table 23–1) and the hospital management engineering department's layout improvement service, incorporating a systematic layout planning methodology. The following nine steps were used in the design process:

- *Step 1*—clarification of goals
- *Step 2*—assessment of customer needs
- *Step 3*—understanding the existing process
- *Step 4*—creation of the ideal design
- *Step 5*—planning for implementation
- *Step 6*—development of a monitoring tool
- *Step 7*—implementation of the ideal design
- *Step 8*—monitoring
- *Step 9*—follow-up

Table 23–1 Process Redesign Method: Sarasota Memorial Hospital

Step 1 Clarification of Goals	Step 2 Assessment of Customer Needs	Step 3 Understanding Existing Process
Identify goals to be achieved. Define terms.	Customers are vital to reengineering. Identify internal and external customers.	Make a flowchart of the *basic* steps in the current process. The team must scrutinize the existing process to determine *what the process is trying to accomplish.*
Identify boundaries of the project.	Complete customer needs assessment. Identify product and service needs and customer expectations. Prioritize.	Identify elapsed and actual times of each step. Graph in stacked-bar diagram for comparisons.
Identify organizational barriers to prepare for change.	Identify owner (stakeholder) of reengineering process and owner needs and expectations.	Identify steps in process that take the greatest amounts of time and "must have" vs. "nice to have."
Questions to ask: Why are we here? Where are we going?	Identify satisfaction and/or dissatisfaction levels by use of surveys or interviews.	Identify strengths and weaknesses of current process. List gaps between existing process and customer needs. Determine what part of the process has the greatest impact. Address those items first. Determine whether the improvement needed requires reengineering or whether incremental changes (problem solving) can improve the process.
Suggested tools: Strategic plan Patient satisfaction survey Outcomes management systems	**Suggested tools:** Brainstorming Surveys, interviews Pareto diagram	**Suggested tools:** Brainstorming Flowcharts Bar charts Pareto diagram

continues

Table 23–1 Continued

Step 4 Creation of Ideal Design	Step 5 Planning for Implementation	Step 6 Development of Monitoring Tools
Determine which state and federal requirements and regulations relate to the new process. Identify boundaries (social, economical, technological) and challenge them. Define who, what, where, when, and how and ask "What if?"	Validate new process with stakeholders if they are not team members.	Create a tool to measure attainment of design goals, customer responses, targets, and improvement in work environment. Customer surveys measure satisfaction levels. Control charts monitor targets.
Conduct site visits to benchmark hospitals and industrial sites to find existing innovative systems. Set targets (costs, FTEs, LOS, supplies).	Address magnitude of change and organizational resistance. What effects reflect on customer needs and other processes?	Set up a monitoring schedule and assign responsibilities.
Assess technology requirements and enhancements. Use technology to develop new process, not to speed up steps in the process.	Develop written plan including: 1. Implementation time lines 2. Responsibilities 3. Skills 4. Reward system 5. Resources 6. Plan to manage change	Review the reward system to provide incentives for change.
Create alternative designs incorporating steps with greatest impact and "must haves." Compare designs with customer needs and criteria selected in Step 2.	Create education and training: 1. How staff will fit in 2. What's expected of them 3. Improved work environment 4. Risk taking 5. Cross-training. (Do matrix.) 6. Curriculum requirements	Continue hospital-wide communication.
Select the ideal design and make a flowchart of basic steps.	Develop plan for ongoing training.	

continues

Table 23–1 Continued

Step 4 *Creation of* *Ideal Design (continued)*	Step 5 *Planning for* *Implementation (continued)*	Step 6 *Development of* *Monitoring Tools (continued)*
Identify work steps and align job functions and policies. Create job descriptions aligned with job functions. Address possible fluctuation and backup systems for new process	Plan and communicate organization-wide.	
Suggested tools: Brainstorming Benchmarking Flowcharts Site visits Surveys	**Suggested tools:** Brainstorming Matrices and grids Pilot program Change management Techniques	**Suggested tools:** Brainstorming Survey tool Check sheets Control charts

Step 7 *Implementation of* *Ideal Design*	Step 8 *Monitoring*	Step 9 *Follow-Up*
Conduct pilot period and reassess. Realign training model.	Monitor areas identified in Step 6.	Continue monitoring
Develop system audit and maintenance process.	Make adjustments as needed.	Continue hospital-wide communication.
Begin implementation sequence developed in Step 5.	Continue hospital-wide communication.	Develop "lessons learned" list.
Continue hospital-wide communication.		
Suggested tools: Communication tool	Suggested tools: Survey tools Control charts Communication tool	Suggested tools: Survey tools Control charts Communication tool "Lessons learned" list

Step 1—Clarification of Goals

The goal of the project was identified by the quality council, and a team was initiated with representation from all areas under study. The team included staff from all modalities of the imaging services department, including nuclear medicine, magnetic resonance imaging (MRI), computed tomography (CT), and general radiology. Team members were technicians, registered nurses, transporters, physicians, and clerical staff from imaging services and the emergency department. A management engineer served as the team's facilitator.

The goal proposed by the quality council was "to identify the most efficient use of the dedicated space." The team clarified and agreed on the goal and understood that, at any time during the process, they could request a modification of the goal from the quality council.

Also in step 1, the team agreed on the definition of all terms used in the process and analyzed internal and external barriers to the project. Brainstorming techniques were used for those activities.

Step 2—Assessment of Customer Needs

The second step, one of the most important, is identification of the imaging services department's customers. The team identified the external customers as patients, family members, and physicians. The internal customers were Nursing Units, Medical Records, Admitting, Surgery, Endoscopy, Respiratory Therapy, Emergency Department, physicians, technologists, nurses, file clerks, transporters, coordinators, supervisors, and management.

The following concerns of our patients were identified:

- environmental issues related to appearance and temperature
- wait time: specific to actual waiting time and lack of explanation for waiting
- accessibility of parking and of other departments within the hospital
- staff politeness, professionalism, and confidentiality
- privacy in examination rooms and changing rooms
- admission process: specifically related to the imaging services and admitting departments
- film loan accessibility, duplication process, and checkout procedures
- education prior to examination
- complications due to medications
- teaching related to postprocedure effects

- access to a patient liaison
- ease of finding the imaging services department

This step is particularly important in helping the team focus away from individual or turf issues. Going back to this step is helpful when the customer is forgotten and personal agendas enter the process.

Step 3—Understanding the Existing Process

The team followed four steps to understand the existing process. First, current square footage of the department was calculated, compiled, and segregated by functional area. The imaging services department currently utilizes 14,000 square feet. (See example of current and proposed square footages in Table 23–2.)

Second, the team began to understand the use of existing space by making a flowchart of the movement of patients and staff through the department. The step of making a flowchart is very lengthy in a process team initiative. The team found that spending time on these flowcharts was counterproductive and used a great deal of team time. Instead, the team found that making flowcharts of the *basic* steps in the existing process was more helpful and familiarized the team with what they were trying to accomplish. These flowcharts were primarily used to familiarize the team members with the activities and locations involved in a patient's management within the department.

The team completed flowcharts for

- inpatients who required a radiological procedure
- outpatients coming into the hospital for a radiological procedure (see example in Figure 23–1)
- radiological examination for an emergency department patient

Third, the highest volume imaging procedures were identified. The team constructed work-flow diagrams showing the physical movement of staff and patients through the department during these procedures. (See example work-flow diagram in Figure 23–2.) The work-flow diagrams highlighted five main problems with the current department layout.

- There is limited access to the light room directly from a hallway. The limited access causes employees to cut through examination rooms to reach the light room (see location A).
- The hallways were identified as a "storage" area both for supplies and for waiting and recovering patients (see location B).

- The long distance between the MRI area and the rest of the imaging services department was noted as difficult for access to film records and transport of patients (see location C).
- The location of the radiologists' offices was noted as segregated from the examination room for all modalities (see location D).
- The long distances between nuclear medicine, and the CT examination rooms, and the inpatient waiting room causes patients and technicians to transverse the perimeter of the light room (see location E).

Fourth, management engineering completed a volume trend analysis for the CT scan, nuclear medicine, and general radiology modalities. Procedure volume for the years 1990 through 1994 were collected from service charge analysis report downloads. The procedure volumes were classified by inpatient and outpatient volumes. Projections on yearly volumes through the year 2000 were made on the basis of average annual percent increase by modality (see Table 23–3). The average volume growth for the imaging services department as a whole is approximately 4 percent. Currently, the overall department procedure volume averages a 62 percent inpatient, 38 percent outpatient mix.

Step 4—Creation of the Ideal Design

The imaging services team followed five steps in creating their ideal department design.

1. Identify issues of concern.
2. Determine spatial relationships of department areas.
3. Assess equipment utilization.
4. Identify needs for new space.
5. Study the need and feasibility of acquiring new technology.

Issues of Concern

The team identified issues of concern to the department. These issues were divided into four major categories: layout, operational, personnel, and equipment. (See Table 23–4 for examples of the issues pertaining to the layout category.) The issues were then ranked on an importance scale of 1 to 5 (5 being most important). The concerns about layout will be utilized by architects as evaluation criteria when alternate layouts are considered. Process improvement teams will be formed to address the operational, personnel, and equipment issues that were identified.

Spatial Relationships

The spatial relationships identified in the work-flow diagrams were used to complete a Muther Chart. (See Figure 23–3 for example of the Muther Chart

Table 23-2 Radiology Redesign Team—Space Requirements

Radiology Area	Current		Proposed		Variance	Explanation
	No. of Rooms	Sq. Ft.	No. of Rooms	Sq. Ft.		
X-ray Rooms						
Angiography	2	1,288	2	1,288	0	Combine with catheterization laboratory in future?
Mammography	1	150	1	200	50	Increase for video area; move toward outpatient area.
Chest X-ray	1	230	1	230	0	Inpatient area
Ultrasonography	1	368	2	400	32	Divide 1 room into 2 smaller rooms next to each other.
General	6	1,894	7	2,182	288	Add a general room to outpatient area. Dedicated pediatric room?
Darkroom	2	252	2, 4	186	–66	Convert 1 current darkroom to daylight processing area; add 1 small darkroom to outpatient area.
Equipment Room	1	110	1	110	0	Vendor storage space
Light Room	1	414	2	714	300	Add small light room for outpatient area to service ultrasonography, nuclear medicine, etc.
Stat Reading Room	1	102	2	204	102	1 for inpatients, 1 for outpatients?
Changing Rooms	1	105	2	210	105	1 for males, 1 for females
Daylight Processing Area	0	0	1	125	125	Implement new technology.
Total		**4,913**		**5,849**	**936**	

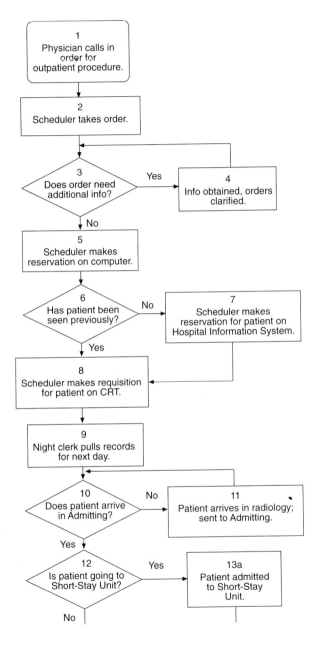

continues

Figure 23–1 Radiology Quality Team–Outpatient Flowchart, Sarasota Memorial Hospital.

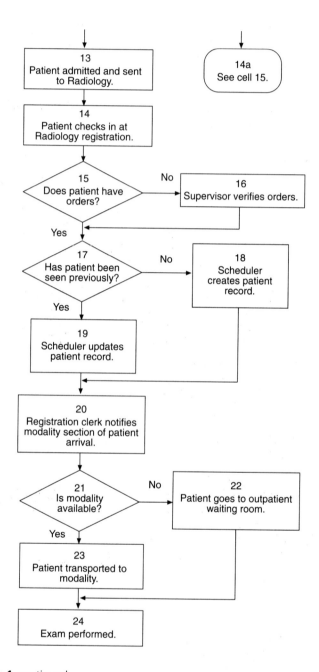

Figure 23–1 continued

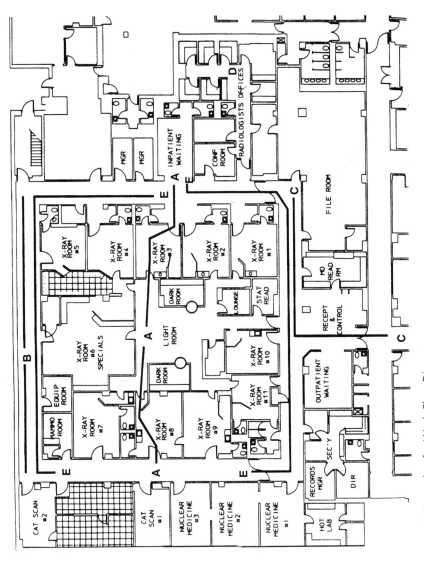

Figure 23–2 Example of a *Work-Flow Diagram*

Table 23–3 Radiology Reengineering—Imaging Services Volume Trend Analysis

| Year | CT Scan Procedures | | |
	Inpatient	Outpatient	Total
1990	4,847	3,108	7,955
1991	5,366	3,617	8,983
1992	6,152	3,725	9,877
1993	6,001	3,828	9,829
1994 Budget	6,193	4,087	10,280
1995*	6,559	4,206	10,766
1996	6,948	4,329	11,276
1997	7,359	4,455	11,814
1998	7,794	4,585	12,379
1999	8,255	4,719	12,974
2000	8,744	4,856	13,600

| Year | Radiology Procedures | | |
	Inpatient	Outpatient	Total
1990	58,291	28,419	86,710
1991	59,382	30,026	89,408
1992	63,509	31,922	95,431
1993	61,734	35,046	96,780
1994 Budget	64,034	38,086	102,120
1995*	65,302	41,270	106,572
1996	66,595	44,720	111,315
1997	67,914	48,458	116,372
1998	69,259	52,509	121,768
1999	70,631	56,898	127,529
2000	72,030	61,655	133,684

| Year | Nuclear Medicine Procedures | | |
	Inpatient	Outpatient	Total
1990	2,267	1,563	3,830
1991	2,548	1,616	4,164
1992	2,793	1,561	4,354
1993	2,295	1,730	4,025
1994 Budget	2,405	1,796	4,201
1995†	2,415	1,860	4,275
1996	2,425	1,926	4,351
1997	2,435	1,995	4,430
1998	2,445	2,066	4,511
1999	2,455	2,139	4,594
2000	2,465	2,216	4,681

continues

Table 23–3 Continued

<table>
<tr><th></th><th>MRI Procedures[‡]</th></tr>
<tr><th>Year</th><th>Total</th></tr>
</table>

Year	Total
1990	3,875
1991	3,553
1992	3,471
1993	3,440
1994 Budget	3,385
1995*	3,331
1996	3,278
1997	3,226
1998	3,175
1999	3,125
2000	3,075

*Projected volume based on average yearly increase between 1991 and 1993 volumes.
[†]Projected volume based on average yearly increase between 1990 and 1993 volumes.
[‡]MRI, magnetic resonance imaging.

used.) This chart illustrates the relative necessity for closeness between department areas by using a scale of absolute, essential, ordinary, important, unimpor-
tant, and undesirable closeness. These relationships were entered into a computer program that generates options of layouts. Computer-generated layouts
were developed showing idealistic spatial relationships, which are helpful in for-
mulating a realistic layout design. The layouts are assigned a score based on a
function of the distance between area pairs and their associated closeness rating.
Using this principle, the lower the layout score, the better the layout. (See Figure
23–4 for four examples of the layouts.)

Equipment Utilization

An equipment utilization analysis was performed to determine the number of
machines and associated rooms required for CT and nuclear medicine examinations.

CT Scanners. Currently, the hospital has two CT scanners and is planning to
purchase replacement or additional scanners. To determine how many machines
to purchase, management reengineering conducted an equipment utilization
analysis of the current CT scanners. The analysis considered the current equipment and three scenarios involving new equipment: one current scanner and one
new scanner; two new scanners; or two new scanners and one current scanner.
Annual procedure volumes, examination times, and equipment downtimes were

Table 23-4 Radiology Redesign—Issues of Concern

Item No.	Area	Score	Description of Need
58	All	4.56	Radiologists more centrally located
16	All	4.33	Outpatient and inpatient waiting rooms side by side, centrally located
10	Reception	4.33	Reception/front desk more open and welcoming
2	All	4.22	Larger and less cluttered working areas
55	All	4.11	More rest rooms, especially needed for employees
57	All	4.11	Parking nearby
32	Reception	4.00	More room at reception desk so that receptionist can move around easily
15	All	3.89	Access to outside
39	All	3.89	Loan department near outside entrance
72	All	3.89	Supplies not easily accessible
49	CT Scan	3.89	Direct entrance to light room instead of through examination room from CT area
33	Nursing	3.89	Centralized nursing area
31	Scheduler	3.89	Need of schedulers for office space other than in light room
61	All	3.78	Computers not easily accessible
74	All	3.78	Outside entrance
5	All	3.67	Dislike cutting through rooms
25	All	3.67	Central file room
50	All	3.67	Door for easy access from file room to central room
82	All	3.67	Central waiting room
59	Nursing	3.67	Office/storage space
73	Nursing	3.67	Holding area for patients before and after angiography
34	Reception	3.67	Reception area for radiology with permanent counters instead of mobile furniture
60	All	3.56	Rest rooms for patients

LOCATION	X-Ray Room—General	X-Ray Room #4/5—Angio	X-Ray Room #6—Angio	X-Ray Room #8—U/S	Equipment Room	Mammography Room	Rest Room	Office—Clinical Instructor
	1	2	3	4	5	6	7	8
1 X-Ray Room—General								
2 X-Ray Room #4/5—Angio								
3 X-Ray Room #6—Angio	U	A 1,2,4						
4 X-Ray Room #8—U/S	U	U	U					
5 Equipment Room	O	O	O	O				
6 Mammography Room	O 7	U	U	O 7	U			
7 Rest Room	A 3,6	A 6	A 6	A 6	U	A 6		
8 Office—Clinical Instructor	I 5	U	U	U	U	O	O	
9 Darkroom	A 1,4	A 1,4	A 1,4	U 10	U	A	U	O
10 Light Room	A 1,4,9	I 2,3	I 2,3	I 2	O	E 4	O	U
11 Stat Reading Room	E 2,4	U	U	I	U	U	U	U
12 Changing Rooms	A 6	A 6	A 6	A 6	U	A 6	A 6	U
13 CT Exam Rooms	I 3,4,7	E 1,4,7	E 1,4,7	I 7	O	U	A 3,4	U
14 CT Control Room	I 3,4,7	E 1,4,7	E 1,4,7	A 1,10	O	U	A 3,4	U
15 NM Exam Rooms	I 3,4,7	U	U	I 7	U	U	A 3,4	U
16 NM Hot Lab	X 8	X 8	X 8	X 8	U	X 8	O	X 8
17 Waiting Room—Outpatient	E 3,4	I	I	A	U	E 3,4	A	U
18 Waiting Room—Inpatient	E 3,4	O 3,4	O 3,4	E 3,4	U	E 3,4	A	U

Legend box: A / 2

Note: Angio, angiography; U/S, ultrasonography; CT, computed tomography; RR, rest room.

Figure 23–3 Radiology Reengineering Team—Muther Chart

9	10	11	12	13	14	15	16	17	18
Darkroom	Light Room	Stat Reading Room	Changing Rooms	CT Exam Rooms	CT Control Room	NM Exam Rooms	NM Hot Lab	Waiting Room—Outpatient	Waiting Room—Inpatient

Closeness Rating	
A	Absolute
E	Essential
I	Important
O	Ordinary
U	Unimportant
X	Undesirable

Closeness Rating Reason	
1	Equipment
2	Communication
3	Patient Convenience
4	Staff Efficiency
5	Students
6	Need RR or Changing Room
7	Myelogram—Dual Examination
8	Film Fogger
9	On Deck Area for Employees
10	Pending Laser Hookup
11	A Lot of Paperwork
12	Pulling Past Examination Films
13	Film in Darkroom

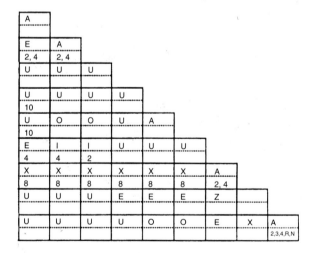

Figure 23–3 continued

Computer-Generated Layout—Option 1
Score = 20825

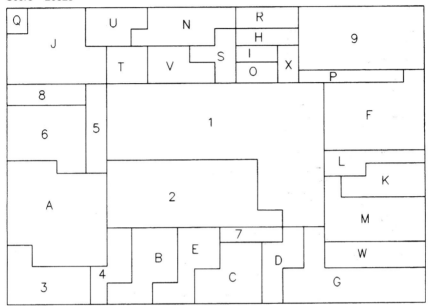

INDEX

2 = X-Ray Room—Angio
3 = X-Ray Room—U/S
4 = Mammography Room
5 = Darkroom
6 = Light Room
7 = Stat Reading Room
8 = Changing Rooms
9 = CT Exam Rooms
A = NM Exam Rooms
B = Waiting Room—Outpatient
C = Waiting Room—Inpatient
D = Transcription Room
E = Reception
F = File Room
G = Radiologist Offices
H = Office Space

I = Office Space
J = Conference Room
K = MRI Reception
L = MRI Waiting Room
M = MRI Scan Room
N = MRI Computer Room
O = MRI Medicine Room
P = MRI Records Room
Q = Telecommunications Area*
R = Scheduling Area*
S = Supply Room*
T = Nurse Area*
U = Team Leader Area*
V = Pre/Post Op Holding Area*
W = Referring Phys View Room*
X = Film Drop-Off/Pick-Up Area*

*Indicates proposed new area

Figure 23–4 Radiology Redesign

Computer-Generated Layout—Option 2
Score = 20854

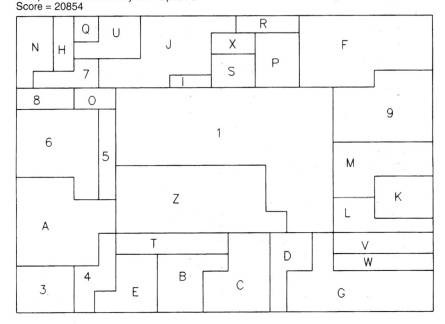

INDEX

2 = X-Ray Room—Angio
3 = X-Ray Room—U/S
4 = Mammography Room
5 = Darkroom
6 = Light Room
7 = Stat Reading Room
8 = Changing Rooms
9 = CT Exam Rooms
A = NM Exam Rooms
B = Waiting Room—Outpatient
C = Waiting Room—Inpatient
D = Transcription Room
E = Reception
F = File Room
G = Radiologist Offices
H = Office Space

I = Office Space
J = Conference Room
K = MRI Reception
L = MRI Waiting Room
M = MRI Scan Room
N = MRI Computer Room
O = MRI Medicine Room
P = MRI Records Room
Q = Telecommunications Area*
R = Scheduling Area*
S = Supply Room*
T = Nurse Area*
U = Team Leader Area*
V = Pre/Post Op Holding Area*
W = Referring Phys View Room*
X = Film Drop-Off/Pick-Up Area*

*Indicates proposed new area

Figure 23–4 continued

Computer-Generated Layout—Option 3
Score = 22005

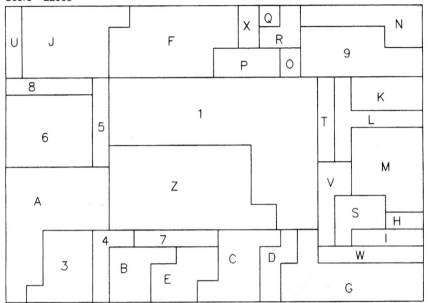

INDEX

2 = X-Ray Room—Angio
3 = X-Ray Room—U/S
4 = Mammography Room
5 = Darkroom
6 = Light Room
7 = Stat Reading Room
8 = Changing Rooms
9 = CT Exam Rooms
A = NM Exam Rooms
B = Waiting Room—Outpatient
C = Waiting Room—Inpatient
D = Transcription Room
E = Reception
F = File Room
G = Radiologist Offices
H = Office Space

I = Office Space
J = Conference Room
K = MRI Reception
L = MRI Waiting Room
M = MRI Scan Room
N = MRI Computer Room
O = MRI Medicine Room
P = MRI Records Room
Q = Telecommunications Area*
R = Scheduling Area*
S = Supply Room*
T = Nurse Area*
U = Team Leader Area*
V = Pre/Post Op Holding Area*
W = Referring Phys View Room*
X = Film Drop-Off/Pick-Up Area*
*Indicates proposed new area

Figure 23–4 continued

Computer-Generated Layout—Option 4
Score = 24584

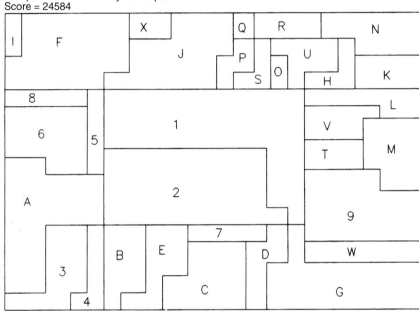

INDEX

2 = X-Ray Room—Angio
3 = X-Ray Room—U/S
4 = Mammography Room
5 = Darkroom
6 = Light Room
7 = Stat Reading Room
8 = Changing Rooms
9 = CT Exam Rooms
A = NM Exam Rooms
B = Waiting Room—Outpatient
C = Waiting Room—Inpatient
D = Transcription Room
E = Reception
F = File Room
G = Radiologist Offices
H = Office Space

I = Office Space
J = Conference Room
K = MRI Reception
L = MRI Waiting Room
M = MRI Scan Room
N = MRI Computer Room
O = MRI Medicine Room
P = MRI Records Room
Q = Telecommunications Area*
R = Scheduling Area*
S = Supply Room*
T = Nurse Area*
U = Team Leader Area*
V = Pre/Post Op Holding Area*
W = Referring Phys View Room*
X = Film Drop-Off/Pick-Up Area*
*Indicates proposed new area

Figure 23–4 continued

collected for calculation of the required machine-hours per day and the associated utilization percentages (see Table 23–5). According to the analysis, the current equipment is utilized 60 percent of the total available time. However, during February and March 1994 (the busiest time of the year for the hospital), the machines attained a utilization percentage of 99 percent during peak hours of the day. At the current volume, the scenarios yield the overall utilization percentages shown in Table 23–6. The proposed equipment will have improved scanning times; examination times are decreased, allowing more patients to be processed per day on each scanner. Therefore, the purchase of two replacement scanners will be adequate for the current and projected procedure volumes, and additional space will not need to be allocated for more than two scanners.

Nuclear Medicine Cameras. Currently, the hospital has nuclear medicine cameras in two departments; four cameras in imaging services and three cameras in cardiovascular diagnostic services (CVD). Both departments are evaluating the purchase of replacement cameras. Data on annual procedure volumes, examination times, and equipment downtimes were collected in order to perform an equipment utilization analysis. Detailed results can be found in Tables 23–7 and 23–8. The current overall utilization percentages for the two areas are shown in Table 23–9.

After analysis, it was determined that any nuclear medicine cameras purchased should be for *replacement* purposes; thus, no increase in the space is required for nuclear medicine. In addition, the equipment utilization analysis indicates that the hospital would realize efficiencies in space, labor, and equipment resources by locating the nuclear medicine cameras in closer proximity to each other.

Need for New Space

The team identified new space needs of the imaging services department: a daylight processing area, a nurse area, a team leader area, a preexamination and postexamination holding area, additional conference room space, a telecommunications and scheduling area, and a film drop-off/pick-up area. Proposed square footages for the new areas were developed as a guideline for the architects (see Table 23–2). The additional proposed department space amounts to approximately 3,000 square feet, for a proposed department total of 17,000 square feet (excluding corridors and rest rooms). The proposed square footages do not reflect space changes that would be required for acquisition of new technology.

Need and Feasibility of Acquiring New Technology

New technology in the imaging field will radically change all activities in the imaging services department, including how an image is acquired, communi-

Table 23-5 Technology Assessment of Imaging Services—Machine Utilization Analysis—CT Scanner Current System: 2 Scanners

Fiscal Year	No. of Annual Procedures	Average No. of Procedures/Day[3]	Required Machines[4]	Required Machine-Hours/Day	Machine Capacity Hours/Day[5]	Machine Utilization %[6]
1990	7,955	21.8	0.9	18	39	46
1991	8,983	24.6	1.0	21	39	52
1992	9,877	27.1	1.1	23	39	58
1993	9,829	26.9	1.1	22	39	57
1994[1]	10,280	28.2	1.1	23	39	60
1995[2]	10,764	29.5	1.2	25	39	63
1996	11,271	30.9	1.2	26	39	66
1997	11,802	32.3	1.3	27	39	69
1998	12,357	33.9	1.3	28	39	72
1999	12,939	35.5	1.4	30	39	75
2000	13,549	37.1	1.5	31	39	79

ASSUMPTIONS:

Days / Year: 365
Staffed Hours / Room / Day: 21
Downtime Hours / Day: 1.4
% Annual Procedure Growth: 5%

Average Exam Time:
Room Setup Time: 10 min.
Patient Prep Time: 10 min.
GE9800 Equipment Time: 30 min.
HiSpeed Equipment Time: 15 min.

NOTES:
1. Figures for 1994 are based on 1994 budget values.
2. Volumes for 1995–2000 are calculated at a 5% annual increase based on 1991–1993 figures.
3. Average no. of procedures per day for February and March 1994 was 33.8. This value corresponds to 72% utilization of the 2 current machines.
4. Required machines and machine-hours per day are based on a weighted average of the current hours of operation: Monday thru Friday: 24 hrs/day, Saturday and Sunday: 12 hrs/day, and on Average Exam Time.
5. Practical Machine Capacity = Staffed hours per day – Downtime hours per day.
6. Machine Utilization % = Required hours per day / Practical machine capacity.

Table 23–6 Utilization of CT Scanners

Projected Scenario	Overall Utilization (%)	Utilization in Year 2000 (%)
Current CT Scanners	60	79
Scenario 1 (1 current, 1 new)	51	67
Scenario 2 (2 new)	42	55
Scenario 3 (2 new, 1 current)	28	37

cated, and visualized; how reports are documented and distributed; and how images are archived and retrieved. These technologies include digital equipment, computed radiography, optical disk storage, and teleradiology.

Due to the financial expense of these technologies, few institutions have begun to install them. Most hospitals are waiting to get more information on the products and for reports of the experiences at other locations after installation of the products. It is beneficial, however, to estimate the impact of these technologies on space utilization in the future. Two primary areas that will be affected are space required for viewing films and for storage of films.

One of the implications of the new digital equipment is the space required for a physician to complete film reading and reporting functions. Currently, films are viewed by utilizing view boxes in the radiologist offices, the referring physicians' viewing room, and the "stat" reading room. With digital equipment, viewing will occur on computer monitors, usually with a set of two to four monitors per workstation. A consideration will be where to locate the viewing areas: close to each modality, in centralized viewing room(s), in radiologist offices, or in remote locations outside the hospital. In addition, workstations will also be required on selected nursing units. If the option of remote film viewing is available, space required for film viewing will decrease.

Space will also be required for a computer room, which will ultimately replace space currently occupied by the file room. The square footage required will depend on the amount of films to be stored on site, and the type of storage system employed. One storage option is to utilize optical disks. Optical disks holding current patient data could be stored in "jukeboxes" for rapid retrieval, and disks containing older information could be stored on wall shelving. The square footage required by the jukeboxes will depend on the size and type of jukebox chosen. SMH's current file room is approximately 926 square feet, which is ample space for implementation of the optical disk storage technology.

Moving to storage that is completely "filmless" in the near future may not be feasible, but some vendors are presenting alternatives to a filmless environment. Vendors have been identified who will digitize the files "as needed" and transmit the image back to the requesting institution. This service implies that the imaging

Table 23-7 Technology Assessment of Imaging Services

Machine Utilization Analysis—Nuclear Medicine Camera
Current System: 4 Cameras

Fiscal Year	No. of Annual Procedures	Average No. of Procedures/Day[3]	Required Machines[4]	Required Machine-Hours/Day	Machine Capacity Hours/Day[5]	Machine Utilization %[6]
1990	3,830	14.7	1.6	17	42	41
1991	4,164	16.0	1.7	19	42	44
1992	4,354	16.7	1.8	20	42	46
1993	4,025	15.5	1.6	18	42	43
1994[1]	4,201	16.2	1.7	19	42	44
1995[2]	4,537	17.5	1.9	20	42	48
1996	4,900	18.8	2.0	22	42	52
1997	5,292	20.4	2.2	24	42	56
1998	5,715	22.0	2.3	26	42	60
1999	6,173	23.7	2.5	28	42	65
2000	6,666	25.6	2.7	30	42	71

ASSUMPTIONS:

Days / Year:	260
Staffed Hours / Room / Day:	11
Downtime Hours / Day:	0.4
% Annual Procedure Growth:	8%

Average Exam Time:

Room Setup Time: 10 min.
Patient Prep Time: 10 min.
Average Current Equipment: 50 min.

NOTES:
1. Figures for 1994 are based on 1994 budget values.
2. Volumes for 1995–2000 are calculated at a 8% annual increase based on 1991–1993 figures for Nuclear Medicine and CVD combined.
3. Average no. of procedures/day for February and March 1994 was 17.5. This corresponds to 48% utilization of the 4 current machines.
4. Required machines and machine-hours per day are based on a weighted average of the current hours of operation: Monday thru Friday: 11 hrs/day (6:30 A.M.–5:30 P.M.), Saturday and Sunday: on call, and on Average Exam Time.
5. Practical Machine Capacity = Staffed hours per day – Downtime hours per day.
6. Machine Utilization % = Required hours per day / Practical machine capacity.

Table 23-8 Technology Assessment—CVD

Machine Utilization Analysis—Nuclear Medicine Camera
Current System: 3 Cameras

Fiscal Year	No. of Annual Procedures[3]	Average No. of Procedures/Day[4]	Required Machines[5]	Required Machine-Hours/Day	Machine Capacity Hours/Day[6]	Machine Utilization[7]
1992	1,076	4.1	0.5	4	23	18
1993	1,580	6.1	0.7	6	23	26
1994[1]	1,990	7.7	0.9	7	23	33
1995[2]	2,149	8.3	1.0	8	23	35
1996	2,321	8.9	1.1	9	23	38
1997	2,507	9.6	1.2	9	23	41
1998	2,707	10.4	1.3	10	23	44
1999	2,924	11.2	1.4	11	23	48
2000	3,158	12.1	1.5	12	23	52

ASSUMPTIONS:
Days / Year: 260
Staffed Hours / Room / Day: 8
Downtime Hours / Day: 0.4
% Annual Procedure Growth: 8%

Average Exam Time:
Room Setup Time: 10 min.
Patient Prep Time: 10 min.
Average Current Equipment: 38.3 min.

NOTES:
1. Figures for 1994 are based on 1994 budget values.
2. Volumes for 1995–2000 are calculated at a 8% annual increase based on 1991–1993 figures for Nuclear Medicine and CVD combined.
3. 98% of CVD procedures require 2 tests (pre/post stress test).
4. Average Procedures/Day for February and March 1994 was 12.1. This corresponds to 52% utilization of the 3 current machines.
5. Required machines and machine hours per day are based on a weighted average of the current hours of operation: Monday thru Friday: 8 hrs/day (8:00 AM–4:30 PM), and on Average Exam Time.
6. Practical machine capacity = Staffed hours per day – Downtime hours per day.
7. Machine utilization % = Required hours per day / Practical machine capacity.

Table 23–9 Utilization of Imaging and Cardiovascular Diagnostic Services

Area	Current Overall Utilization (%)	Projected Utilization in Year 2000 (%)
Imaging Services	44	71
Cardiovascular Diagnostic Services	33	52

services department would have the technology necessary to receive and transmit the digitized images.

Step 5—Planning for Implementation

The team met with the architects to discuss the findings of the project. The renovation timetable, based on the team's work, is currently being discussed.

Step 6—Development of a Monitoring Tool

The layout issues identified by the team in step 4 will be used as criteria for evaluating the new facility. Specific evaluation will be performed with respect to travel distance for patients and staff.

Steps 7 to 9—Implementation, Monitoring, and Follow-Up

After the first six steps have been completed, steps 7 to 9 are easy to do. However, a word of caution is required here: the team must remain disciplined throughout all of the steps. Because steps 7 to 9 are a more familiar type of work (no new tools or "tricks"), the team may not concentrate on or work through these steps. If these steps are not completed with as much focus and commitment as steps 1 to 6, the end result will fall short of expectations. If this occurs, there is a tendency to refocus the team's efforts on steps 1 to 4, thus missing the real flow in the process, which should occur in steps 7 to 9.

OUTCOME OF THE PROCESS

Our team completed the first five steps of the redesign process and made a presentation to the quality council. The team's preliminary layouts were made and shared with the architects. Additional positive results coming from the team process are as follows:

- computer-generated, "ideal" layouts based on spatial relationships identified from the work-flow diagrams and results of the Muther Chart
- a detailed list of issues for layout evaluation criteria
- an identified list of patient and employee satisfaction issues, which will be a base line of information for follow-up studies, once the new facility is in place
- a list of additional space needs
- a volume trend analysis for all modalities
- an equipment utilization analysis determining the number of CT scanners and nuclear medicine cameras required

GETTING STARTED—MAXIMIZING RESULTS

The most important measurable change resulting from this reengineering process is a new approach for employees regarding what their jobs are and who their customers are, as well as a genuine eagerness toward change. Often, employees resist change. What occurs through this process is not only a clear sense of "teamwork," but also an impatience with the "status quo" and a commitment toward improving the workplace. Employees who have been involved on a team use the skills learned in the process in their daily roles and are eager to participate in the process again. They now regard assessment of both processes and customer feedback as essential to the overall evaluation of their department.

The four key points for achievement of results in process redesign and overall organizational change are:

1. education
2. team composition
3. utilization of the appropriate process, combined with the flexibility to incorporate expertise from the organization
4. provision of ongoing consultation to the facilitator, team leader, and team members

Education

We have utilized a just-in-time approach to education. When a team is formed, they are taught meeting skills and group dynamics prior to holding team meetings. This approach has proved to be a valuable tool. Meetings become much more productive, and natural conflict is understood and not encouraged or discouraged. Meeting skills that team members learn are

- team member roles, including facilitator, team leader, recorder, and time-keeper
- use of agendas and of time frames for agenda items
- group dynamics, including balanced participation from all team members, team interventions for specific behavior types, and good communication and listening skills
- techniques to refocus the team toward goals and customer focus when personal agendas or fears come into the team process

Group Dynamics

The teams utilize group dynamic techniques from Joiner & Associates' *The TEAM Handbook*. The stages of team growth discussed in this book have been particularly helpful in allowing teams to understand the normal process of forming, storming, norming, and performing. This knowledge helps the teams when they experience the conflicts and discomforts associated with the brainstorming phase.

Facilitator and Team Leader Education

Facilitators and team leaders are provided education prior to being assigned to a team. Two days of role responsibilities, the meeting process, group dynamics, and intervention skills are taught initially. Following that session is another two-day workshop on the scientific approach, with emphasis on quality tools and techniques for problem-solving and redesign processes.

Team Composition

We have found that facilitators can be management or staff level employees who are not part of the process under study. With the proper education and coaching, a manager involved in the process can serve as team leader, but the manager should not be a team member because this role could lead to problems relating to staff level employees who are also team members. Managers who are not involved on teams have the advantage of encouraging empowerment and developing self-directed work teams, and they also have the opportunity to practice newly acquired skills of coaching and strategic planning. Teamwork brings staff with different roles together to look at being proactive versus reactive. Another very important consideration in the process is to access the expertise available to the teams from within the organization. In this reengineering effort, the facilitator was a management engineer who brought tools and techniques not known by the others to the process: the Muther Chart, work-flow designs, and computer-generated layout methodology.

Ongoing Consultation

Providing ongoing consultation services for team leaders, facilitators, and team members is imperative. Educational seminars and just-in-time training are effective tools in preparing a team for the redesign process, but assistance should always be available to the team when they begin to experience the feelings of frustration, impatience, rush to accomplishment, and dealing with group behaviors. As the team completes a problem-solving or redesign process for the first time, the amount of consultation services required begins to diminish, and self-directed work teams take over.

CONCLUSION

In our journey to becoming a quality managed organization, we learned that, as one brings the scientific methods of Juran, Crosby, or Deming into the organization, one must also practice the art of management. Tools and techniques can only be useful if people are rewarded for honestly using them and if the organization supports risk taking with the knowledge that not all changes will be successful. Vital in this art is a good communication system, sound education and training, ongoing review of the process and feedback, and alignment of recognition and reward systems with the mission, vision, and goals of the program.

BIBLIOGRAPHY

1. Adams H, Arora S. *Total Quality in Radiology.* Delray Beach, FL: St. Lucie Press; 1994.
2. Salvendy G. *Handbook of Industrial Engineering.* 2nd ed. New York: Wiley; 1992.
3. Scandura T. *Voice of the Business.* Presented at the Quality Management Certificate Program; 1994; University of Miami, FL.
4. Scholtes P. *The TEAM Handbook.* Madison, WI: Joiner & Associates; 1988.

■ 24 ■

An Update—
The Ambulatory Treatment Unit

Judy M. Lanigan, MA, RN
Linda Bartkowski-Dodds, MS, RN
Jody Mechanic, MS, RN

Like many other hospitals, Stanford University Hospital has restructured and reengineered care delivery systems in response to the many changes in health care. One major change has been the trend toward outpatient ambulatory care services. This trend, driven by economic and technological forces, requires a significant change in the way hospitals do business and promotes new opportunities for alternatives to traditional inpatient care.

As a component of the overall patient-centered care strategy at Stanford University Hospital, the ambulatory treatment unit was developed to provide a seamless continuum of care directed toward an evolving outpatient population. New programs were designed to enhance access, improve quality and service, and contribute to more efficient use of resources. These contributions are evidenced by the development of programs such as a one-time registration process, eliminating the need for repeated patient registrations, as well as expansion of unit hours and locations to more appropriately bring services to the patient. The ambulatory treatment unit employs a unique complement of nursing staff to meet the needs of a diverse patient population. To provide more responsive patient service, nurses with different specialty backgrounds are cross-trained in other areas to redesign roles and best support the newly reengineered patient care environment. This cross-training provides increased efficiency and flexibility and greater response to multiple patient care needs.

Implementation of the ambulatory treatment unit began as a staged process to incrementally build in new services over time. This process has allowed for the development of new protocols, integration of patient care standards, and professional education of staff.

Today, the ambulatory treatment unit continues to diversify its services and has set a precedent for development of future innovative patient care delivery systems in a rapidly changing health care environment.

The Ambulatory Treatment Unit— An Innovative Model

Judy M. Lanigan, MA, RN
Linda Bartkowski-Dodds, MS, RN
Jody Mechanic, MS, RN

The ambulatory treatment unit (ATU) at Stanford University Hospital was designed originally to meet the health care needs of the following two unique patient populations: (1) those requiring medical support therapy, such as newly discharged bone marrow transplant patients or oncology patients receiving prolonged chemotherapy treatments, and (2) those undergoing invasive diagnostic/therapeutic procedures on an outpatient basis. Before the opening of the ATU, these patients would have been admitted to an inpatient bed or treated in a clinic. If these patients were admitted, they were often denied reimbursement by insurance carriers demanding that patients receive ambulatory care. Lengthy infusions often create delays in a clinic setting. These practices decrease clinic productivity and provide suboptimal accommodations for patients and families.

The ATU has provided an answer to this dilemma by accommodating chemotherapy patients for the time required to complete the therapy and discharging these patients within a 23-hour period, allowing for reimbursement on an outpatient basis.[1] Patients undergoing invasive/therapeutic procedures, such as cardiac catheterization, are processed and receive recovery care on an outpatient basis instead of being admitted and risking insurance denial. These practices simplify the admission/discharge procedure.

More recently, the drive to decrease hospital length of stay, combined with the development of new technology making surgical procedures less invasive, has stimulated the need for comprehensive ambulatory services. New patient populations have continued to surface, and the ATU has diversified its services concurrently to accommodate these demands for diversification. Figure 24–1 illustrates this evolution in the first 4 years after the inception of the ATU.

To enhance convenience and access to ambulatory services, the ATU is located on the first floor of the hospital, adjacent to the emergency department and the clinics. Here, the ATU has one large infusion room, with a capacity to treat six patients simultaneously. In addition, one large room contains three pheresis sta-

Source: Reprinted from Lanigan, J.M., Dodds, L., and Mechanic, J., The Ambulatory Treatment Unit, *Journal of Nursing Administration*, Vol. 24, No. 4, pp. 41–44, with permission of J.B. Lippincott Company, © 1994.

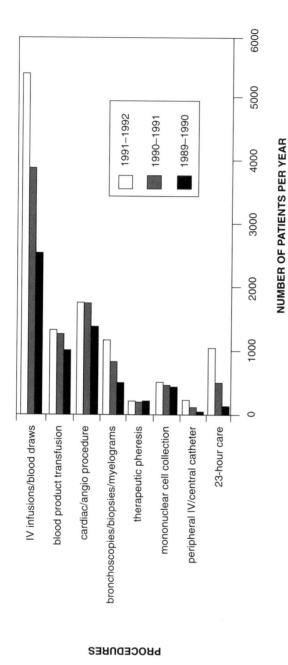

Figure 24–1 Population Growth in the ATU

tions and a total of 21 beds, including semiprivate rooms that provide gurney and bed space for lengthy day or overnight treatments and several private rooms to accommodate special patient needs. Additionally, a satellite is located on the second floor of the hospital, adjacent to the catheterization/angiography department, for processing patients undergoing catheterizations or angiograms. Post-procedure recovery occurs in the main ATU, however, where patients and families can be accommodated more comfortably.[2]

Because of the diverse needs of these patient populations, the ATU nursing staff must undergo cross-training within at least two specialty areas. For example, a nurse experienced in cardiac care would be assigned primarily to pre- and post-catheterization care and cardioversion, but would also be cross-trained to administer chemotherapy and provide symptom management. Other staff members with oncology experience would provide the medical resources when necessary, creating a complementary and collaborative atmosphere. With the increased proficiency of clinical nursing skills required and the recent expansion of the program, the nursing staff has had a continual need to increase the scope of their practice and add to their professional challenge through the creation, adoption, and implementation of innovative nursing practice.[3]

PROGRAM IMPLEMENTATION AND INNOVATIONS

Patient-Focused Care

The ATU emphasizes service orientation. Patient scheduling needs are accomplished through expanded hours, including weekend, evening, and holiday coverage, enabling patients to be seen during hours that are less likely to conflict with careers or personal agendas.[1]

The ATU is based on the creation of innovative programs to fulfill both patient and organization needs. From a patient perspective, unit management and staff members have simplified the admission to and discharge from the unit, facilitating frequent visits from patients requiring medical support therapies on an ongoing basis. For example, bone marrow transplant patients require blood product support until their transplanted bone marrow matures to the point at which blood counts are stabilized.

Institutional Strategic Support

The ATU supports the organizational innovations of the hospital in several ways. First, as the trend toward outpatient services is increasing, the ATU has established an environment that allows for the expansion of new as well as existing programs throughout the institution. In addition to the bone marrow and heart/lung transplant programs, other programs include the stereotaxic treatment program, the 23-hour care program for ambulatory surgery patients, and outpatient nursing care for research protocols involving experimental drug therapy. The ATU services also encompass a large component of both pre- and post-care for invasive procedures that are required for specific patient populations. This includes pre- and post-care for patients undergoing cardiac catheterization, liver and heart biopsies, complicated endoscopy procedures, and bronchoscopies. Additionally, the ATU resolved the problems associated with elective, outpatient cardioversions by providing an ambulatory setting for this procedure, as opposed to the use of an inpatient bed. This has facilitated improved compliance with state regulatory requirements and improved hospital reimbursement.[4]

Second, the ATU has improved appropriate use of health care services by providing care delivery on an outpatient basis that would not be reimbursable through traditional, inpatient care. It has reduced saturation in the emergency department by providing an observation care program for stabilized, post-trauma patients, thereby improving use of hospital resources.

Finally, the participative leadership style provided by the nurse manager has promoted increased responsibility and accountability among staff members and has facilitated collaboration with physicians and hospital departments. This has been accomplished through the ATU nurse council. The purpose of the council is to collaborate with the nurse manager regarding operation issues, provide recommendations for the improvement of patient care, and assist in identifying unit cost containment activities. A second example, the ATU advisory group, comprised of representatives from departments that interface with the ATU, provides an opportunity for input from physicians and interdepartment staff members on unit issues.

At the beginning of each fiscal year, the entire unit participates in an annual planning meeting with the nurse manager and the assistant director of nursing. At this time, unit goals and an overview of unit financial status for the following year are discussed as a component of the overall hospital goals. This information is then used as a foundation for the ATU nurse council agenda.

The ATU participated recently in a department-wide survey to assess the degree of job satisfaction of staff. Although the results of overall department scores were positive, the ATU results revealed higher scores in several areas related to professional staff development issues. Figure 24–2 illustrates comparative mean scores in six key areas for 1992 and 1993.

DEVELOPMENT OF SPECIALTY PROGRAMS

Staff development also is facilitated through the role of specialty program liaison nurse. This role can include responsibilities such as the development of poli-

KEY ISSUES	MEAN SCORES			
	ATU		ALL PATIENT CARE AREAS	
	1992	1993	1992	1993
Flexibility in scheduling	4.2	4.3	4.0	4.0
Recognition of work from peers	4.1	3.9	3.4	3.8
Control over what goes on in work setting	3.5	3.2	3.0	3.1
Participation in organizational decision making	3.3	3.2	3.0	3.0
Control/responsibility	3.6	3.4	3.2	3.4
Opportunities for career advancement	3.5	3.5	3.2	3.3

Figure 24–2 Job Satisfaction Scores. Mean scores based on 5-point Likert scale with 5 representing "very satisfied" and 1 representing "very dissatisfied."

cies and procedures, patient teaching tools, discharge instructions, and participation in staff education. Three of these programs, including the peripheral intravenous central catheter (PICC) program, the cardiac catheterization program, and the therapeutic pheresis program, are discussed in further detail.

Vascular Access Devices: The PICC Line Program

To maintain state-of-the-art proficiency in the use of vascular access devices and to reduce the repeated need for venipunctures in patients requiring intermediate length intravenous therapies and blood drawing, a staff nurse-initiated program was created on the unit to begin use of the peripheral intravenous central catheter (PICC) line.

With the assistance of an outside consultant, the nurse proposed a group of ATU nurses to complete a certification process for PICC insertion. Additionally, because the program represented a procedure traditionally performed by physicians, the nurse developed hospital-wide policies and procedures that required numerous presentations to respective committees, advisory boards, interdisciplinary practice groups, and the legal office. Thus, the nurse's knowledge of the innovative use of the PICC and her commitment to improving the quality of patient care on the unit led to the adoption of this innovation not only on the ATU unit, but on other hospital units as well.

To date, the nurse has participated in a house-wide education of staff, developed comprehensive discharge instructions for patients and families, and created a nursing quality assurance form to ensure appropriate follow-through and use. Maintenance policies are updated annually, and staff education continues on an ongoing basis. This program represents how a nursing innovation is operationalized continually and confirmed as an integral component of quality patient care.

The Cardiac Catheterization/Interventional Radiology Program

The outpatient cardiac catheterization program was developed in response to the cardiac catheterization laboratory's request to ensure that patients are ready for their procedures in a timely manner. The primary populations served include patients undergoing interventional radiology procedures, such as cardiac catheterizations, percutaneous transluminal coronary angioplasties, cerebral angiograms, stent changes, and tube changes for biliary obstruction. On the morning of the scheduled procedures, patients and families are given pre-procedural education, sign informed consents, and have the necessary laboratory tests performed. On completion of the procedure, patients are returned to the ATU for recovery. Although the majority of patients are discharged within 8 hours after a procedure is completed, if necessary, they may remain for additional observation by using the 23-hour care program.

The Therapeutic Pheresis Program

The therapeutic pheresis program began as an adjunct to the inpatient bone marrow transplant program and has expanded to meet the needs of a larger group of patient populations. These populations include patients with a diagnosis of multiple myeloma, breast cancer, lymphoma, Hodgkin's disease, and leukemia. Typically, these patients undergo stem cell collections for 4 hours each day, until adequate stem cells have been collected. The ATU nurses maintain a close communication with the bone marrow transplant unit and attend multidisciplinary rounds to enhance continuity between the two units.

In addition to stem cell collections performed for the bone marrow transplant patients, the therapeutic pheresis program was developed to provide plasma and red cell exchanges and platelet and white cell depletions for patients diagnosed with various diseases, including Guillain-Barré syndrome and idiopathic thrombocytopenia purpura.

Currently, the ATU staff includes five nurses who are highly trained in pheresis therapy and are on call to provide evening and weekend coverage to meet the specialized needs of these diverse patient populations. Each staff member is involved in the development of policies and procedures, documentation and patient teaching tools, and quality assurance for the program.

Twenty-Three Hour Program

The Twenty-Three Hour Care Program on the ATU provides overnight care for patients recovering from outpatient surgery who require additional nursing support, such as pain or nausea management, intravenous antibiotics, or hydration. Typical surgical patients using this service include orthopedic patients, such as those undergoing meniscectomies and arthroscopy repairs; gynecologic patients, such as those undergoing laser laparoscopies; and patients undergoing plastic surgery, hand reconstruction, hernia repair, cataract surgery, nasal septoplasty, and other surgeries appropriate for outpatient care. Recently, preoperative admissions requiring bowel preparations or intravenous antibiotics before surgery have been added to this service. This is an excellent example of another innovative mechanism to avoid preoperative, inpatient surgical stays and reduce the overall hospital length of stay.[5]

CONCLUSION

The ATU provides an alternative setting and an adjunct for patient care delivery in the hospital arena. Programs have been designed to augment and enhance existing patient care services and maximize benefits for the patient. In addition, the ATU provides an environment that enhances professional development and job satisfaction among nursing staff. With the trend toward increasing outpatient services in care delivery, the ATU remains a unique entity in the acute care setting and a nursing care innovation at Stanford University Hospital.

REFERENCES

1. Weisman E. Observation units hold promise for outpatient care. *Hospitals.* 1990;64(12):66.
2. Anderson H. Convenient care a top priority for new center. *Hospitals.* 1991;65(8):66, 68.
3. Hermann CE. Diversified nursing practice in ambulatory care. *Nurs Econ.* 1993;11(3):176–179.
4. Matson TA. *Restructuring for Ambulatory Care: A Guide to Reorganization.* Chicago: American Hospital Publishing Inc; 1990;41–43.
5. Flory J. *Ambulatory Care: A Management Briefing.* Chicago: American Hospital Publishing Inc; 1990:9–11.

∎ 25 ∎

An Update—
Development of an Innovative
Nursing Care Delivery System

Susan D. Guild, MS, RNC, NNP, PNP

Care delivery is a system of interdependent processes. Current delivery systems too often support activities that are disjointed, archaic, and process oriented, rather than outcome oriented. Since reengineering focuses on process innovation and redesign to achieve defined outcomes, it offers the ideal framework for development of care delivery systems. Its concepts are evident throughout this obstetric care project at Strong Memorial Hospital.

As a leader in the obstetric health care community, Strong Memorial Hospital's competitive market position and commitment to innovative, family-centered care demanded a leap beyond the product to the process, beyond facility design to care delivery. The creation of a new vision for obstetric care delivery required an empowered team, working with a clear mandate and few boundaries. A well-defined work plan, organized around process-oriented topics, provided a comprehensive multidisciplinary perspective of obstetric care delivery. Based on this information, the project report affirmed the tenets of reengineering, calling for a collaborative team approach to delivering care in a natural order or continuum, with patient-focused processes as the guiding principle.

Implementation was delayed one year to permit major changes in the original facility design that were based on project report recommendations. Multidisciplinary work groups have now begun the task of bringing the vision to reality. Staffing will be redesigned around multiskilled workers. A competency-based, cross-training program for nursing staff will ensure flexibility and recognize expertise. Initiatives in patient education and home care will link inpatient and outpatient areas in a continuum of patient-focused care. A triage system will guide patient placement, with single-room maternity care offered as the standard. An expanded case management model and an interdisciplinary policy and standard of care manual will enhance collaboration and continuity of care. Formal partnerships between nurse managers and advanced practice nurses will ensure comprehensive leadership and quality care throughout the transition. Finally, a newsletter, staff forums, and community focus groups will allow ongoing communication with internal and external customers during each phase of the project.

Breakthrough thinking is essential to futuristic health care planning and the systems that will define it. Reengineering offers an exciting framework for innovation to ensure their success.

Development of an Innovative Nursing Care Delivery System

Susan D. Guild, MS, RNC, NNP, PNP
Rebecca Wrede Ledwin, MS, RNC, PNP
Deborah M. Sanford, MBA, RN
Terri Winter, MS, RN

Strong Memorial Hospital is a tertiary care facility with over 700 beds that provides care and consultation to a ten-county region in upstate New York. The Ob-Gyn department offers a complete spectrum of women's health services. The inpatient service—comprising labor and delivery, the birth center, the newborn nursery, the high-risk obstetrics unit, gynecologic/gynecologic oncology units, and the gynecologic operating room—is affiliated with an active outpatient/referral service with several specialty clinics.

Following national trends, births at Strong Memorial Hospital have increased over the past decade to 4,300 deliveries per year. This has resulted in rising occupancy, with significant doubling of patients during peak census. Root causes include the following: (1) a substantial increase in high-risk births within socially, economically, and medically disadvantaged minority and teenage populations;

Source: Reprinted from Guild, S.D., Ledwin, R.W., Sanford, D.M., and Winter, T., Development of an Innovative Nursing Care Delivery System, *Journal of Nursing Administration,* Vol. 24, No. 3, pp. 23–29, with permission of J.B. Lippincott Company, © 1994.

Acknowledgments: The authors thank the following additional members of the Nursing Care Delivery Task Force: Pamela Cate, MS, RN; Kathryn Flynn, BSN, RN; Maureen Freedman, MS, RN; Susan Howlett, RN; and Sara Weller, BSN, RN. A special thanks is given to Ann Dozier, MS, RN, Director of Ob-Gyn Nursing, for her support and mentorship.

(2) an increase in births to older women, many of whom have high-risk problems; and (3) a decrease in available obstetric specialty care in surrounding rural communities. Moreover, trends toward a shortened length of stay for low-risk obstetric patients, single-room maternity care as the obstetric standard, managed care, and emphasis on the patient as consumer also required consideration. These factors, as well as the increased demand for tertiary level services, provided the impetus for an evaluation of facilities and care delivery.

A proposal for obstetric bed expansion and facilities renovation was submitted to the New York State Department of Health; it was approved in December 1992. Counterpart to this initiative, an Ob-Gyn nursing task force was convened in June 1992 to evaluate the system of nursing care delivery and develop recommendations for a new system.

Over the next 8 months, the task force gathered information on nursing care delivery systems through an extensive review of the literature, internal interviews, and a survey of targeted hospitals across the country. Based on this information, knowledge of the current delivery system, and philosophy of obstetric nursing at Strong Memorial Hospital, the task force developed recommendations for a new system of care delivery. Once implemented, this new system will complement facilities designed to successfully meet the current and future challenges of a changing, more demanding health care environment.

The following sections address the development of this system.

THE PROJECT TEAM

Selecting the Team

Selecting a project team with representation from all sectors of Ob-Gyn nursing was key to the success of the project. Membership included nine representatives who reflected a cross-section of management/clinical, staff/leadership, and inpatient/outpatient perspectives. Led by an advanced practice nurse, the team included clinical nurse specialists from the birth center and high-risk obstetrics unit, the Ob-Gyn project management specialist, nurse managers from labor and delivery and the birth center, an assistant nurse manager from the newborn nursery, a staff nurse from the high-risk obstetrics unit, a nurse practitioner from the outpatient area, and the Ob-Gyn night nursing supervisor.

An informal luncheon meeting hosted by the director of Ob-Gyn nursing provided the official project kickoff and the expected deadline. The team received its charge, reviewed essential background information, and socialized, beginning the team building process.

Organizing the Team

Orienting team members to the project presented the next challenge. Each member came with diverse experiences and expectations; therefore, initial meetings were used to establish a baseline of information within the team. This included review of the original facilities proposal, as well as existing nursing care models, such as case management and mother/baby nursing.

An organization framework for project activities was then established. Team members set time frames for each phase of the project, agreed on meeting behaviors, set a meeting schedule, identified lines of communication, such as format for minutes and directory of members, and reviewed roles within the group, such as chair and recorder. In addition, each member was given a binder for project information. Vested and organized, the team was ready to develop a work plan.

THE PROJECT WORK PLAN

Developing a Work Plan

The next phase involved identifying and organizing a plan for gathering information on obstetric care delivery systems. The group began by brainstorming the ideal system of care delivery. This process was facilitated by use of an outline/mapping wheel (Figure 25–1). The new care delivery system lies at the core of the wheel; its spokes represent the multiple facets of care essential to an effective system. A patient- and family-centered philosophy of care rests at the top of the wheel, representing the guiding principle for the system. Aspects (or spokes) are then delineated, based on the themes of continuity, comprehensiveness, collaboration, effectiveness, and efficiency, as stated in this philosophy. Once established, this vision of the ideal system served as a guide and focal point for project activities.

Discussions then focused on strategies for obtaining information necessary for recommendations. The group identified several ways to accomplish this: a literature review, a survey of hospitals around the country, interviews of key (institution) personnel, review of internal statistics, and review of regulatory statements and professional standards. Once the work plan was identified, the team set a 6-week schedule for organizing the process and a 2-month schedule to complete it.

Literature Review

A literature search provided information published over the past five years on care delivery systems, as well as trends and practices in obstetric health care. Key

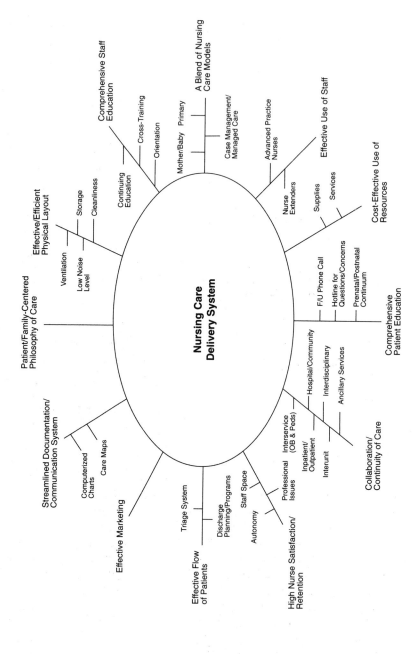

Figure 25–1 The Outline/Mapping Wheel for the New Care Delivery System

words were identified to guide the search, and a process of cataloging and reviewing articles was established. One person was assigned to generate a computerized bibliography, which included journal articles, newspaper items, and conference overviews. Articles were distributed to the task force, reviewed and summarized during project meetings, and coded to the bibliography with title, journal, date discussed, and overview. The articles, summaries, and bibliography were placed in each team member's notebook, which provided a quick reference list to use throughout the project.

Thirty-five articles were reviewed by the group. Although information on obstetric issues was readily available, little was found in the literature on care delivery systems, with a few noteworthy exceptions.[1–3] Once completed, the literature survey provided an overview of trends, themes, and innovations in obstetric care and guided development of survey and interview questions.

External Hospital Surveys

The task force developed a plan to survey hospitals noted for their active obstetric services and progressive approaches to care across the country. These surveys would provide a picture of each obstetric care delivery system from administrative, management, and clinical perspectives. A list of hospitals, contact names, and phone numbers was compiled from fellow members of hospital consortiums, article citations, contacts from conferences, and personal networking. Thirty-six hospitals were identified for the survey.

After a review of patient/nurse satisfaction surveys and other instruments used to collect institutional data, a prototype was developed. Building on these examples, the finished questionnaire addressed key issues identified in the ideal system of care delivery (Exhibit 25–1). A triage format, with four variations of the tool, allowed focused input from obstetric nursing administrators, nurse managers, staff nurses, and other providers, such as physicians, advanced practice nurses, and nurse extenders. The tools were trialed within the Ob-Gyn department to refine questions, test ease of completion, and evaluate information reliability. They also were reviewed with the director of Ob-Gyn nursing and the planning and marketing department of the hospital before implementation.

To begin the process, a cover letter from the director of Ob-Gyn nursing and a sample survey were sent to the obstetric nursing administrator at each hospital. The letter stated the survey purpose, requested participation, and promised an overview of results. A task force member then called within the next 1 to 2 weeks to verify participation and schedule a phone interview. In anticipation of this call, administrators were requested to review the survey and begin identifying other contacts to be interviewed within their institution, such as nurse managers. After

Exhibit 25–1 Survey Content

Administrator
  General hospital statistics
  Number and distribution of OB beds
  Average LOS for type of delivery
  Classification of the hospital
  Staffing patterns on the various units
  Model of nursing care
  Use of cross-training
  Patient mix on units
  Educational programs offered
  Discharge planning
  Recovery areas of various patients
  Physician coverage
  Use of nurse extenders
  Cost-effectiveness of current system
  Advantages/disadvantages of the current system
  Changes planned for the future
Staff nurse survey
  Rated effectiveness of the following: layout, location of supplies, documentation system, patient/staff ratio of care, patient teaching, discharge planning, support from ancillary services, collaboration between nurses and other providers, in-service education, and cross-training programs.
  In addition, staff nurses were asked about the impact of various nursing activities on the amount of time required to do that activity.
Nurse manager survey
  Patient mix on the unit
  Physical layout/conduciveness to care delivery
  Definition of patient population by risk level
  Staffing patterns
  Cross-training pattern/program
  Type/frequency of mandatory in-services/continuing education programs for nursing staff
  Model of nursing care
  Documentation system
  Patient education program
  Location of recovery for C-section patients
  Discharge planning
  Collaboration with other professionals
  Use of nurse extenders
  Attending physician/resident coverage
  Type/use of ancillary personnel
  Satisfaction/cost-effectiveness of the current system
  Changes planned for the future
Additional personnel survey
  Asked the provider to describe their role and responsibilities.

Exhibit 25–2 Interview Content

Likes and dislikes in the current delivery system
Preferred changes
Perceptions about consumer needs/desires for care
Effectiveness of communication and collaboration between:
  Inpatient/outpatient areas, hospital and community, the various ancillary services, and obstetric and pediatric departments
Suggestions regarding staffing levels
Changes to be considered in the organization of units
Perspectives on cross-training, nursing educational programs, and documentation systems
Suggestions for improving discharge planning and patient education

the administrative survey, the other contacts were called to set up a time for actual interview.

Task force members were given four to five hospitals to survey. Each person completed a pilot survey from one of the assigned hospitals. The group reviewed this first set of responses to clarify questions, ensure consistency between interviewers, and determine ease of information retrieval from the tool. No problems were found, and the process continued.

Most hospitals responded with enthusiasm and, as a result, a 70 percent participation rate was achieved. Establishing an accurate list of obstetric nursing directors for each hospital and sending a cover letter with a sample survey ensured a smooth and timely response. This enabled appropriate administrators to review the tool and forward it to their staff members, allowing preparation time and decreasing interview time. Administrative surveys lasted 30 to 40 minutes, nurse manager/advanced practice nurse surveys took 40 to 90 minutes, and staff surveys lasted 20 to 30 minutes.

The greatest percentage of interviewees were administrators and nurse managers. Advanced practice nurses often provided the most detailed perspective of programs and clinical issues. Administrators identified few nursing staff or nurse extenders and no physicians as contacts for interview. Initial completion time of the surveys was 4 weeks; however, this was extended to 8 weeks because of difficulty in arranging initial contacts with a few key hospitals and scheduling interview times with busy administrators and managers.

Internal Interviews

Obtaining the perspective of key individuals within Strong Memorial Hospital and the community was essential in developing a new care delivery system. Approximately 40 individuals, who represented diversity in scopes of practice, specialty areas, practice sites, and viewpoints essential to care delivery, were identified. These included obstetricians, pediatricians, perinatologists, residents, pediatric and Ob-Gyn nurse practitioners from the hospital and community, nurse midwives, clinical nurse specialists, staff nurses at all levels, newly hired staff nurses with work experiences at other hospitals, social workers, community health nurses, consumer advocates from the community and hospital consumer advisory board, ancillary personnel, such as dietitians and housekeepers, and personnel from the hospital planning and marketing department.

Interviews followed the surveys in November 1992. Using a similar process, they built on survey information. Interviewers queried individuals on what they liked about the current delivery system, what they wanted to see changed from the perspective of their roles, and what innovative ideas they might offer from their experiences or networking (Exhibit 25–2).

In preparation, a cover letter stating the purpose of interviews, requesting participation, and informing contacts of possible interview topics was sent out again. The assigned task force members then performed one-to-one personal interviews using the tool as a guide and focusing on those questions pertinent to the interviewees. Lastly, they completed the tool, summarizing the interview.

Each member was assigned four to five individuals to interview based on clinical interest or prior acquaintance. No problems with process or tool were identified with the first set of interviews. Interviews lasted approximately 30 minutes. Proximity and a vested interest in the care delivery system at Strong Memorial Hospital contributed to a 90 percent participation rate and to completion of interviews within the allotted 3-week time frame.

Statistics

Statistics provided the backdrop for planning a care delivery system. Obtained from the hospital database, they included length of stay for major patient populations, number of deliveries, number of admissions and discharges, number and type of clinic patients, and patient use of educational programs and resources. Expected bed capacity and configuration of units in the proposed renovation plan also were reviewed.

Statistics contributed to an understanding of patient population and flow, which helped establish recommendations. However, most of the data obtained were not analyzed. Statistics were found to be more helpful during actual program development.

Standards and Regulations

Compliance with professional standards and statements of regulatory agencies is essential to any care delivery system. The New York State Department of Health code, the Joint Commission on Accreditation of Healthcare Organizations standards, the American College of Obstetricians and Gynecologists/American Academy of Pediatrics perinatal guidelines, and the Association of Women's Health, Obstetric and Neonatal Nurses standards were all reviewed by the project team. Again, this information was more essential to the development and implementation phases of the project.

THE PROJECT REPORT

Collating Data

Extensive information obtained from surveys, interviews, and literature review required a system of organization for collating and analyzing data. A list of topics that were developed by the project team and encompassed the major areas of care delivery provided the necessary framework (Exhibit 25–3).

Using this list of topics, two members, assigned to organizing and writing the report, began the task of placing information into a computer database. Many strategies were used to accomplish this. Because surveys and interviews were written in the interviewer's shorthand, each member met with the collating team to code information into the database. This approach facilitated the collating process and provided an opportunity for initial review of information prior to large group discussions. When a meeting was not possible, each member provided a summary of the survey or interview, organized according to the list of topics. The collating team also placed article summaries from the literature review into the database.

The report generated from this database presented an organized overview of surveys, interviews, and articles. Each section of the report reviewed pertinent information on a specific topic, coded by source, with space provided at the end of that section for writing questions, issues, ideas, and recommendations.

Developing Recommendations

A retreat day was organized for project team members to provide a forum for discussion of information and development of recommendations. In laying the groundwork for productive discussion, each individual was given the 170-page report 3 weeks before the retreat. Members were asked to review this packet thoroughly, identifying issues and organizing recommendations for each topic. In addition, the last few project meetings were devoted to discussion of topics addressing potentially sensitive issues that were not well understood by the group or that contained multiple issues requiring preliminary sorting.

To ensure an organized and thorough review of the issues, a timed, sequenced agenda was established. Similar topics were grouped and prioritized, with each

Exhibit 25–3 Care Delivery Topics

Triage areas/early labor lounges
Labor and deliveries/LDRs
MFICUs
C-section operating rooms/recovery rooms
LDRPs
Postpartum units
Antepartum units
Nurseries
Interunit collaboration
Outpatient service
Inpatient/outpatient collaboration
Hospital/community collaboration
Staff orientation
Staff continuing education/inservices
Cross-training
Patient education
Nursing care delivery systems/models
Clinical nurse specialists
Nurse midwives
Nurse practitioners
Attending physicians/residents
Interdisciplinary collaboration
Ancillary services
Documentation systems
Discharge planning/programs
Professional issues
Marketing/consumer issues/patient satisfaction
Nurse satisfaction
Miscellaneous

member leading discussions on a set of topics. Leaders prepared points to be addressed for each topic, which were written on poster paper and displayed during discussion. In addition to discussion leaders, the project team also identified a timekeeper, a facilitator, and a recorder to assist with retreat activities. For accurate documentation of ideas, proceedings were tape-recorded and entered simultaneously into a word processor. A poster display of the retreat objective, definitions of care delivery and philosophy of care, facilities information, and the template of an ideal care delivery system were additional visual cues for discussion. These preparations resulted in a thorough review of all topics and the identification of several innovative ideas for nursing care delivery.

Writing the Report

Recommendations were incorporated into a report organized by topics. Each section presented an overview of the current system at Strong Memorial Hospital; a synopsis of information gathered from surveys, interviews, and articles; and specific recommendations listing pros and cons. A draft of this report was reviewed and finalized by the project team after the retreat. In March 1993, the report was distributed to nursing leadership for initial review. In addition to this internal report, survey results were sent to participating hospitals.

In April 1993, a summary of the report was used by the director of Ob-Gyn nursing in discussions with the service leadership group to develop consensus for future directions. Two consecutive meetings addressed an overview of the report and a review of the implementation timetable and work plan. In May 1993, these meetings were followed by forums with staff members to discuss plans for implementation and to clarify their role in this process. Work groups, identified by the director of Ob-Gyn nursing during this phase, are reviewing recommendations currently. They will begin the process of program development and implementation for a new nursing care delivery system. Members of the project team will be consultants during this process.

The New System

The new system envisioned by the task force will echo the themes set forth in the philosophy of care. Quality, holistic patient- and family-centered care will be provided on a continuum through the collaboration of a team of care providers. This team will offer all levels and aspects of care-giving skills, tailored to ensure a seamless, individualized, health care experience for each patient. Roles will be innovative and flexible, using blended positions and placing expertise in pivotal functions within critical areas. A blend of nursing models, which include case management, primary nursing, and mother/baby nursing, will be chosen to meet the specific needs of each care site and patient population. Defined mechanisms for collaborative care and enhanced communication will connect all caregivers and care sites at interdisciplinary, interunit, interservice, inpatient/outpatient, and hospital/community levels. Linked by these mechanisms, care and education will begin during prehospitalization and continue through hospitalization and home recovery. Care will be delivered in an environment designed with the patient as the central focus, using a system of single-room maternity care to bring services to the patient, as well as efficient and effective triage and discharge planning programs to move patients smoothly through the system. Together, the renovated environment and new care delivery system will represent a redesigned service line for women's health care at Strong Memorial Hospital.

Lessons Learned

The success of this project was due largely to the process described. This included a vested project team with balanced and diverse representation, a clearly stated purpose and time frame, careful organization of the process, ongoing project evaluation, effective use of resources, and development of a user-friendly system of data organization.

However, lessons can be learned with any project. In retrospect, some of the following measures would have contributed to quality and efficiency:

1. Incorporating total quality management (TQM) principles into project activities from the start—TQM, an approach to quality espoused at Strong Memorial Hospital, had not been fully implemented at the start of the project. Formally orienting the project team to this approach would have provided a number of useful tools for problem solving and team building, as well as a framework of organization and philosophy of approach for the project.

2. Involving more staff members—Team size was limited to maximize efficiency and ensure an easy coordination of activities. Membership was weighted with leadership because of expertise or responsibility for care delivery. Inclusion of more staff members would have provided an additional unique and essential perspective, removing the weight of this responsibility from the shoulders of the one staff member assigned.

3. Providing for member turnover—As with any project extending over time, team members come and go. In this case, two members had to leave the project at points critical to their participation. Because no provisions were made for their replacement, other members assumed their responsibilities; however, their singular perspectives and contributions were lost to the group. The identification of alternates for each member early in the project may have avoided these later adjustments.

4. Eliminating statistics—In a project of this kind, knowledge of basic statistics, such as number of deliveries, are important initially to paint a background or scenario on which to make recommendations; however, significant time should not be spent in collecting and analyzing statistics during the creative phase of recommendations and idea building. Analysis can be left for work groups to deal with during actual program development and implementation.

5. Streamlining the review of standards and regulations—Although it is important to know standards and requirements of regulatory agencies, this is work more appropriate to later stages of the project, when programs must finally be shaped out of recommendations.

CONCLUSION

New delivery systems provide the foundation for the coming renaissance in health care. The nursing profession has the opportunity to assume a central role in planning this next generation of health care systems. Architects of these new systems need a clear sense of purpose and a resolve to network and collaborate within all facets of the health care industry. The process requires organization, creativity, and commitment. It demands an appreciation of the best in current systems, sensitivity to trends, and critical analysis of future requirements. The opportunity is ours to fashion.

REFERENCES

1. Armstrong DM, Stetler CB. Strategic considerations in developing a delivery model. *Nurs Econ.* 1991;9(2):112–115.
2. Manthey M. Delivery systems and practice models: A dynamic balance. *Nurs Manage.* 1991;22(1):28–30.
3. Phillips CR. Single-room maternity care for maximum cost-efficiency. *Perinatology-Neonatology.* 1988;12(2):22–31.

■ 26 ■

Reengineering Patient Care Operations in a Mid-Sized Hospital

Leanne M. Hunstock, MBA, MEd, RN, CS, CNAA

REENGINEERING PATIENT CARE OPERATIONS

West Boca Medical Center (WBMC) is a 200-bed acute care hospital located in a residential neighborhood in Boca Raton, Florida. The hospital is owned by a multifacility proprietary national health care system. The hospital had a traditional structure both clinically and administratively. With the hospital's good reputation for patient care quality and profitability, the administrators began looking to the future in regard to positioning themselves for increased competition and managed care. In the past, they had responded to the specialty market to the degree that there was an exceptionally broad range of specialties for a small mid-sized community hospital; the only tertiary services were in the maternal child area. The hospital houses general and multispecialty services (Exhibit 26–1).

In *Reengineering the Corporation: A Manifesto for Business Revolution,*[1(p.32)] Hammer and Champy define reengineering as "the fundamental rethinking and radical redesign of business processes to achieve dramatic improvements in critical, contemporary measures of performance, such as cost, quality, service and speed." Reengineering is distinguished from approaches that seek to change outcomes by modifying or redesigning existing processes. In contrast, the reengineering process is based on an approach of designing operations from the ground up, disregarding tradition and old mental models. Keeping this premise in mind, the hospital set out to take an objective look at how they would like to see their operations function to support the mission of the hospital. The initial step was to determine the goal of the project that would help to guide the planning of the decision-making process.

At the outset, the goal of the reengineering project was to develop a patient care delivery system that would meet the following objectives:

- improve patient care outcomes
- enhance physician, patient, and employee satisfaction

Exhibit 26–1 Original Patient Services Configuration

Unit	No. of Beds	Floor
General Surgical	42	2nd
General Medical	12	3rd
PCU/Telemetry	28	3rd
General Pediatric	12	4th
Pediatric ICU	8	1st
Obstetric	14	1st
Labor and Delivery	8	1st
Newborn Nursery	14	1st
Newborn Intensive Care (NICU)	8	1st
ICU/CCU	16	1st
Emergency Department	50 visits per day	1st

Note: PCU, Progressive care unit
Source: West Boca Medical Center, Boca Raton, Florida.

- increase the efficient use of all resources
- reduce the number of inefficient interventions received by patients
- decrease length of stay and billing lag time

The reengineered units' staff organizational structure, position control, and budget were to include all of the labor required to provide the following services to patients on a 24-hour basis:

- nursing care
- admission and discharge
- blood and other specimen collections
- respiratory treatments
- electrocardiograms (EKGs)
- arterial blood gas (ABGs) determinations
- discharge planning
- infection control
- quality assurance
- risk management
- chart completion
- menu completion and administration of nourishment

- patient room housekeeping (excluding heavy floor work in corridors and common areas)
- cleaning and simple maintenance of equipment

To reengineer the hospital operations, the project focused on the components of operations that included the use and deployment of labor, the organizational structure, the distribution of supplies, reengineering of systems and documentation, and the use of technology.[2] Basic tenets were as follows:

- Redesign work roles both in the patient-focused clinical areas and in the remaining ancillary and support departments. Cross-train staff and evaluate on the basis of performance competency.
- Streamline documentation through the development of an interdisciplinary document that integrates critical pathways, care plans, and a format for charting by exception.
- Reduce the number of times a patient is transferred and/or transported.
- Reallocate up to 75 percent of labor and supply resources required for patient care to the patient care unit.
- Organize the reporting structure and departments to support the predominant patient groups served.
- Manage costs on the basis of cost per unit rather than hours per unit or full-time equivalent per unit.
- Utilize ancillary department managers as expert consultants with collaborative accountability to the new department managers for the quality of care and service provided.
- Reduce the number of policies and procedures, moving toward integrated processes with outcome accountability defined.

The hospital wanted to accomplish the objectives without the capital remodeling expense experienced in many reengineering projects.[3] The first step was to complete a comprehensive operational and financial assessment. This assessment required meetings with key stakeholders such as medical staff leaders, the governing board, department heads, and the administrative team, which consisted of the chief executive officer (CEO), chief financial officer (CFO), and three assistant administrators. The administrative team functioned as the steering committee and included other key personnel as needed and determined by the team. The author served as a consultant and, to expedite planning and model development, provided the conceptual framework for reengineering to the administrative team/ steering committee. The administrative team/steering committee participated in approximately eight hours of education on the reengineering framework and exercises to determine the mission and objectives for operations reengineering.

Initially, the administrative team met with the governing board, which included the medical staff executives regarding the goals and conceptual model. After gaining support from the governing board, the CEO and assistant administrator of patient care services met with the medical staff in the medical department meetings and at the annual meeting of the entire medical staff to discuss the conceptual model with them. As the planning proceeded, the medical staff participated through their department meetings with the CEO and assistant administrator of patient care services.

Next, the conceptual model was developed into an operational and financial model that the administrative team/steering committee believed made sense for their hospital, was affordable, and would assist them in reaching their goals. Development of this model was accomplished through feasibility studies, workload analyses, and cost-benefit analyses on the projected models. This process was accomplished through the joint efforts of the assistant administrators, the CEO, and the department managers. Once the administrative team/steering committee approved a model, a patient-focused care unit director was hired and the department managers were recruited to participate in the planning for implementation.

The staff was involved early in the planning process through monthly informational meetings with the administrative team/steering committee. The CEO also presented the initial concept to them through around-the-clock open forums to explain the rationale for change, the need to reengineer the work processes, and patient care and hospital operations. Later, staff were brought actively into the process as they served in work groups for designing some of the new roles and developing new job descriptions and a new multidisciplinary documentation system.

REENGINEERING PROCESS AND STRUCTURE

The process of reengineering began with determination of which services in the hospital would be included in the project. It soon became apparent that, in order to reach the outcome of a fully integrated service, the project had to include as many services as possible from the clinical ancillary and support services. The process included a view to inpatient or ambulatory services and all the inpatient services noted above. A process of zero-based analysis[2(p.236)] was undertaken. This process was used to analyze data on all patients by services either directly consumed or indirectly received during hospitalization and the expectations of patients regarding services and quality of care. The patient types were then aggregated into similar groups on the basis of the most prevalent characteristics, such as services consumed and expected. The unit placement was then determined. The final consideration was the availability of technology and hospital requirements to support the new aggregations of patients.

Because no capital budget existed to support the project, it was limited to current facilities, with the exception of cardiac monitoring, which was planned to have additional cardiac monitors. All units were equipped with an automated order entry system and computerized pharmacy and laboratory systems. It was determined that five new units would become the patient-focused units, as shown in Exhibit 26–2.

To expedite services to the patient in the most efficient and effective manner, it was decided that the direct caregivers needed to plan, coordinate, implement, evaluate, and most important, control and be accountable for the provision of services the patient required. For this reason, it was determined that reengineering of processes should enable 75 percent of the patient-consumed services to be provided on the patient care unit. As a result, the processes that were reengineered initially were environmental maintenance, supply distribution and stocking, clinical pharmacy, medication dispensing, medication education and consultation, medication administration, respiratory therapy, nursing, equipment cleaning, storage and distribution, staff orientation and education, food service ordering and distribution, clinical case management, utilization and risk management, social services, discharge planning, patient admission and discharge, diagnostic testing, patient transportation, all specimen collection, clinical documentation, and medical record management.

To organize work and processes around patient aggregates, the following initial roles were determined:

- **Department director**—The department director has 24-hour accountability for hiring, firing, and evaluating the multidisciplinary staff; staffing the unit; marketing the unit to physicians; and ensuring customer satisfaction,

---

Exhibit 26–2 Newly Designated Patient-Focused Units

Patient-Focused Units	Unit Size (No. of beds)	Floor
Medical/Surgical/PCU/Telemetry	82	2nd, 3rd
Pediatric/PICU/NICU	28	4th
Labor, Delivery, Recovery, Postpartum/Obstetrics/Nursery	36	1st
Emergency/ICU/CCU	16	1st
Ambulatory Services		1st

Source: West Boca Medical Center, Boca Raton, Florida.

standards of care, and financial management of the unit within the budget. This position shares clinical accountability through a collaborative relationship with existing expert department heads in areas such as the pharmacy, laboratory, respiratory care, dietary services, housekeeping, medical record management, utilization review, education, and admitting. These experts serve as consultants in the hiring and evaluation of the staff performing duties pertinent to their clinical specialty.

- **Clinical specialist/educator**—This specialist is responsible for ongoing education and orientation of all staff, quality assurance, hands-on intervention, and support of staff with clinical competencies. This position is salaried and has visibility on all shifts. The educator works one shift per month, with direct care staff responsibilities, to maintain clinical skills and to function as role model and preceptor for staff members.

- **Registered nurse (RN)**—The RN functions as a primary care leader for five or six patients monitored in the progressive care unit (PCU), for eight to ten patients in the medical/surgical unit, or for patients from both units. Each RN works with a patient care assistant (PCA) to assist in the care of those patients. The RNs and PCAs are intended to work in partnership teams of two. The partners share similar schedules, and the RN participates in the performance evaluation of the PCA. The RN assesses, plans, coordinates, supervises, delivers, and evaluates patient care, drawing on the expertise and assistance of other caregivers and clinicians based on the unit. The RN demonstrates competency in phlebotomy, electrocardiograms (EKGs), simple respiratory care, ABG specimen collection, delegation, and supervision.

Patient care assistant—The PCA assists the patient in activities of daily living; makes beds; maintains a clean patient environment; takes and records vital signs, phlebotomy, EKGs, and collects specimens as ordered for diagnostic testing. Additionally, the PCA transports patients, charts patient data and observations, collects intake and output data, ambulates the patient, provides range-of-motion exercises, incentive spirometry, chest percussion, oxygen setups, and other duties as assigned. The PCA is supervised and evaluated by the RN.

- **Cardiopulmonary clinician**—The role of this clinician expands the traditional respiratory therapist role to include collection of ABGs, obtaining EKGs and vital signs, and performing phlebotomy. This clinician performs all maintenance of specialized patient care equipment, such as intravenous fluid pumps, oximeters, hypothermia blankets, and special beds. Other responsibilities include daily rounds, consultation with physicians, provision of education for other patient care providers on simple respiratory interventions, and administration of the patient-related interventions assigned under the supervision of an RN. Partnership teams assume responsibility for starting routine oxygen and incentive spirometry and monitoring their patients on oxygen and aerosol to free the clinician for specialized procedures and collaboration with physicians and clinical experts on complex cases.

- **Unit attendant**—This unit-based housekeeper cleans patient care rooms, passes trays, runs errands, transports patients and supplies, passes nourishments and coffee, cleans specialized equipment, and stocks supplies.
- **Concierge**—This staff member answers telephones, assists visitors, assists staff and visitors at the desk, transcribes physician's orders, and participates in patient admission and discharge.
- **Administrative case manager**—This case manager is an RN or licensed vocational nurse trained to do concurrent quality improvement monitoring, utilization review, infection control screening, discharge planning, and admission and discharge, and to assist with critical pathway development.
- **Charge nurse**—The charge nurse or shift manager oversees operations of the shift; serves as a resource person to physicians, staff, and families; and manages conflicts. He or she assists in care of patients with special needs such as newly admitted patients and difficult patients.
- **Unit-based clinical pharmacist**—The clinical pharmacist is stationed at the desk and enters all orders, checks medication administration records, and consults with physicians and nurses on the most cost-effective and appropriate medications. He or she dispenses first doses and missing medications via a unit-based portable stock of drugs and checks and procures all unit-dosed medications for the assigned unit.
- **Information specialist**—This position is responsible for concurrent chart completion and coding, for monitoring critical pathway variances, and for assisting with general clerical or administrative duties related to care of patients.
- **Monitor technician**—This technician is cross-trained to function in a variety of unit clerical support roles, in addition to monitoring cardiac patients.

Staff and department managers participated in implementation and systems coordination teams to determine streamlined processes and systems that supported the newly unit-based activities and work. For example, a new process needed to be developed for all specimens collected by the unit-based staff that had to be transported, logged in, and processed in the laboratory. These procedures required that orders be processed differently. Labels and work lists had to originate and be handled on the unit instead of being routed through the laboratory department where they were processed and returned to the unit for execution. All supplies needed to be ordered, processed, delivered, and stocked by one department, instead of three or four different departments providing various components of the whole process for their products. Once the new roles and processes were determined, staff designed the clinical training programs. By virtue of meeting the goal of unit basing 75 percent of the patient services, numerous systems and processes were automatically identified for reengineering.

REORGANIZATON

For the integration of services to be complete, the administrative team was required to consider a reorganization of responsibilities as a prerequisite of the reengineering project. The existing structure of three assistant administrators needed to be radically changed to support the new operations. The recommendation was to divide the services along the lines of inpatient and outpatient services. In this model, the departments of pharmacy, utilization review, dietary services, quality resources, social services, respiratory care, electrocardiography, electroencephalography, pulmonary care, education, and inpatient nursing would report to the inpatient administrator. The departments of laboratory, radiology, cardiopulmonary care, housekeeping, operating rooms, outpatient surgery, biomedical engineering, and rehabilitation services including physical therapy, occupational therapy, and speech therapy would report to the outpatient assistant administrator. Because of the highly political nature of these changes, the decision was made by the executive leadership to transition into this structure. Eventually, one of the assistant administrators left the hospital. Then the staff for services that primarily supported the inpatient services reported to the assistant administrator for patient care services, and the outpatient clinical departments reported to the other assistant administrator, who was promoted to chief operating officer, while the CEO moved to cover two hospitals.

It was recommended that future projects make this organizational change prior to implementation of new processes, in order to minimize resistance to the restructuring of departments to support the new operation. It was determined that, at the very least, the departments of laboratory, pharmacy, respiratory therapy, housekeeping, and dietary services should report to the inpatient assistant administrator for the planning, implementation, and transition periods. Following full implementation, those areas that relinquish most of their direct inpatient support functions to the patient-focused care units, such as pharmacy, laboratory, respiratory care, electrocardiography, and housekeeping can reorganize and report to the outpatient administrator.

Some cross-functional areas such as medical record management, the business office, and human resources were divided between the CFO and the outpatient assistant administrator. The reasons for this recommendation were that, in order to swiftly accomplish the fully integrated model being proposed, it was essential that alignment of authority within the newly integrated services occur immediately, for the greatest impact on planning and retraining. It was also determined that the organizational structure should remain in place for at least six months after the implementation, to solidify the new model. Without this shift, the resistance would not only be strong, but cemented, as a result of maintaining the traditional authority structure, which would then supersede the new clinical and operational integrated structure. This scenario was evidenced in this project, in which the traditional structure prevented the full integration of the pharmacy and delayed the full integration of some of the laboratory functions such as phlebotomy and cross-training. The political nature of the reengineering was by far the most delicate factor and the element most laden with potential for undermining and defeat of the reengineering efforts.

REALLOCATION OF LABOR

Approximately 60 full-time equivalents (FTEs) or 47 percent of the budgeted FTEs in the affected ancillary and support departments were allocated and converted into approximately $2 million of productive salary, which was used to fund the new roles on the patient-focused units. The departments affected by the allocation were phlebotomy, respiratory care, electrocardiography, electroencephalography, pharmacy (which increased positions), dietary services, housekeeping, pulmonary care, medical records management, utilization review, social services, education, and transportation. The amount of allocation was based on the amount of work being unit based and the amount of work remaining in the centralized department. The remaining FTEs in the ancillary and support departments were used to combine functions into the ambulatory services departments and the outpatient-focused departments of laboratory, pharmacy, cardiopulmonary care, and diagnostics. Adjusted productive cost per unit of service targets were set up for all departments and built into staffing matrices for day-to-day operational cost monitoring. Sample staffing for the medical/surgical/progressive care unit (PCU) appears in Exhibit 26–3.

IMPLEMENTATION

All positions were treated as new positions for the new roles, with job postings, interviews, and hires. The plan was to phase in the start up for all the units. The first unit (phase 1) to be implemented was the medical/surgical/PCU/telemetry combination. These units combined the three largest general medical-surgical inpatient areas on two different floors into one larger administrative patient-focused unit with one staff and one department director. These units

Exhibit 26–3 Sample Staffing Pattern for Medical/Surgica/ Progressive Care Unit

Day Shift (7:00 am to 7:00 pm)	No. of staff (hr/wk)	Night Shift (7:00 pm to 7:00 am)	No. of staff
Department Director	1 (40)		
Charge Nurse	2	Charge Nurse	2
Case Manager	1 (40)		
Clinical Educator	1 (40)		
Clinical Pharmacist	2 (10)		
Housekeeper	2 (16)		
Monitor Technician	1	Monitor Technician	1
Concierge	2	Concierge	1
Cardiopulmonary Clinician	1	Cardiopulmonary Clinician	1
Registered Nurse	10	RN	8
Patient Care Assistant	10	PCA	8

Source: West Boca Medical Center, Boca Raton, Florida.
Note: Census: 62 (20 PCU, 14 medical, 28 surgical).

formerly had been administered as three separate units with three separate staffs and managers.

The three units were too large to place on one contiguous floor, and therefore some consideration for the two floors was made in the staffing plan. Specifically, the surgical patients were centered primarily on the second floor, and the beds for patients monitored by telemetry were to be increased from the 20 existing beds to all the medical beds on the third floor and then to those on the surgical floor if the necessity arose. The nursing staff was cross-trained to care for medical, surgical, and telemetry patients, so that patients could be admitted to any third floor bed and not have to be moved again unless they moved to an intensive care unit bed. Later plans included expanding cardiac monitoring capability on both floors to further enhance the flexibility of patient placement.

The goal was to minimize the dislocation of the patient by increasing the flexibility of the staff and hospital, as the focus of organizing care. All staff were trained to perform basic housekeeping, to allow for general surface cleaning to facilitate keeping the patient areas and the unit clean and tidy. They were also trained to turn over beds in a rapid manner, fill out and process menus, process laboratory specimens, handle paperwork, provide phone support, process orders, and perform services valued by patients, such as providing snacks, personal interaction, leisure activities, and customer communication.

The nonlicensed staff, primarily the PCAs, were trained for approximately eight weeks. This training included time to incorporate all clinical aspects of the certified nursing assistant tasks, which include simple respiratory care, transport, phlebotomy, and electrocardiography. The nursing staff were trained, if necessary, for phlebotomy and respiratory care and cross-trained to other nursing specialties such as EKG interpretation and monitoring. The nurses, educators, monitor technicians, concierges, respiratory therapists, and PCAs were cross-trained to perform phlebotomy and obtain EKGs and vital signs, do charting, and assist with basic patient care, such as transfers and activities of daily living, although some of these tasks were not to be primary duties for all staff. Prior to implementation, all team members were provided training in team dynamics. The nurses were provided training in delegation, and nurses and PCAs underwent training and in-service training to learn to work in partnerships. Classes were designed to enhance planning, teamwork, and the transition from primary nursing to partnerships with a nonlicensed partner. During implementation, the leadership staff was on the unit around the clock to support the staff. The next phase of implementation occurred three months later and included the remaining specialty units and the ambulatory services.

THE REENGINEERED MODEL

The reengineered model shifted the labor to the patient care unit. The patient care functions followed the new reengineered form or structure of services. The former functionally centralized ancillary and support departments of pharmacy, laboratory, respiratory care, electrocardiography, dietary services, housekeeping, and social services are now smaller support departments with department managers who function as consultants and service suppliers to the new director of the reengineered patient-focused unit. The departments are now service departments whose customers are truly the patients in the units. The services now provided by those departments can be provided through internal or contracted external means, which changes the customer-supplier relationship. Patient services are driven by the patient care unit rather than by centralized remote departments. Staff are cross-trained to avoid passing off work to another department or discipline if they have been trained to perform it. There is collaborative accountability for successful and efficient operations among the department directors of the ancillary and support departments and the patient unit director. There is a 50 percent increase in the number of staff members working out of a large central station on the patient care unit (see staffing in Exhibit 26–3). Services that may be integrated in future phases are medical record management and admitting. The respiratory therapy department has been converted to a cardiopulmonary diagnostic department with responsibility for phlebotomy and specimen collection, EKGs, electroencephalograms, cardiac rehabilitation, and respiratory therapy for outpatients.

Table 26–1 Outcome and Process Indicators for Medical/Surgical/Progressive Care Unit

	February 1993	*April 1993*	*January 1994*
Outcome Indicators			
No. of Incident Reports	44	53	12
Patient Satisfaction (%)	64	90	91
Physician Satisfaction (%)	73	84	92
Employee Satisfaction (%)	64	76	87
Nosocomial Infection Rate (%)	2.1	1.55	1.3
Process Indicators			
Medication Errors	30	4	20
Average Hospital LOS	4.4	5	4
Response to Call Lights within 5 min (%)	NA	80	98
Average First-Dose of Antibiotics	NA	38 min	28 min

Note: LOS, length of stay; NA, not available.
Source: Courtesy of West Boca Medical Center, Boca Raton, Florida.

OUTCOMES

Outcome indicators were set up and measured prior to implementation of phase 1 in February 1993 and periodically thereafter for a one-year period, as indicated in Table 26–1.

Since the reengineered model was planned and implemented after the budgets for the fiscal years 1993 and 1994 were approved and in place, the patient-focused care unit (PFCU) budgeted salary expenses were adjusted on the basis of productive salary cost per unit of service targets, which were developed for all departments affected by the allocation of resources. A listing of these departments can be found in Table 26–2. As noted earlier, some ancillary and support departments reduced staff, while some increased staff. The PFCU increased staff, compared with the budget allotment, as a result of the additional staff in new and expanded roles who were based on the PFCU and paid from the patient unit cost center.

Departmental cost comparisons for the first three months of phase 1 (medical/surgical/PCU/telemetry) are detailed in Table 26–2.

This table compares the budgeted cost per unit of service in each department affected by the allocation and the reduction in workload, as a result of the elimination or shift of functions in the PFCU, with the adjusted target salary cost per unit of service based on the provision of the same number of services in both periods. The totals demonstrate the overall comparisons of providing the same amount of service under the budgeted cost, compared with the previous fiscal

Table 26–2 Salaries, Wages, and Benefits—Actual Cost Compared to Budget and Prior Year on the Basis of Unit of Service

	Actual Cost		Budget
Department	March to May 1992	March to May 1993	March to May 1993
PFCU			
PFCU (2nd floor)	$518,944	$542,313	$567,538
PFCU (3rd floor)	$389,353	$397,461	$323,771
Laboratory	$454,915	$346,770	$478,666
Dietary Services	$6,447	$6,655	$8,153
EKG	$36,902	$78,633	$46,716
Pulmonary	$101,199	$89,812	$103,525
Pharmacy	$163,596	$136,770	$203,299
Respiratory	$178,842	$141,085	$300,712
Utilization Review	$100,106	$75,317	$97,334
EEG	$10,025	$10,213	$15,992
In-service Program	$41,884	$30,061	$42,415
Transport	$29,081	$14,155	$37,427
Total (SWB x FY 93 units)	$1,950,303	$1,814,815	$2,129,715

Notes: SWB, Salaries, Wages, and Benefits

Departmental cost per unit service multiplied by the number of units delivered in each department in March through May of fiscal year 1993. Includes all departments affected by phase 1 reeingineering (medical and surgical units, progressive units, and telemetry units).

Source: Courtesy of Leanne Hunstock and National Medical Enterprises Executive Information Service, Santa Monica, California.

---

year and the actual cost in the reengineered model. The estimated cost for phase 1 was $48,000 for new staff training and orientation and was captured through the savings gained by the allocation of labor from ancillary and support departments.

At the end of fiscal year 1994, the productive salary cost per adjusted patient-day for the hospital was 2.2 percent below budget on a year-to-date basis and 3.7 percent above the actual cost for fiscal year 1993. The total salary, wages, and benefits for the hospital during the same time was 0.6 percent below budget on a year-to-date basis per adjusted patient-day and 6 percent over the previous year's actual cost. It was anticipated that the nonproductive salary costs would exceed the budgeted cost due to the nonbudgeted increase in FTEs and training costs. However, the nonproductive salary costs for fiscal year 1994 were 1 percent below budget. This may be due to the management of the training process and use of low census days to cross-train current staff to new roles.

RECOMMENDATIONS AND CONCLUSIONS

The political experiences of this reengineering effort demonstrated the need to change the organizational structure prior to implementation, to minimize the potential for sabotage. For example, despite verbalized support for the model, professional departments had difficulty giving up even the simplest functions and expressed that resistance by making some training difficult to access and by fault-finding with the implementation of the function. Some departments refused to assign required specific staff to the unit and insisted on rotating them. The organizational structure, which was implemented later, positioned these departments under line authority in relationship to the assistant administrator of patient care services. This reorganization prior to the implementation would have facilitated the smooth integration of these services. Although this strategy was considered during the planning, it was deemed to be unnecessary until later.

The question of whether or not the level of participation of the department heads has impact on the level of cooperation during the reengineering planning and implementation is often asked. The resistance to change lies not in the process but in the outcome of the change. If the outcome is radically different from the current operational paradigms that exist, particularly for professionals, the resistance behaviors may be consistent in flavor and intensity, regardless of the process. When the complex world of the hospital is reengineered, old habits die hard. The swift and radical changes required for positioning for the future require a comprehensive operations approach rather than a limited view of expanding the role of the nurse. Any other approach will likely yield only incremental, but no doubt more comfortable, change.

REFERENCES

1. Hammer M, Champy J. *Reengineering the Corporation: Manifesto for Business Revolution.* New York: HarperBusiness; 1993:32.
2. Strasen L. Redesigning hospitals around patients and technology. *Nurs Econ.* 1991;9(4):233–238.
3. Weber D. Six models of patient-focused care. *Healthcare Forum.* 1991;July–August:23–30.

■ 27 ■

Creating a New System of Health Care

Tim Porter-O'Grady, EdD, PhD, RN, FAAN

The key work for the future of health care, as for any other component of the work of American society, is integrating the system. Whatever leads to appropriate outcomes will be essential to the work of redesigning and reengineering the health care workplace. A number of initiatives will be essential to making the emerging system work well. The realities of the future of health care in a reformed system challenge our ability to manage it effectively. These realities call for the leadership to view the system differently and to construct approaches to reflect the new realities.

REALITY 1

It is the continuum that will define the activities in health care for at least the next two decades. A capitated noninstitutional model for health care delivery that seeks the health of the subscriber is the linchpin of any emerging system. Subscriber approaches demand the best value for the dollar spent. In health care, this means that designated dollars are to be spent for a specified list of benefits available to the subscriber. It is in the best interest of the service entity to reduce the per unit costs of its benefits in order to ensure maximization of its available resources and reduce the costs of service.

Reformatting the way in which service gets delivered in a capitated system will challenge notions of reengineering.

1. The continuum means moving focus away from institutional services to a range of services not dependent on high intervention and institutional processes.

2. Disciplines that have historically been employed exclusively in hospitals will have to do better career planning. The hospital jobs shrink as health care

expands into other settings. Career mobility will be essential to the professionals of the future.

3. Reengineering around the hospital patient is just a first small step in the systems change of moving to where the patient lives instead of the traditional practice of bringing the patient to where the provider works. Making health-based services convenient and available means moving many of the services to where the patient is and providing preventive services that keep this person from needing hospital services.

4. The intent of capitated, subscriber-based approaches is to save as much high-intensity spending as possible. Staying well and preventing illness may soon be one of the major priorities of the health care system. In it is the opportunity to reduce cost and to maximize resources.

5. The key emphasis in health care will be primary services. This focus will call for a reemphasis on practitioners who have the requisite skills. Linking these providers into the service systems and creating primary "gatekeeper," case management, or care coordinator roles will be essential to the cost and service effectiveness of the system.

REALITY 2

Information is becoming increasingly vital to the success of operating a continuum-based health care system.[1] Computerized clinical data base approaches will be essential to the documenting and validating of clinical approaches, quality outcomes, and cost variables in ways that can result in good management of the system. Value will depend on the level of data available, its quality, and its accuracy.

1. Documentation and critical clinical information regarding the patient's health journey will be the cornerstone of patient care. The vehicle of documentation and the integration of clinical, cost, and quality data will indicate the value of service and its viability for both patient and provider. Manual systems simply cannot cope with the integration complexity required to ensure efficacy and effectiveness.

2. The clinical path will increasingly define the activities of the provider and patient along the service continuum. Integration of the roles and processes within the life circumstances of the patient will require a clear notion of the roles of the various players and the fit of those roles with regard to the patient's clinical profile.

3. The understanding of the culture, resources, and lifestyle of the patient within the care continuum will have accelerating value in health service delivery. A significant proportion of the factors influencing health and ill-

ness can be controlled by understanding and applying the patient's own circumstances and resources to activities that generate health and prevent or delay illness.

4. Building the interdisciplinary team of providers will expand beyond hospital walls and become the requisite for patient-based services in any setting. There will become no unilateral service or discipline-specific departmentalization. Care along the continuum assumes partnership and integration of the disciplines. Team-based approaches will define the character of service delivery for some time to come.

5. Careful clinical technology management will be incorporated into the management processes associated with a more health-prescriptive approach. Better and more efficient use of clinical diagnostics and therapeutics will result from the more primary and preventive focus of health service. Careful assessment processes for acquisition of technology will be a requisite of any health plan.

6. Care will be moderated to the culture of the patient. In many cases, care taken to the customer means providing a basis for the patient's own community to define ways it will address its care needs and service delivery. The role of the provider will be related to support and resource provision to assist the community in adequately addressing its health-related concerns.

REALITY 3

Physicians will be partners in the process in new ways. The physician of the future will not be a free-standing, independent, entrepreneurial entity for much longer.[2] There will be a close systems association requiring a different set of relationships and behavior between physicians and other players in the health system.

1. Larger primary care practices will continue to unfold. Every health plan will have associated directly with it a large and diverse physician group. Physicians will be required to associate with such groups and to direct their practices within the context of the group's expectations.

2. Care expectations will follow particular care pathways and patterns. Physicians will be expected to perform within the clinical norms and cost framework of the group practice and in a way that facilitates their relationship with the health plan.

3. Relationship with other disciplines and care providers will exemplify collateral relationships and colleague interactions. More emphasis on dialogue, team process, and continuum of care will call for more partnering activities from physicians.

4. The physician decision role will be more integrated in the care system and less unilaterally evident in the governance structure than in the past. Placing physicians more fully within the care continuum and the collective framework of clinical policy, protocol, and decision making about practice places them closer to the appropriate patient locus of control and builds partnership among the providers of care.

5. As with the rest of the providers, payment and reward will be more directly related to successful outcomes and subscriber satisfaction than to application of sophisticated practice processes or technology. Since subscriber relationships and reduced care costs will be associated with better clinical outcomes, physician reward systems will be altered. Judicious use of resources will require more discrete judgment regarding patient services and clinical activities.

FUTURE FOCUS OF REENGINEERING

Many reengineering activities are focused on current concepts of patient care delivery. This perspective, however, is short sighted and only begins to prepare the health system for the kind of changes it has yet to confront. Besides the enhancement of data-driven information systems and service integration along the continuum, a number of newer initiatives will influence the future content of service restructure and redesign.

Computer-Based Clinical Information Superhighway. The use of artificial intelligence, holographic images, and international clinical networks will change forever the role and relationship of the doctor in health care. Where technology drives the decision tree with increasingly large complexes of information, the physician facilitates interpretation rather than undertaking the clinical deliberative process soon to be managed by technology. Tying together the clinical systems and physicians from across the world in a network of consultation and collaboration, the ability to make a diagnosis by television and to do surgery from miles away through the use of robotics and other clinical processes changes our understanding of clinical diagnostics and therapeutics. The organization of health care services around these technologies means a different configuration of services and design of hospitals and other health care facilities.

Community Building and Health Care. In the near future the notion of health will expand beyond individual notions of health or illness to more community-based understanding of healthful living. It is becoming clearer just how systems interact to create related outcomes. Violence, poverty, homelessness, shelter, parenting, education, and a host of other social forces act to create conditions for social health or illness. Failure to address any of these issues results in increased use of the illness care structures of society and extends them past their ability to adequately address the public needs. Placing the health care systems and services within the context of community and formatting service structures within that framework change both the configuration and content of health services. Location becomes critical, and the decentralized nature of the process changes the structure and location of service. More community and cultural orientation to the provision of services changes the way, place, and content of the health services provided.

Integration Means Creating Service Networks across the Social and Work Spectrum. There is no need to create rigid institutional models for service delivery. The delivery system will create a service framework that fits the needs of the subscriber and the payers in a way that addresses specific needs. The population-specific health issues can be more adequately addressed by accommodating service to the cultural and structural needs of the segment of the population being served. Individual workplaces that have specific health care needs related to work activity and expectations can have a health focus that addresses a unique set of variables. Designing contracts or frameworks for health care will be essential if health services are to remain competitive and viable. The more specific the health-based service structure, the lower the resource use, and thus the lower the cost. It is here where value issues will play out, articulating cost and quality factors in a service model satisfactory to the customers who access it.

The Role and Character of the Disciplines Will Change Forever. In the old model, each discipline or work group could define for itself what it was and the contribution it made to service delivery. Segmentation of roles, functions, and structure made it possible for this to continue through the current life of the health care system. Integration, however, has changed all that. The issue is now how each discipline contributes to the relationship of the whole and its support of the outcomes expected from the service relationship. Over the horizon, it will be less possible to define the parameters of one discipline without measurably affecting those of another. These processes are primarily exclusionary and, thus, difficult to translate to the new age, in which such processes will be less fruitful. Factors such as standards of practice, protocols, and pathways will drive the providers together to redialogue their roles and functions. Those that cannot survive the test of relationship and value will fall away and simply disappear or become something else. Partnership and linkage are simply not an option.

There Are No More Permanent Structures or Boundaries. Because of the need to design and fashion organizations to reflect their milieu, it is important to note that there will not be permanently configured structures or services. The culture, community, and vagaries of change, as well as population characteristics and needs, automatically trade away stable context for variable processes. The world is being dramatically reconfigured, and it is challenging to keep up with it. What is happening must now be known in a much more fluid context. As things continue to shift and change, the structures that support health care will have to adapt and adjust. Systems must be flexible and easily shifted to parallel the changes in society. Absolutes in structure and process simply impede the ability of the system to adjust itself in ways that are more effective and meaningful. Reality will define those elements of the service system directed to addressing the needs of a changing world. The system must be able to adapt and adjust response to demand.

CONCLUSION

The world is shifting and changing as we continue to respond to the vagaries and the impact of changes already under way. It is the challenge of the time that we are forever catching up to the demand for change. It is an age that is calling all people out of the industrial mind-set and challenging us to respond to an emerging new paradigm.

It is no longer adequate either to see or to respond to the world as we have grown accustomed to do. What is emerging is not like anything we have previously experienced or even currently know. The new paradigm looks nothing like what we have known. That is the challenge of reengineering.

Not only do we have to continually raise the standard and improve the value of service in health care, we are called to revisualize what it is and how best to integrate it into the changing social fabric in a way that enhances the quality of life and the social good. Fragmented and illness-based notions of what it is and should be are not adequate to the larger vision of health.

Structures within the delivery system and in the greater society call for a different set of relationships among the providers, payers, and other customers. Changes in structure, process, and outcomes demand a different framework within which to conceive and live out relationships among all the players in the health care relationship.

Reengineering should really be identified as "new engineering," since much of what is necessary calls for a total rethinking of the concepts and processes associated with the delivery of health services. Using old notions of the delivery of health services simply won't address the demands of an emanating prototype for health. Everyone is encouraged to identify with newer definitions of health and care and to ask questions about impact and appropriate response. Health care reforms is speeding these questions to the forefront and providing a challenging context for the dialogue.

The challenge for all leadership is a willingness to create a new health care system. A fundamental requisite for reengineering is the mind-set that challenges the status quo and the purposes of current methodology. An innovative and pioneering personality reminiscent of other historical moments in America's past is valuable in undertaking this major initiative.

As with all major change, it is the requirement of leaders that they listen to the winds of change and assess the impact of change for the greater good. Through this process, the fashionable and trendy can be sorted from the substantive and meaningful. With this strategy as a foundation, the efforts to create and build will always reflect principle and value and, thus, will become sustainable and advance the social good. In the final analysis, it is to that end that all sound reengineering efforts should be directed.

REFERENCES

1. Rheingold H. *The Virtual Community: Homesteading on the Electronic Frontier.* New York: Addison-Wesley; 1993.
2. Ludden J. Doctors as employees. *Health Manage Quart.* 1993;15(1):7–11.

Index